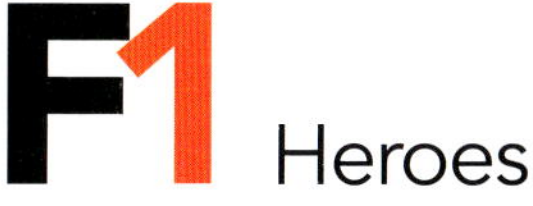

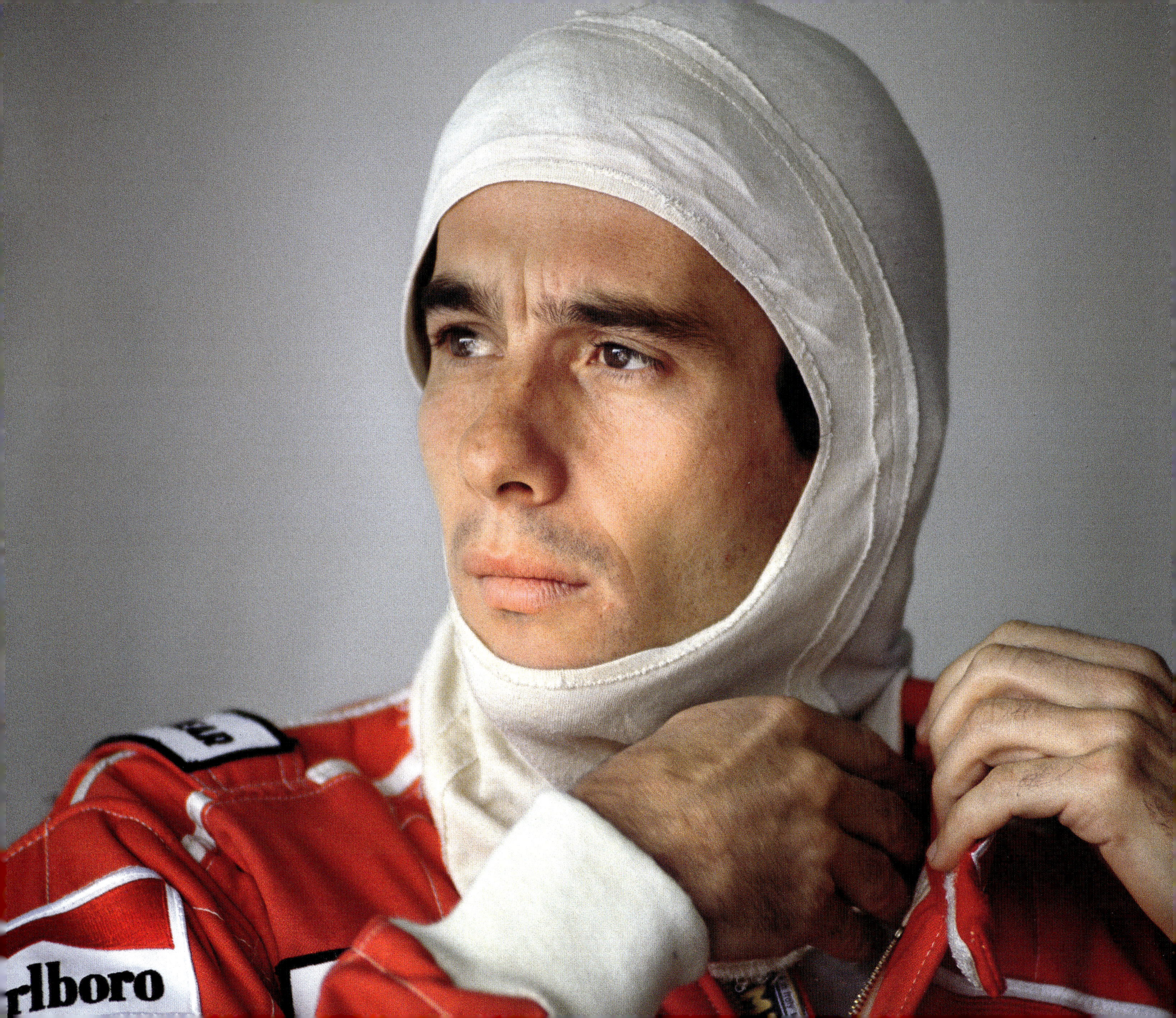
rlboro

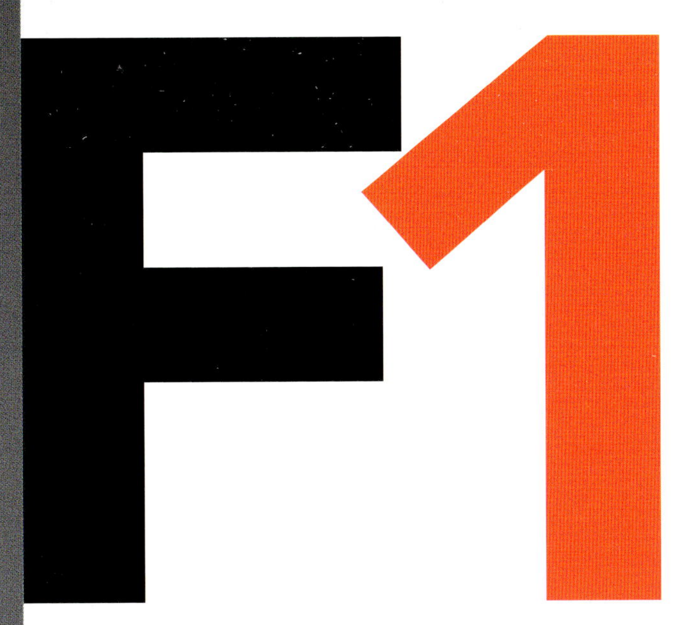

F1 Heroes

Champions and Legends
in the Photos of Motorsport Images

edited by
Ercole Colombo
Giorgio Terruzzi

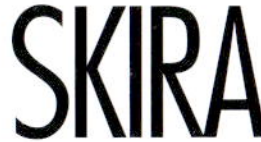

SKIRA

The Salt of Passion

A long and exciting adventure. Every F1 Grand Prix offers a double show, a double opportunity: drivers and cars from the present that hark back to the past, to other faces, to other single-seaters. Our attention is constantly renewed, combining ancient heroes and old loves with the new; it moves our memories along for kilometers at high speed; it connects historic circuits like Silverstone, Spa, Monza, to more recent settings; it constantly unearths similarities. Clark and Senna, Schumacher and Hamilton, Fangio and Lauda, Leclerc and Stewart, Mansell and Verstappen… Thanks to our love for racing, we can all travel with our imagination when we watch a live competition.

Thus, we are speaking of a privilege, of our privilege, enhanced by this extraordinary gallery of recounted images. Ercole Colombo and Giorgio Terruzzi—bound to one another since time immemorial and since time immemorial dear to me—were able to accomplish a journey through Motorsport Images' collection of photographs. A unique "archive of archives," it comprises the works of many prestigious, and invaluable photojournalists, preserving the expressions, the gestures, and the most memorable, spectacular actions of a competitive, human, and technological story more than 70 years long: the history of Formula 1, the first chapter of which dates back to 1950.

I believe that every reader, every spectator will have the opportunity to find the salt of their passion in this volume, what triggered this curiosity for the first time, this interest, this emotion and that which continues to feed hopes, tensions, ambitions, and disappointments. The champions that marked a day or an era with their courage, their talent, and on occasion with their sacrifice. Figures that have kept, and still keep us company, displaying the significance of their dedication and determination.

I am speaking of something that has involved me, too, since I was a boy. I believe that the most fitting word, in this case, is "intensity." This is the key ingredient of Formula 1, but also of life. You will find it in every one of the photographs before you, as well as in your memory. It is what has led and still leads the men and women active on the track to do better, improving themselves as well as—I think and hope—each and every one of us does in our everyday lives. Passion, intuition, acting on impulse and out of genius, but also perseverance, dedication, and concentration. At the beginning of this adventure as well as today, in this very delicate time of transition, which I am certain will lead to new scenes, new surprises, and new wonders.

A good journey, then, to all of you, to all of us, in the company of our heroes, our Formula 1 Heroes.

Stefano Domenicali
President and CEO

The great Juan Manuel Fangio once observed that there are two types of people: those who like a quiet life and the "adventurers." Racing drivers, he said, and especially the champions, are the ultimate adventurers because the harder something is the greater the satisfaction they derive from taking that challenge.

Drivers are the focal point of Formula 1 and this fascination with their adventure is the core appeal of the sport.

It has always been this way.

In the days from Fangio, through Villeneuve, to Senna, the risks meant that it could be a beautiful, but also brief, life. More recently with the welcome advances in safety, the driver remains the hero and his or her skill in dominating a machine of unimaginable power can be appreciated as an entertainment and a sport.

Photography has always been the most powerful medium for carrying this adventurer narrative.

Motorsport Images is the world's largest motorsport image library, with over 28 million images in the collection, including the world's only unbroken visual history of Formula 1 racing, with images of every Grand Prix.

The collection comprises the archives of LAT, Rainer Schlegelmilch, Studio Colombo, Sutton Images, Giorgio Piola, and Maggi & Maggi.

We are proud, in partnership with the Comune di Monza and Vidi srl, to produce this powerful exhibition, *F1 Heroes*, skilfully curated by our much loved colleague and Monza local, Ercole Colombo, and the highly respected Giorgio Terruzzi. It brings together the best images of heroic drivers taken by the best photographers.

We hope you enjoy *F1 Heroes* and that it leaves a lasting impression.

James Allen
President, Motorsport Network

www.motorsportimages.com

Cover
Bahrain GP, 2020. Romain
Grosjean (Haas VF-20 Ferrari)
emerges from flames after
a horrific accident on the
opening lap of the race.
Photo: Andrew Hone

On page 2
Phoenix, United States GP,
1991. Ayrton Senna puts on
his balaclava and does up his
fireproof suit in the McLaren
garage as he prepares to
head onto circuit.
Photo: Rainer Schlegelmilch

On page 10
Silverstone, British GP, 2016.
Lewis Hamilton celebrates
with his home fans.
Photo: Glenn Dunbar

Design
Marcello Francone

Editorial Coordination
Eva Vanzella

Copy Editor
Maria Conconi

Layout
Sara Marcon

Translations
Cristina Popple

First published in Italy in 2021 by
Skira editore S.p.A.
Palazzo Casati Stampa
via Torino 61
20123 Milano
Italy
www.skira.net

Printed and bound in Italy. First
edition

ISBN: 978-88-572-4667-3

Distributed in USA, Canada,
Central & South America by
ARTBOOK I D.A.P. 75 Broad
Street Suite 630, New York, NY
10004, USA.
Distributed elsewhere in the
world by Thames and Hudson
Ltd., 181A High Holborn, London
WC1V 7QX, United Kingdom

Contents

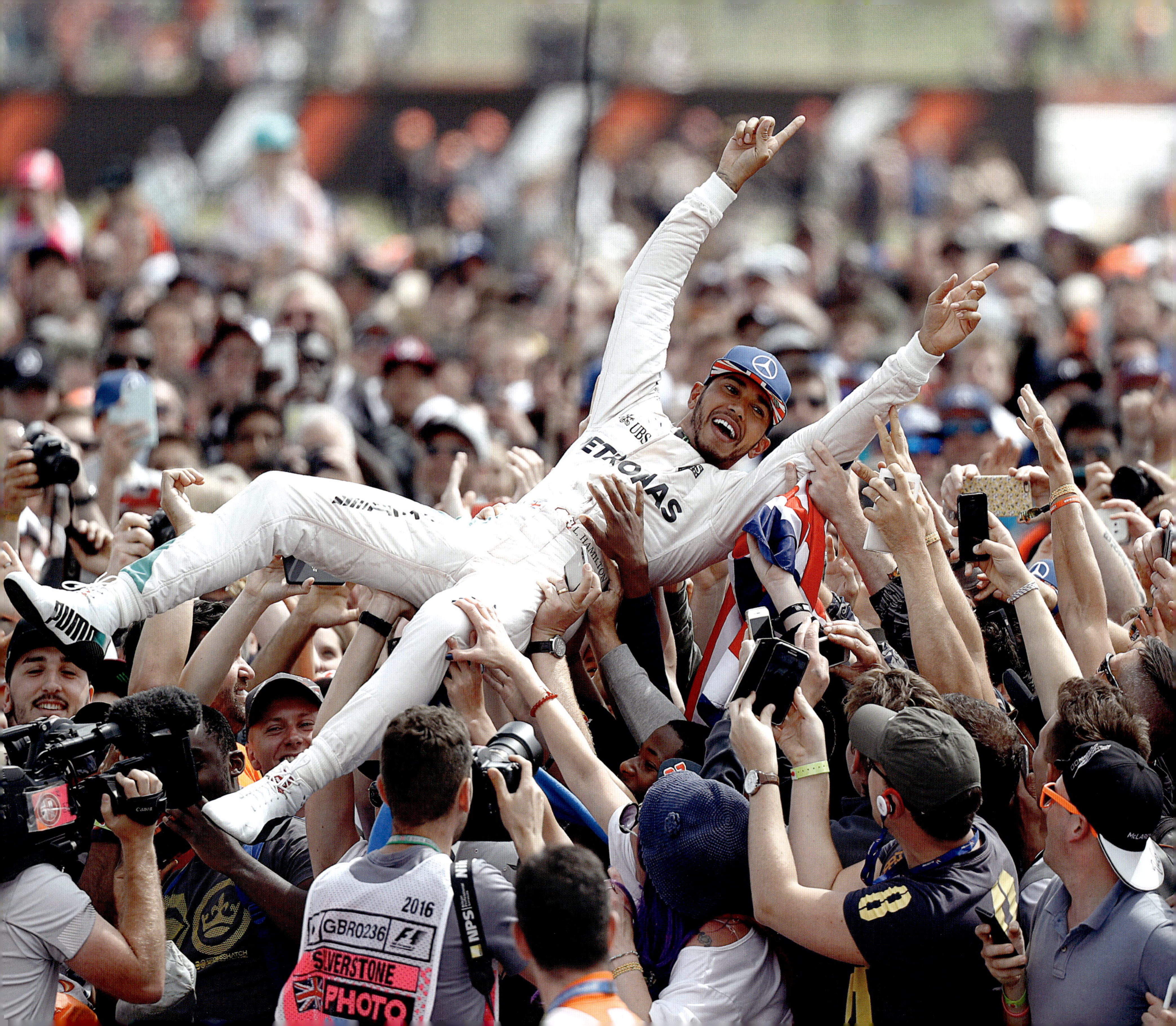

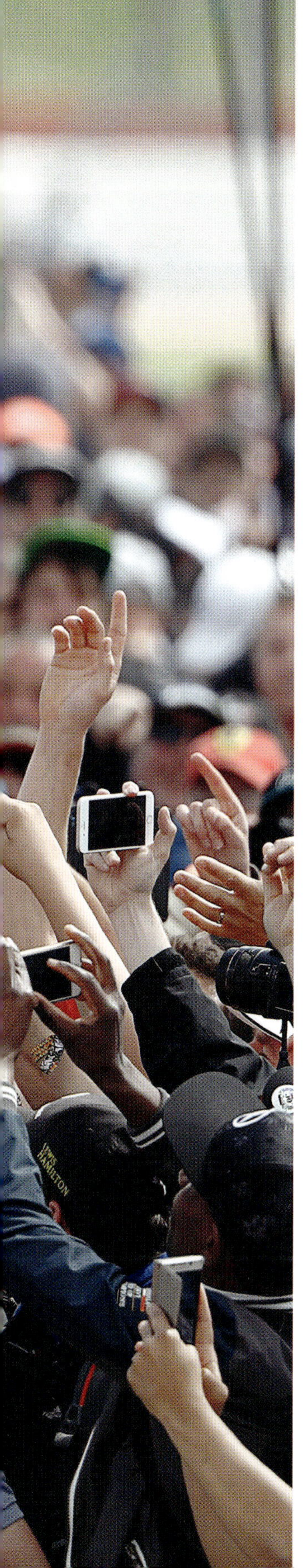

Shiny paint jobs. Fleeting images that trigger unparalleled passions. Surprising, baffling cars, capable of going so fast that they cause a turmoil of emotions, of imagination. Extremely powerful mechanical horses. Mechanics and electronics combined in such a staggering hyperbole that they become incomprehensible.

The allure of Formula 1 is the key ingredient of an adventure that has lasted over seventy years, and has never ceased to amaze and enthral different generations, captivated by the power of a competition made of great endeavors and tragedies. There is a figure at the center of this scenario, there has always been. The driver. The champion. These are people capable of accomplishing extraordinary, magnificent, arduous feats. Anomalous athletes consecrated to a profession that is by and large incomprehensible, since racing means you are putting your life, as well as your talent, on the line. These are their stories. The stories of figures that marked an era and the history of motor racing. The winners and the defeated, brought together in a gallery in which each of us may recognize a face, a gesture, an instant of our own lives. Champions in their moment of triumph, champions who have lost. All of them loved because they are bearers of excitement, of unforgettable joy, of deep sorrow.

Travel companions for the children we once were, as they are for today's younger generation. Always capable of amazing us, of dashing fearlessly along the narrow edge where the mystery of our existences resides.

Champions. For a number of happy days belonging to different time periods. Those who won everything, who won so much. But even those who gave it their all, sharing an ambition, a dream with every experienced, enthusiastic spectator young or old, male or female. Thus becoming the objects of a profound gratitude, be it openly displayed or cherished in secret. Emotions, feelings. Racing hearts. Revealed and offered up, as it always happens when sports become the most truthful reflection of life.

1950–1959
A Winning Formula

Monaco GP, 1950. Juan Manuel Fangio, winner of the race, on the podium with Prince Rainier. Photo: LAT Images

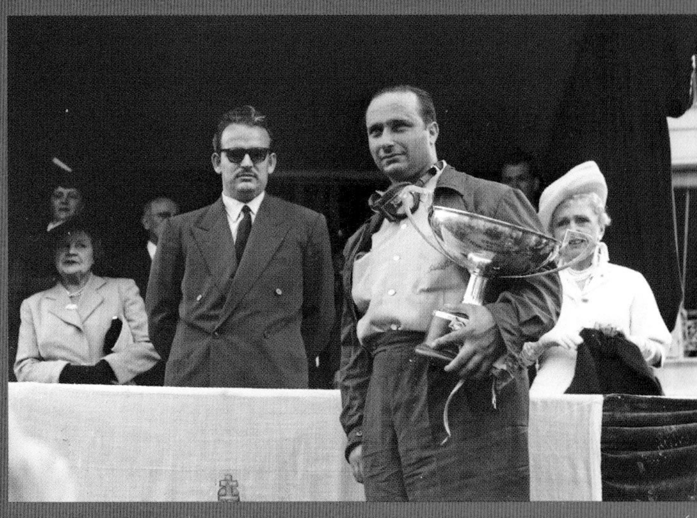

The World Championship, or "Formula 1" as we now know it, was born here. In the mid Twentieth century, the century of the motor. The first race, the first Grand Prix, was held in England, at Silverstone, on May 13, 1950. The first pole position: Giuseppe "Nino" Farina. The first winner: Nino Farina. The first world champion: Nino Farina. Alfa Romeo. Seven races, including one in Indianapolis, already a world unto itself. The wording "Formula 1" dates back to 1948. "Formula" stands for the series of technical rules that are mandatory for all participants in the competition; the number "1" substitutes the letter "A" used in the open-wheel competitions held in 1946.

There was a strong Italian presence in this first decade of great motor racing. Farina (1906–1966), a Turinese of boundless courage, started off the adventure, then came one who left his mark on history like few others, Juan Manuel Fangio (1911–1995). His family was originally from Abruzzo, his passport Argentinian. His father had emigrated from Loreto, he was born in Balcarce, south of Buenos Aires, and he came to Europe following in the footsteps of Achille Varzi, the gentleman from Galliate, great rival of Nuvolari's, who had perished during a practice session in Bern in 1948. Fangio's wonderful flight began in 1951, when he won the title for Alfa Romeo, and continued until 1958, when he retired from competition. Five-time champion. The second win in 1954,

driving Mercedes and Maserati, the third in 1955 with Mercedes, the fourth in 1956 with a Lancia inherited and entered into the competition by Ferrari. His fifth win was in 1957, again with Maserati, when his rival, his double, had already passed away: Alberto Ascari (1918–1955), two consecutive titles, in 1952 and 1953, with Ferrari. Alberto was the son of Antonio, a formidable Alfa Romeo driver from the Twenties, friend and associate of Enzo Ferrari, who died during a race in Montlhéry, France, on July 26, 1925. Fangio and Ascari, seven titles between the two of them over the span of a magnificent albeit cruel decade. The cars themselves were enormous, they bore the traits of a style that belonged to a previous era, interrupted by World War II. They were front-engined, with huge noses and steering wheels. Human and technical hazards, an endless list of victims, including Ascari, who died in Monza on May 25, 1995 while testing his disciple Eugenio Castellotti's Ferrari, though by then he had moved on to Lancia. He wasn't wearing his blue shirt or the helmet that he treated like an amulet. He died in an accident with no witnesses, at the same age as his father, in a similar high-speed left curve, on the 26th day of the month. "Curva Ascari," since then and ever after.

These two, the champions of the Fifties, rational, very skilled at putting their minds into their races. Alberto: 13 victories (with a record of 9 consecutive wins) and 14 pole positions in barely 32

races. Juan Manuel: 24 victories and 29 pole positions over 51 GPs. Fangio was a survivor. He quit in 1958 at age forty-seven. The winner of the 1958 World Championship was Mike Hawthorn (1929–1959), the British Ferrari driver with the iconic polka-dotted bowtie. He died, by a twist of fate, only a few months later in a car crash in Guildford, not far from home. His friend and team mate at Ferrari, Peter Collins, had died in an accident during a race on August 3, 1958, in Germany.

In 1959, the last title of the decade was won by Jack Brabham (1926–2014), an Australian of powerful physique and talent, destined to mark the passage into a new era, as he won the World Championship again in 1960.

There is more to recall. The first Ferrari F1 victory accomplished by José Froilán González (1922–2013) at Silverstone on July 14, 1951. The first woman to run a Grand Prix, Maria Teresa De Filippis (1926–2016), a Neapolitan who came in tenth in Belgium in 1958 driving a Maserati. The tragedies that bore away Luigi Musso (1924–1958) and Eugenio Castellotti (1930–1957), both Ferrari drivers. The long and fruitless pursuit of a title on the part of Stirling Moss (1929–2020), who came in second four times four years in a row, from 1955 to 1958. The era of the Mille Miglia ended in tragedy in 1957, a race that Moss had won in 1955, at the wheel of a Mercedes, setting a legendary record: an average of 157.65 kilometers (97.96 miles) an hour.

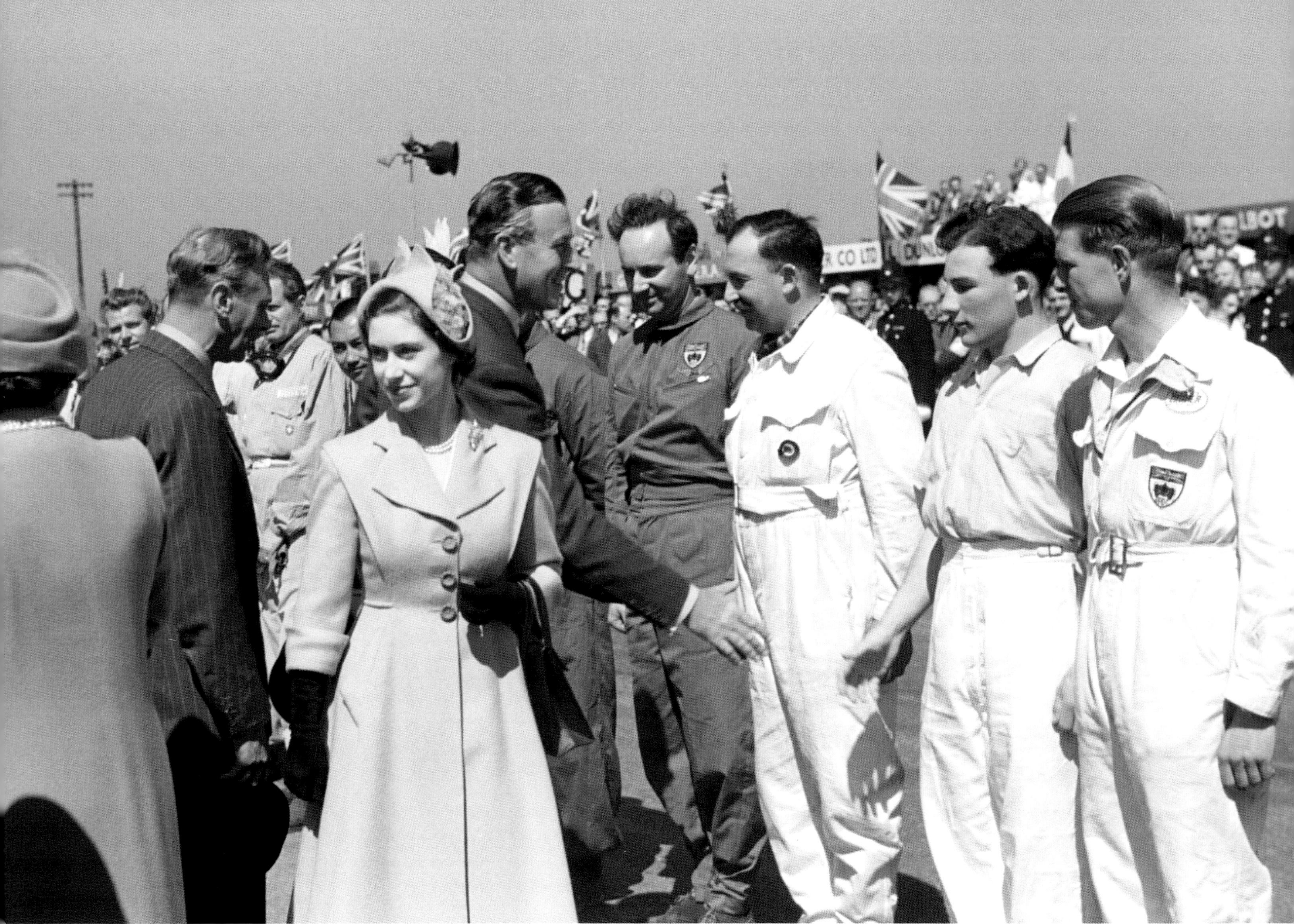

Silverstone, British GP, 1950. Princess Margaret meets the drivers before the start. Photo: LAT Images

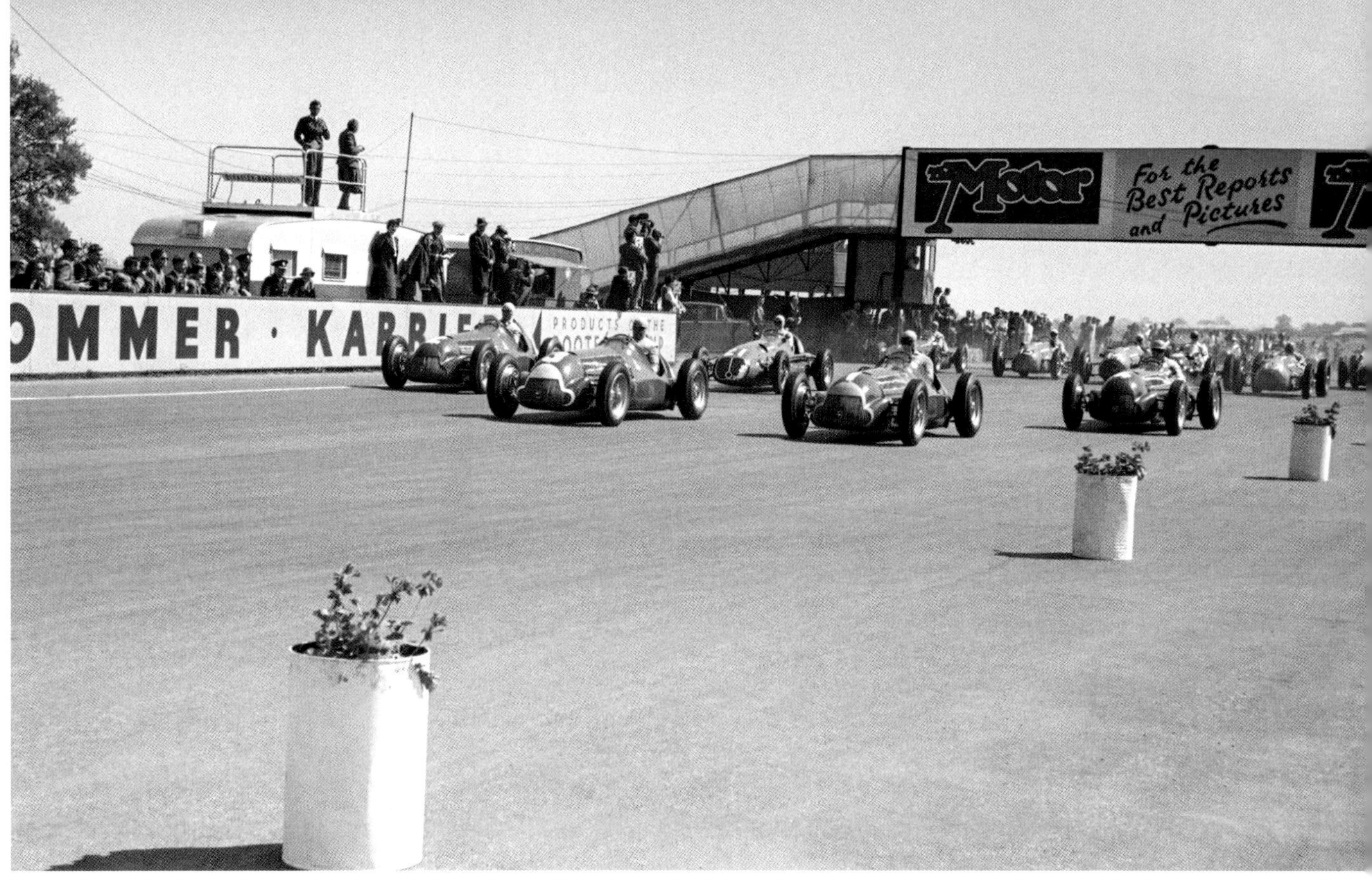

Silverstone, British GP, 1950. Luigi Fagioli (Alfa Romeo 158) leads Giuseppe Farina (Alfa Romeo 158), Juan Manuel Fangio (Alfa Romeo 158), and the Thai driver Birabongse Bhanuban, known as "Prince Bira" (Maserati). Photo: LAT Images

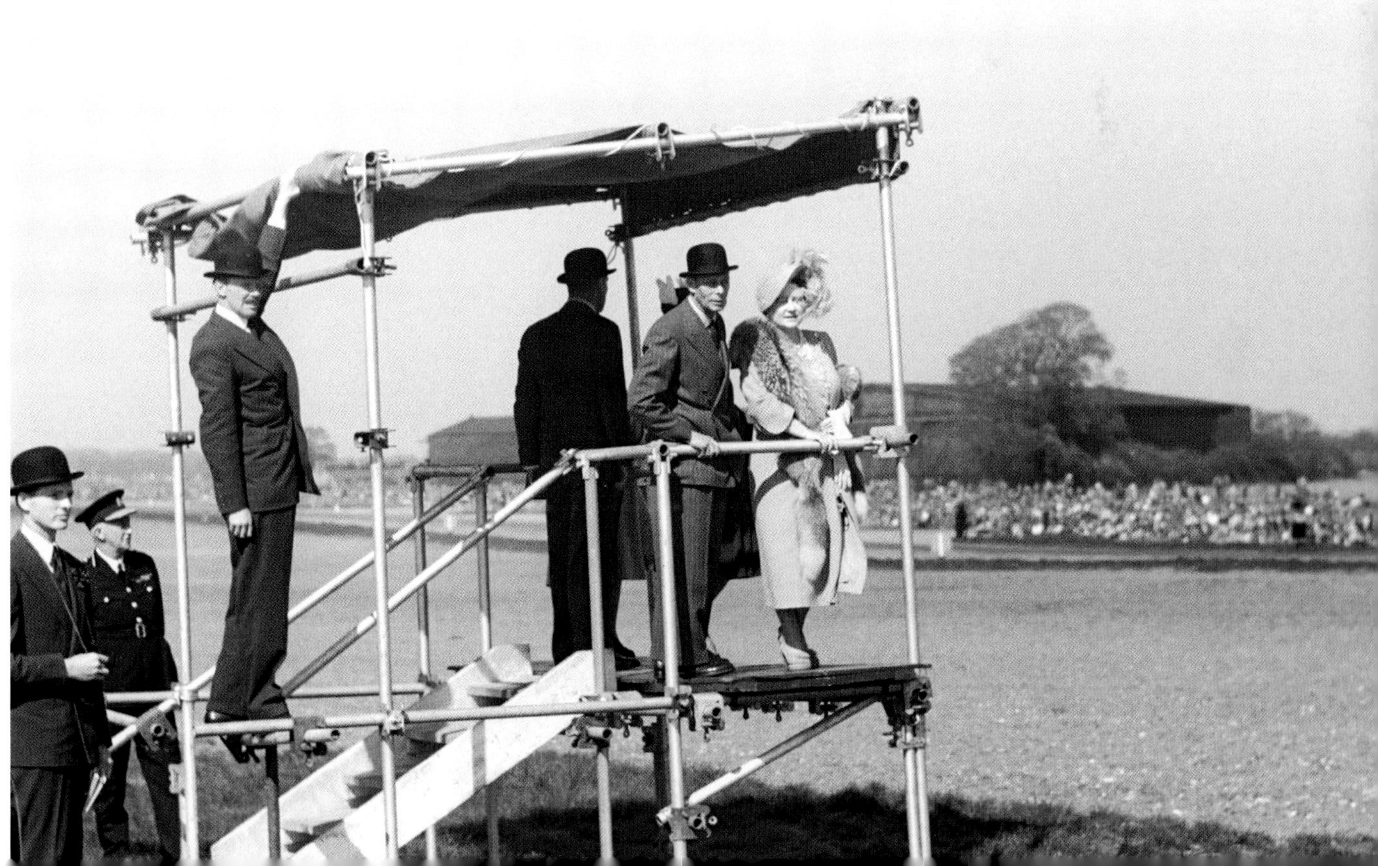

Silverstone, British GP, 1950. King George VI of the United Kingdom and Queen Elizabeth watching the start of the first World Championship race from a makeshift grandstand at Stowe Corner. Photo: LAT Images

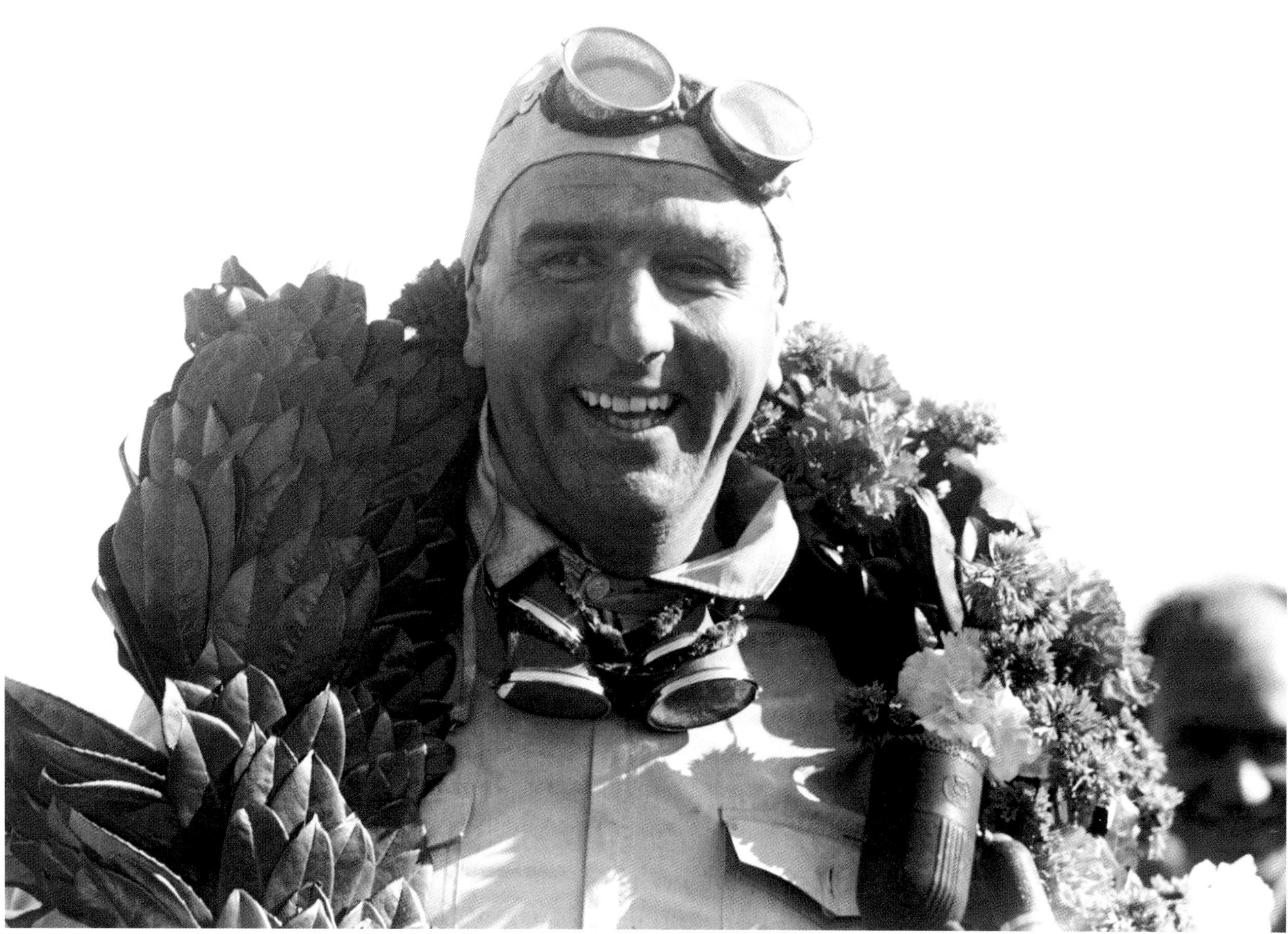

Silverstone, British GP, 1950. Giuseppe "Nino" Farina celebrates winning the first
Formula 1 World Championship race. Photo: LAT Images

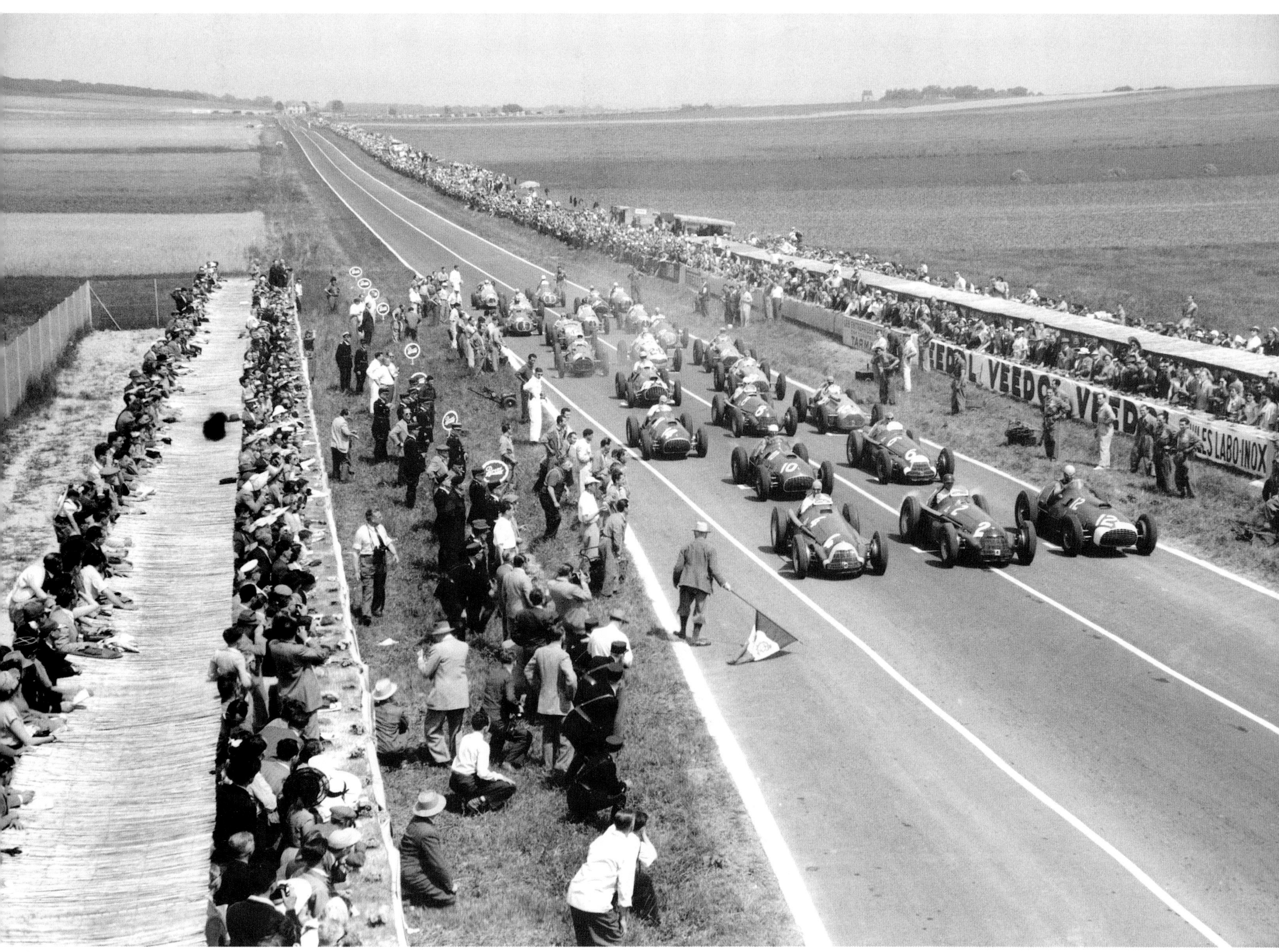

Reims, French GP, 1951. Juan Manuel Fangio (Alfa Romeo 159, number 4), Giuseppe Farina (Alfa Romeo 159, number 2), and Alberto Ascari (Ferrari 375, number 12) on the front row. Photo: Michael Tee

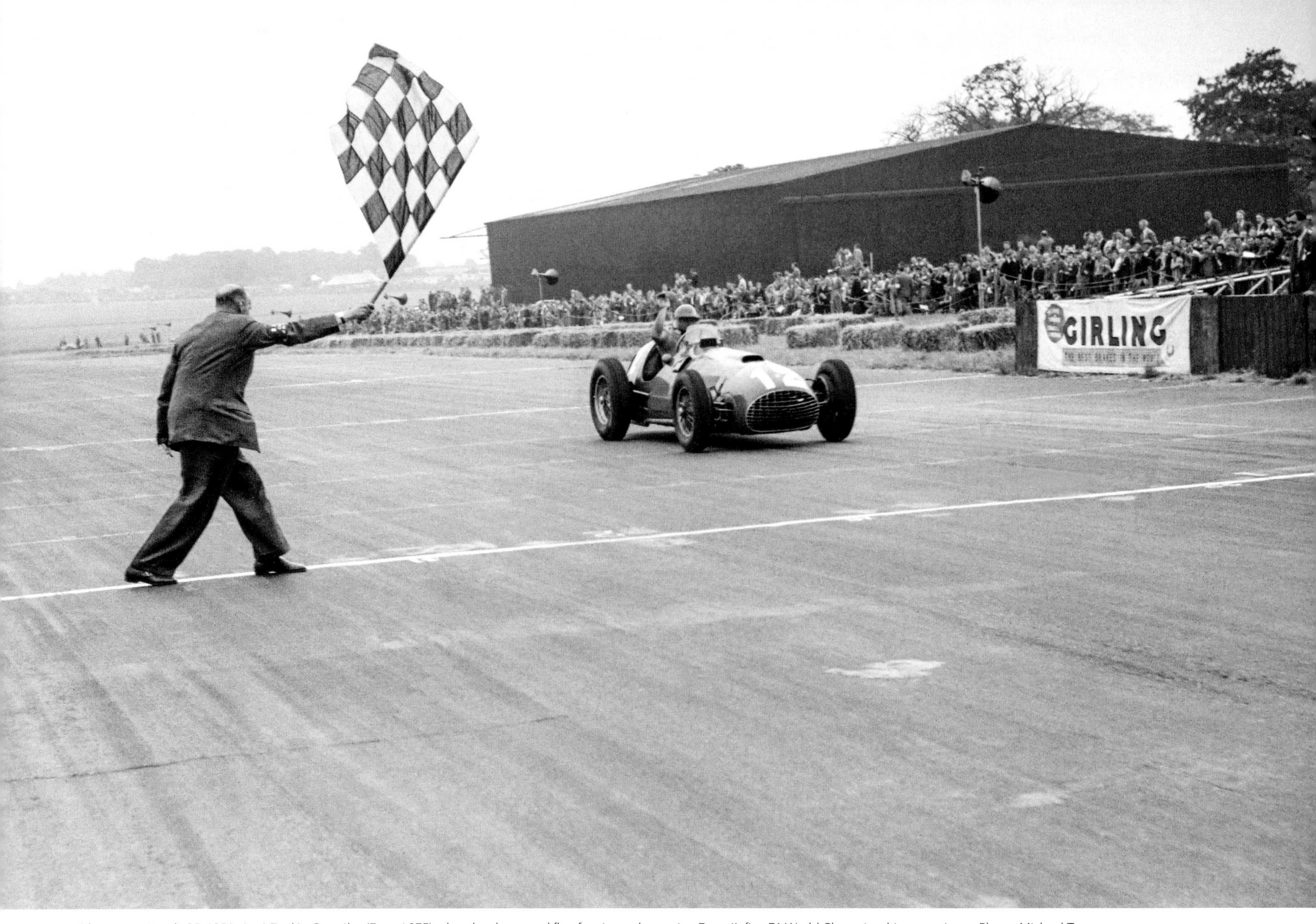

Silverstone, British GP, 1951. José Froilán González (Ferrari 375) takes the chequered flag for victory, becoming Ferrari's first F1 World Championship race winner. Photo: Michael Tee

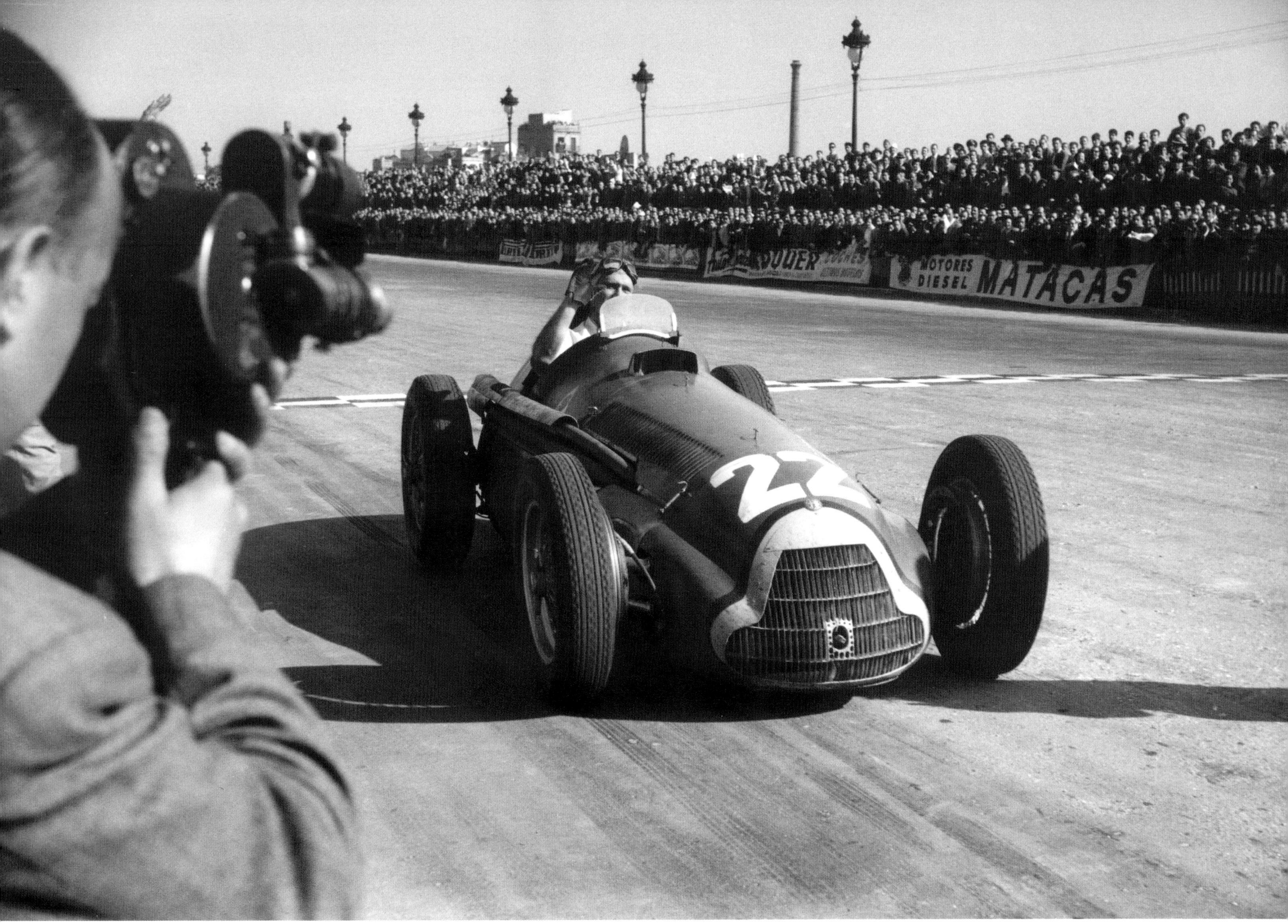

Pedralbes, Spanish GP, 1951. Juan Manuel Fangio (Alfa Romeo 159) celebrates winning the Grand Prix and the World Drivers' Championship for the first time. Photo: LAT Images

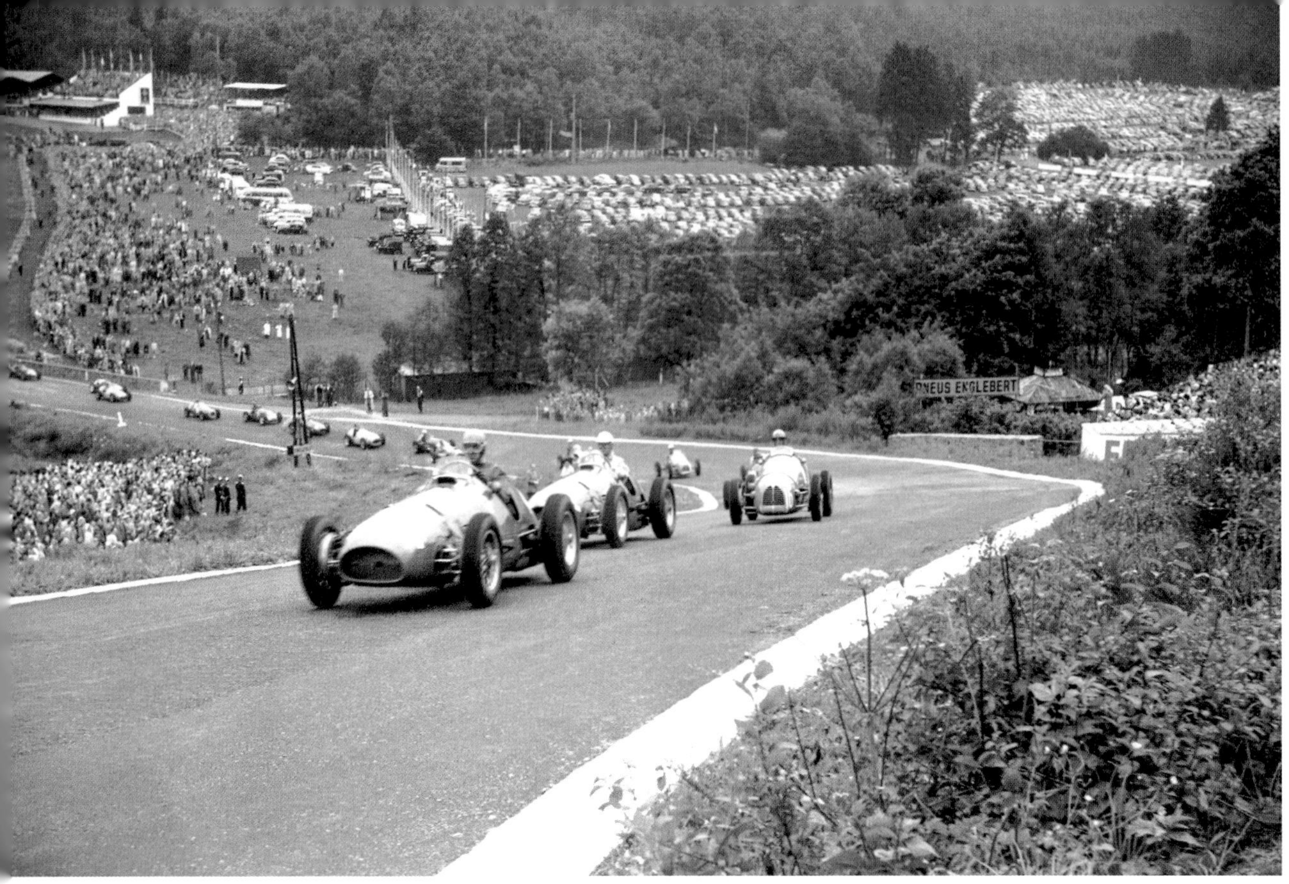

Spa-Francorchamps, Belgian GP, 1952. Alberto Ascari (Ferrari 500) leads Giuseppe Farina (Ferrari 500), and Jean Behra (Gordini T16), up Eau Rouge and Raidillon. Photo: Michael Tee

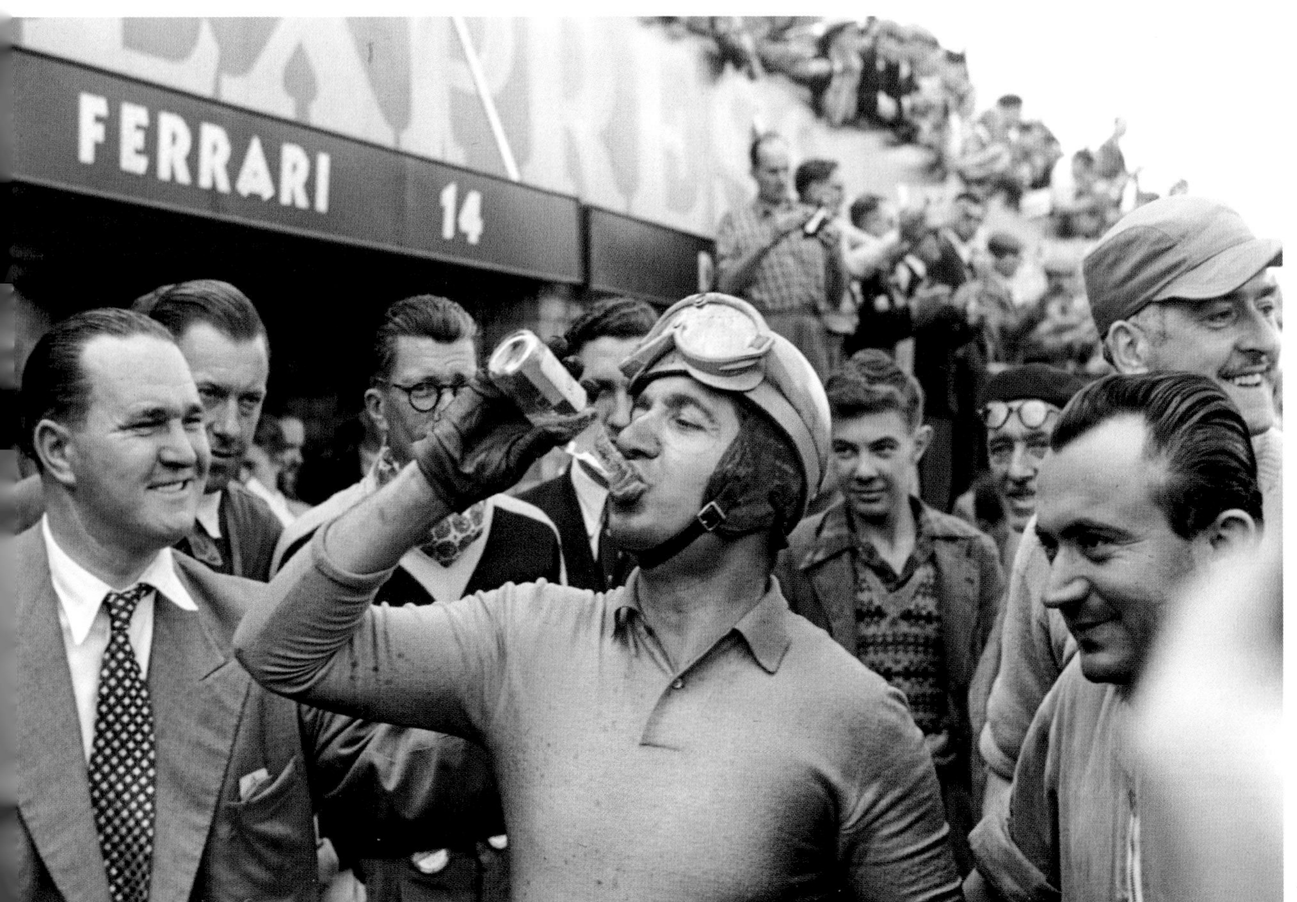

Silverstone, British GP, 1952. Alberto Ascari celebrates winning the race by a lap by drinking a bottle of beer in the pits. Photo: LAT Images

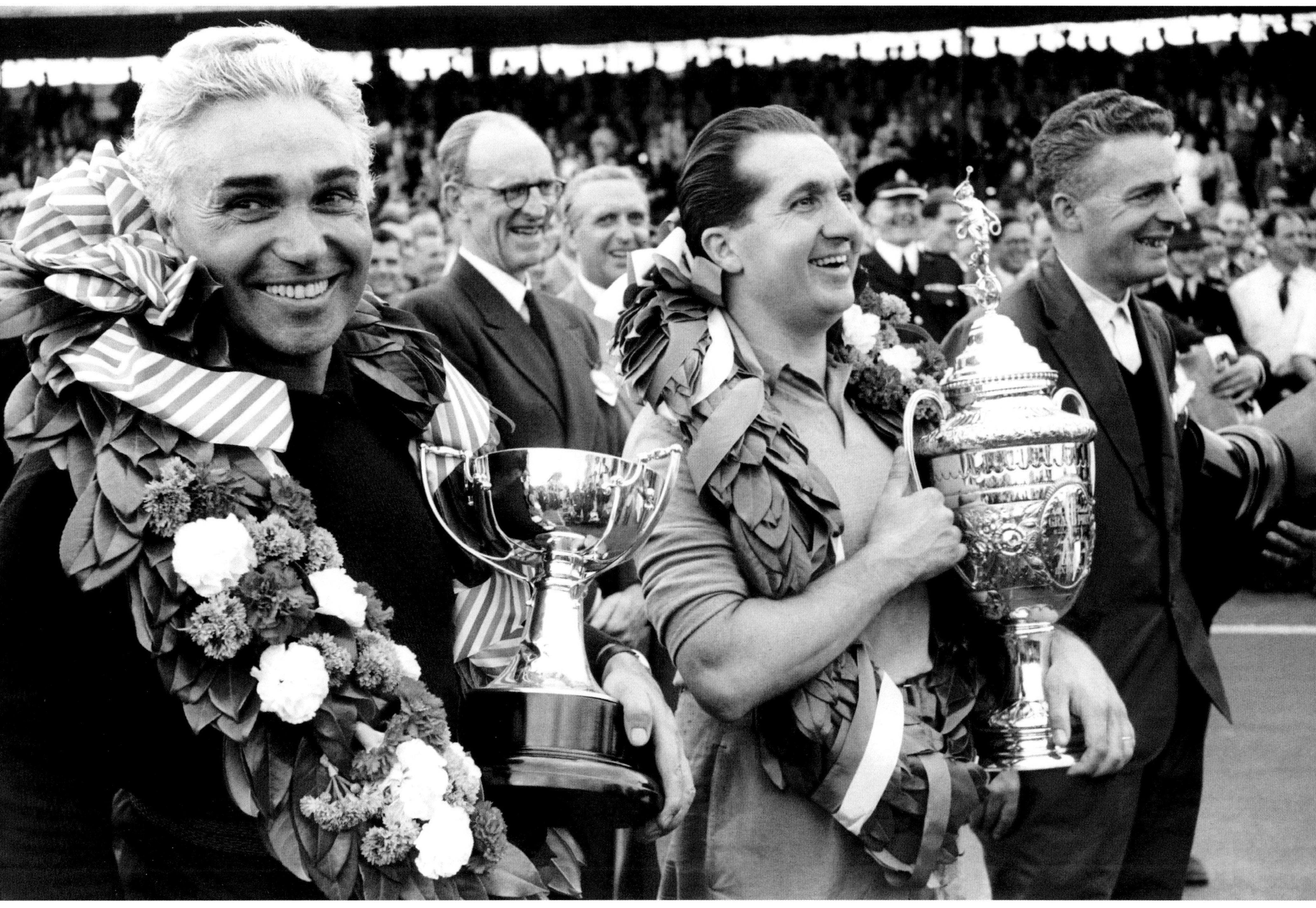

Silverstone, British GP, 1952. Alberto Ascari and teammate Piero Taruffi celebrate first and second place. Photo: LAT Images

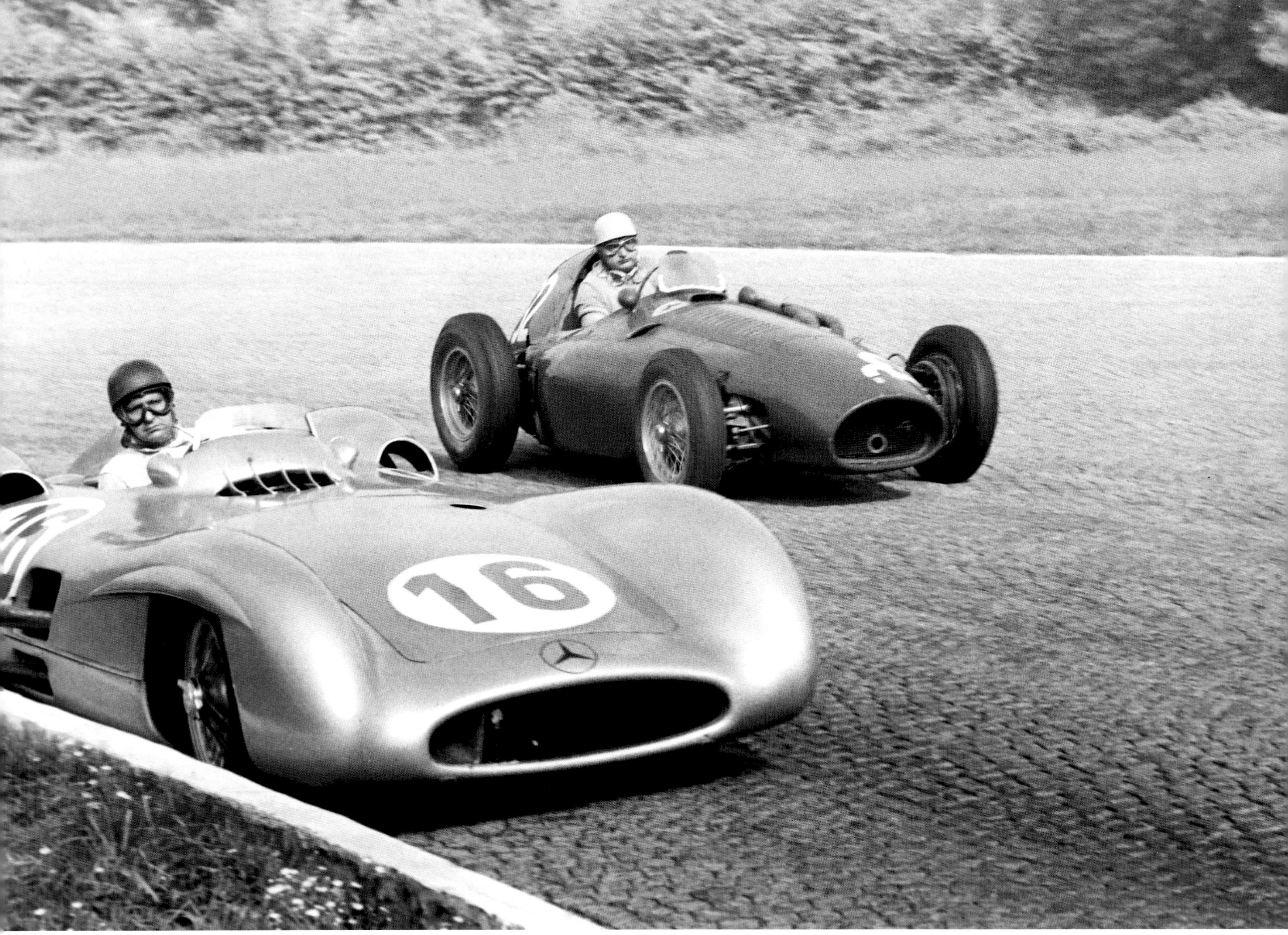

Monza, Italian GP, 1954. Juan Manuel Fangio (driving the streamlined variant of the Mercedes W196) leads José Froilán González (Ferrari 553). Photo: Michael Tee

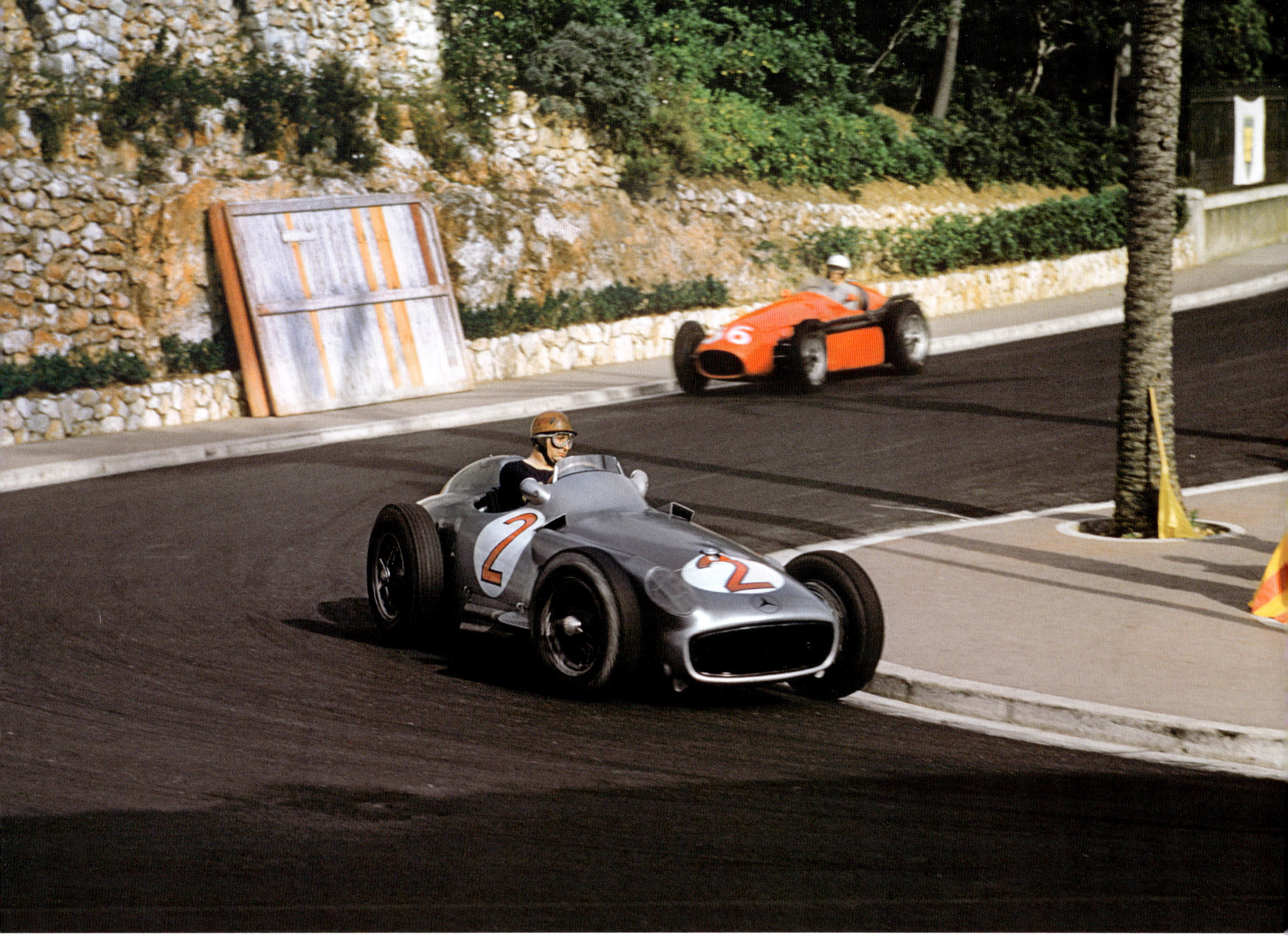

Monaco GP, 1955. Juan Manuel Fangio (Mercedes-Benz W196) leads Roberto Mieres (Maserati 250F). Photo: Michael Tee

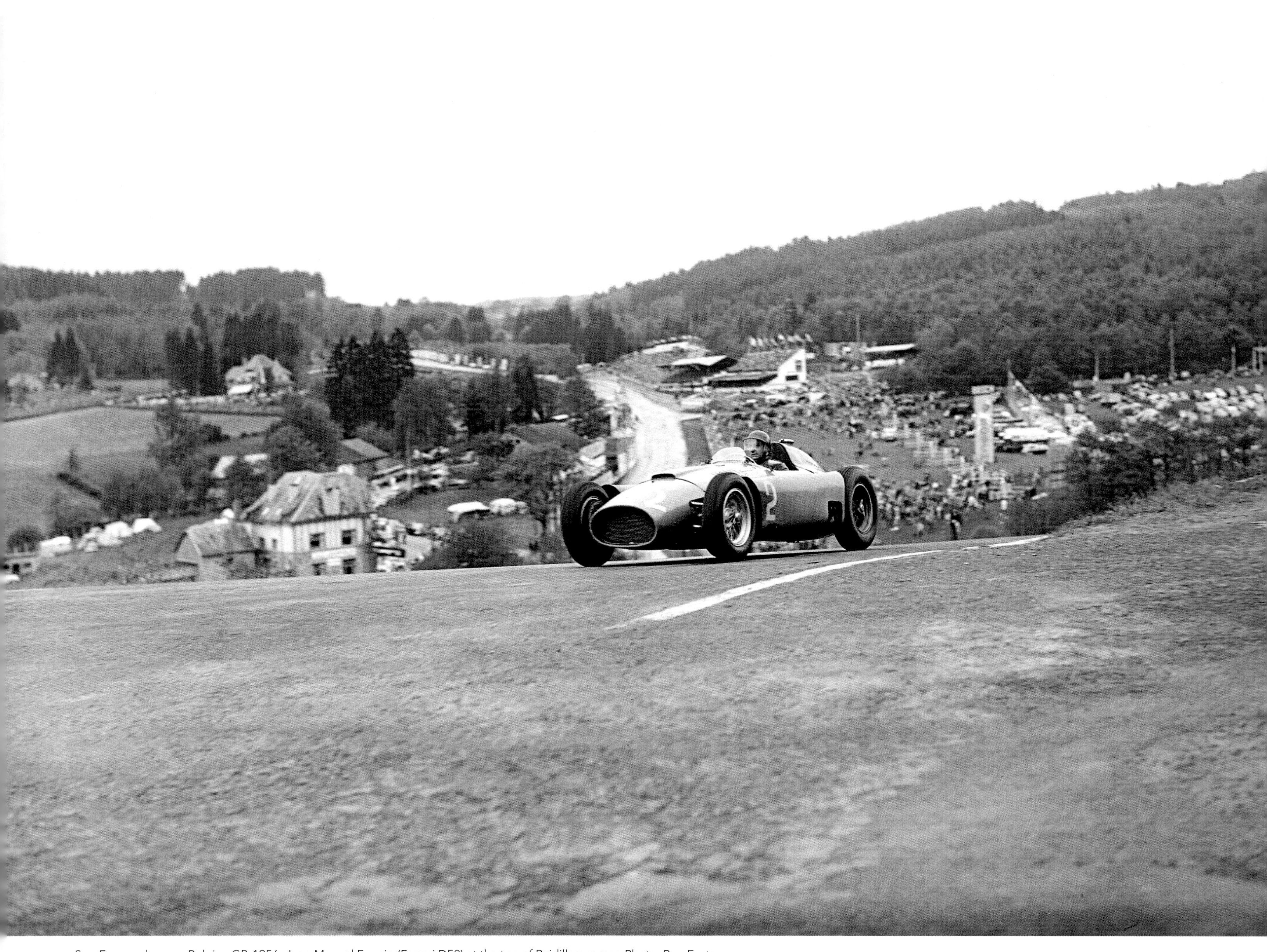

Spa-Francorchamps, Belgian GP, 1956. Juan Manuel Fangio (Ferrari D50) at the top of Raidillon corner. Photo: Ron Easton

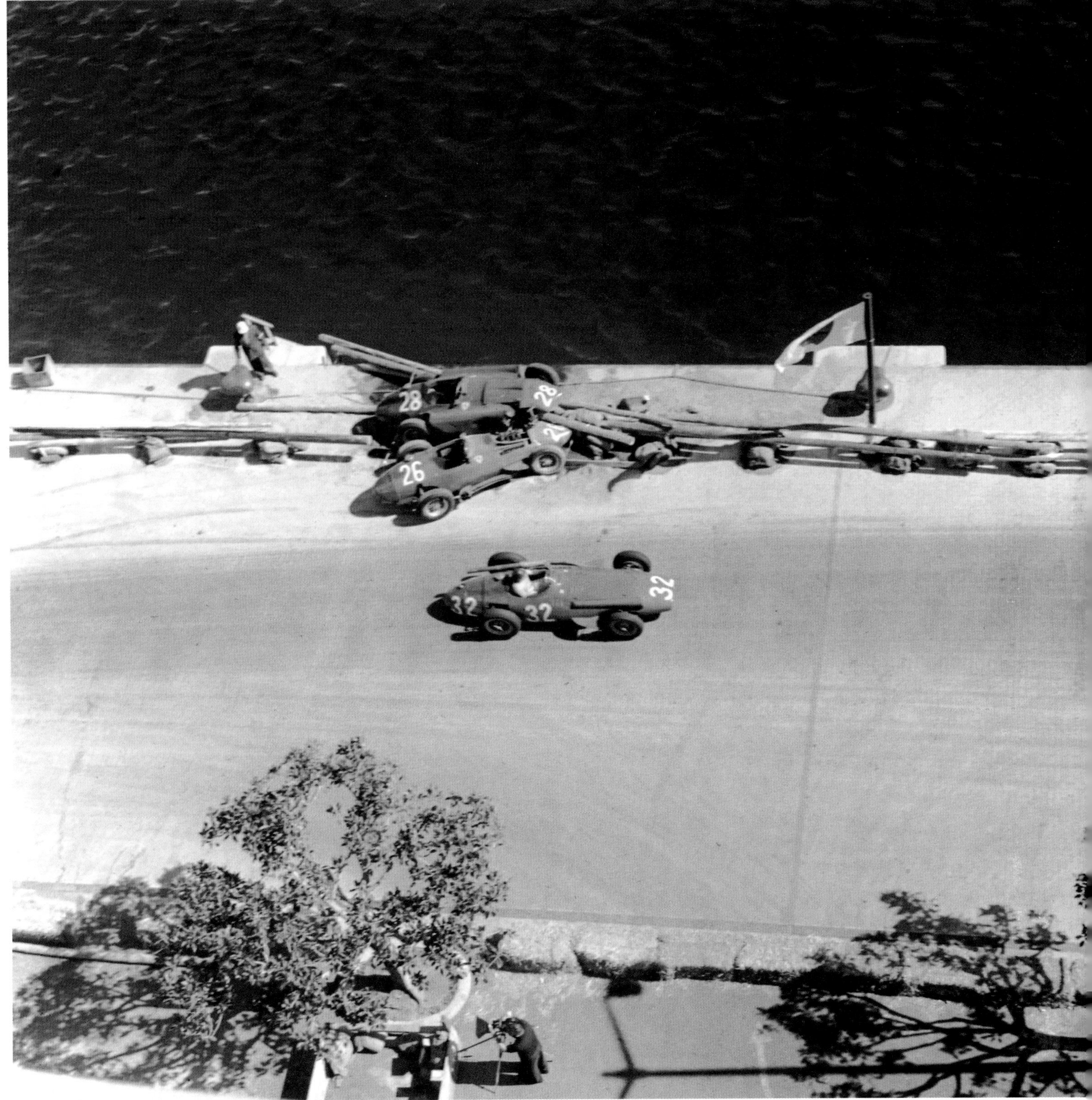

Monaco GP, 1957. Juan Manuel Fangio (Maserati 250F) passes the abandoned Ferrari D50 cars of Mike Hawthorn (number 28) and Peter Collins (number 26). Photo: Michael Tee

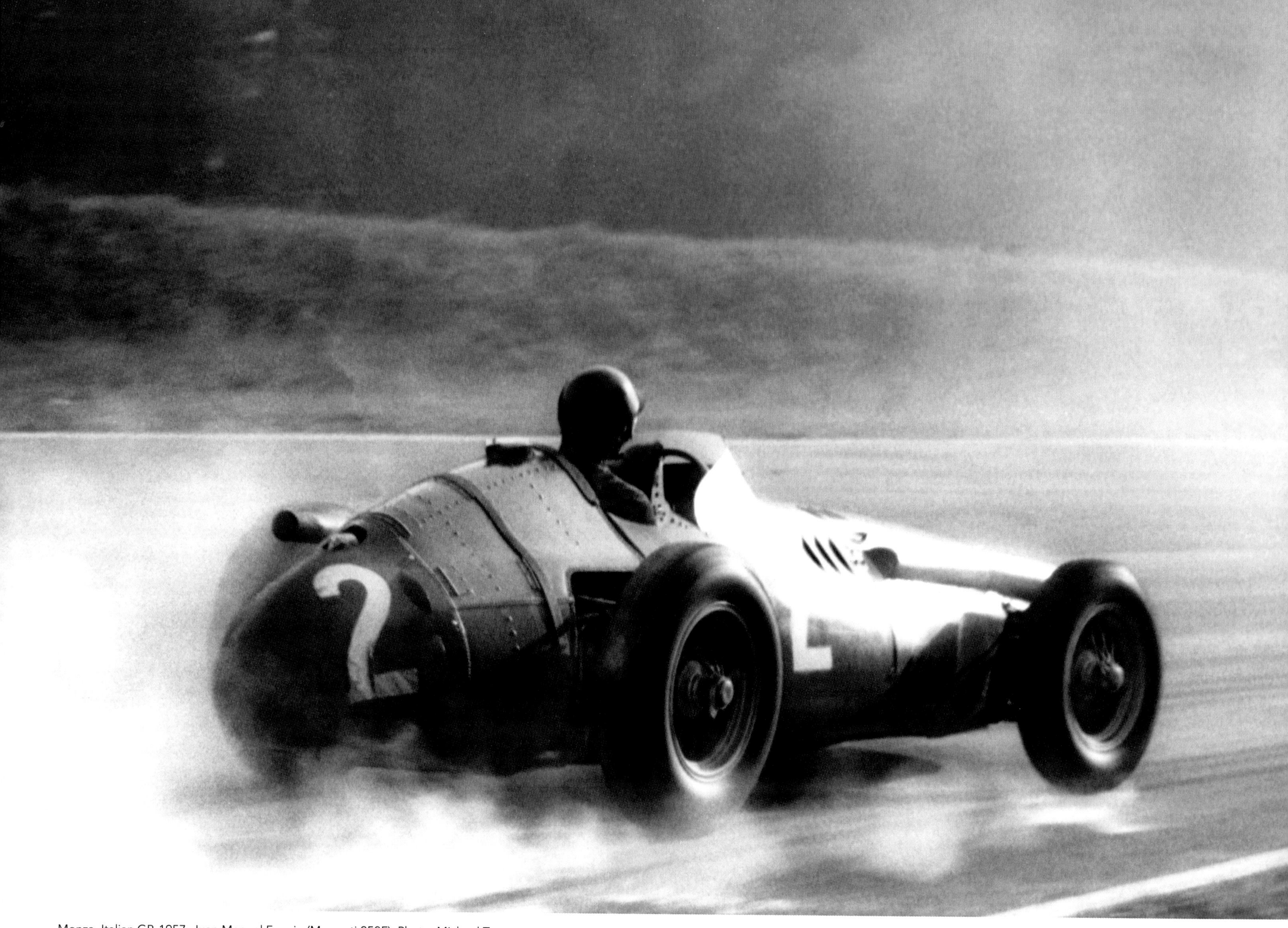

Monza, Italian GP, 1957. Juan Manuel Fangio (Maserati 250F). Photo: Michael Tee

Silverstone, British GP, 1958.
Mike Hawthorn (second),
congratulates teammate and
race winner Peter Collins.
Photo: Ron Easton

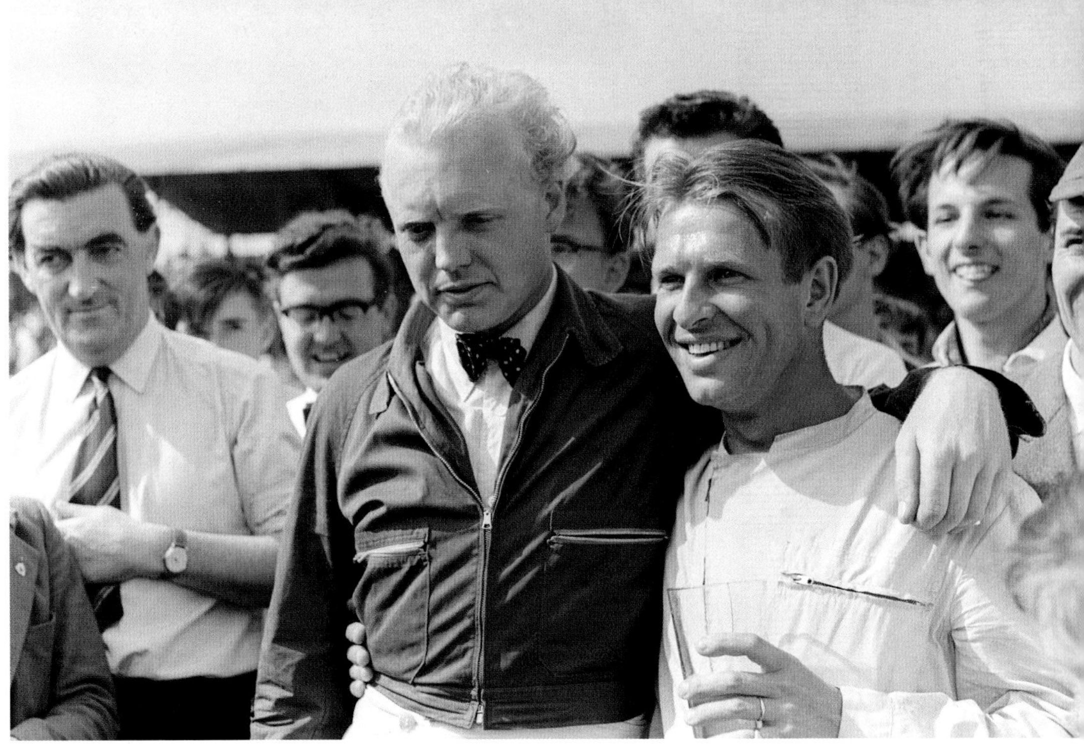

Monza, Italian GP, 1958.
Mike Hawthorn (Ferrari 246)
has a refreshing drink while
mechanics work on a tyre
change during a pit stop.
Photo: Michael Tee

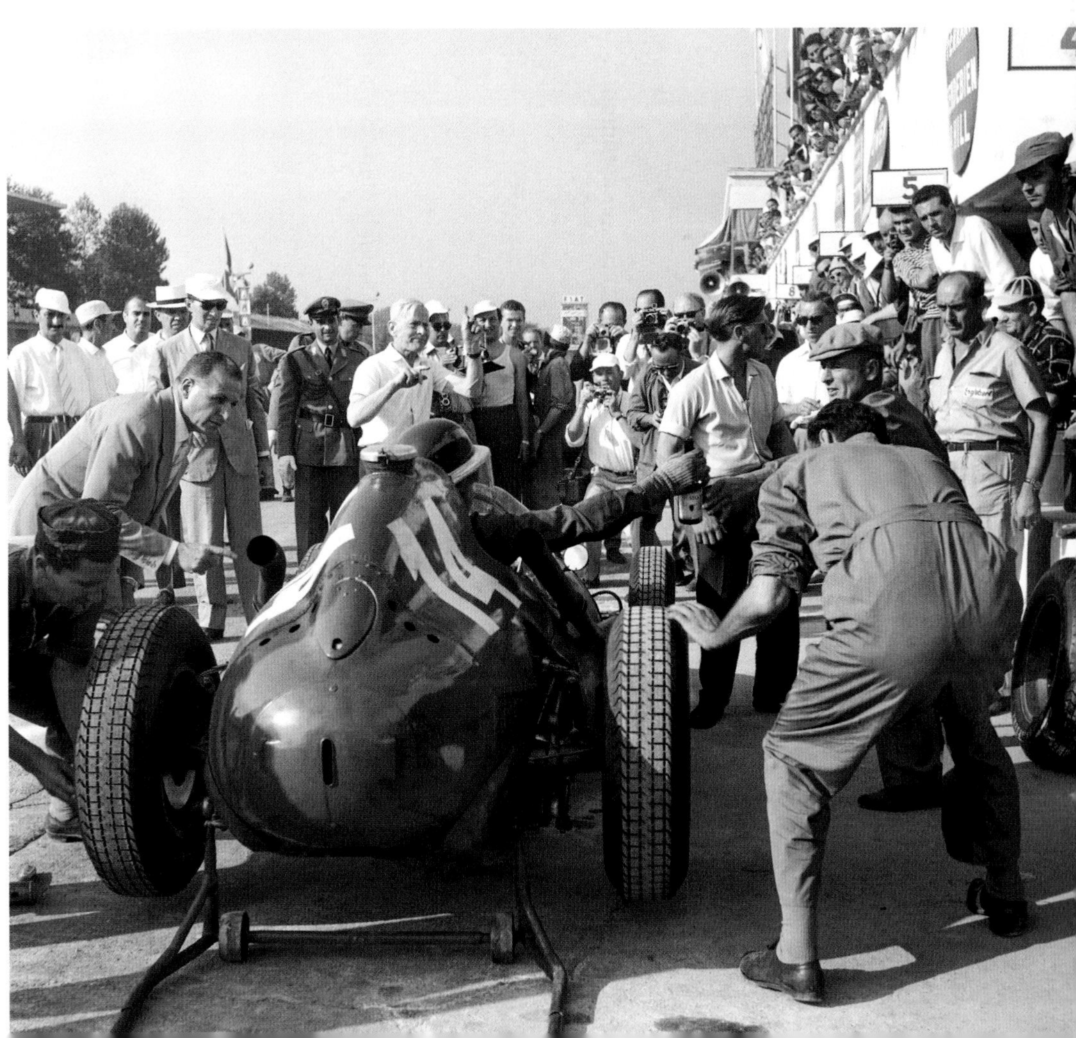

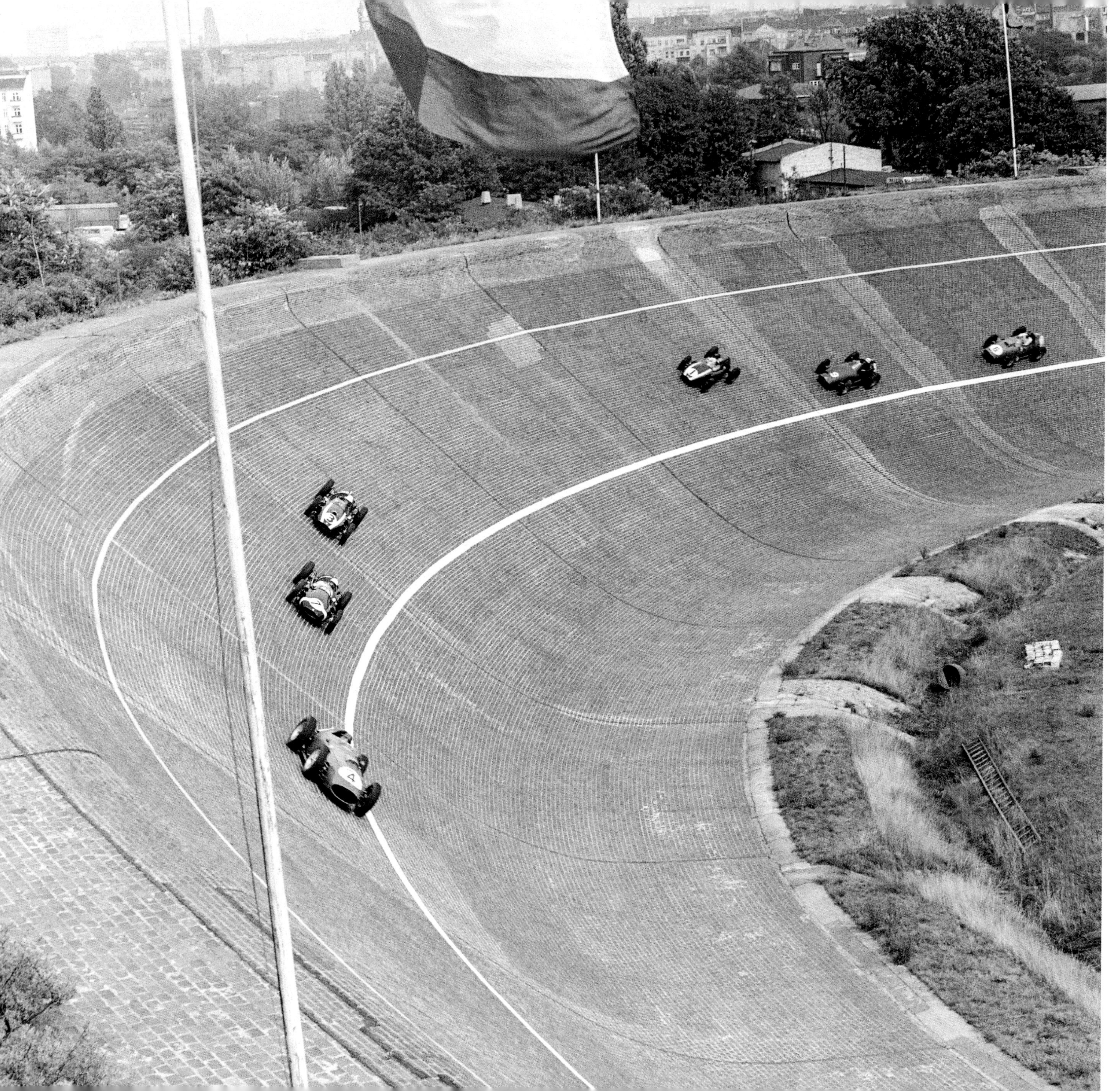

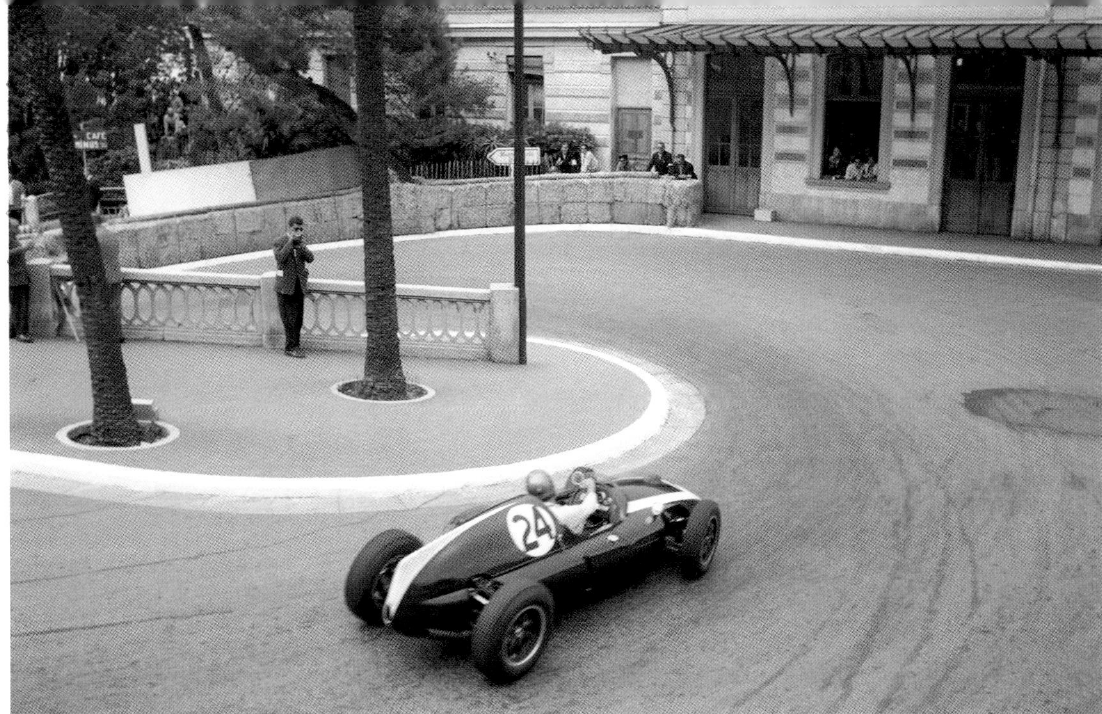

Monaco GP, 1959. Jack
Brabham (Cooper T51 Climax).
Photo: Maurice Rowe

Avus, German GP, 1959.
Tony Brooks (Ferrari 246)
leads Stirling Moss (Cooper
T51 Climax), Masten Gregory
(Cooper T51 Climax), Jack
Brabham (Cooper T51 Climax),
Jo Bonnier (BRM P25), and
Dan Gurney (Ferrari 246).
Photo: LAT Images

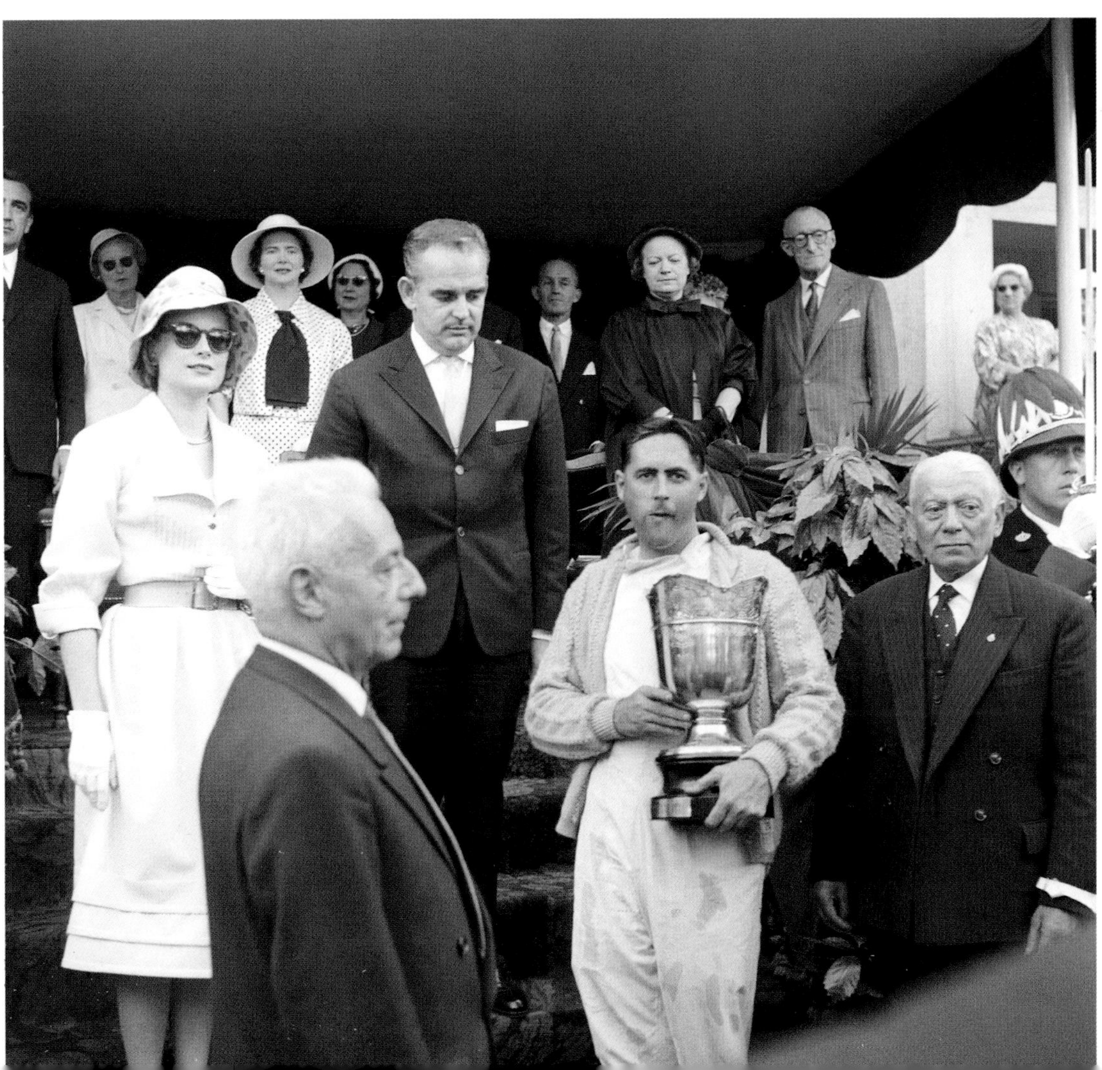

Monaco GP, 1959. Jack
Brabham, winner of the race,
on the podium with Prince
Rainier and Princess Grace of
Monaco. Photo: Michael Tee

1960–1969
The First Revolution

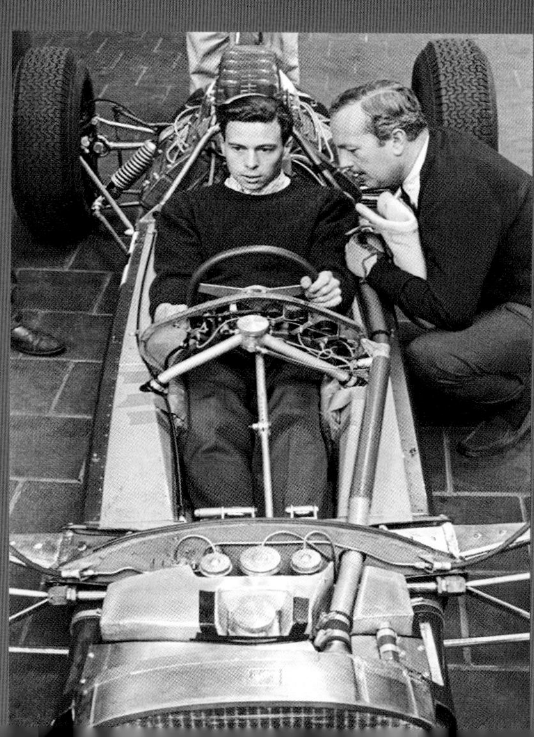

The world changed; details, customs, habits changed. And the cars changed: the street models and the race cars, too. Mostly "Made in England." The Sixties, a revolution. Extremely modern single-seaters, still very dangerous, rear-engined, smaller, wider wheels for the growing popularity of F1. Jack Brabham was the first world champion in a decade full of unforgettable protagonists. Graham Hill (1929–1975) and Jim Clark (1936–1968) stood out among the others, and not only because they both achieved two titles. Hill, born on February 15, 1929 in Hampstead, an area in north London, with that thin, wry mustache, is to this day the only driver to have won the Triple Crown, which alongside the F1 World Championship (accomplished in 1962 with BRM and in 1968 with Lotus), includes the Indianapolis 500 (won in 1966 driving a Lola), the Monaco GP (five wins between 1963 and 1969, his last victory), and the 24 Hours of Le Mans (which Hill conquered in 1972 with the Frenchman Henri Pescarolo, driving a Matra). A champion of intelligence and versatility, his achievements in F1 included: 176 races, 14 wins, 13 pole positions. In 1973 he founded his own team, Embassy Hill, with the intention of launching a new, young, British talent, Tony Brise. They both died in an airplane accident on November 29, 1975, Graham in the cockpit of a Piper Aztec. They crashed not far from London due to very difficult weather conditions. Hill had three children.

The youngest, Damon, would become world champion in 1996.
Jim Clark was Scottish. Born in Kilmany on March 4, 1936. He was quiet and reserved, and a god behind the wheel. His career was tied to Lotus and to Colin Chapman, brilliant and mysterious, designer of the first car with a monocoque chassis, perfect for Jimmy who drove nearly laying down: two world titles (in 1963 and 1965), a victory at the Indianapolis 500 (1965), the first with a rear-engined vehicle. His style was magnificent and effective, and he had a sensational aptitude for speed. Many consider him to be the all-time best, alongside Senna: 72 Grands Prix, 25 victories, 33 pole positions. The numbers of an ace. Paired with an image that induced a heart-rending nostalgia. He died in Hockenheim, in Germany, on April 7, 1968 during a Formula 2 race, in an unfathomable accident.
They—Hill and Clark, along with Brabham—were the giants of a decade that honored other protagonists as well. Phil Hill (1927–2008), an American from Miami, a Ferrari driver, world champion in a dramatic 1961, year of the death of his teammate, Wolfgang von Trips, in Monza, in an accident that cost the lives of 15 spectators. A kart racing enthusiast, he built the small track in Kerpen of which Rolf Schumacher became the custodian several years later, allowing his son Michael to do his first laps behind a wheel. John Surtees (1934–2017), winner of the title in 1964 driving a

Ferrari, the only F1 world champion who also won a motorcycle World Championship. In fact, between 1956 and 1960, John won seven motorcycle world titles in different categories. The third title conquered by Jack Brabham in 1966 set an undefeated record. He was the first and only world champion to drive a single-seater bearing the driver's name.
Denis Hulme, a New-Zealander (1936–1992), also driving a Brabham, won in 1967; Jackie Stewart, another Scotsman, born in Dumbarton on June 11, 1939, obtained his first world title in 1969 driving a Matra-Ford introduced by Ken Tyrrell. He was an admirer and a friend of Clark. Just like Jack Brabham, with his victories he led the way into the following decade.
The names of Italian drivers disappeared from the hall of fame of the World Championship. Lorenzo Bandini, young, sweet, and very much loved, died in Monte Carlo in 1967 in a fire that is still painful to recall. Giancarlo Baghetti, the only driver to win his first F1 race (France, 1961), wasn't able to establish himself. Ludovico Scarfiotti, winner of the Italian GP at Monza in 1966, died two years later during the practice session of a hill climbing event in Rossfeld. They were all Ferrari drivers. Meanwhile, a young New-Zealander, Bruce McLaren (1937–1970), brave and extraordinarily enterprising, had founded his own team. The debut of the first McLaren in F1: Monaco GP, 1966.

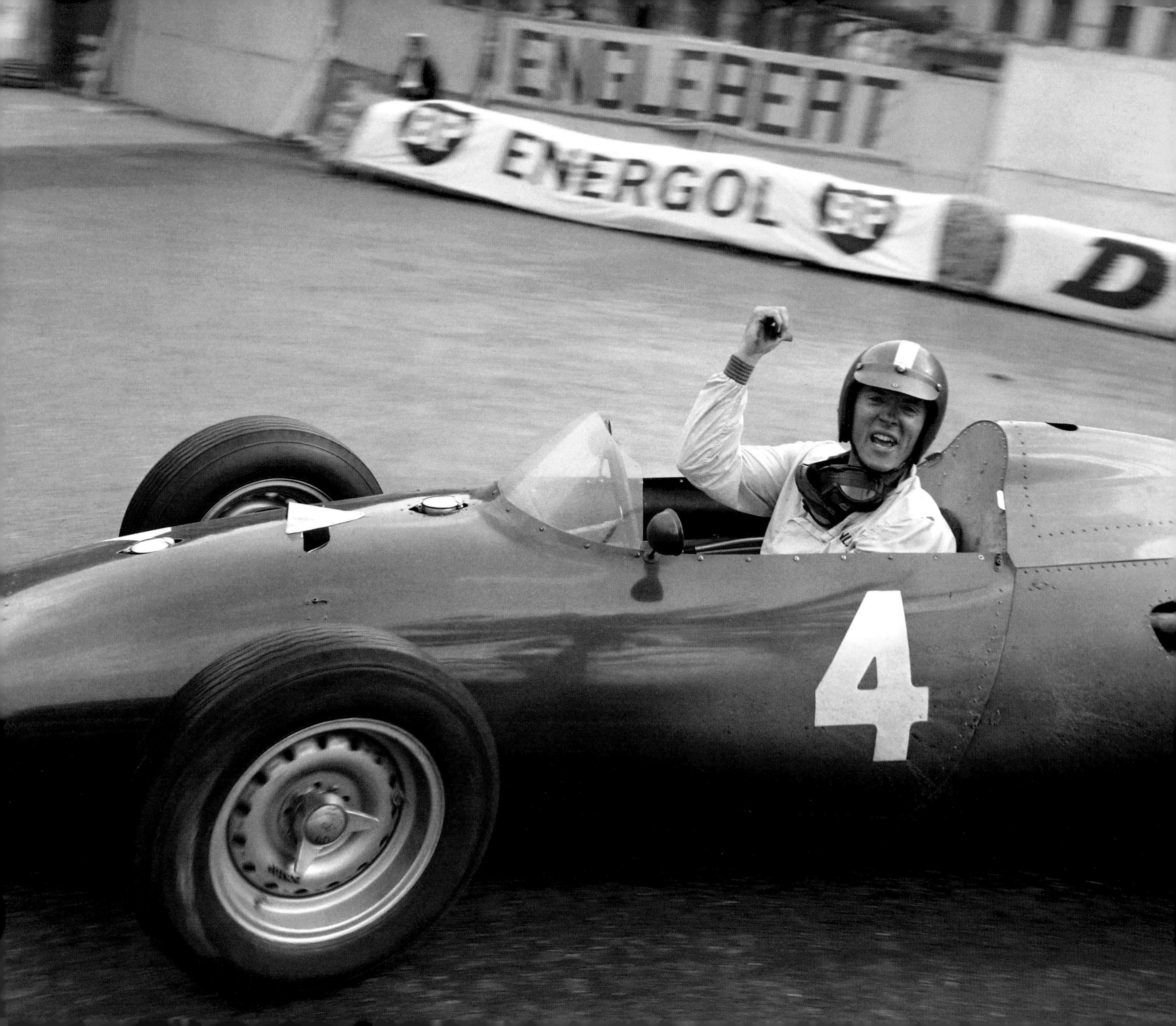
ENGLEBERT
ENERGOL

Monaco GP, 1960. Dan Gurney (BRM P48) waves to Photographer David Phipps. Photo: David Phipps

Silverstone, British GP, 1960. Jack Brabham (Cooper T53 Climax) saws at the steering wheel on his way to victory. Photo: David Phipps

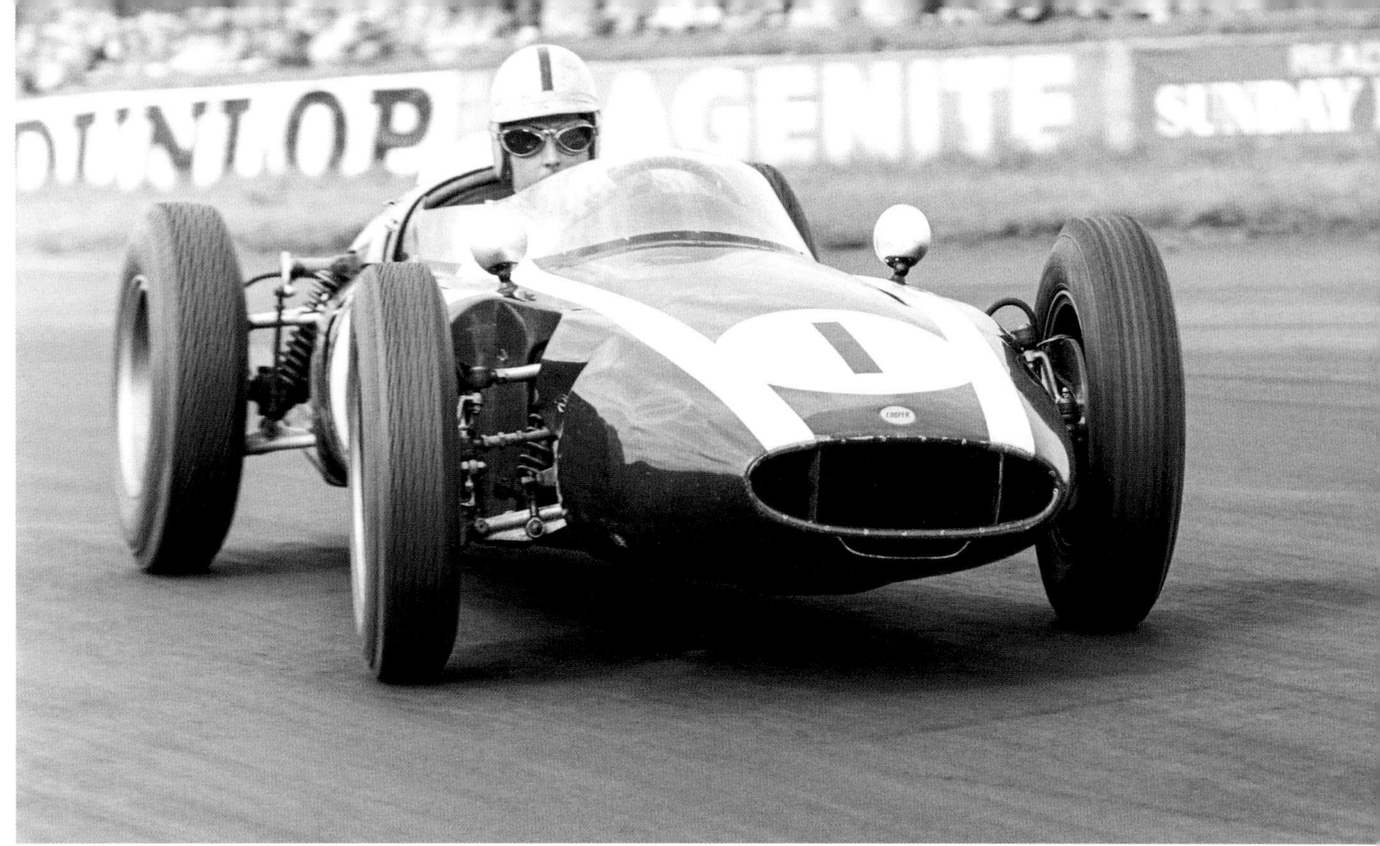

Nürburgring, German GP, 1961. Phil Hill (Ferrari 156) rounds the Karussell. Photo: David Phipps

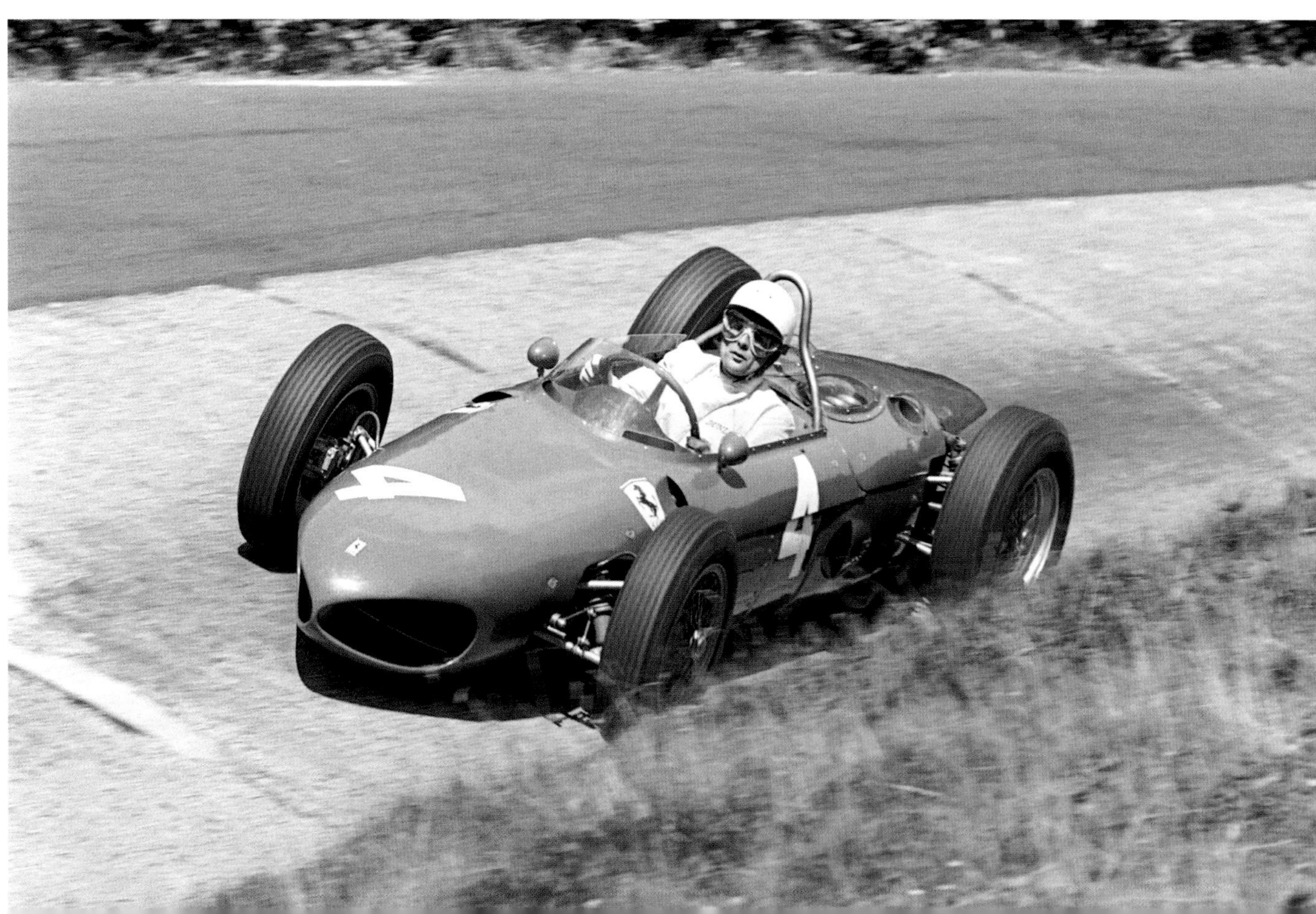

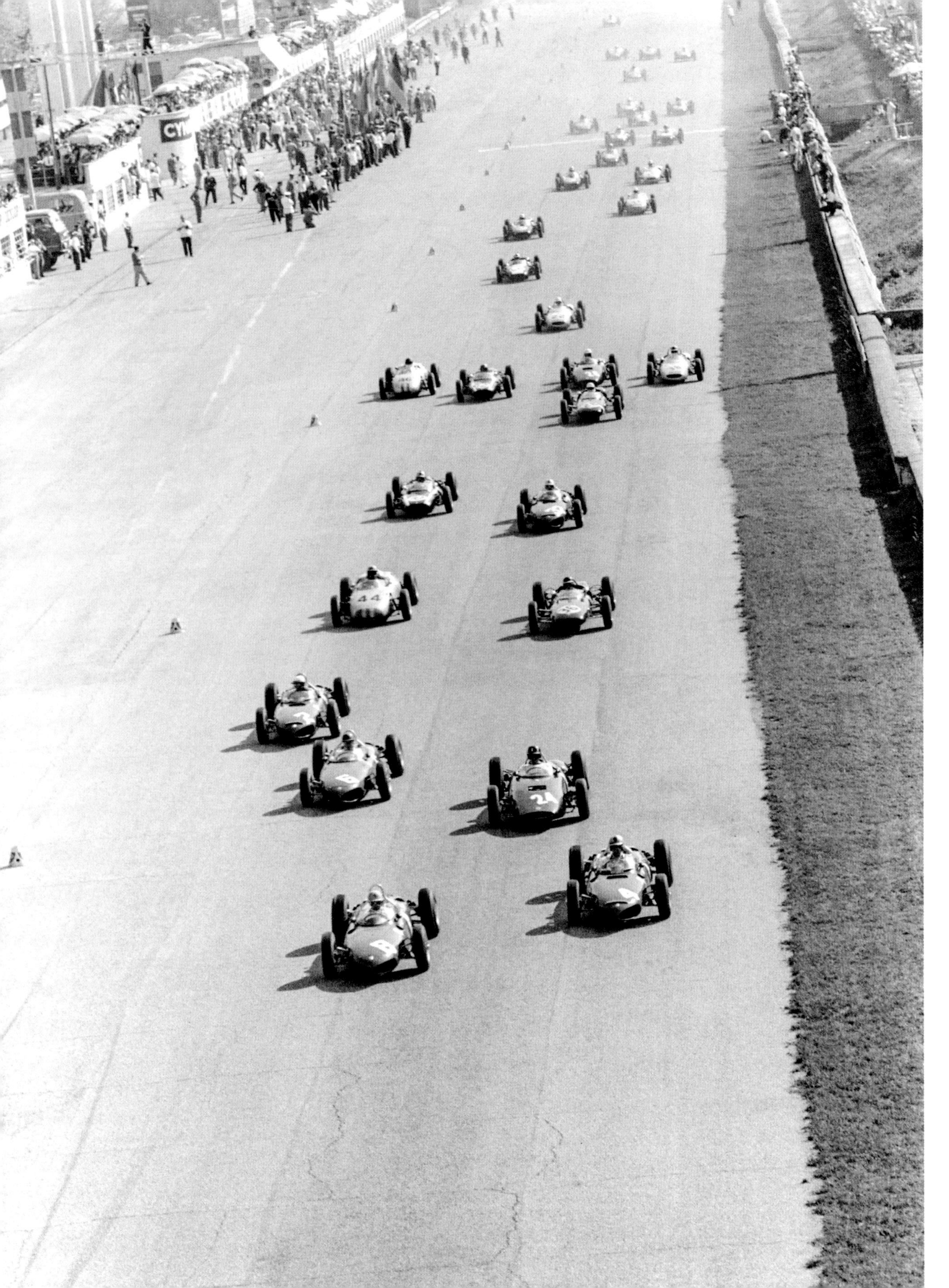

Monza, Italian GP, 1961. The start, with Ricardo Rodríguez (Ferrari 156) leading from Wolfgang von Trips (Ferrari 156). Photo: David Phipps

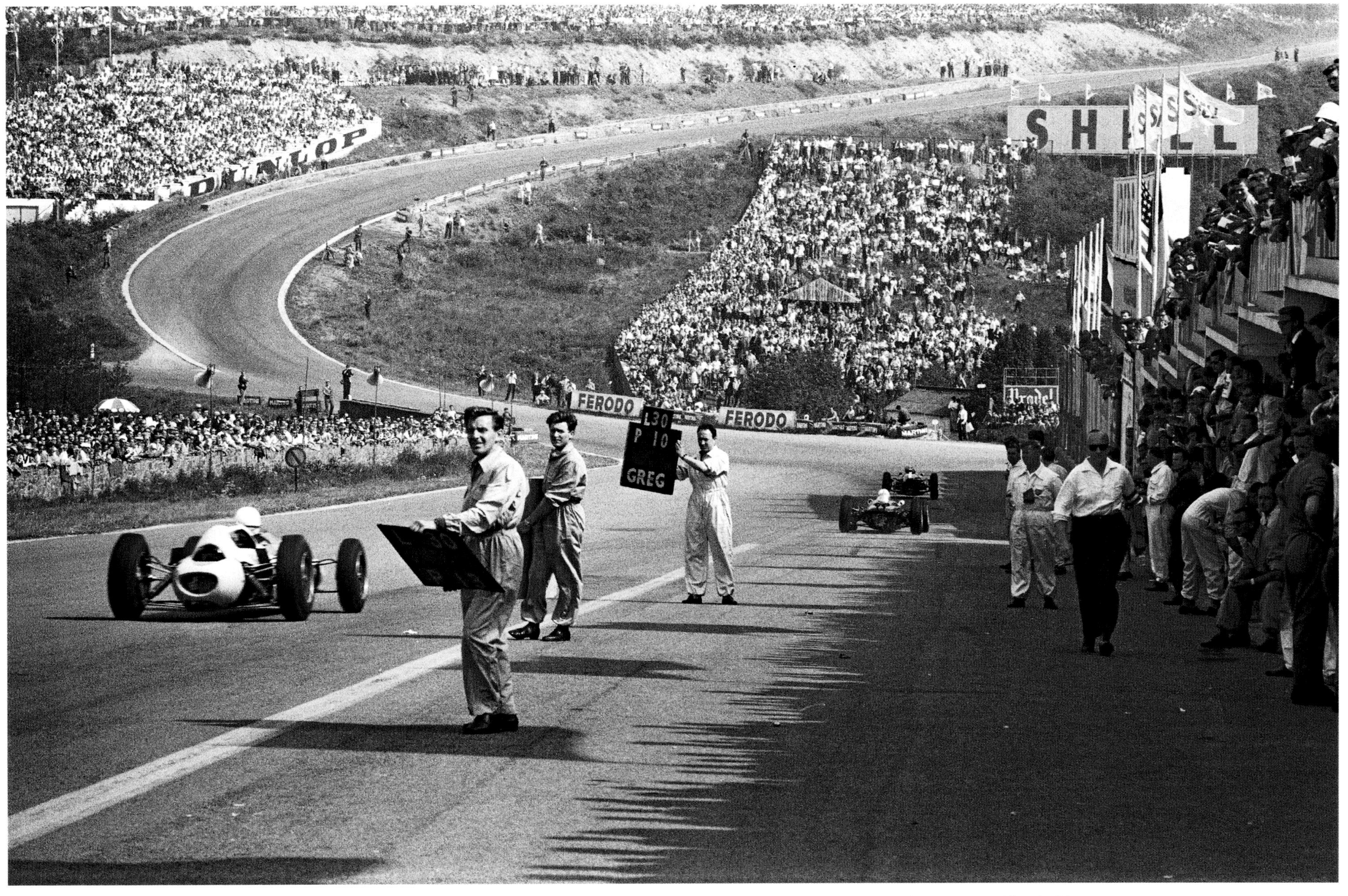

Spa-Francorchamps, Belgian GP, 1962. View from the pits looking downhill towards Eau Rouge, as mechanics hold pit boards to signal to drivers. Photo: Rainer Schlegelmilch

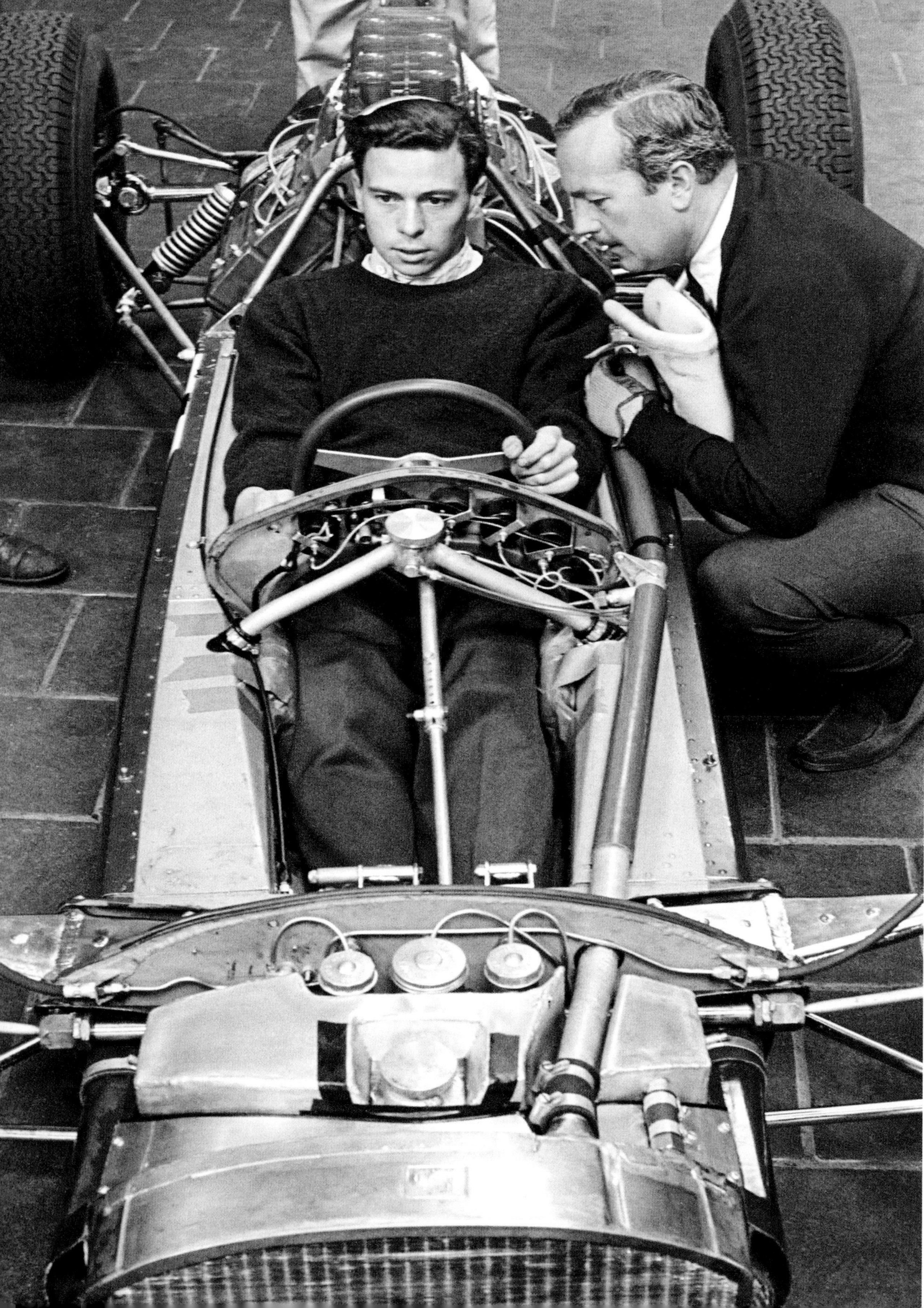

Zandvoort, Dutch GP, 1962.
Jim Clark, sitting in the new
Lotus 25, talks with Colin
Chapman. Photo: David Phipps

Reims, French GP, 1963.
Jim Clark wearing extra plaster
strips to protect against
flying stones. Photo: Rainer
Schlegelmilch

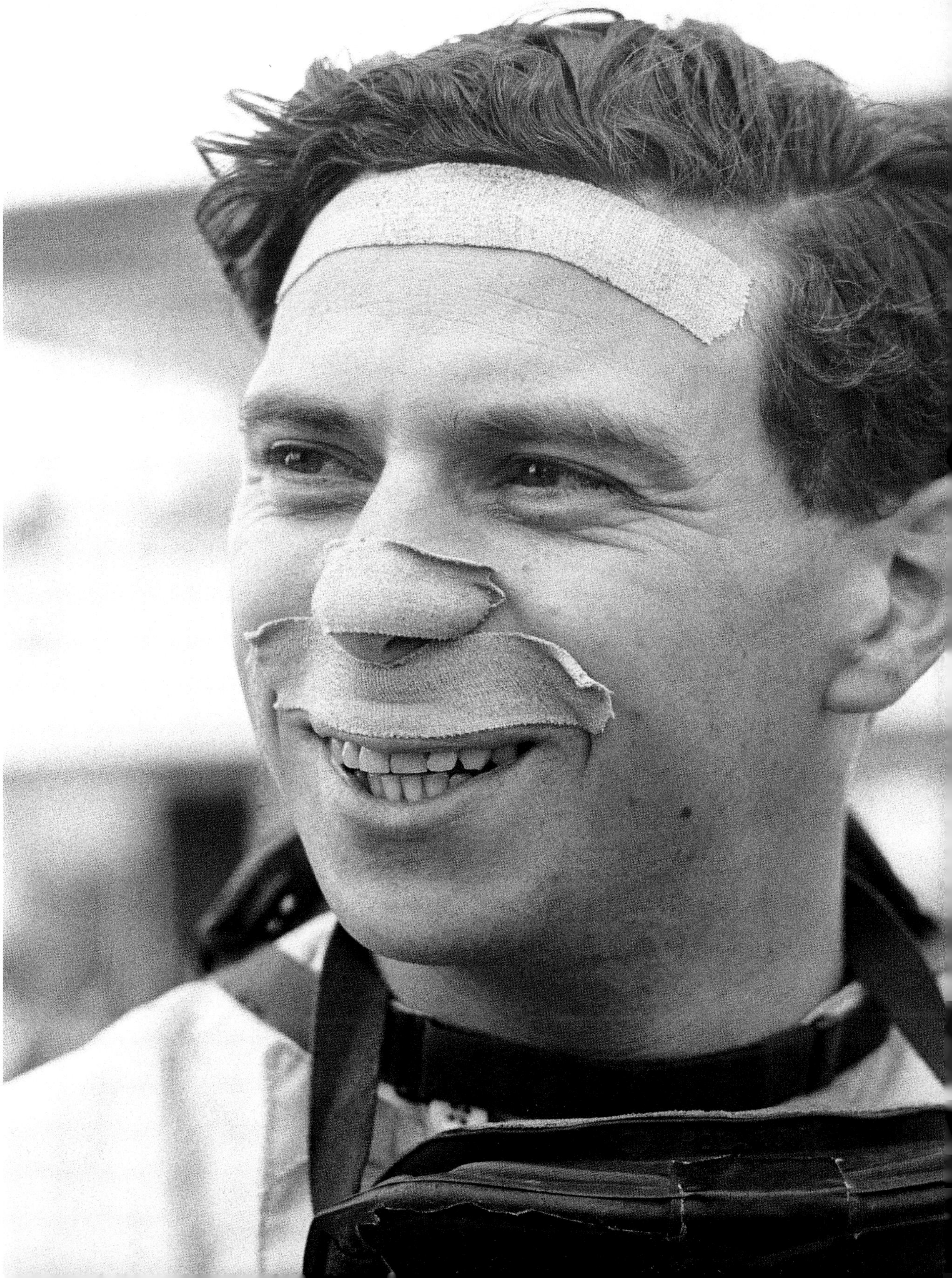

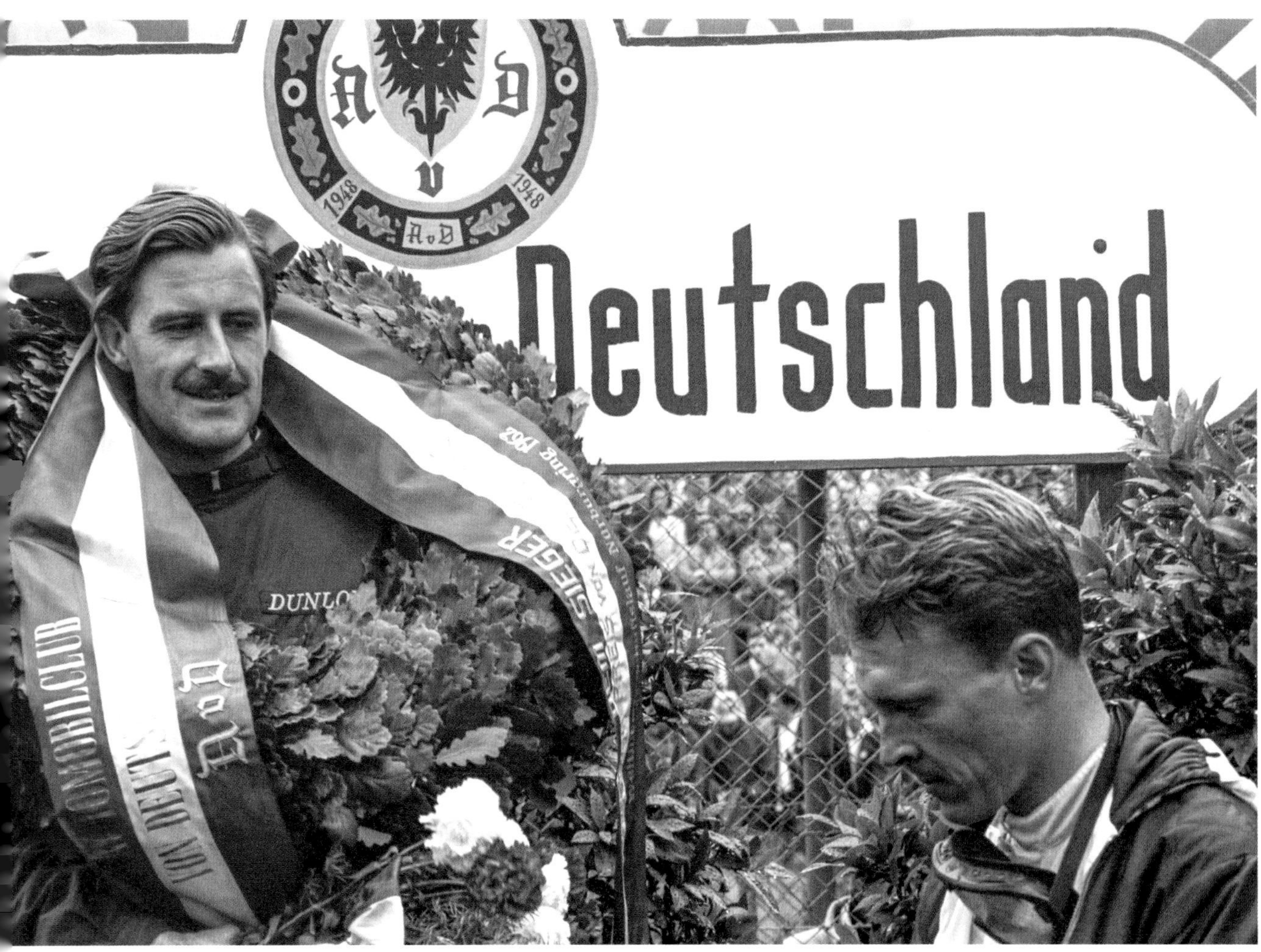

Nürburgring, German GP,
1962. Graham Hill (first) and
Dan Gurney (third), on the
podium. Photo: David Phipps

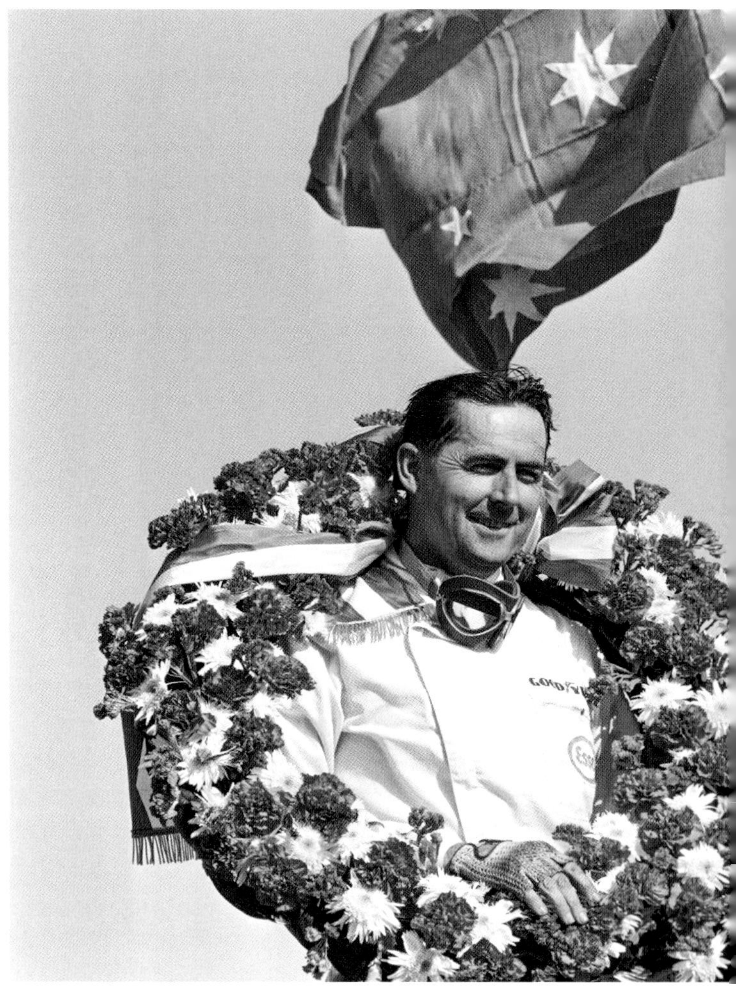

Zandvoort, Dutch GP, 1966.
Jack Brabham celebrates
victory on the podium. Photo:
Ron Easton

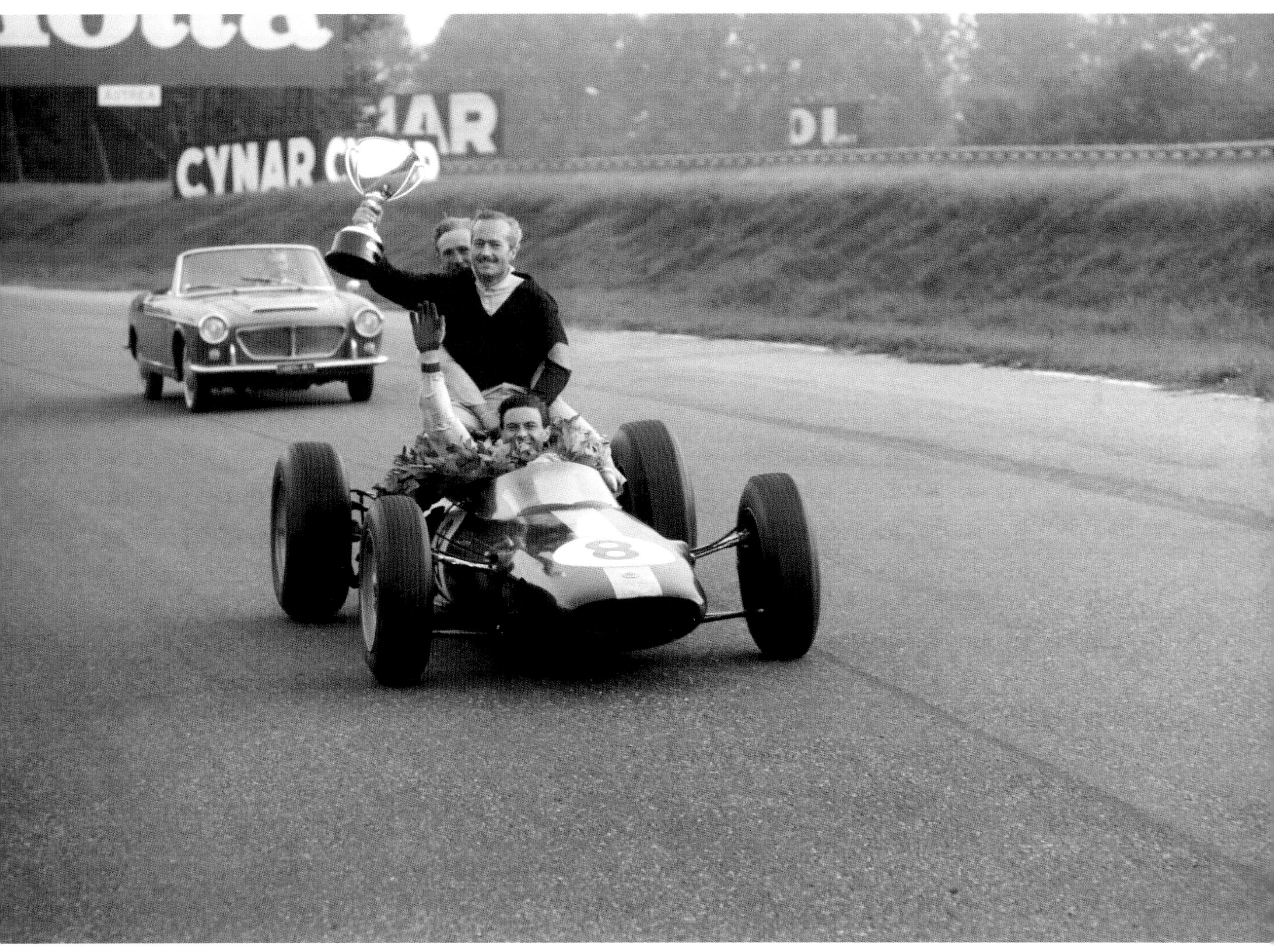

Monza, Italian GP, 1963. Jim Clark (Lotus 25 Climax) with Colin Chapman, holding the winner's trophy on the back. Photo: David Phipps

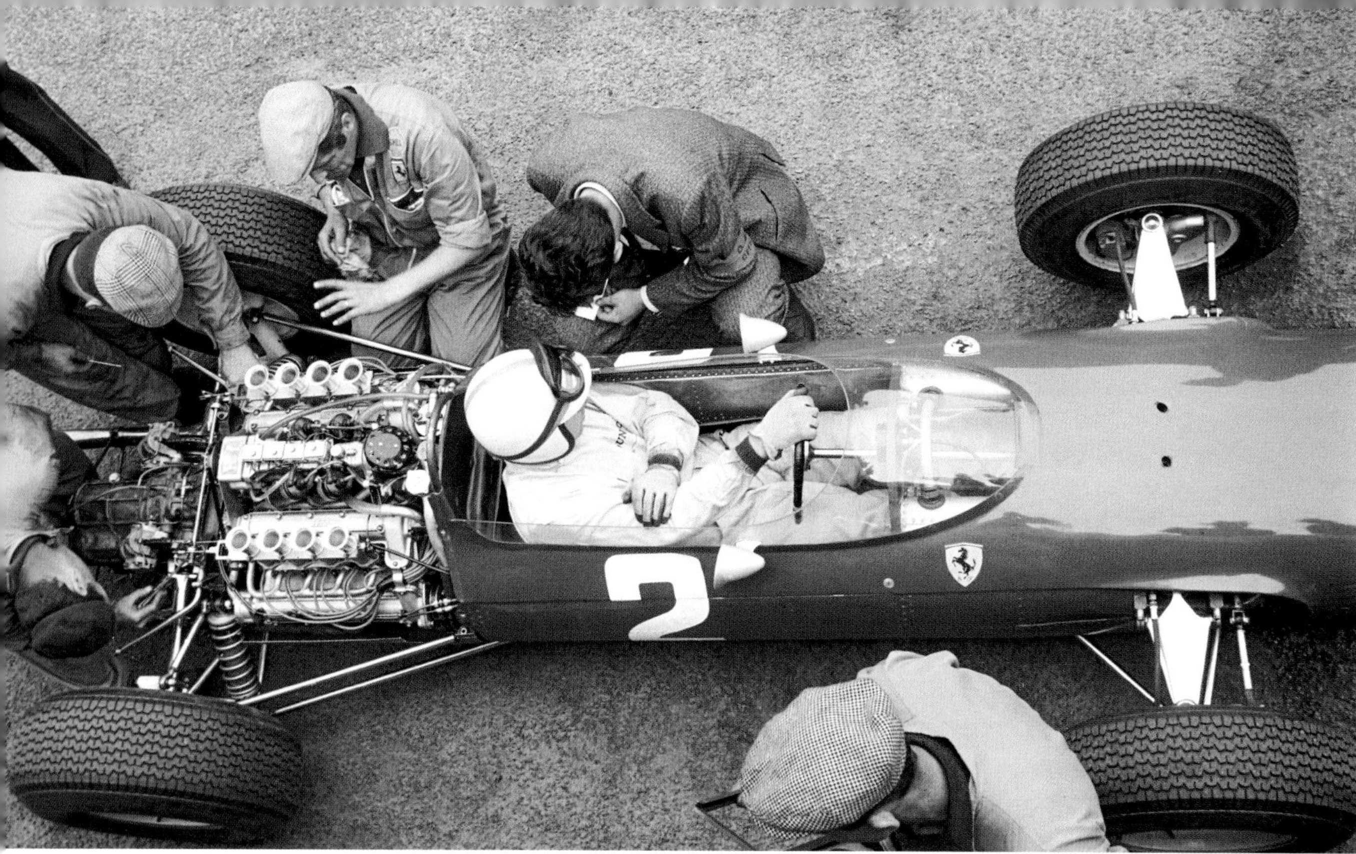

Zandvoort, Dutch GP, 1964.
John Surtees (Ferrari 158).
Photo: David Phipps

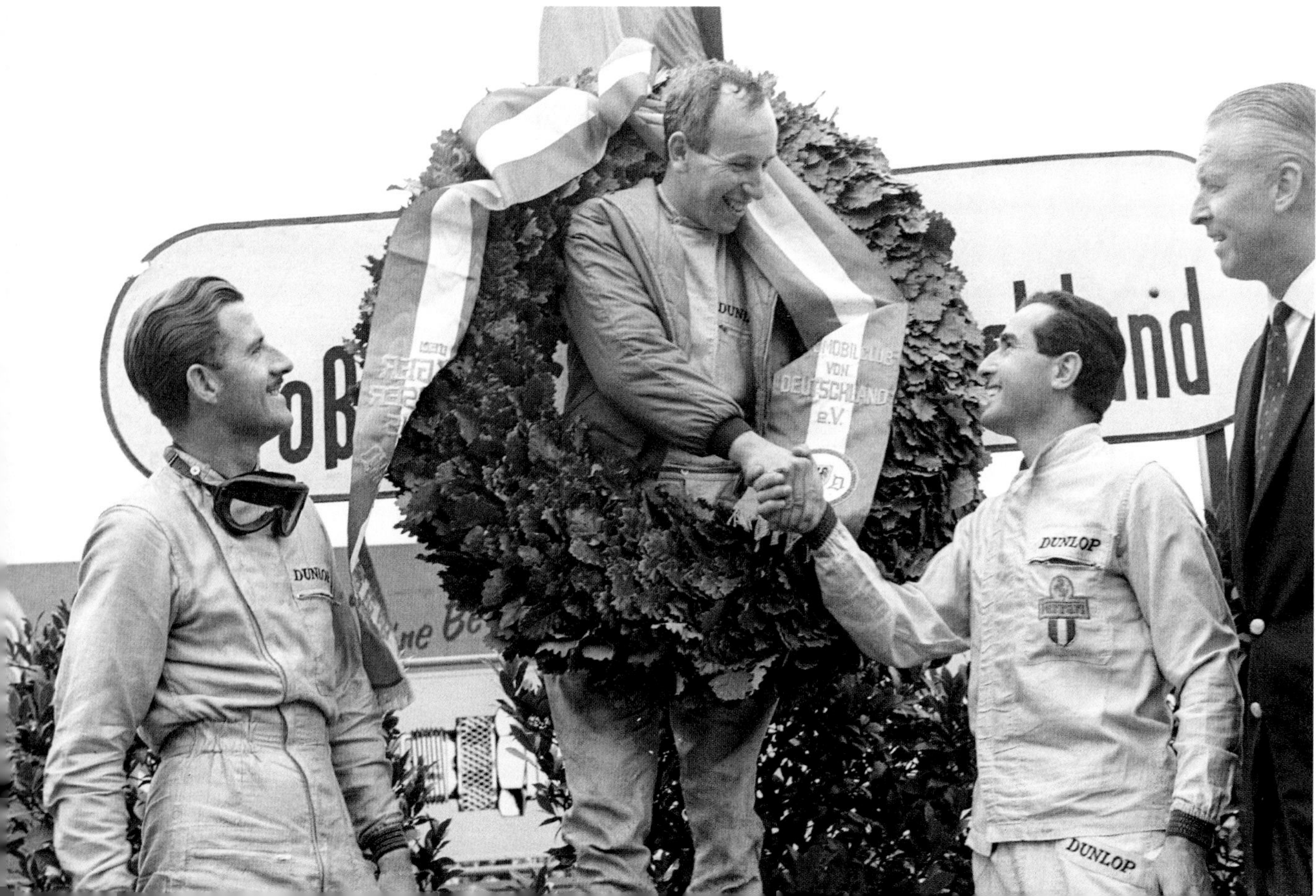

Nürburgring, German GP, 1964. John Surtees (first) celebrates on the podium, with Graham Hill (second), and Lorenzo Bandini (third).
Photo: David Phipps

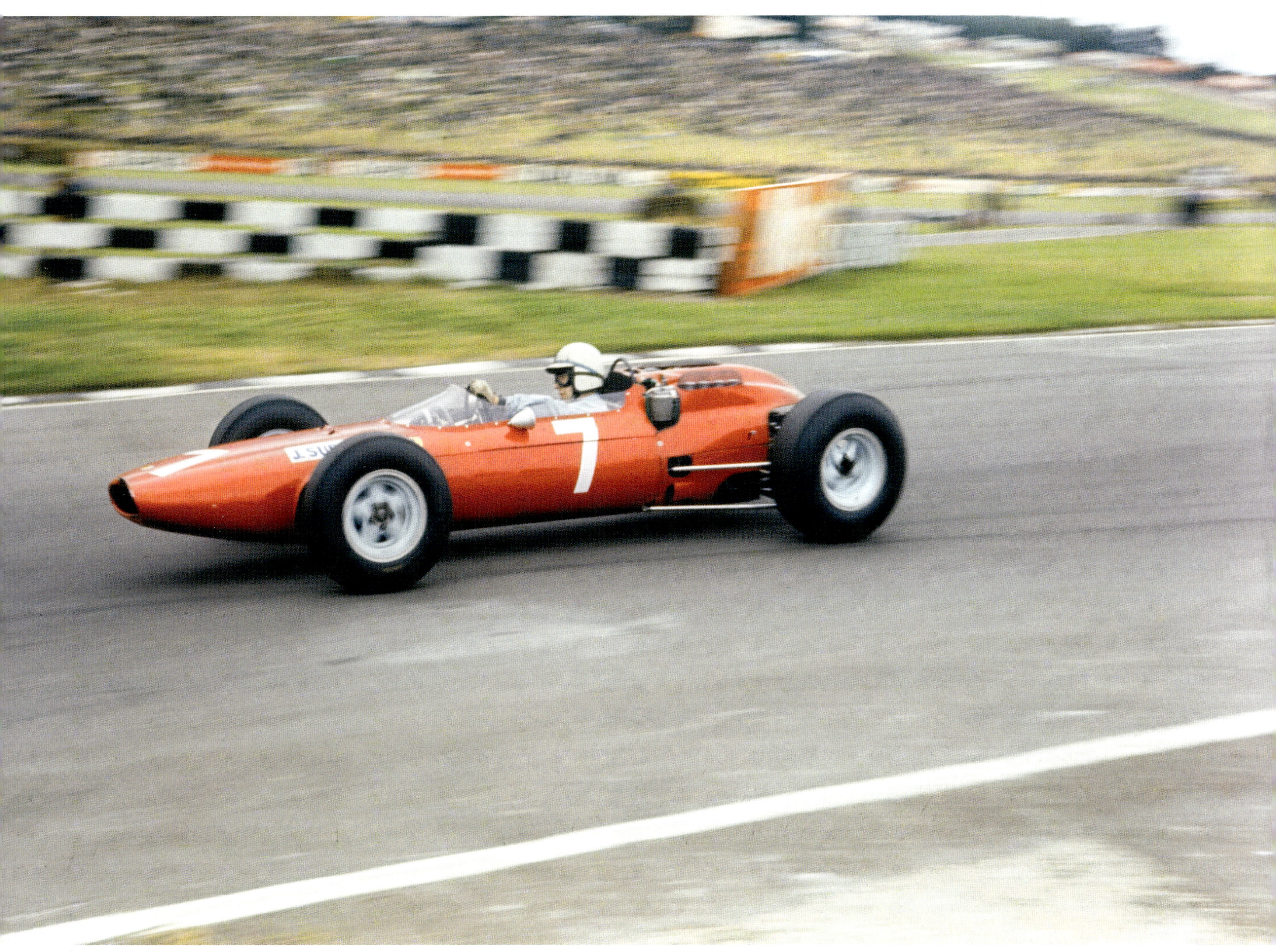

Brands Hatch, British GP, 1964. John Surtees (Ferrari 158) approaches the apex of Paddock Hill Bend. Photo: David Phipps

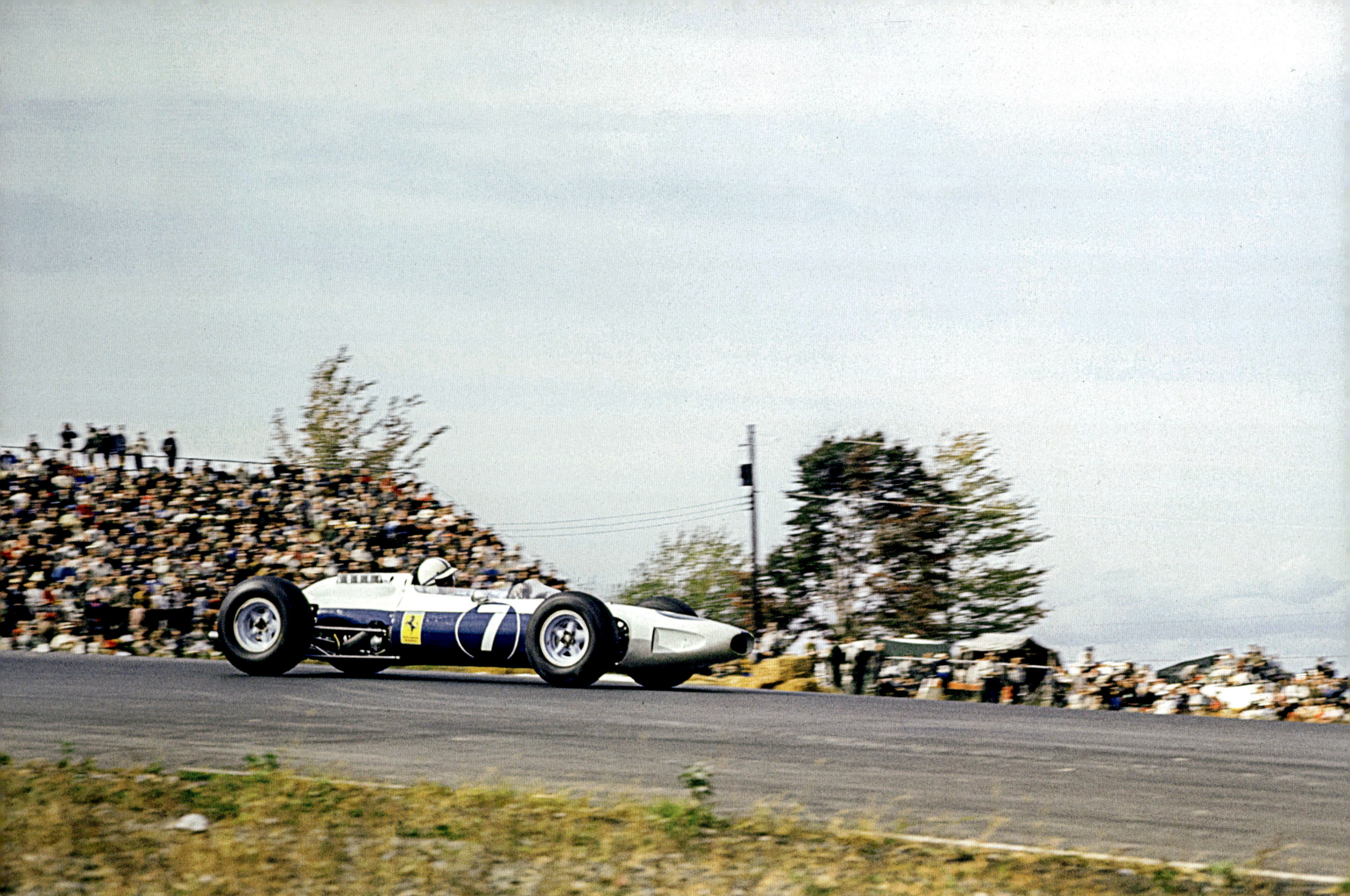

Watkins Glen, United States GP, 1964. John Surtees (Ferrari 158). Photo: Michael Tee

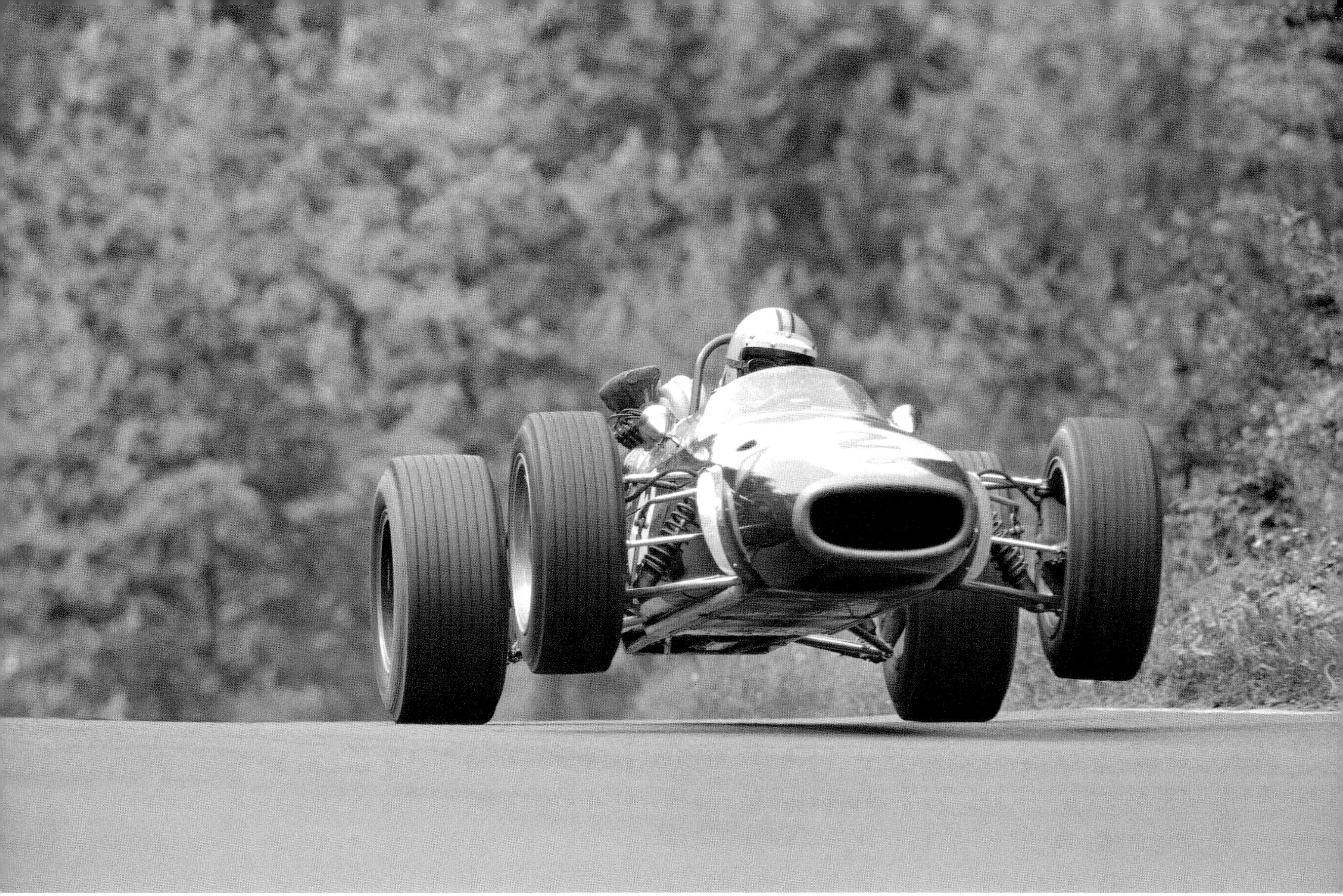

Nürburgring, German GP, 1967. Denny Hulme (Brabham BT24 Repco) at Flugplatz. Photo: Rainer Schlegelmilch

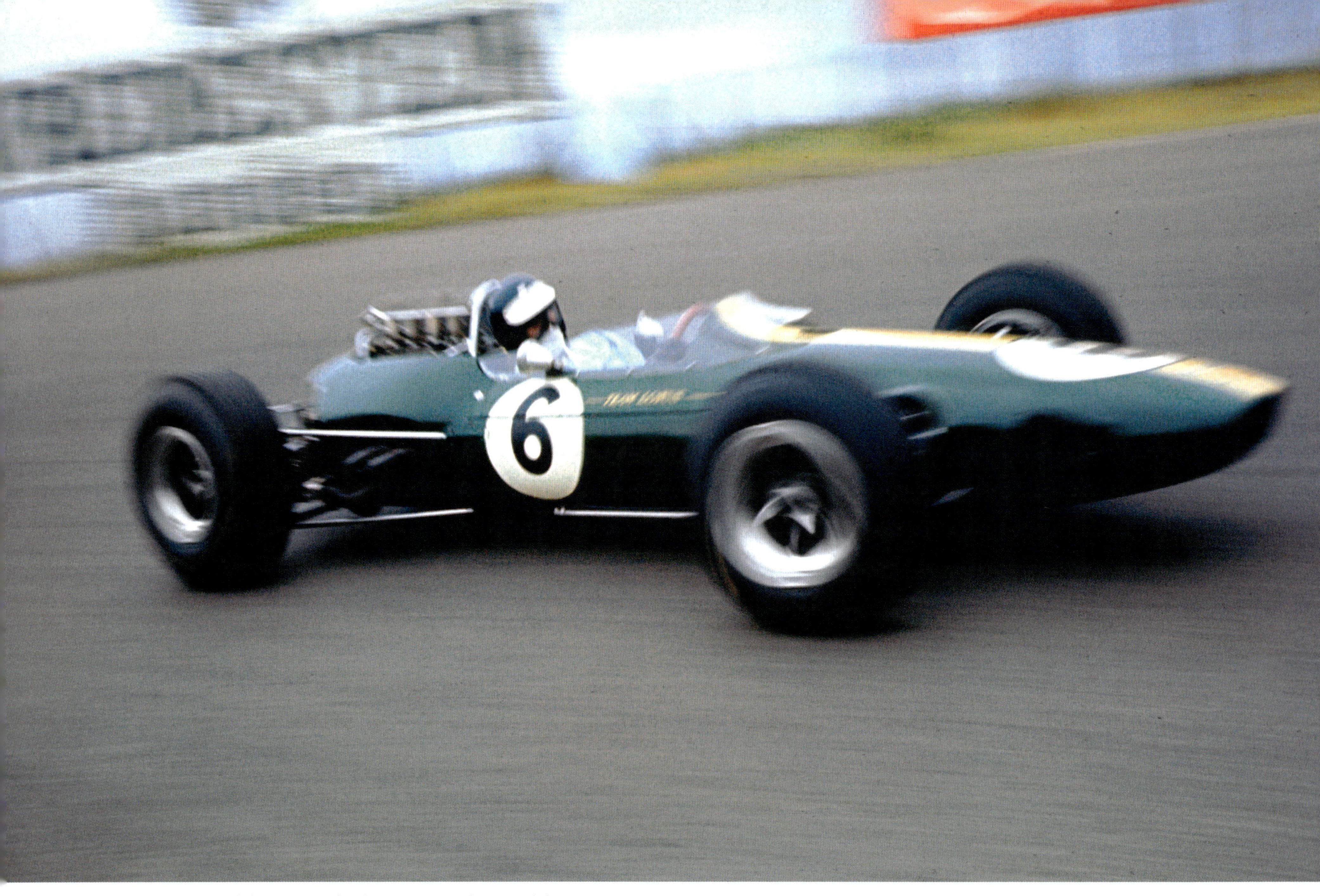

Zandvoort, Dutch GP, 1965. Jim Clark (Lotus 33 Ford) at the Tarzan corner. Photo: David Phipps

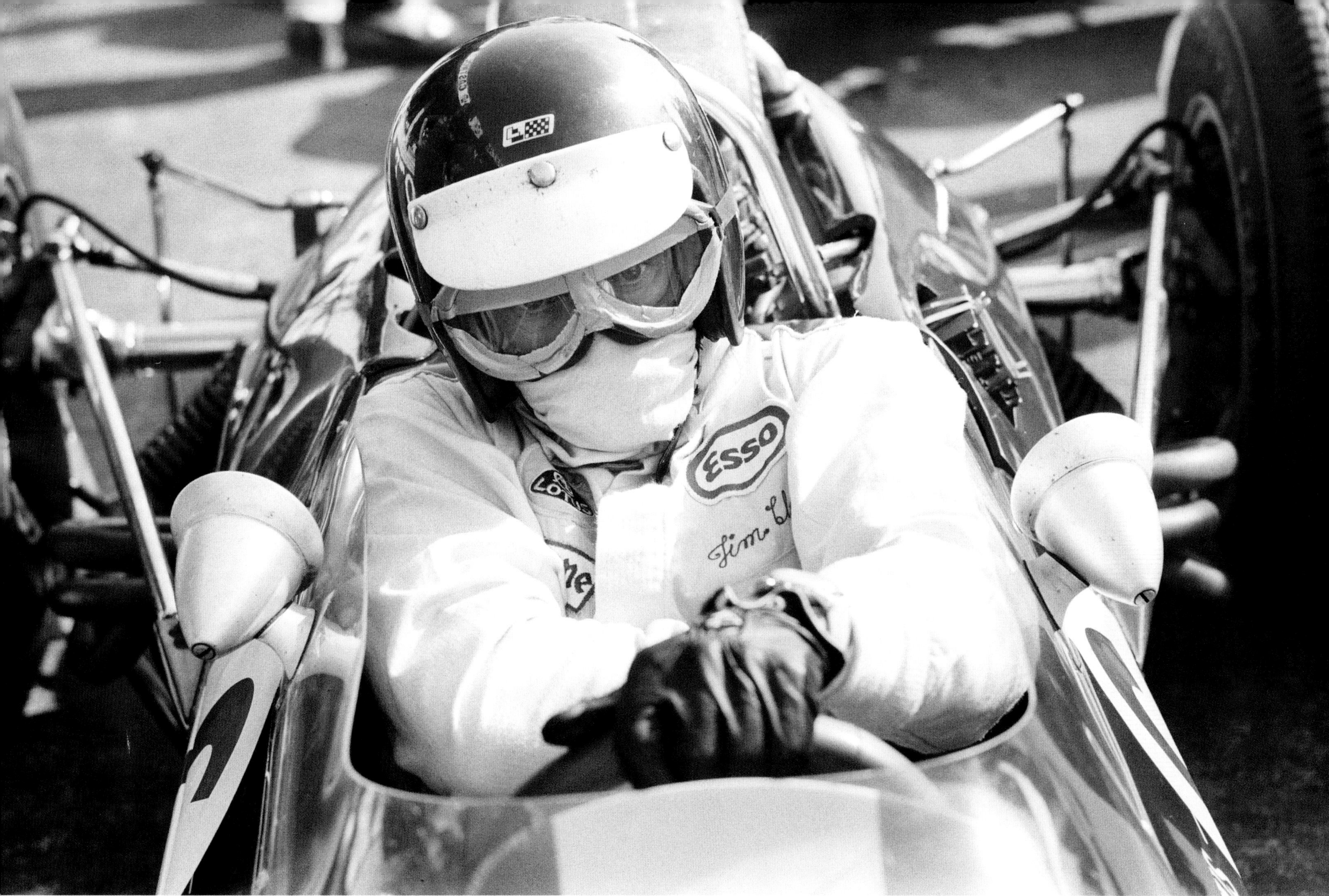

Zandvoort, Dutch GP, 1966. Jim Clark (Lotus 33 Climax). Photo: Rainer Schlegelmilch

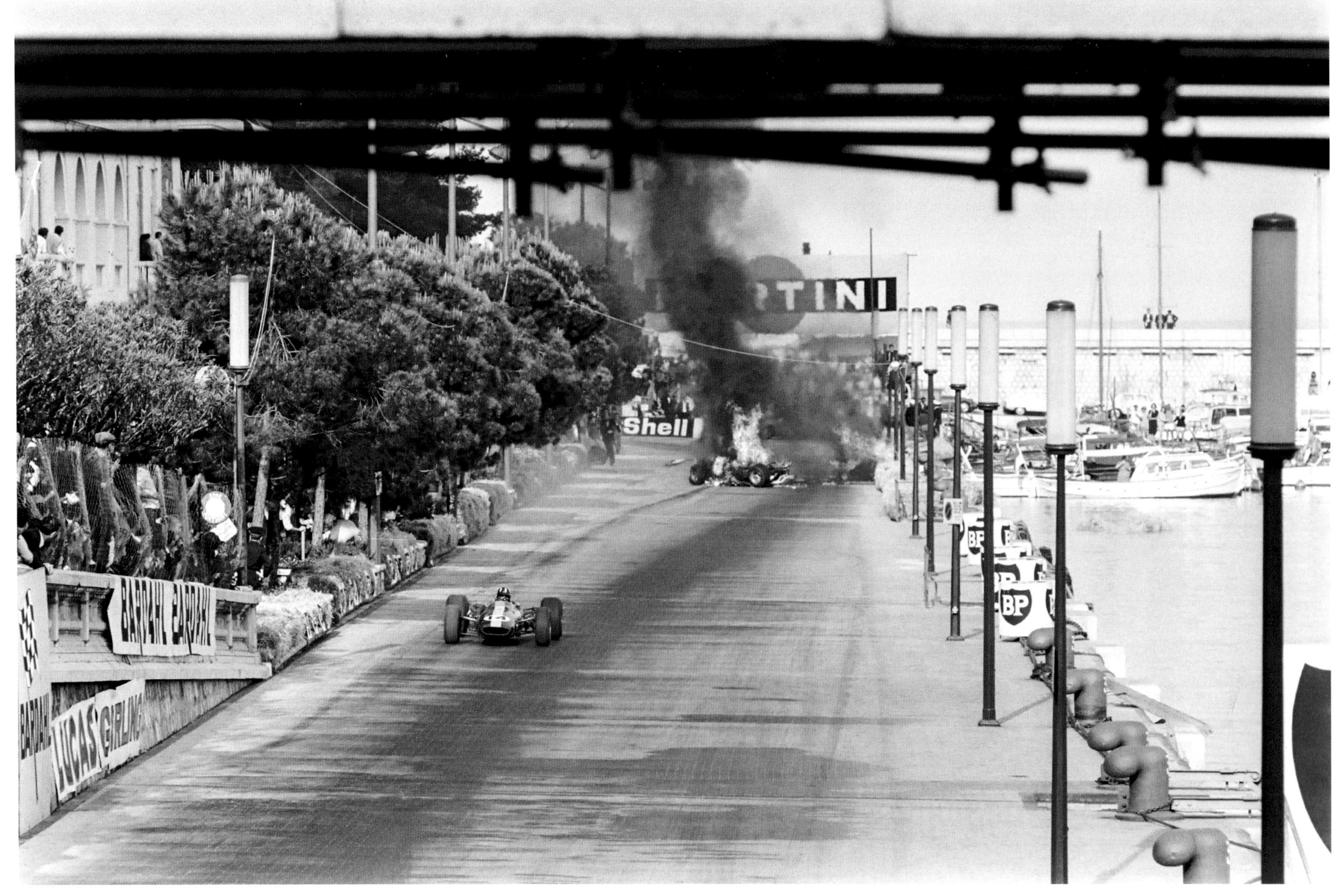

Monaco GP, 1967. Graham Hill (Lotus 33 BRM) passes the crashed car of Lorenzo Bandini (Ferrari 312). Photo: LAT Images

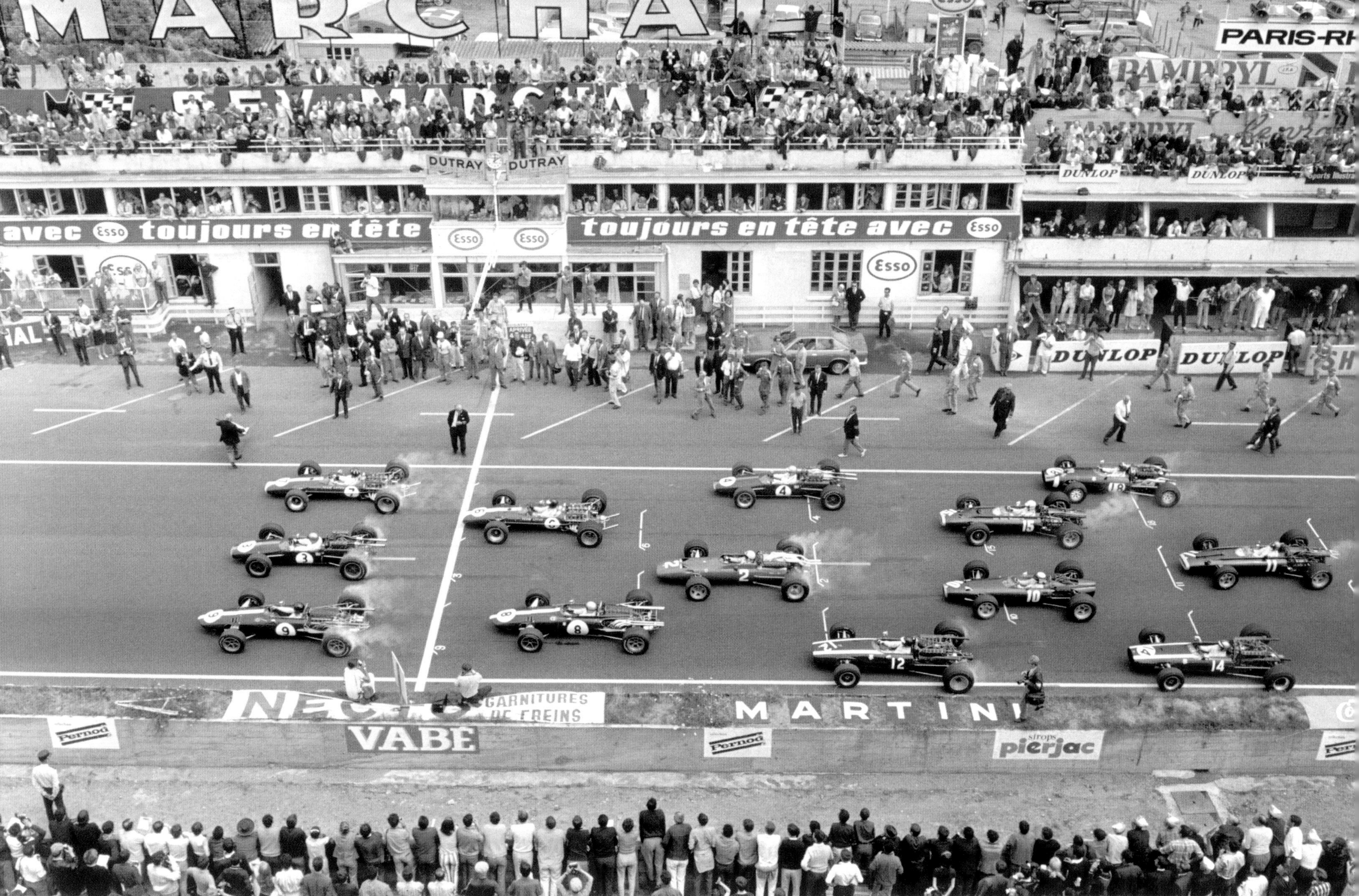

La Sarthe, French GP, 1967. Graham Hill (number 7, Lotus 49-Ford Cosworth), Jack Brabham (number 3, Brabham BT24-Repco), and Dan Gurney (number 9, Eagle T1G-Weslake) lead Jim Clark (number 6, Lotus 49-Ford Cosworth), Bruce McLaren (number 8, Eagle T1G-Weslake), Denny Hulme (number 4, Brabham BT24-Repco), Chris Amon (number 2, Ferrari 312), Jochen Rindt (number 12, Cooper T81B-Maserati), Chris Irwin (number 15, BRM P83), Jackie Stewart (number 10, BRM P261), Jo Siffert (number 18, Cooper T81-Maserati), Pedro Rodríguez (number 14, Cooper T81-Maserati), and Mike Spence (number 11, BRM P83) at the start. Photo: LAT Images

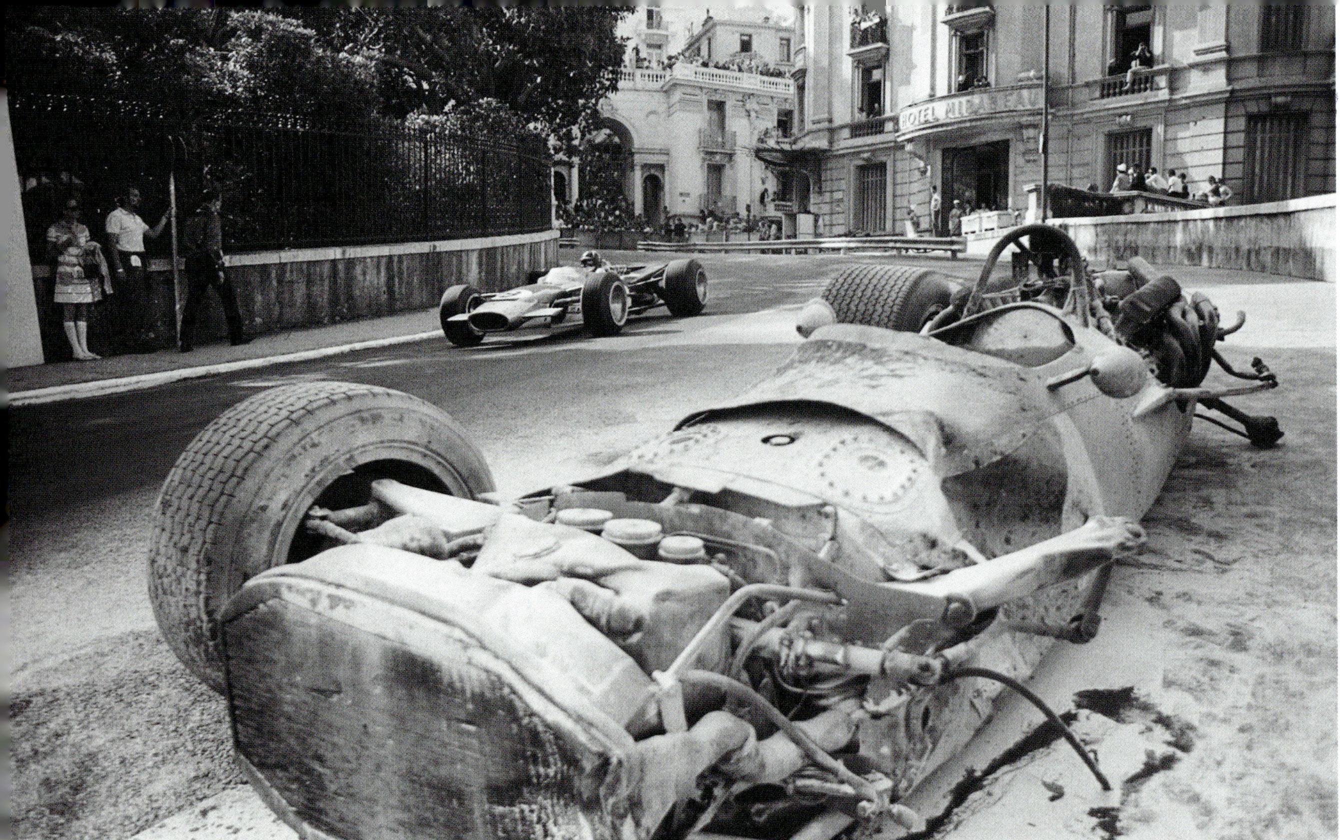

Monaco GP, 1968. Graham Hill (Lotus 49B Ford) passes Pedro Rodríguez's wrecked BRM P133. Photo: Rainer Schlegelmilch

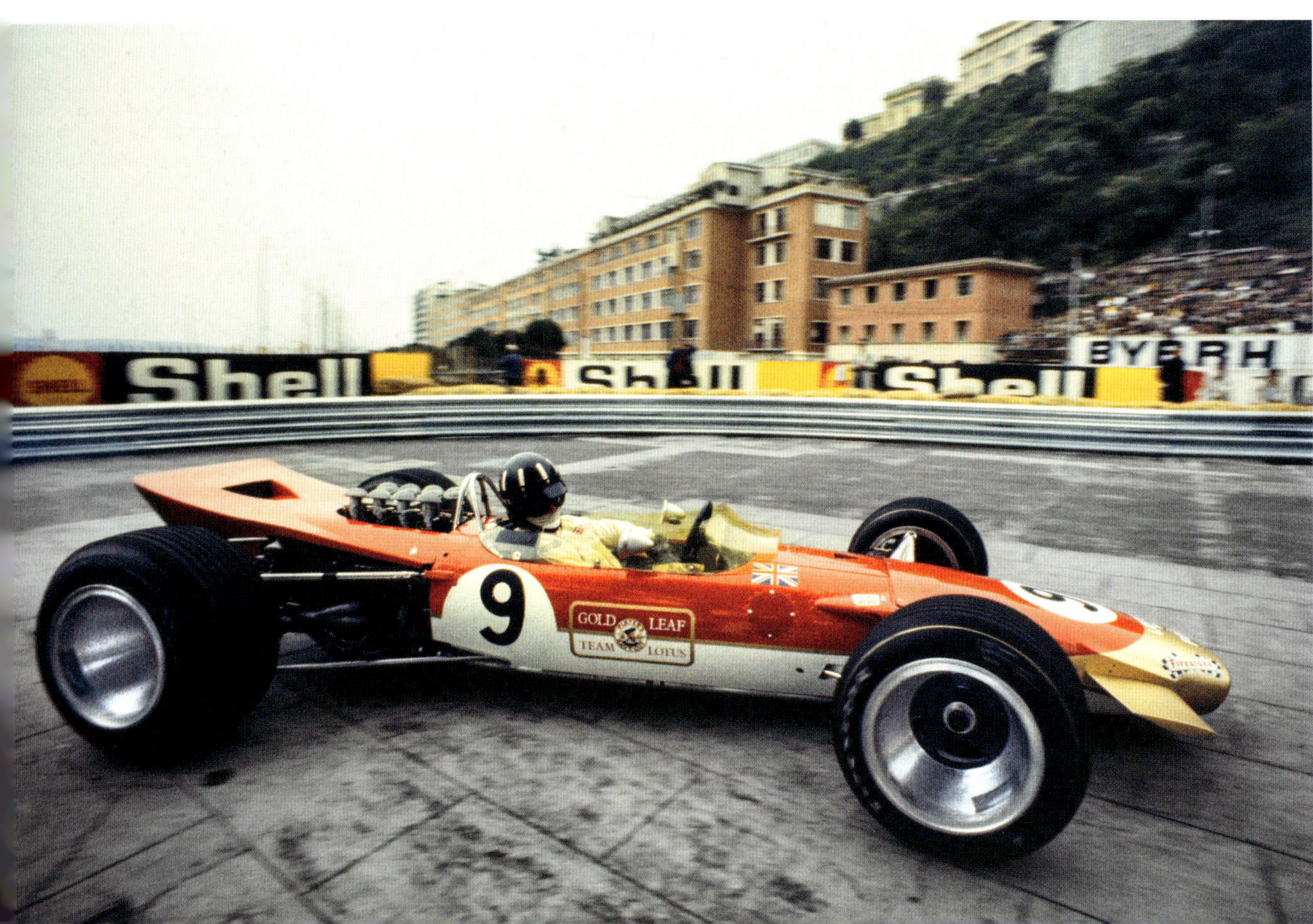

Monaco GP, 1968. Graham Hill (Lotus Ford 49B) on his way to victory on the debut for the car. Photo: David Phipps

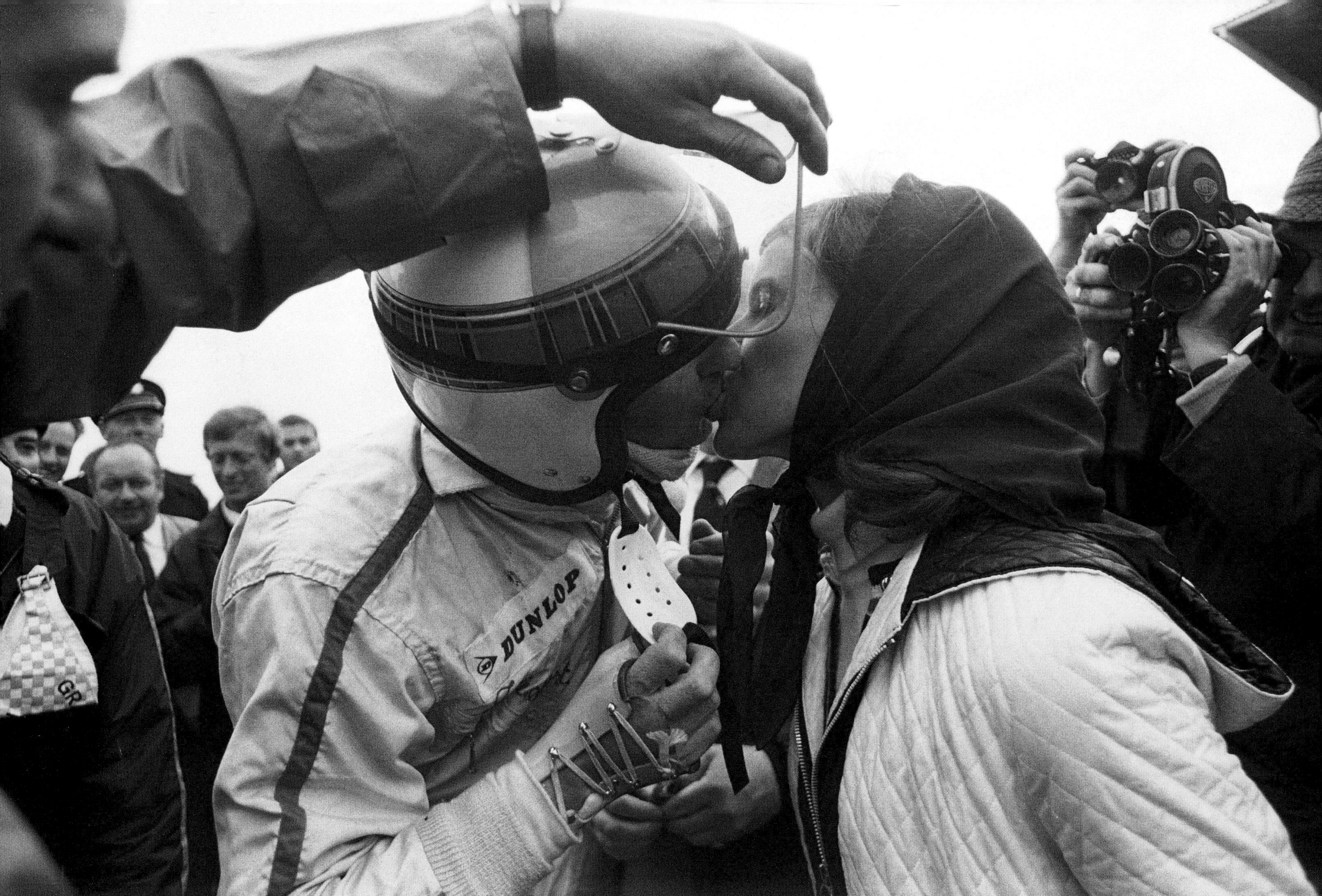

Zandvoort, Dutch GP, 1968. Helen Stewart kisses her husband, Jackie, after his win. Photo: Rainer Schlegelmilch

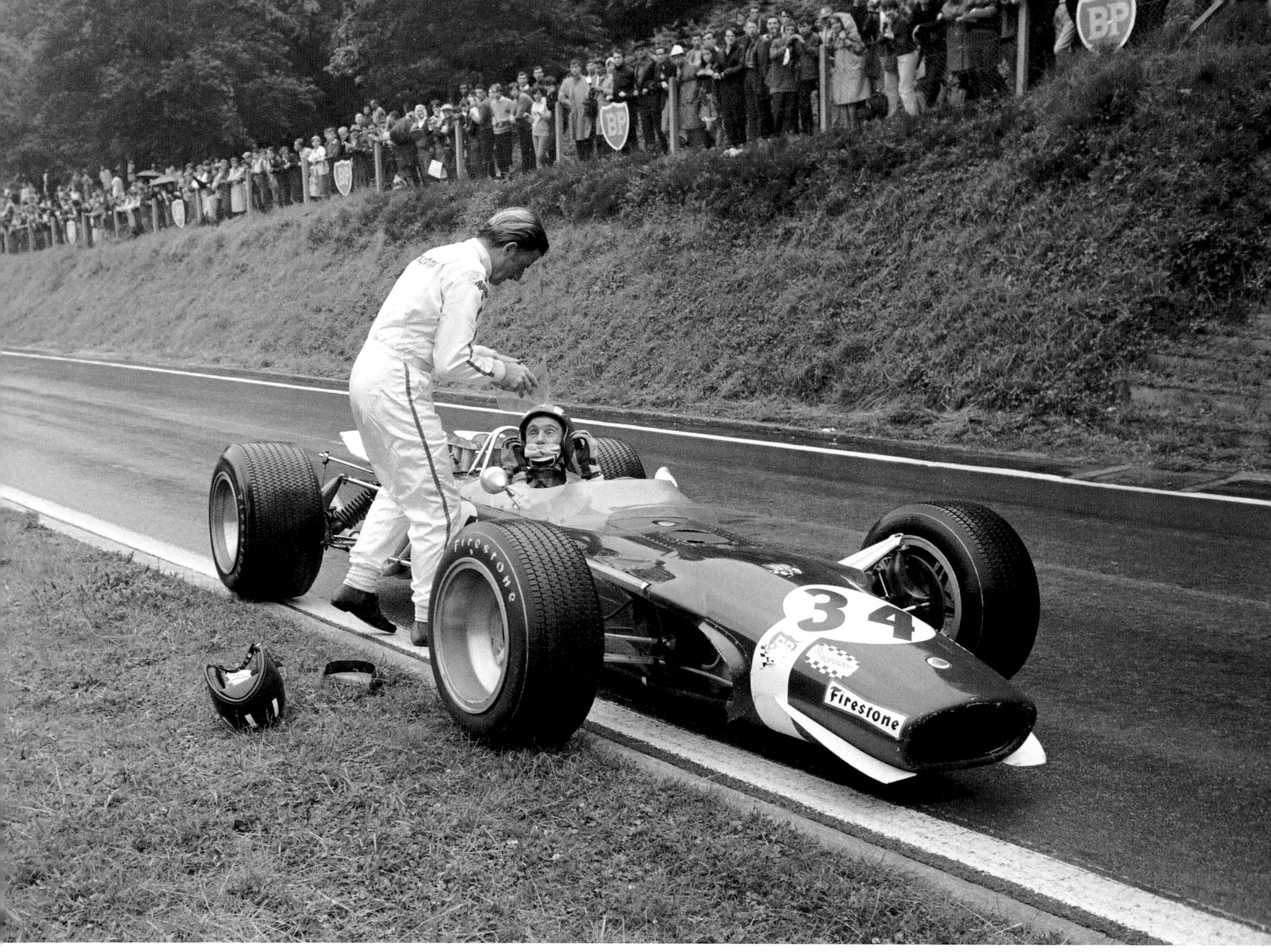

Rouen-Les-Essarts, French GP, 1968. Jo Siffert pulls over in his Lotus 49 Ford to allow a retired Graham Hill to give him his visor to protect against the spray. Photo: Michael Tee

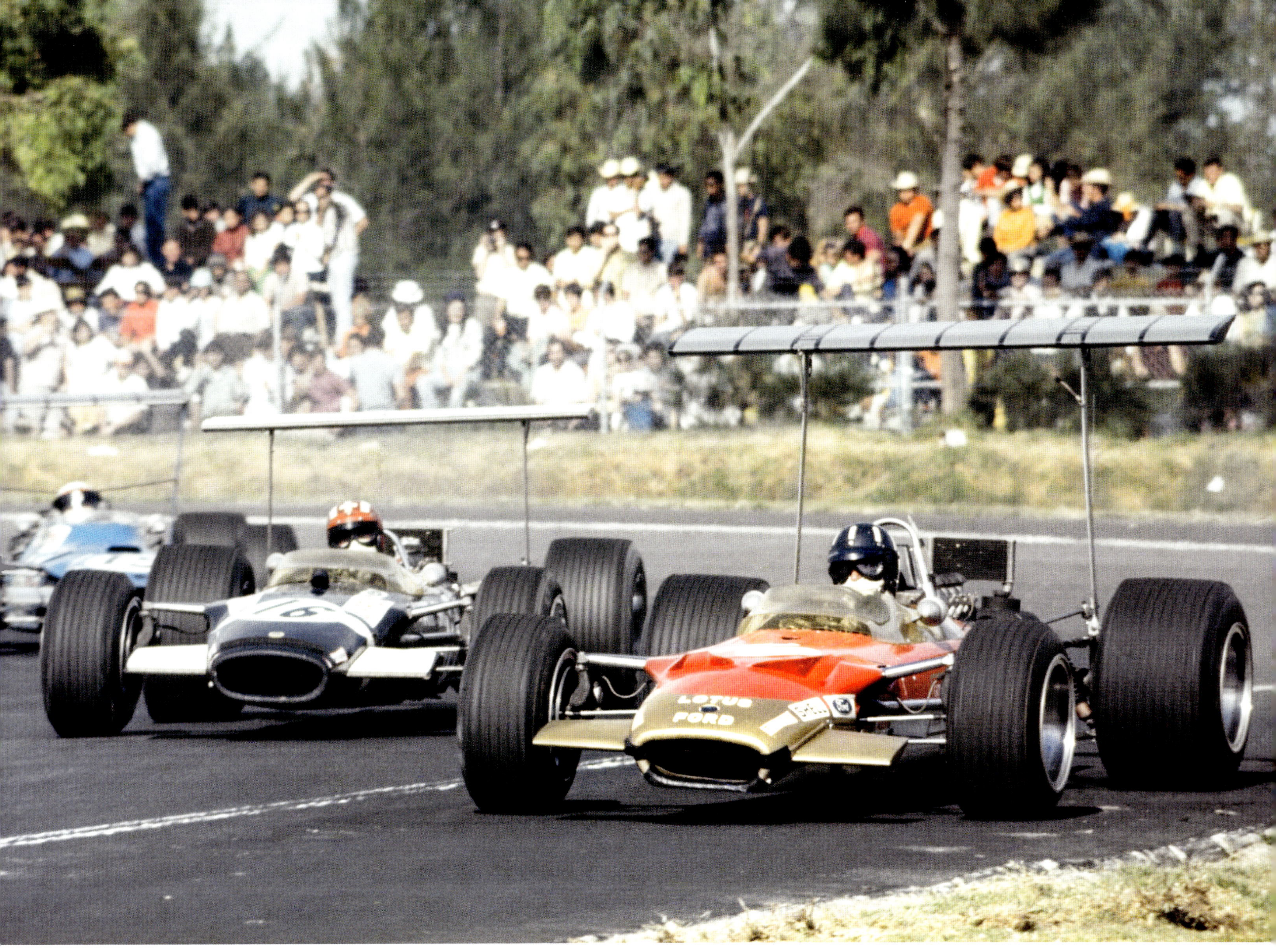

Mexico City, Mexican GP, 1968. Graham Hill (Lotus Cosworth 49B) leads Jo Siffert (in a similar Rob Walker Racing entered car) and Jackie Stewart (Matra Cosworth MS10). Photo: David Phipps

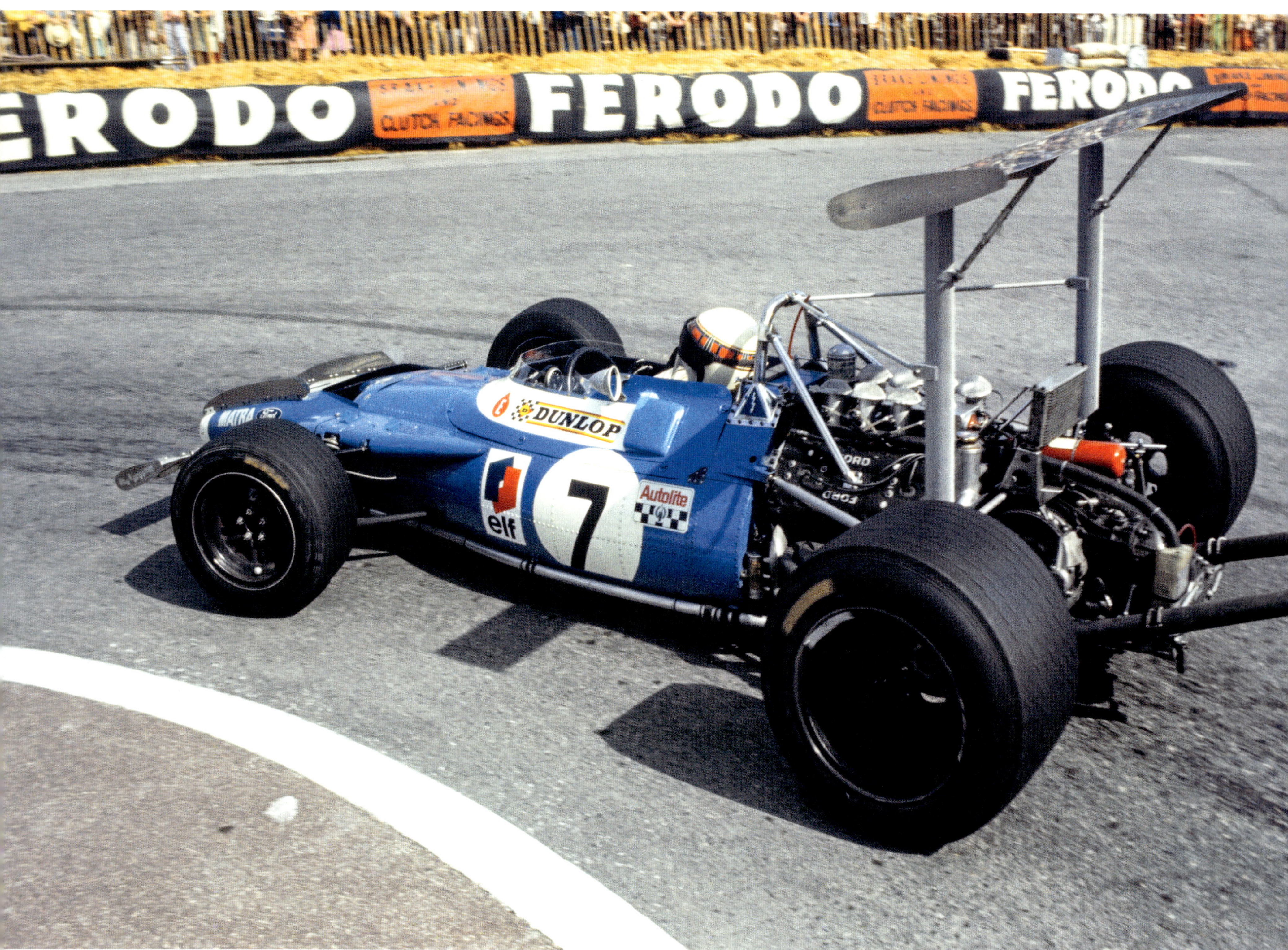

Monaco GP, 1969. Jackie Stewart (Matra MS80 Ford) during practice on Thursday. Photo: David Phipps

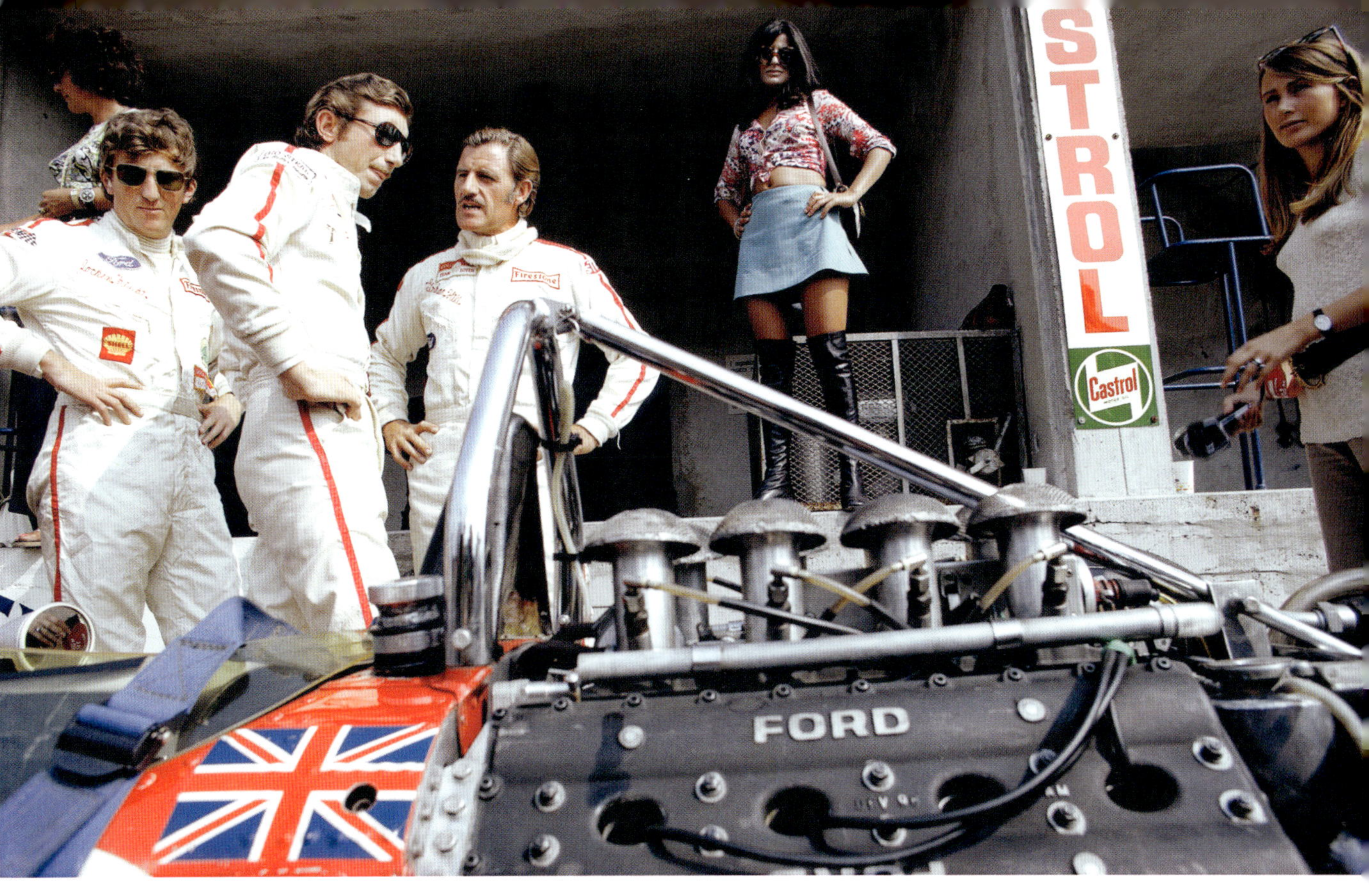

Monza, Italian GP, 1969. From left to right: Bette Hill, Jochen Rindt, Jo Siffert, Graham Hill, Simone Siffert, and Nina Rindt. Photo: Rainer Schlegelmilch

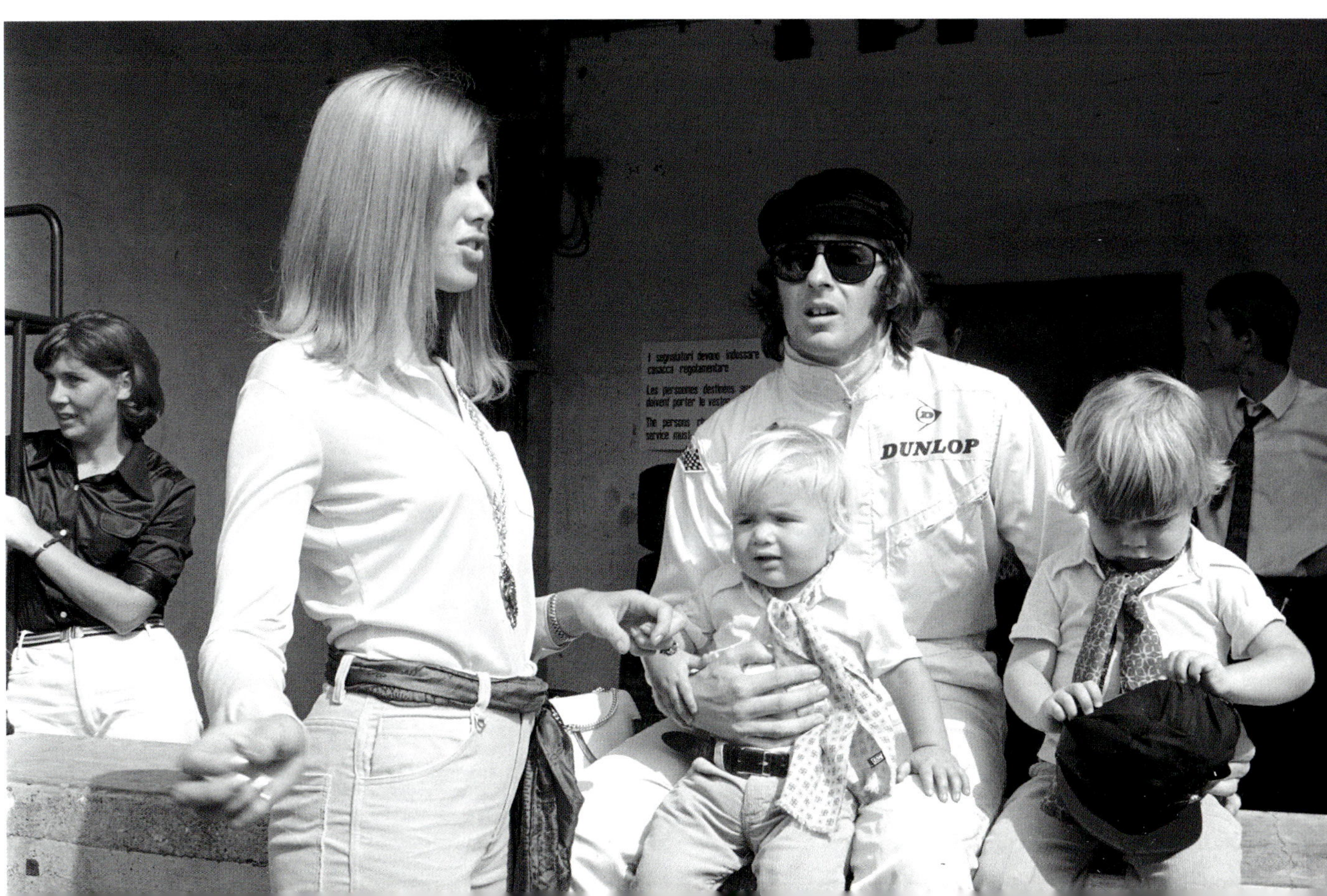

Monza, Italian GP, 1969. The Stewart family, with Helen, Jackie, Paul, and Mark, in the pits. Photo: David Phipps

1970–1979
Champions Like Stars

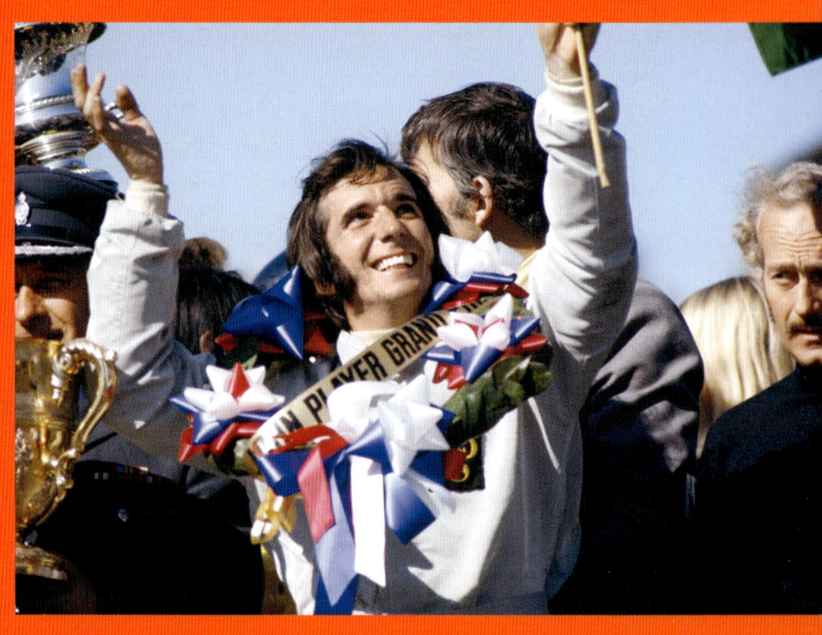

Wings, spoilers, and flaps. Cars like missiles, like upside-down airplanes. An aerodynamic boom. Plus: the debut of the first turbocharged GP engine pioneered by Renault at Silverstone in 1977, the same race in which Gilles Villeneuve debuted with a McLaren. Not only. A surge of excellent protagonists for a telegenic, widely broadcast, and extremely popular F1. In fact, the names of the champions of this decade are unforgettable: Jochen Rindt, Jackie Stewart, Emerson Fittipaldi, Niki Lauda, James Hunt, Mario Andretti, and Jody Scheckter. With endurance racing came the first covered-wheel prototypes for the World Sportscar Championship, offering an alternative to the Grand Prix single-seaters. These were brilliant times, full of faces, forms, and challenges that placed the Seventies in the stratosphere of passion. Rindt (1942–1970), German born but raised in Austria, is the only world champion to be posthumously awarded the title. He died during a practice session at Monza on September 5, 1970, driving a beautiful albeit very dangerous Lotus. His style: aggressive and effective. A capable man, not only on the racecourse. His rival was Jacky Ickx, Belgian teammate of Clay Ragazzoni, drivers of the wonderful Ferrari 312B. His best friend was Jackie Stewart, who after the title achieved in 1969 went on to win two more World Championships in 1971 and 1973, with Tyrrell. Jackie: an absolute ace, a real star, long hair, clothes in line with those worn by the young people thronging universities, streets, and concerts. The Beatles and the Rolling Stones. Stewart retired in 1973 after the death, during a practice session at Watkins Glen, of his heir apparent, the Frenchman François Cevert. His figures: 99 GPs, 27 victories, 17 pole positions. Meanwhile, another formidable young man made his appearance, Emerson Fittipaldi (1946), a Brazilian from São Paulo, two-time world champion. In 1972 with Lotus, in 1974 with the McLaren team for its first world title. Emerson raced alongside his brother Wilson, both destined to become fathers, uncles, and grandfathers of a whole line of drivers who are still racing to this day.

And then, well, Niki Lauda (1949–2019). Champion with Ferrari in 1975, assumed dead after the terrible accident in Nürburgring on August 1, 1976, literally returned to life after 40 days, ready to fight side by side with his friend James Hunt until the last race, in Japan, when under the driving rain he decided to stop in the pits, delivering the world title to the British McLaren driver. He confessed he was afraid. And in displaying his fear, he showed a different, anomalous courage full of humanity. Niki: a real hero. Unforgettable, capable of winning again in 1977, of holding his own against Enzo Ferrari in a challenge between two formidable characters. With a name—Niki Lauda—like a brand, printed in everyone's collective memory, then and forever.

Mario Andretti (1940) won the title in 1978 with an uncatchable Lotus. Born in Motovun, Istria, emigrated to the United States, strong everywhere, with any car, winner in Indianapolis in 1969, he too was the progenitor of a family that brought an astounding number of drivers into the world of motor racing. Jody Scheckter (1950) entered the hall of fame in 1979. South African. During his first years, he pushed his aggressiveness to the limit; he then learned to combine speed and tactics to return the World Championship to Maranello. Andretti and Scheckter's teammates? Ronnie Peterson and Gilles Villeneuve, two irresistible, fearless young men consecrated like few others to speed, who both passed away to soon. Ronnie at Monza in 1978, Gilles in Zolder, Belgium, in 1982. The Seventies: many winners, too many victims. Joseph Siffert (1936–1971), Swiss, born in Fribourg, died at Brands Hatch during a non-championship race. Piers Courage (1942–1970), British, born in Colchester, died at Zandvoort, in the Netherlands. Pedro Rodríguez (1940–1971), Mexican, died at the Norisring in Germany during a covered-wheel car race. Roger Williamson (1948–1973), British, also died at Zandvoort, while his friend David Purley desperately, albeit in vain, attempted to save him from the fire enveloping his March. Peter Revson (1939–1974), American, handsome, rich, friendly, died during a practice session at Kyalami, South Africa, as did Tom Pryce (1949–1977),

a Welshman from Ruthin, who was killed when he ran over a race official who was crossing the track carrying a fire extinguisher. Helmuth Koinigg (1948–1974), an Austrian, died during a race at Watkins Glen. Mark Donohue (1937–1975), American, died in Austria during a practice session. Carlos Pace (1944–1977), a stalwart Brazilian, died in an airplane accident just like Graham Hill and Tony Brise.
Many a sad day. But many moments of brilliance, too. Vittorio Brambilla (1937–2001), from Monza, a two- and four-wheel driver, won an unforgettable Austrian GP under a downpour in 1975. Lella Lombardi (1941–1992) was the only woman to be ranked in the World Championship. Half a point achieved in Spain, in 1975. A March single-seater for both. Many and diverse were the vehicles driven by the Neo-Zealander Chris Amon (1943–2016). His talent as huge as his bad luck: 96 races and not one victory.

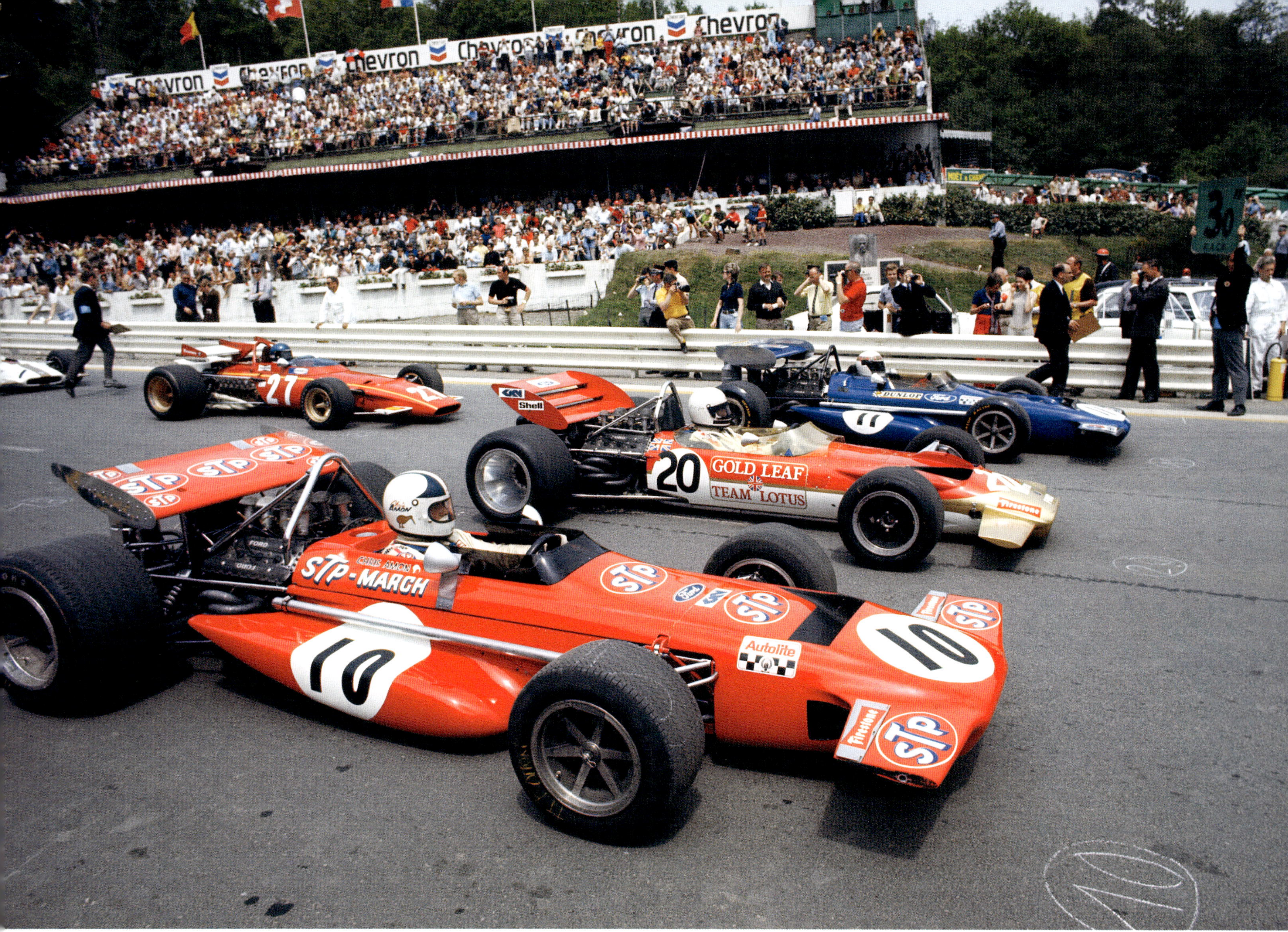

Spa-Francorchamps, Belgian GP, 1970. Jackie Stewart (March 701 Ford) waits on pole position alongside Jochen Rindt (Lotus 49C Ford) and Chris Amon (March 701 Ford), with Jacky Ickx (Ferrari 312B) behind. Photo: Rainer Schlegelmilch

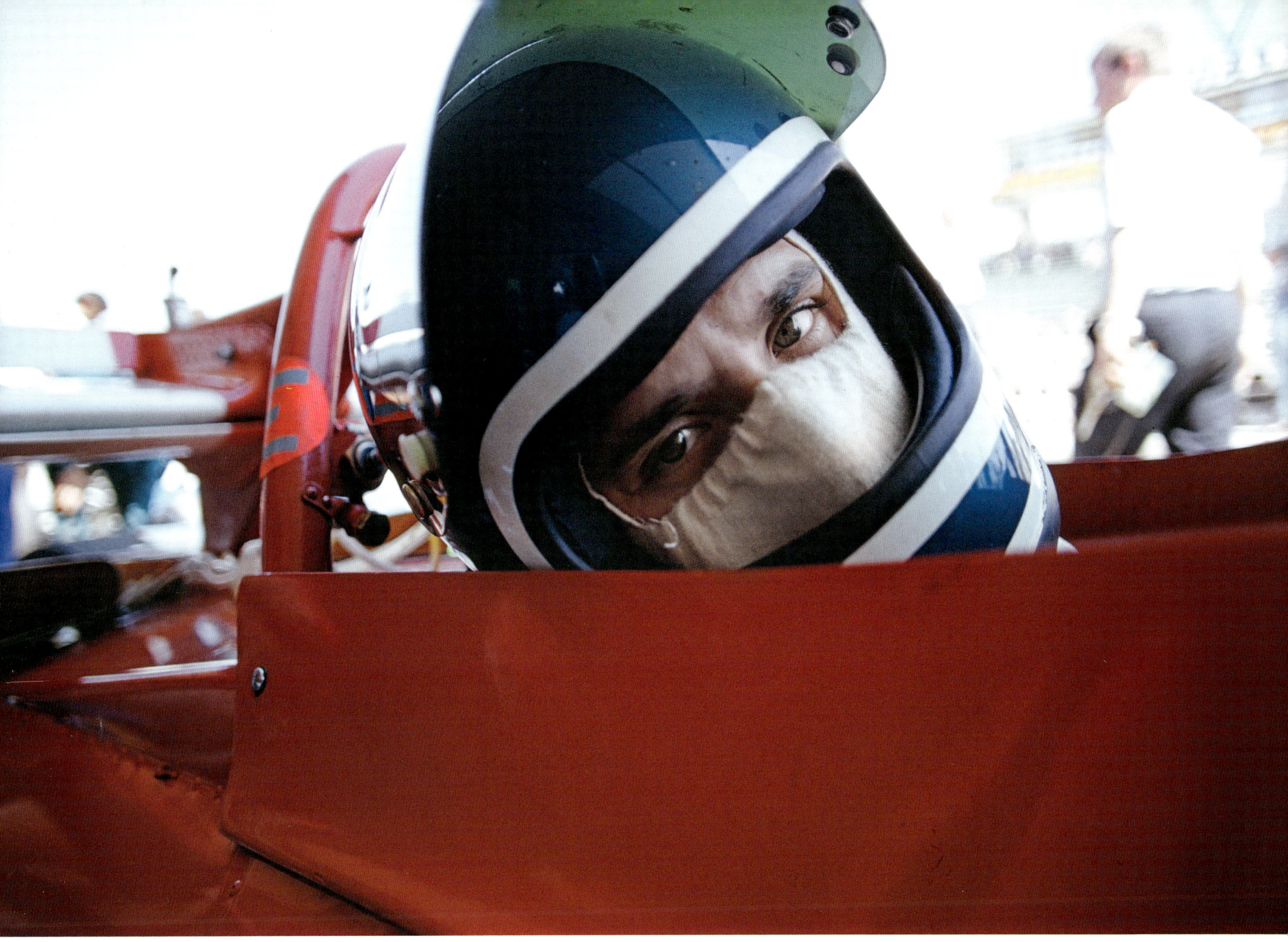

Jarama, Spanish GP, 1970. Jacky Ickx peers over the side of his Ferrari 312B. Photo: Rainer Schlegelmilch

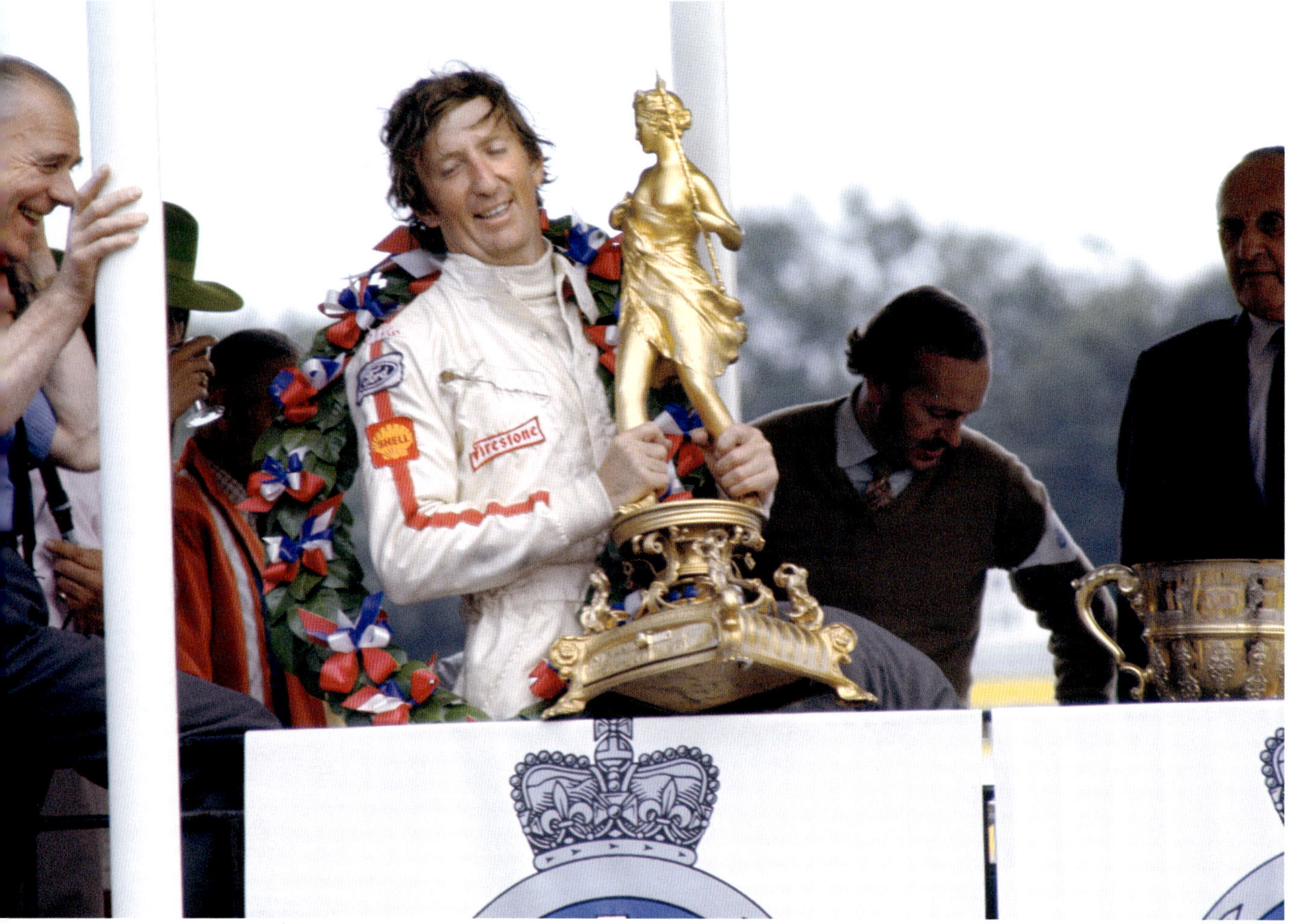

Brands Hatch, British GP, 1970.
Jochen Rindt celebrates victory
on the podium. Photo: Rainer
Schlegelmilch

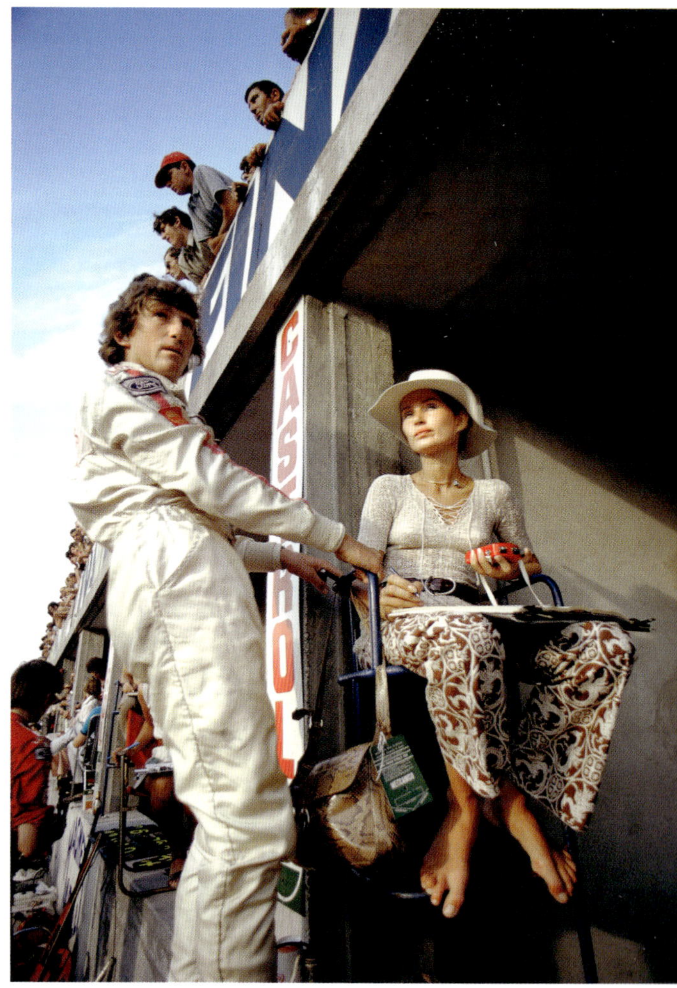

Monza, Italian GP, 1970.
Jochen Rindt in pits with his
wife Nina shortly before he
headed out onto the track
for the final, ill-fated time
during practice. Photo: Rainer
Schlegelmilch

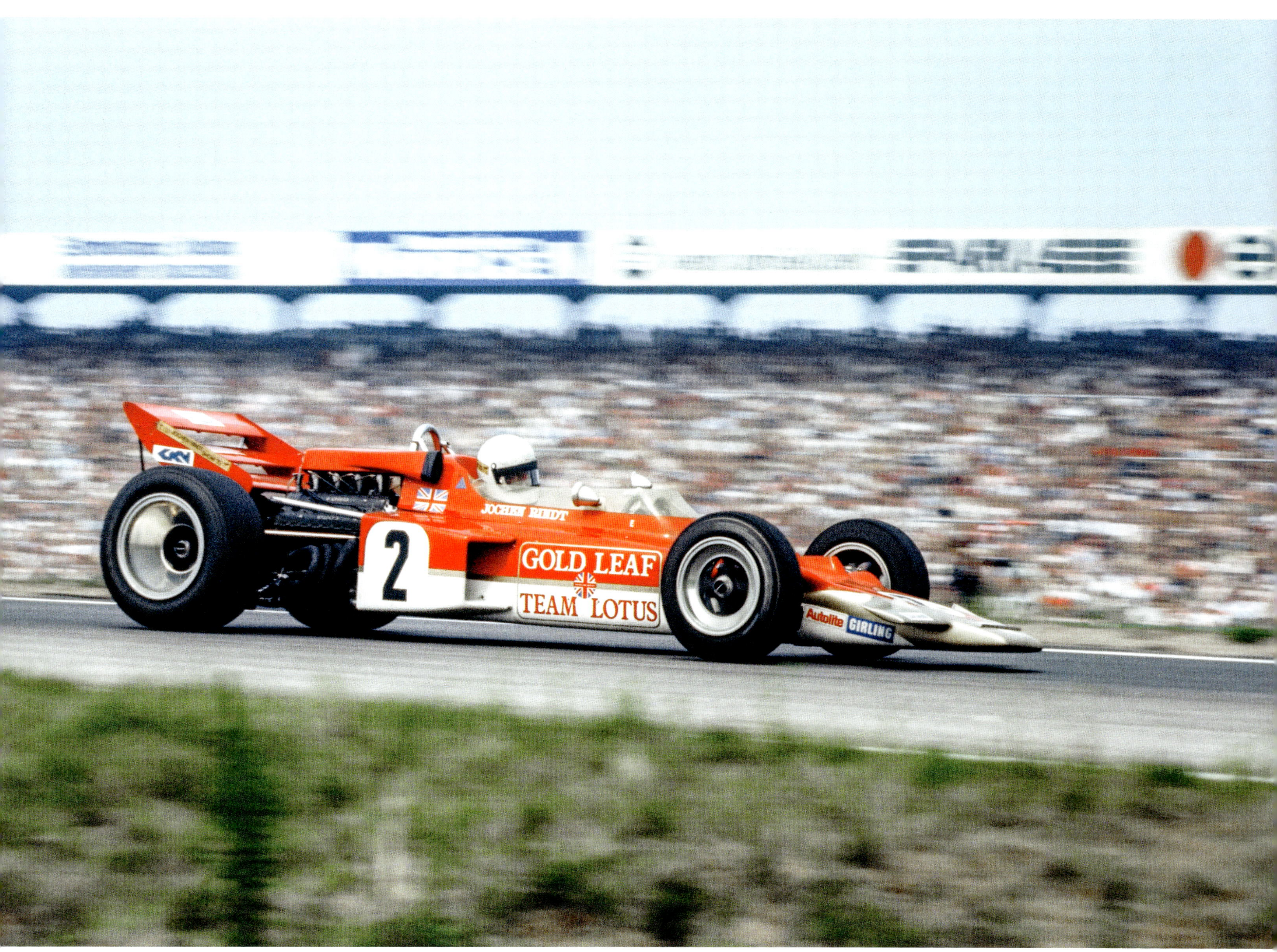

Hockenheim, German GP, 1970. Jochen Rindt (Lotus 72C Ford) in the Stadium. Photo: Michael Tee

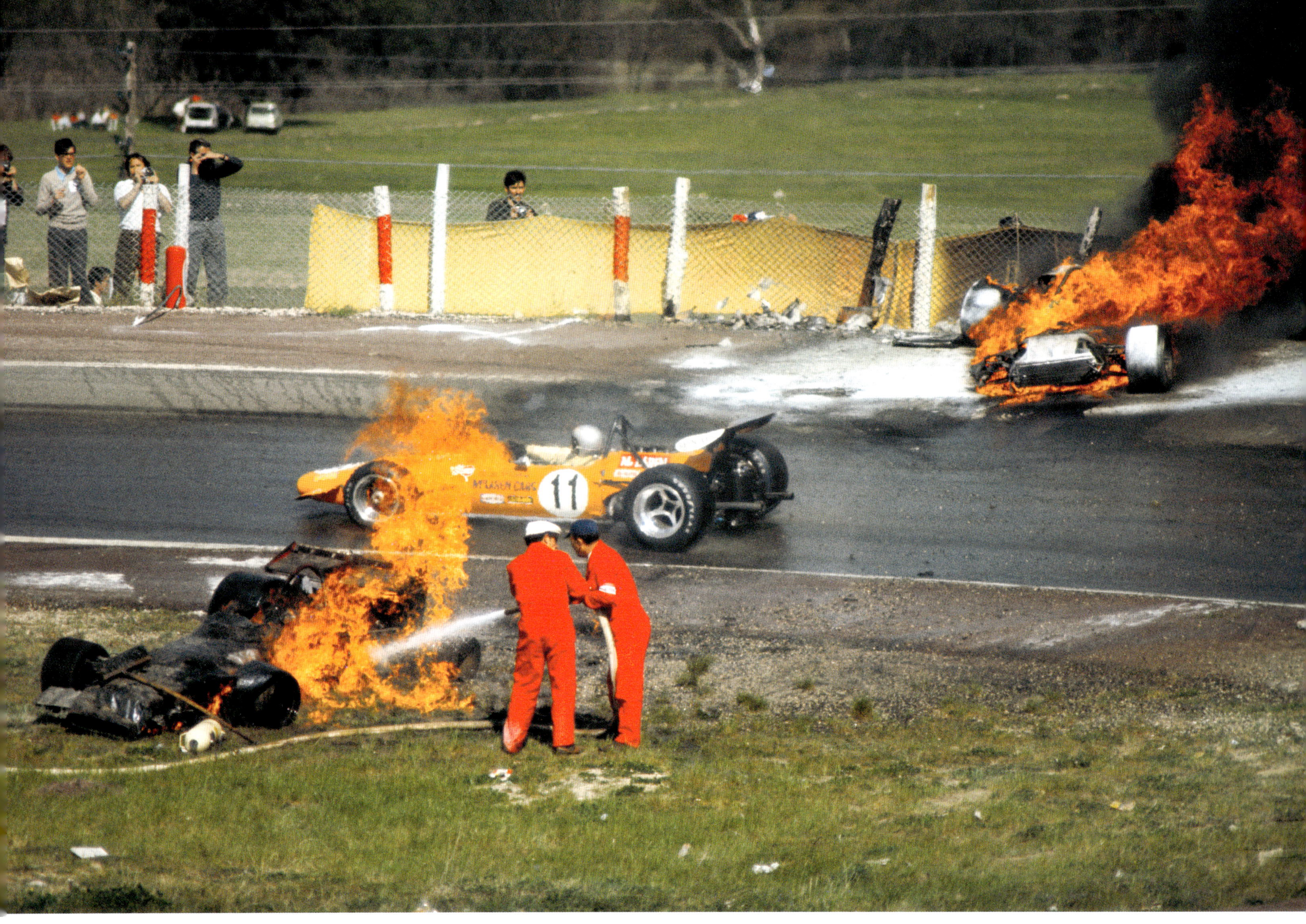

Jarama, Spanish GP, 1970. Bruce McLaren (McLaren M14A Ford) drives between the burning BRM P153 of Jackie Oliver and Ferrari 312B of Jacky Ickx as marshals work to extinguish the flames. Photo: Rainer Schlegelmilch

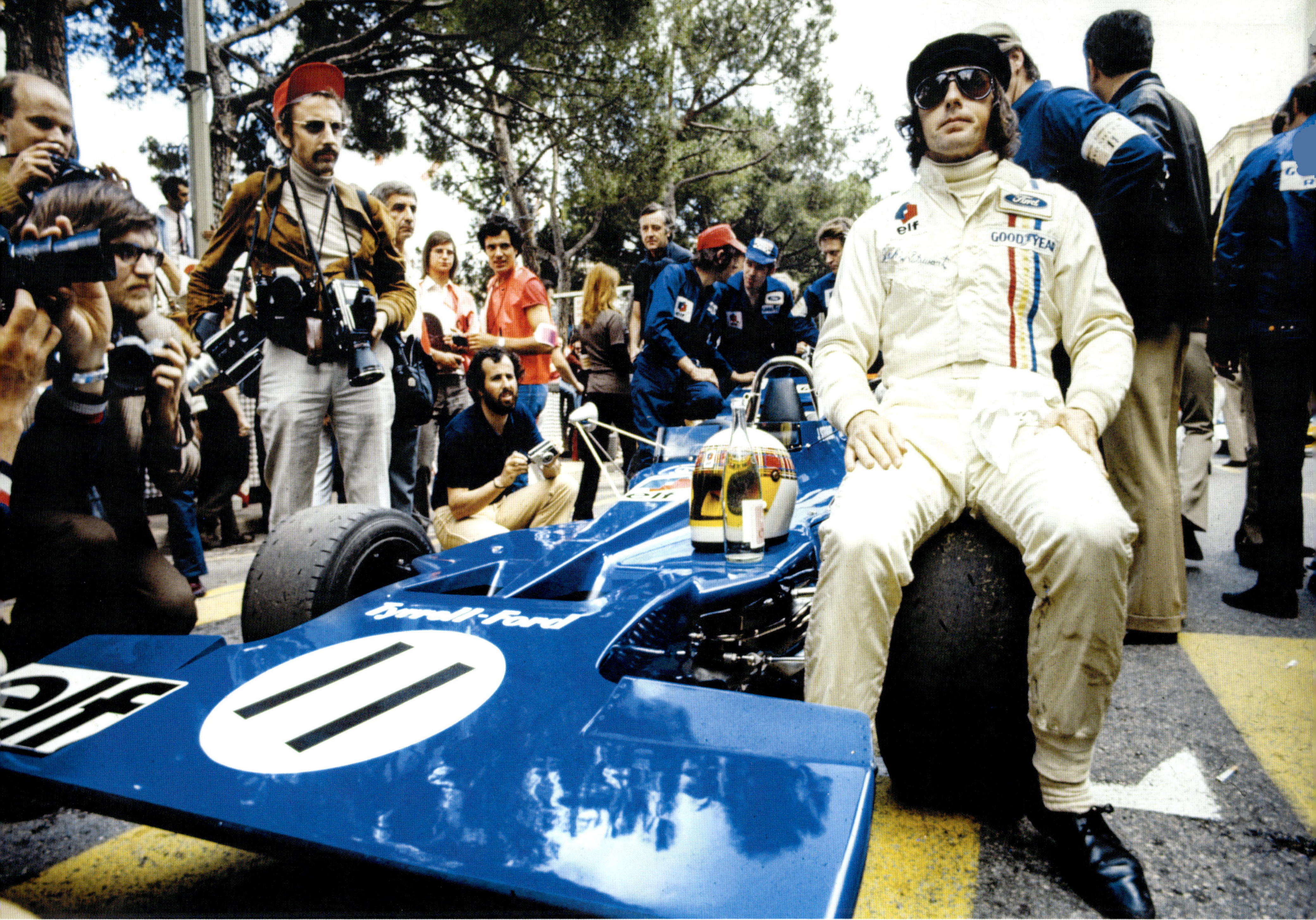

Monaco GP, 1971. Jackie Stewart sits on his Tyrrell 003 before the start. Photo: Rainer Schlegelmilch

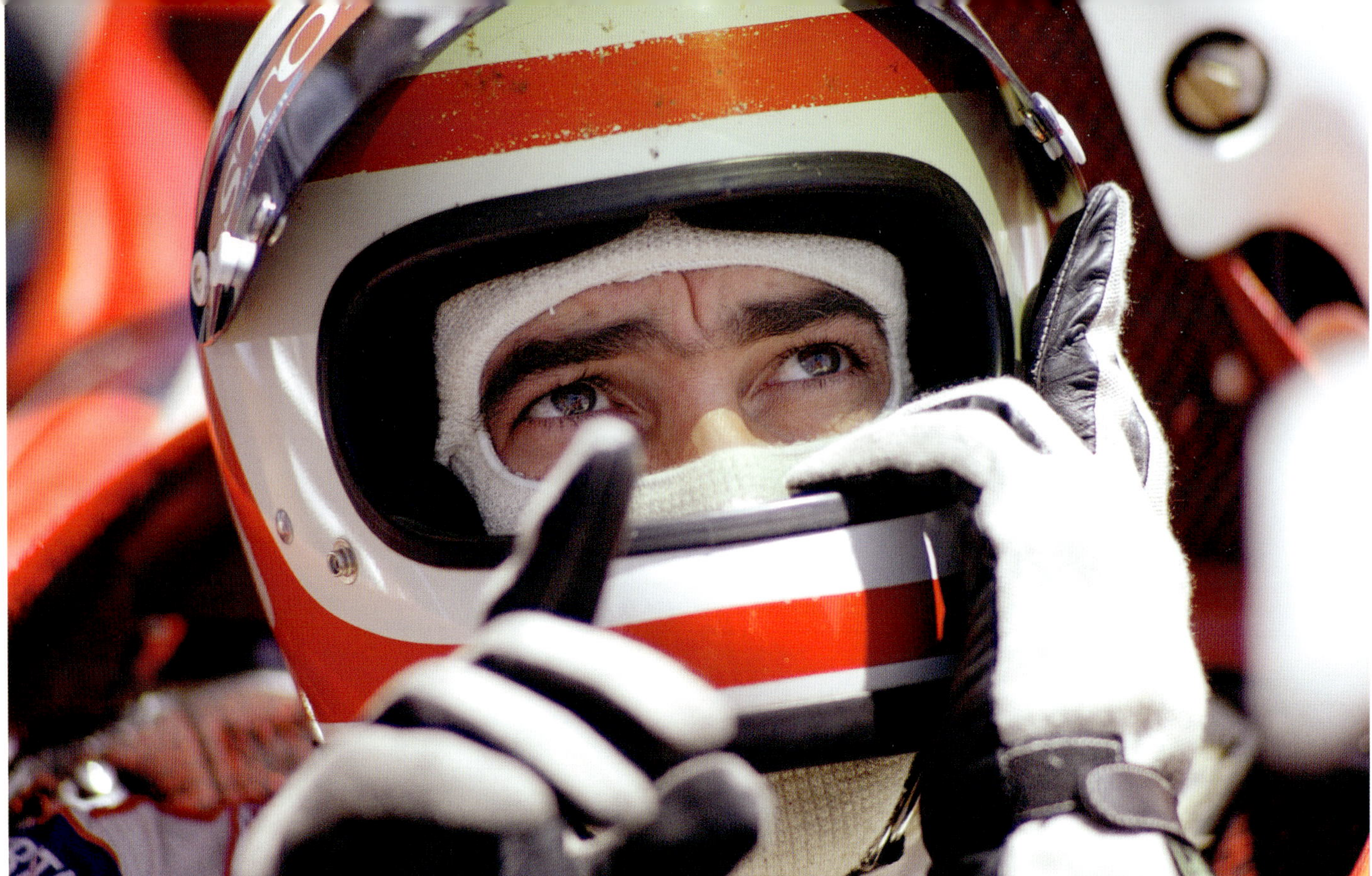

Paul Ricard, French GP, 1971.
Clay Regazzoni (Ferrari 312B2).
Photo: Rainer Schlegelmilch

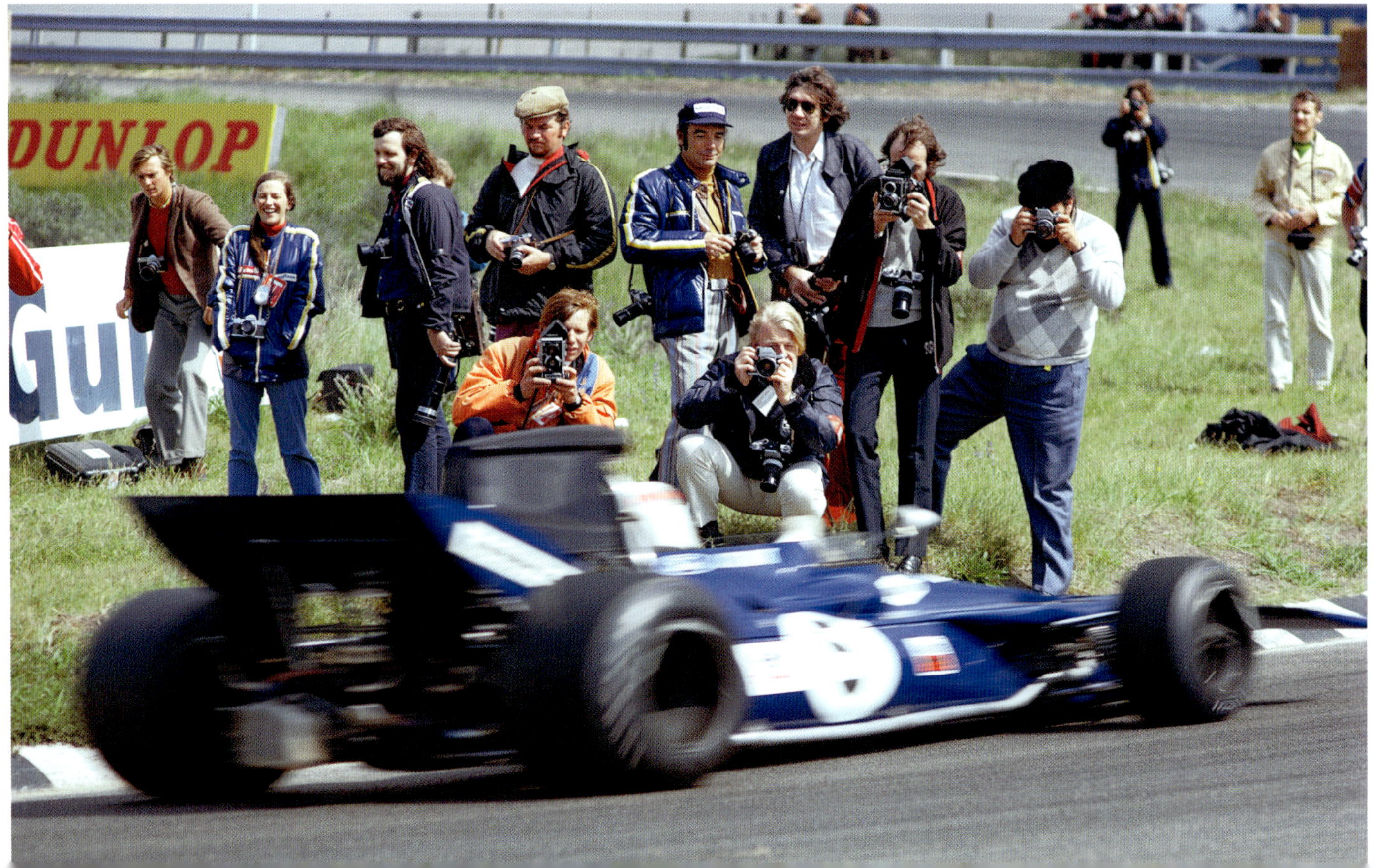

Zandvoort, Dutch GP, 1971.
Photographers standing close
to the action, while Jackie
Stewart (Tyrrell 003 Ford)
passes by. Photo: Rainer
Schlegelmilch

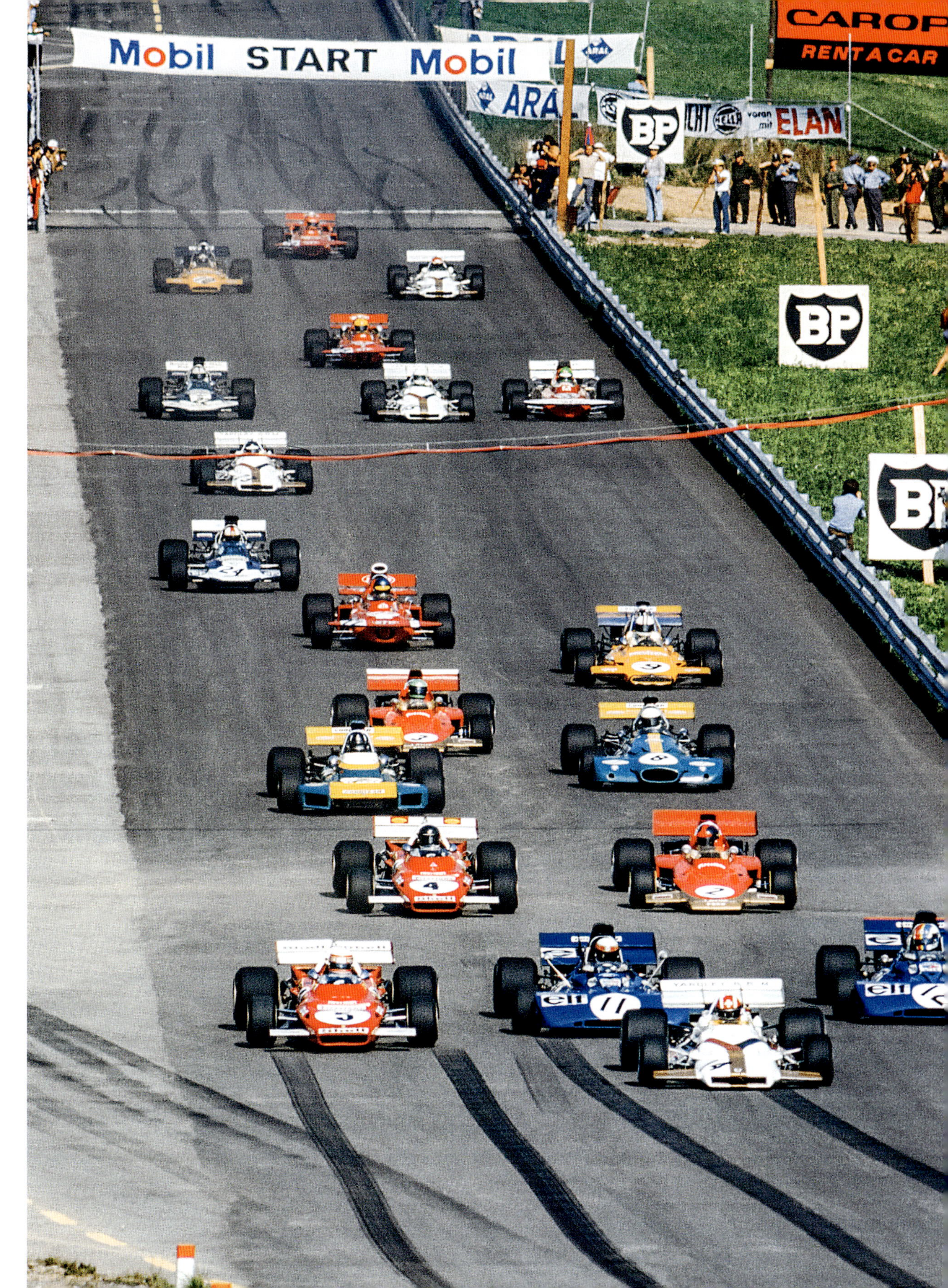

Zeltweg, Austrian GP, 1971.
Jo Siffert (BRM P160) leads
Clay Regazzoni (Ferrari 312B2),
Jackie Stewart (Tyrrell 003
Ford), and François Cevert
(Tyrrell 002 Ford), at the start of
the race. Photo: Laurie Morton

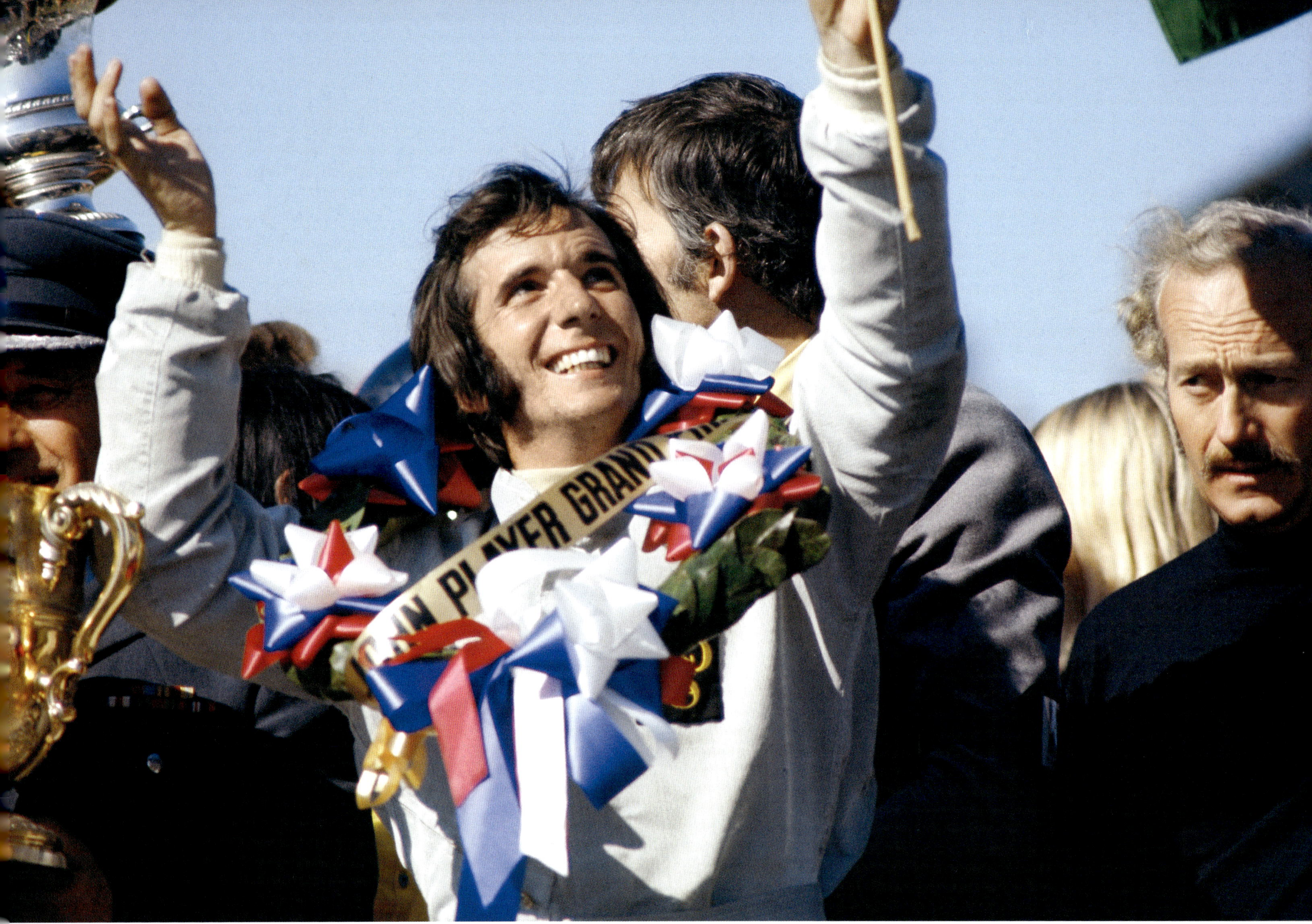

Brands Hatch, British GP, 1972. Emerson Fittipaldi celebrates victory on the podium with Colin Chapman, Lotus Team owner. Photo: Rainer Schlegelmilch

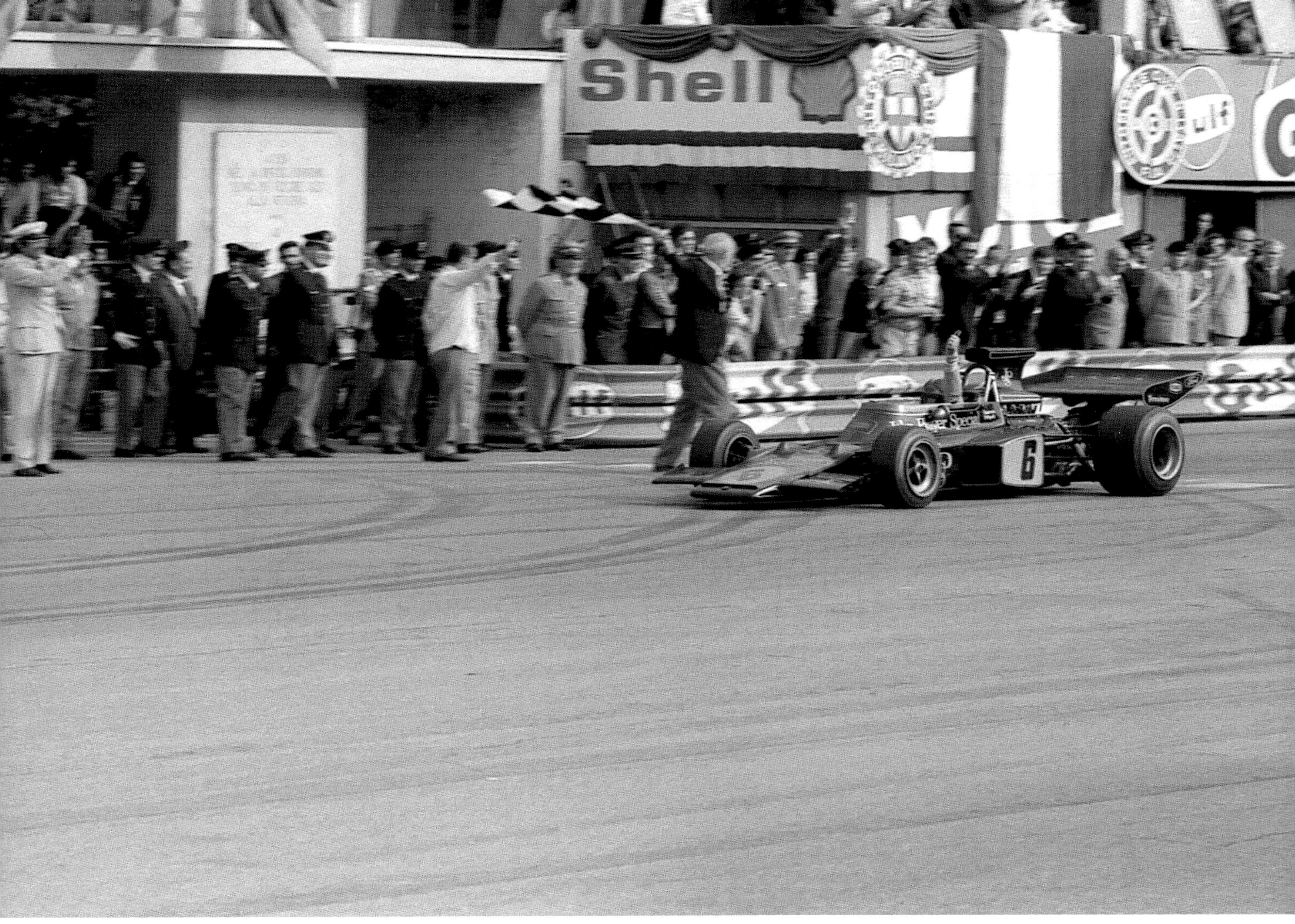

Monza, Italian GP, 1972. Emerson Fittipaldi (Lotus 72D Ford) celebrates victory, becoming the then-youngest champion. Photo: Ercole Colombo

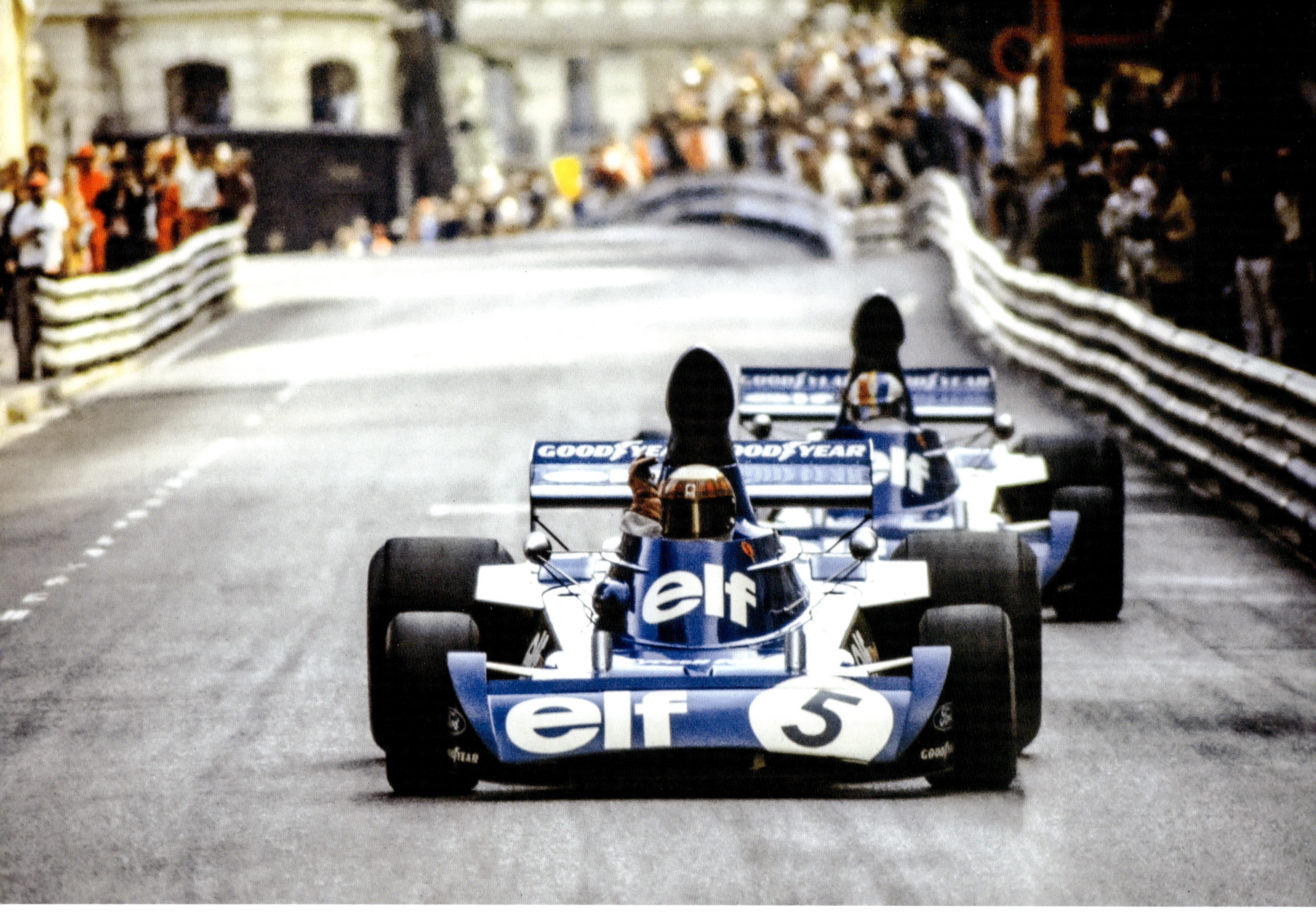 Monaco GP, 1973. Jackie Stewart (Tyrrell 006 Ford) leads François Cevert (Tyrrell 006 Ford) into Mirabeau. Photo: Rainer Schlegelmilch

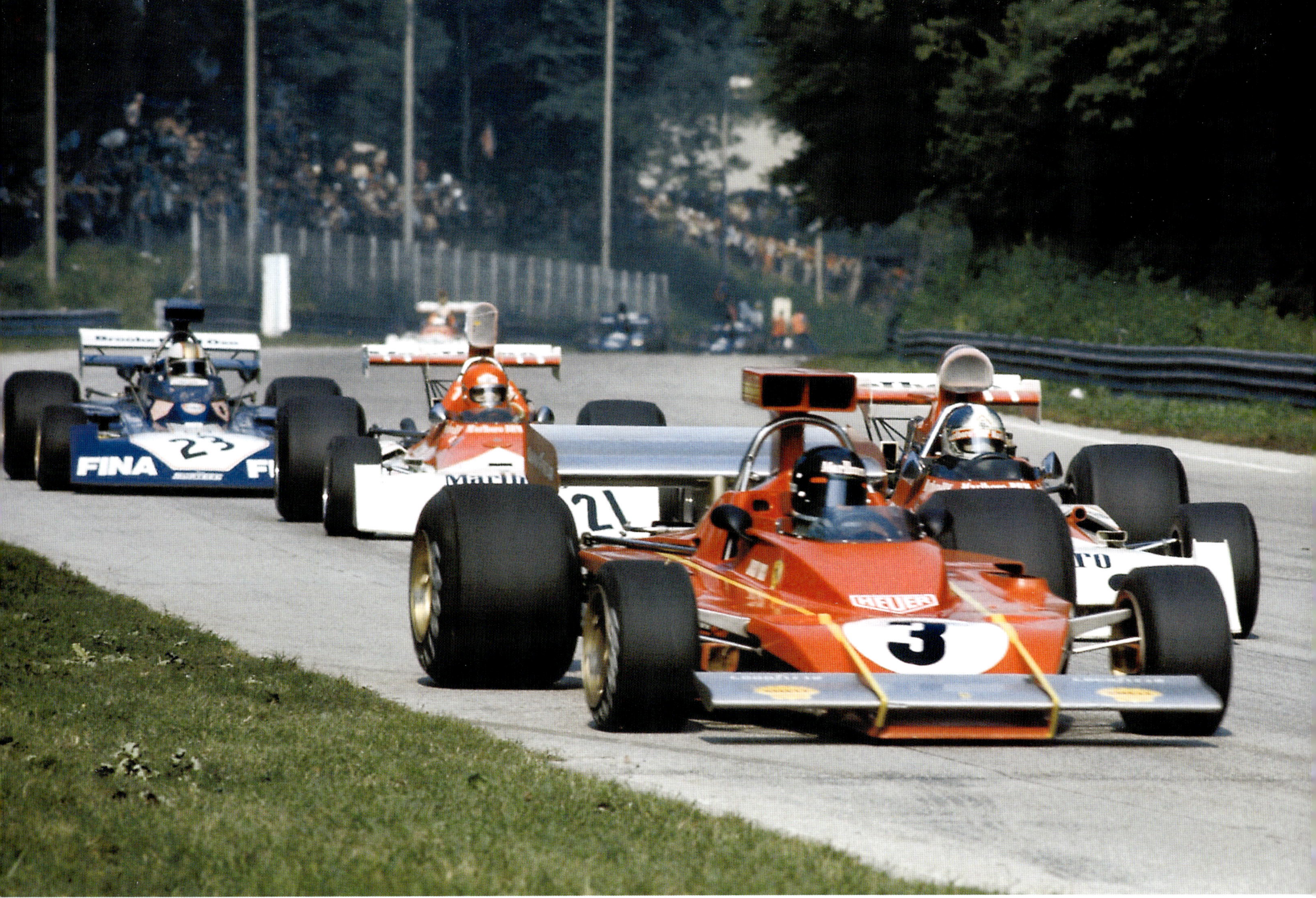

Monza, Italian GP, 1973. Jacky Ickx (Ferrari 312B3) leads Jean-Pierre Beltoise and Niki Lauda (BRM P160E), and Mike Hailwood (Surtees TS14A). Photo: Ercole Colombo

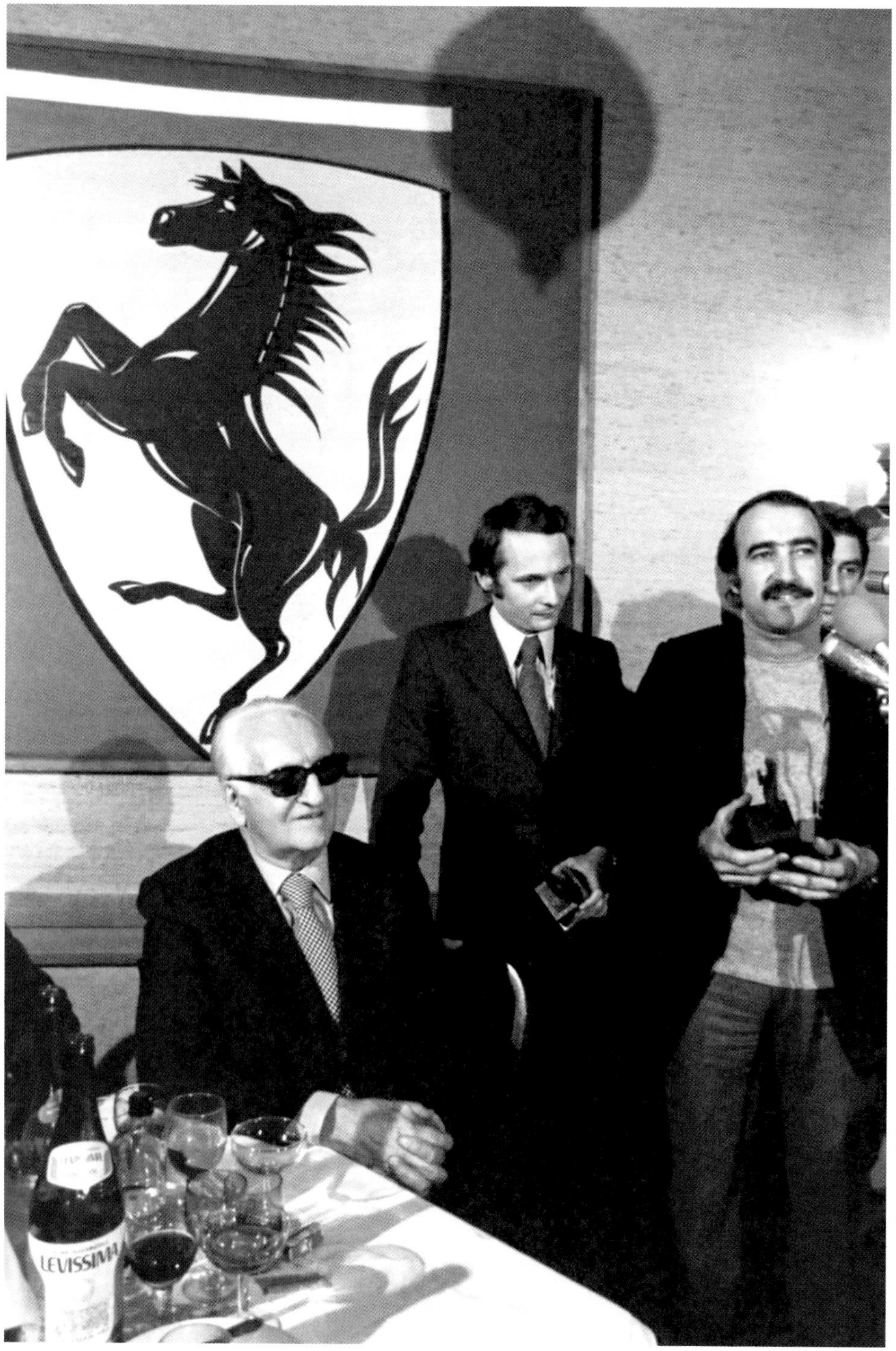

Modena, 1975. Enzo Ferrari with his drivers Niki Lauda and Clay Regazzoni. Photo: Ercole Colombo

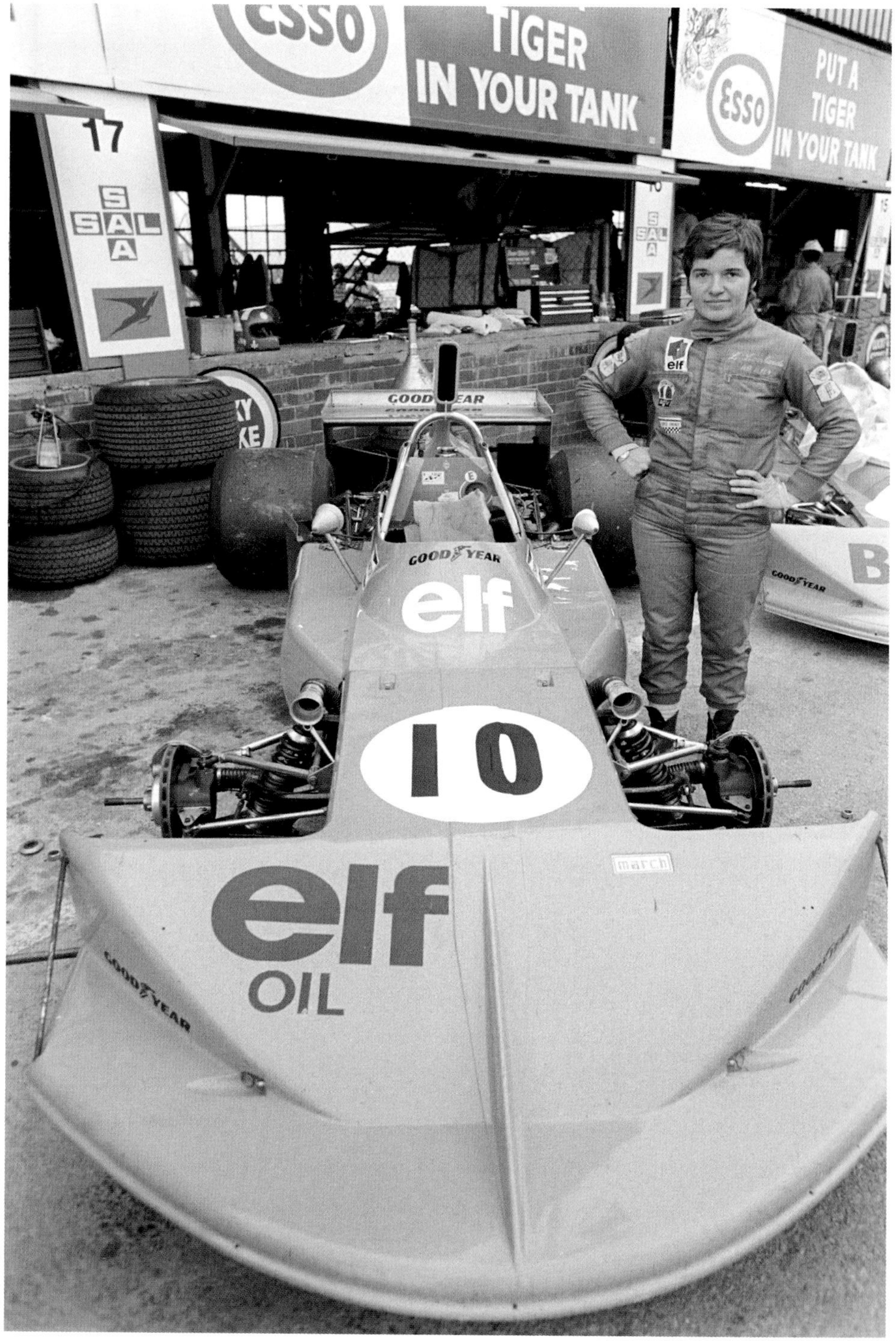

Kyalami, South African GP, 1975. Lella Lombardi stands next to her March 741 Ford after becoming the first female to qualify for a Grand Prix since 1958. Photo: David Phipps

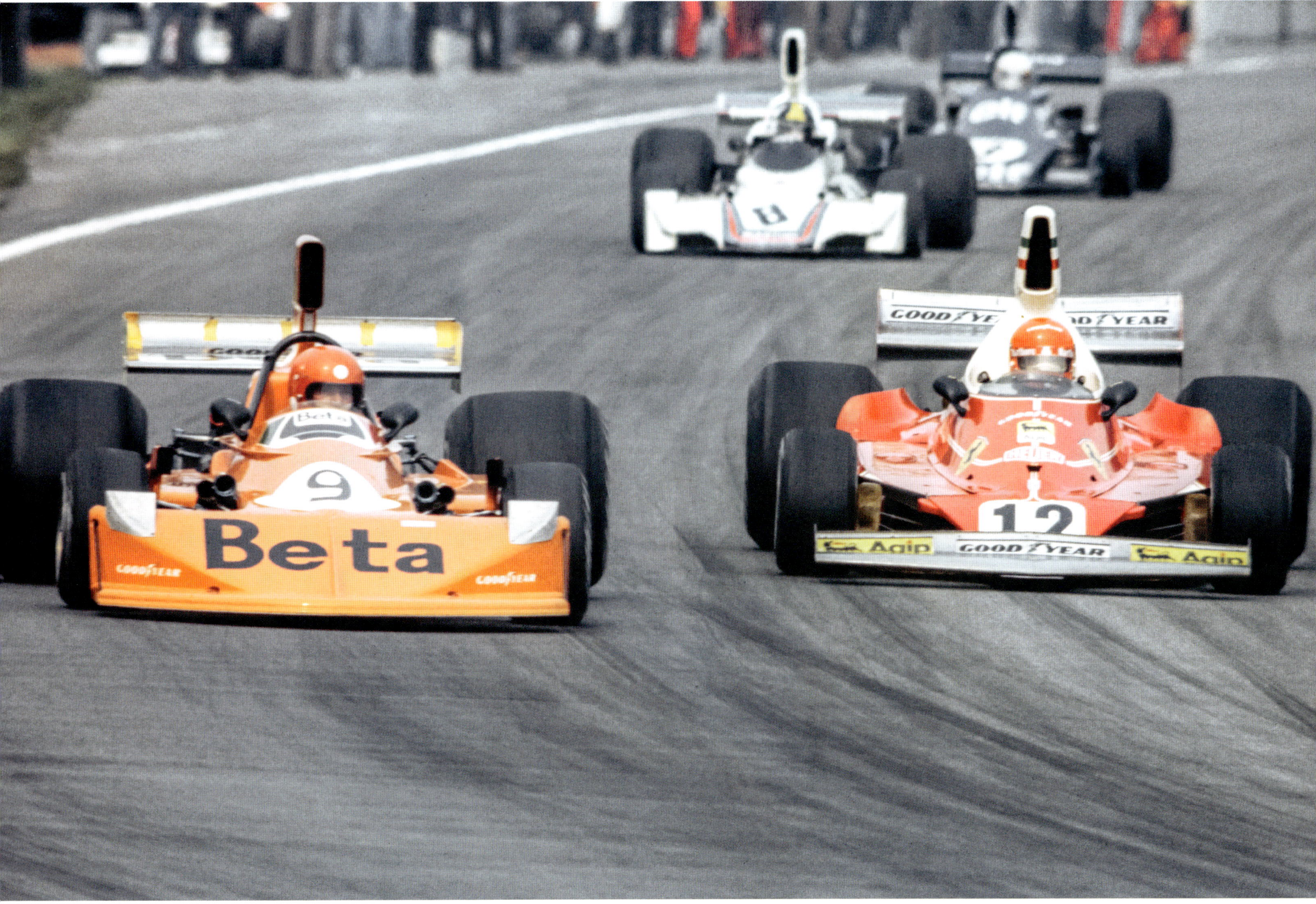

Zolder, Belgian GP, 1975. Vittorio Brambilla (March 751 Ford) battles with Niki Lauda (Ferrari 312T) ahead of Carlos Pace (Brabham BT44B Ford). Photo: Ercole Colombo

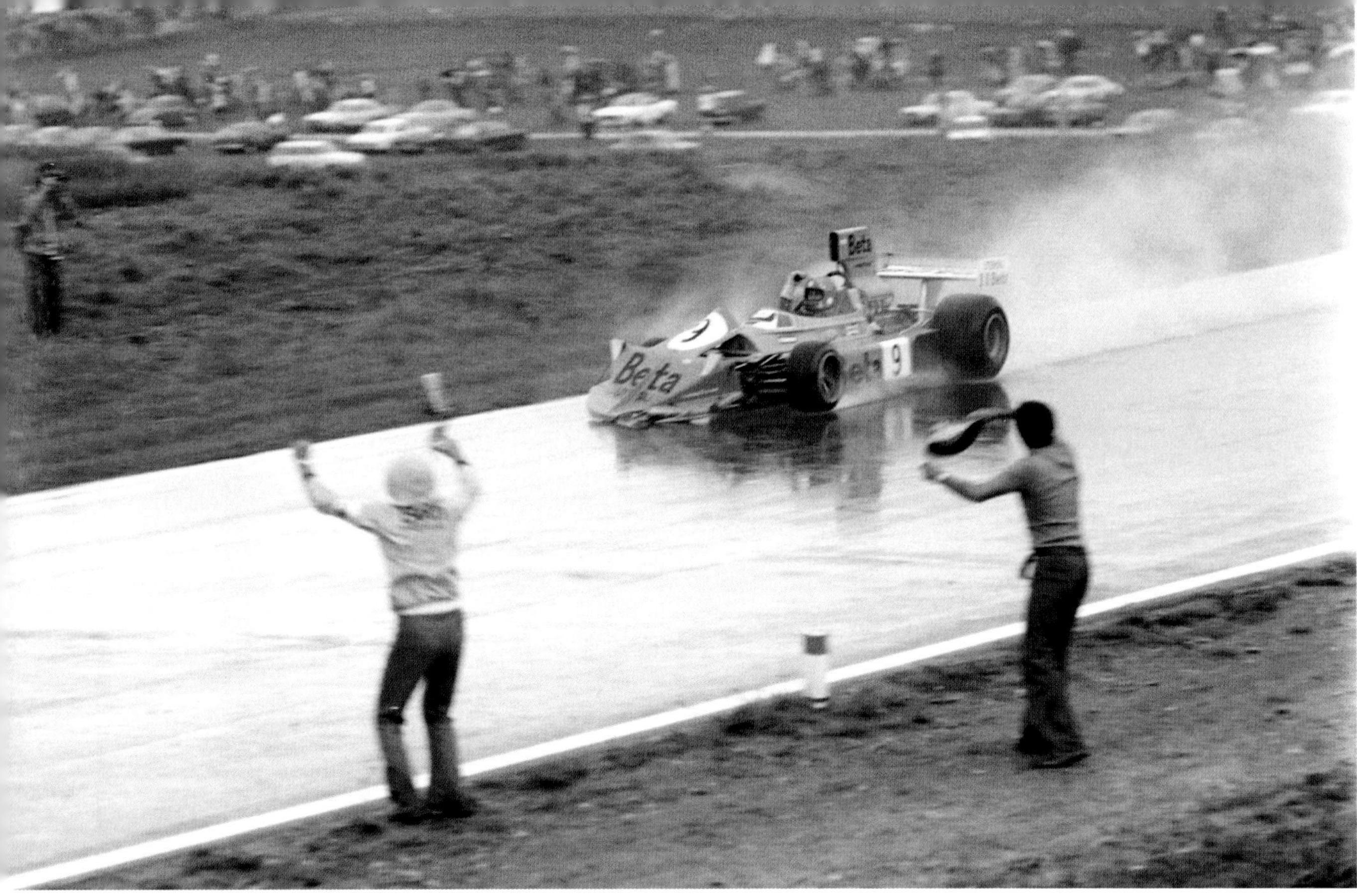

Zeltweg, Austrian GP, 1975. Vittorio Brambilla (March 751) takes his first victory in a rain-shortened race. Photo: David Phipps

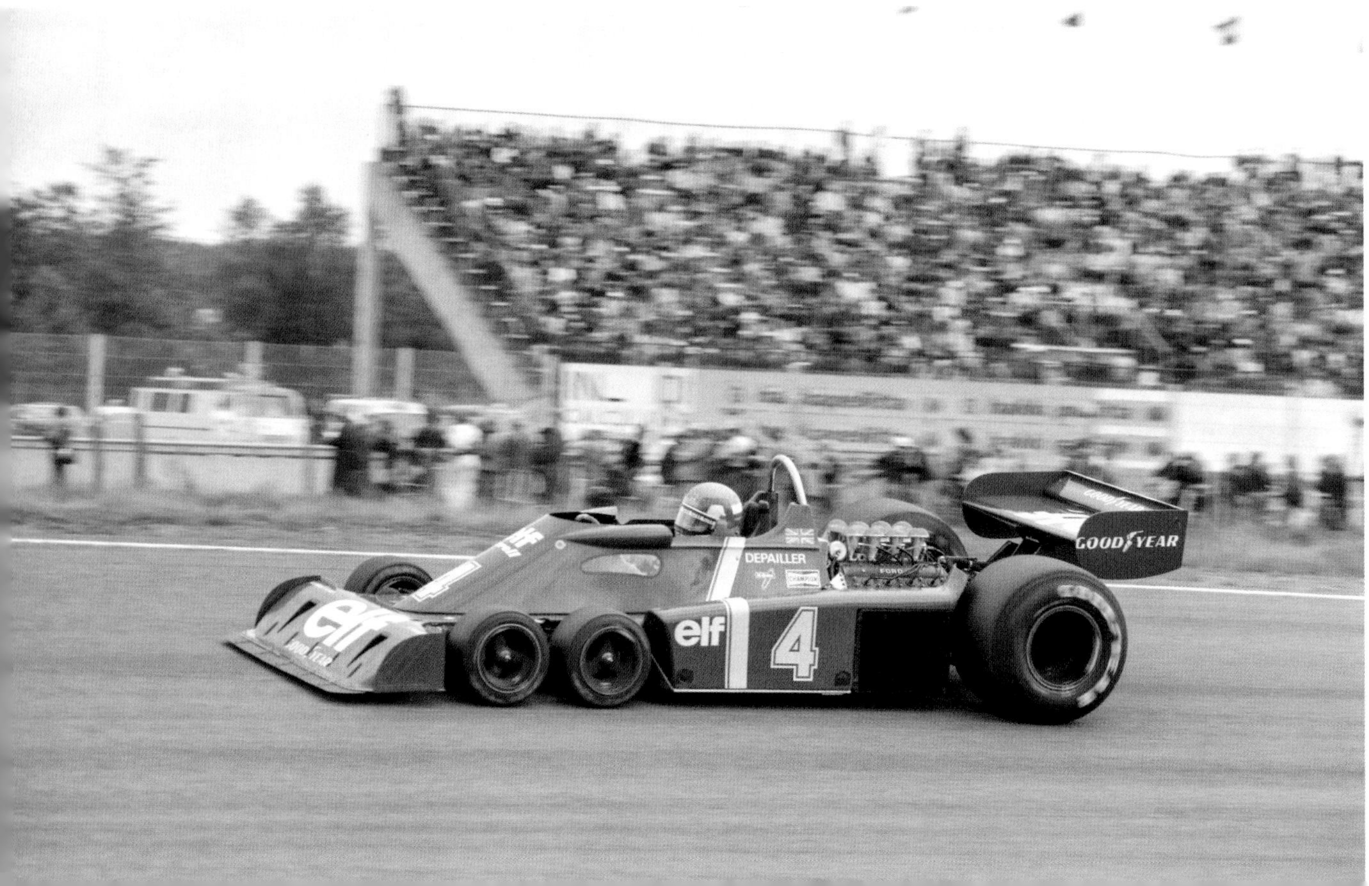

Swedish GP, 1976. Patrick Depailler (Tyrrell P34 Ford). Photo: Ercole Colombo

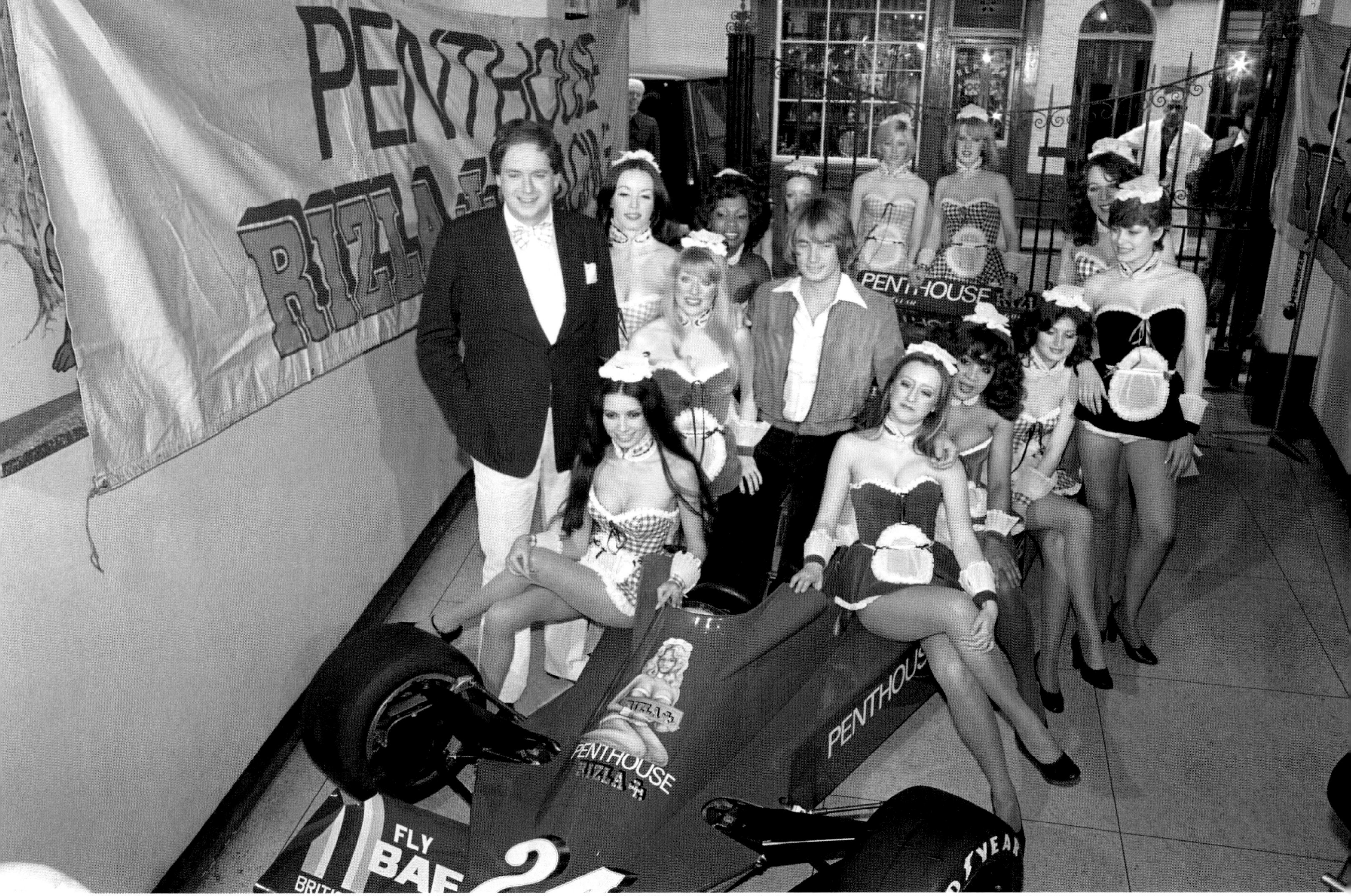

1977. Lord Alexander Hesketh (left), Hesketh Team owner, and 1977 driver Rupert Keegan, in his car, with the Penthouse Pets at the branding launch of Penthouse Rizla Racing Hesketh 308E. Photo: David Phipps

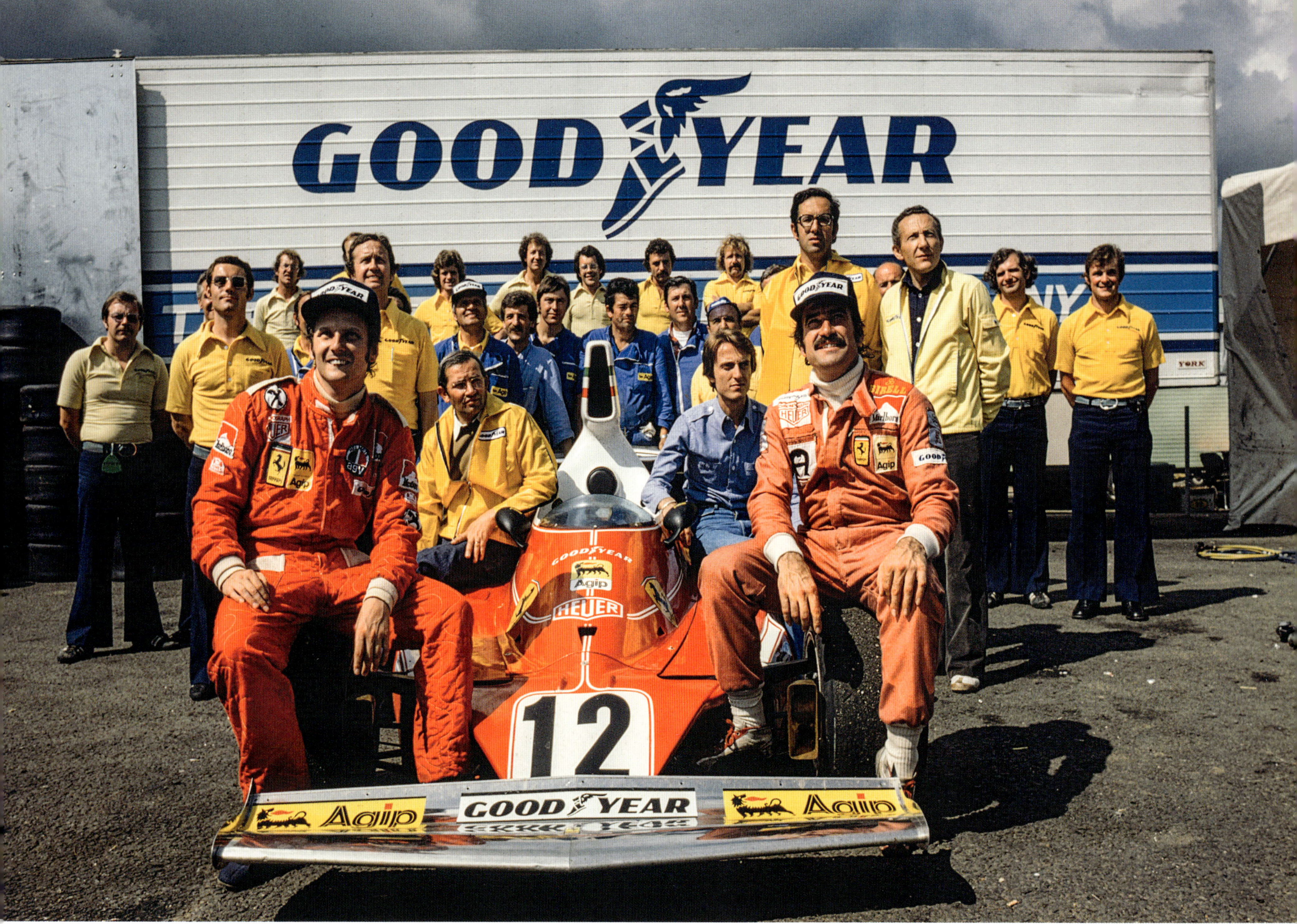

Silverstone, British GP, 1975. Ferrari team photo with drivers Niki Lauda and Clay Regazzoni, engineer Mauro Forghieri, and team President Luca di Montezemolo with the Ferrari 312T. Photo: David Phipps

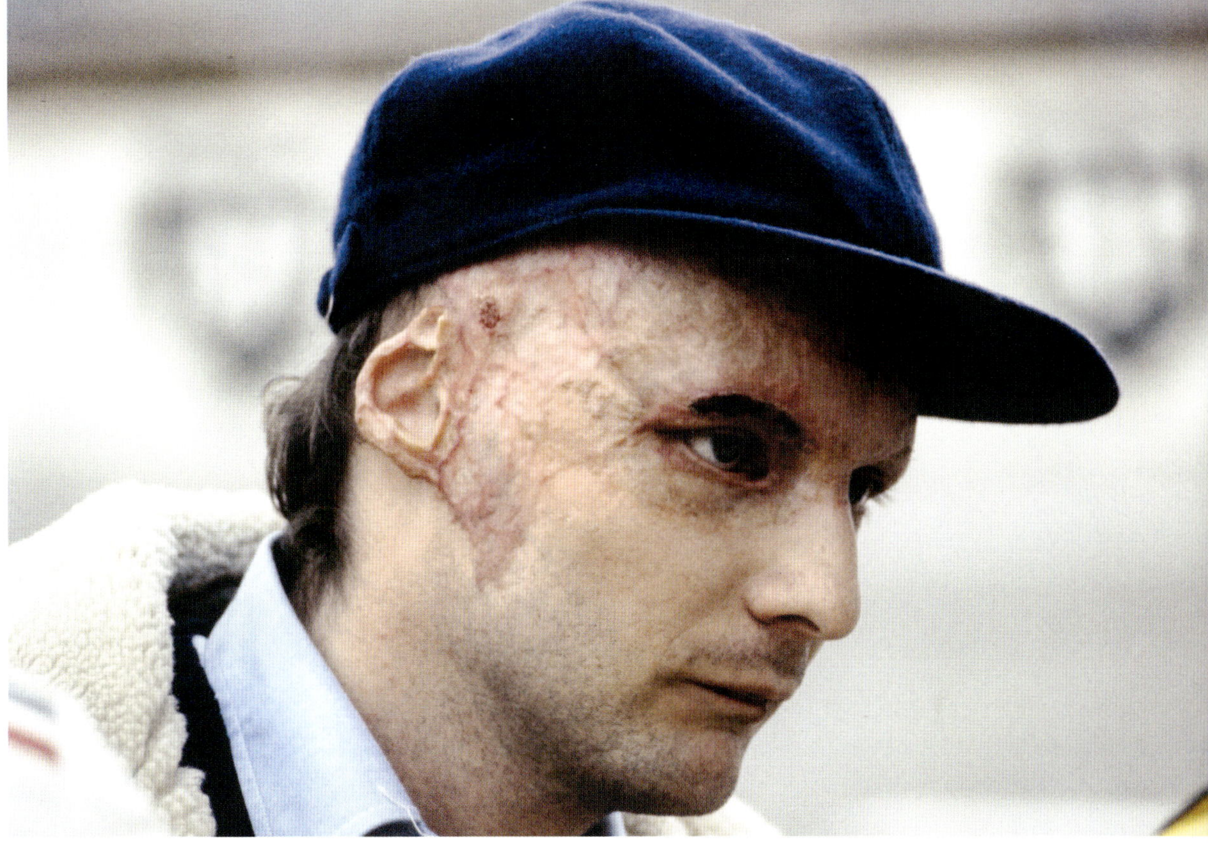

Monza, Italian GP, 1976. Niki Lauda with the visible burns and scars he sustained in his near-fatal crash just six weeks before. Photo: Ercole Colombo

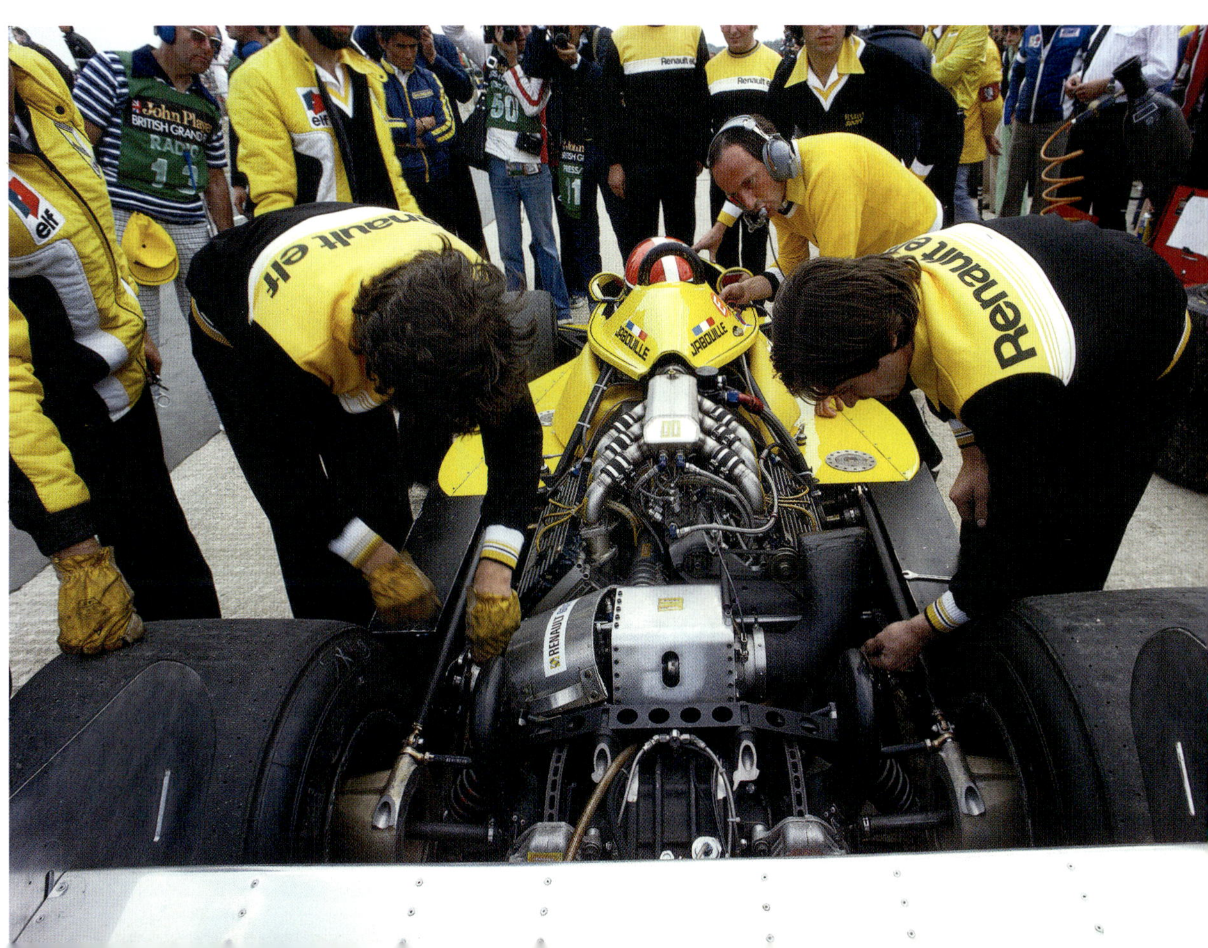

Silverstone, British GP, 1977. Mechanics check the turbocharged engine in Jean-Pierre Jabouille's Renault RS01 ahead of their debut. Photo: Rainer Schlegelmilch

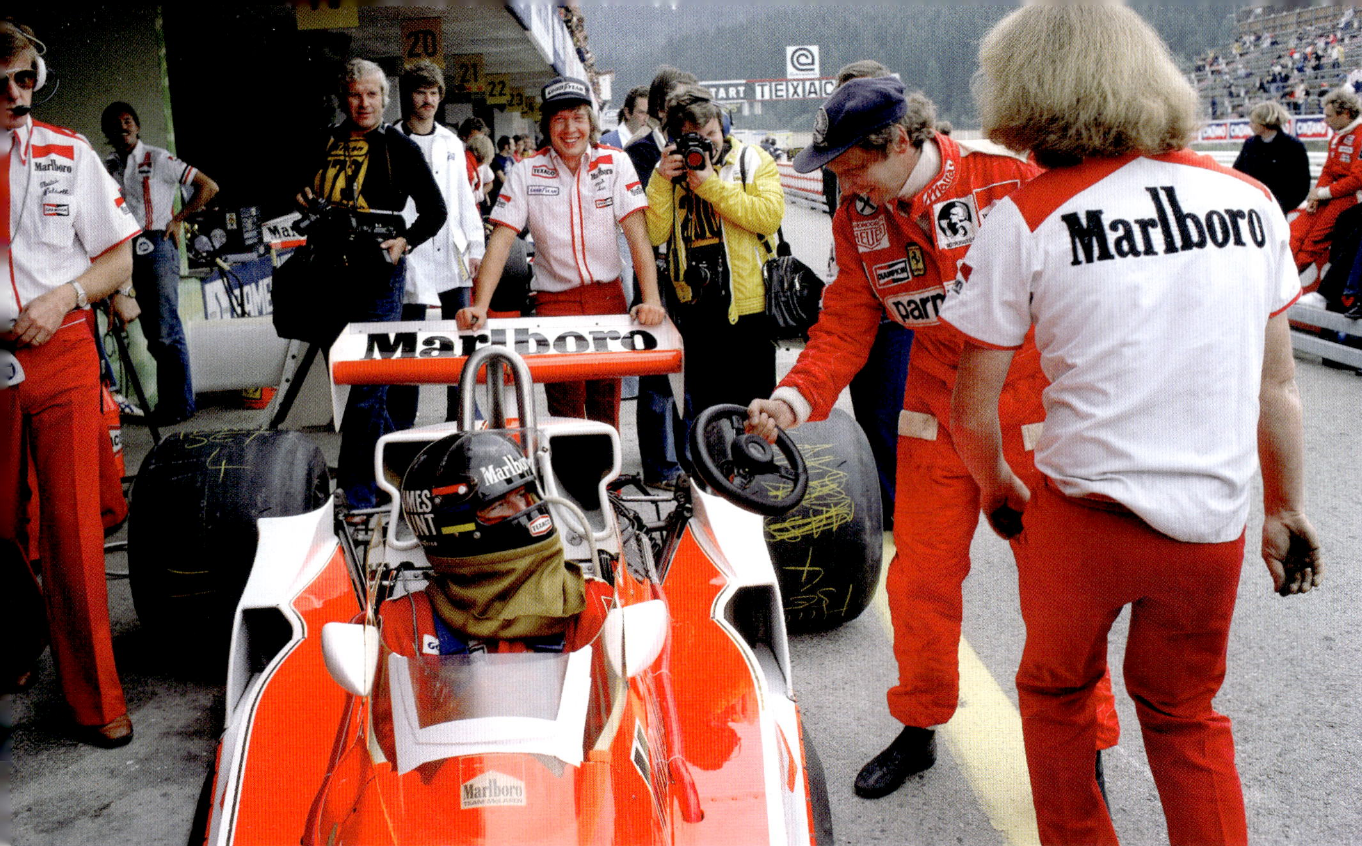

Zeltweg, Austrian GP, 1977.
Niki Lauda handing over
James Hunt's steering wheel.
Photo: Rainer Schlegelmilch

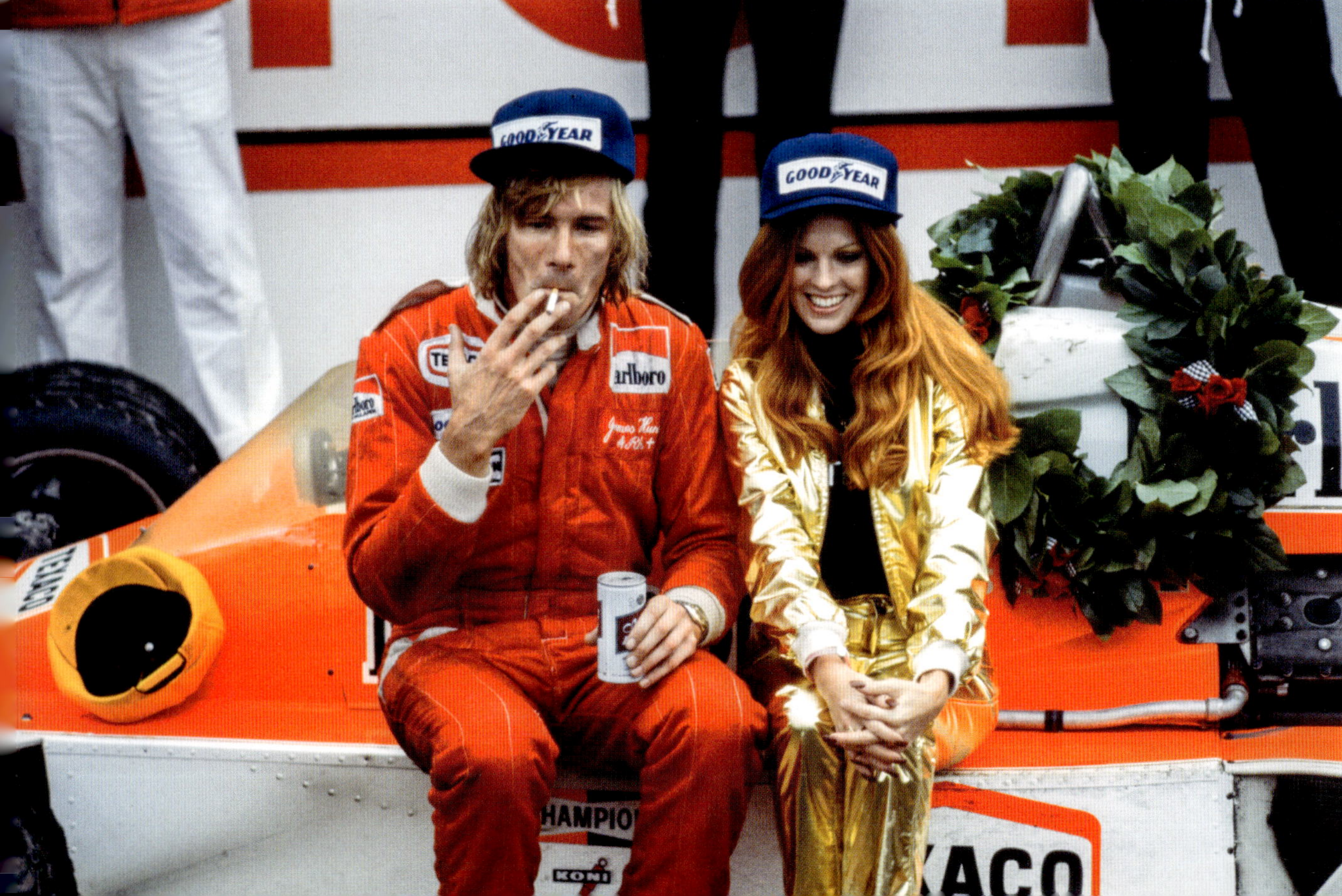

Watkins Glen, United States
GP East, 1977. James Hunt
(McLaren M26) celebrates his
victory with a cigarette and a
beer. Photo: David Phipps

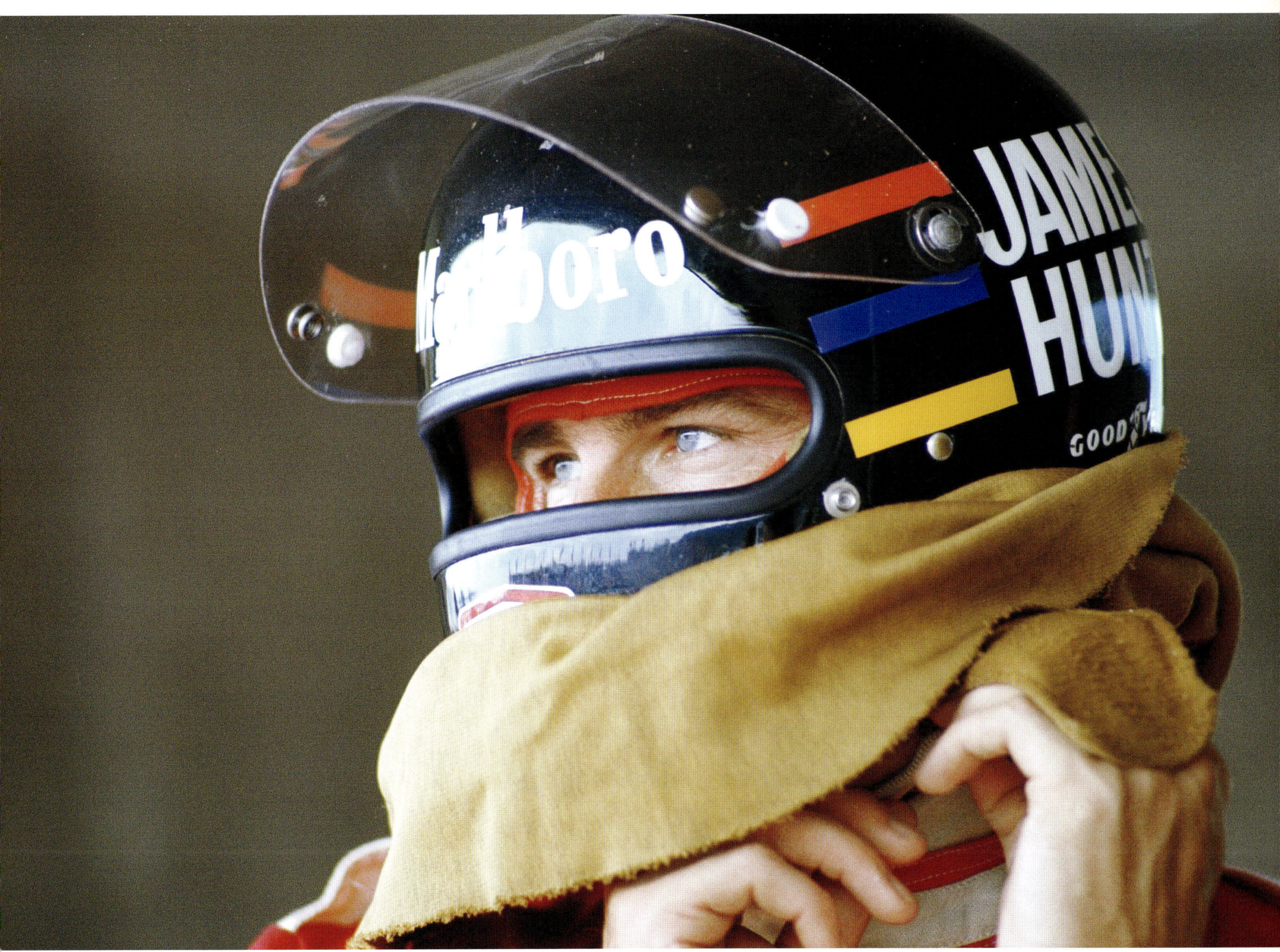

Zeltweg, Austrian GP, 1977. James Hunt. Photo: Rainer Schlegelmilch

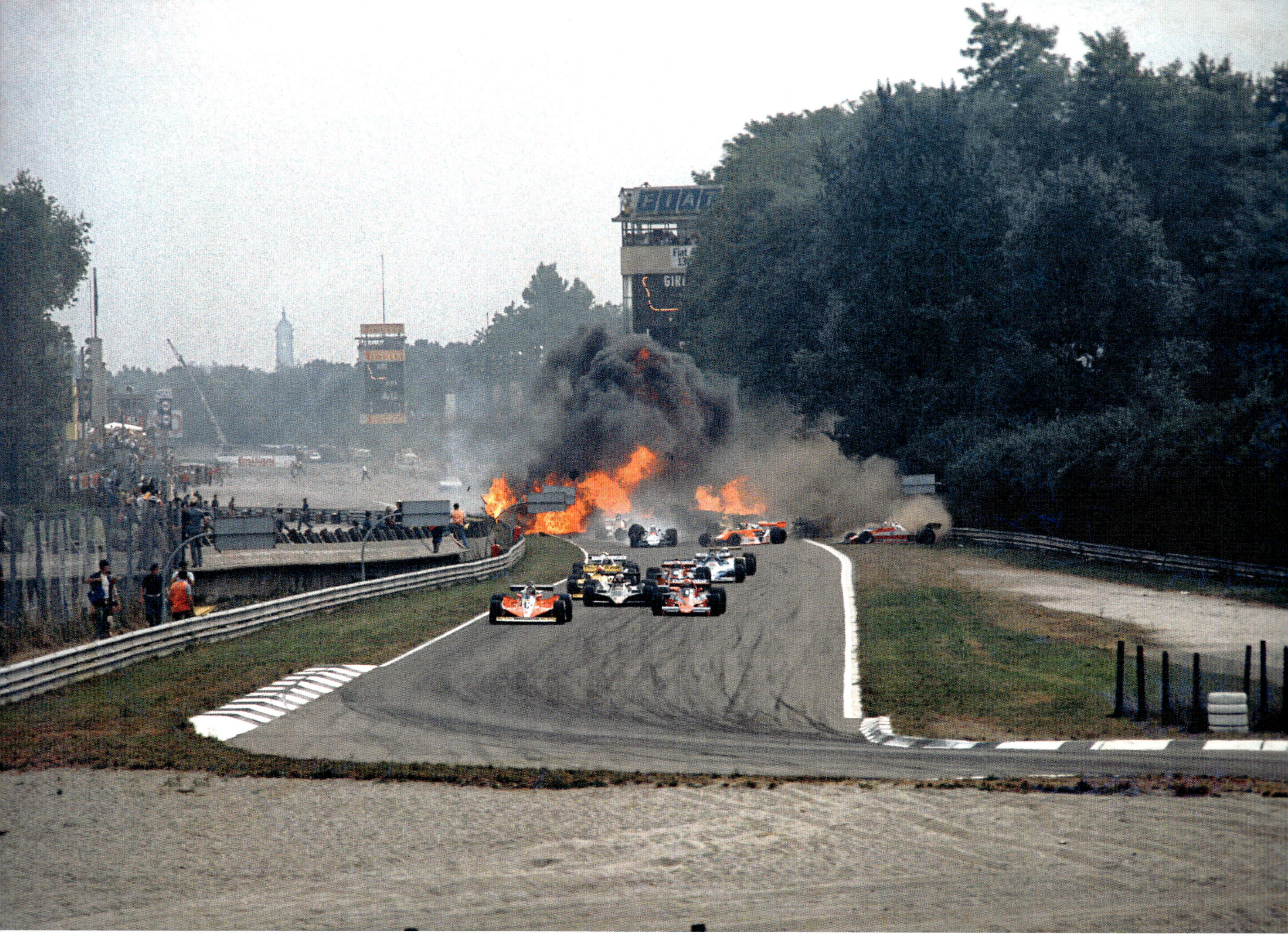

Monza, Italian GP, 1978. The crash at the start in which Ronnie Peterson lost his life. Gilles Villeneuve (Ferrari 312T3), Niki Lauda (Brabham BT46, Alfa Romeo), and Mario Andretti (Lotus 79 Ford) lead as the accident takes place behind them. Photo: Ercole Colombo

Zandvoort, Dutch GP, 1978.
Mario Andretti (Lotus 79
Ford) leads teammate Ronnie
Peterson. Photo: David Phipps

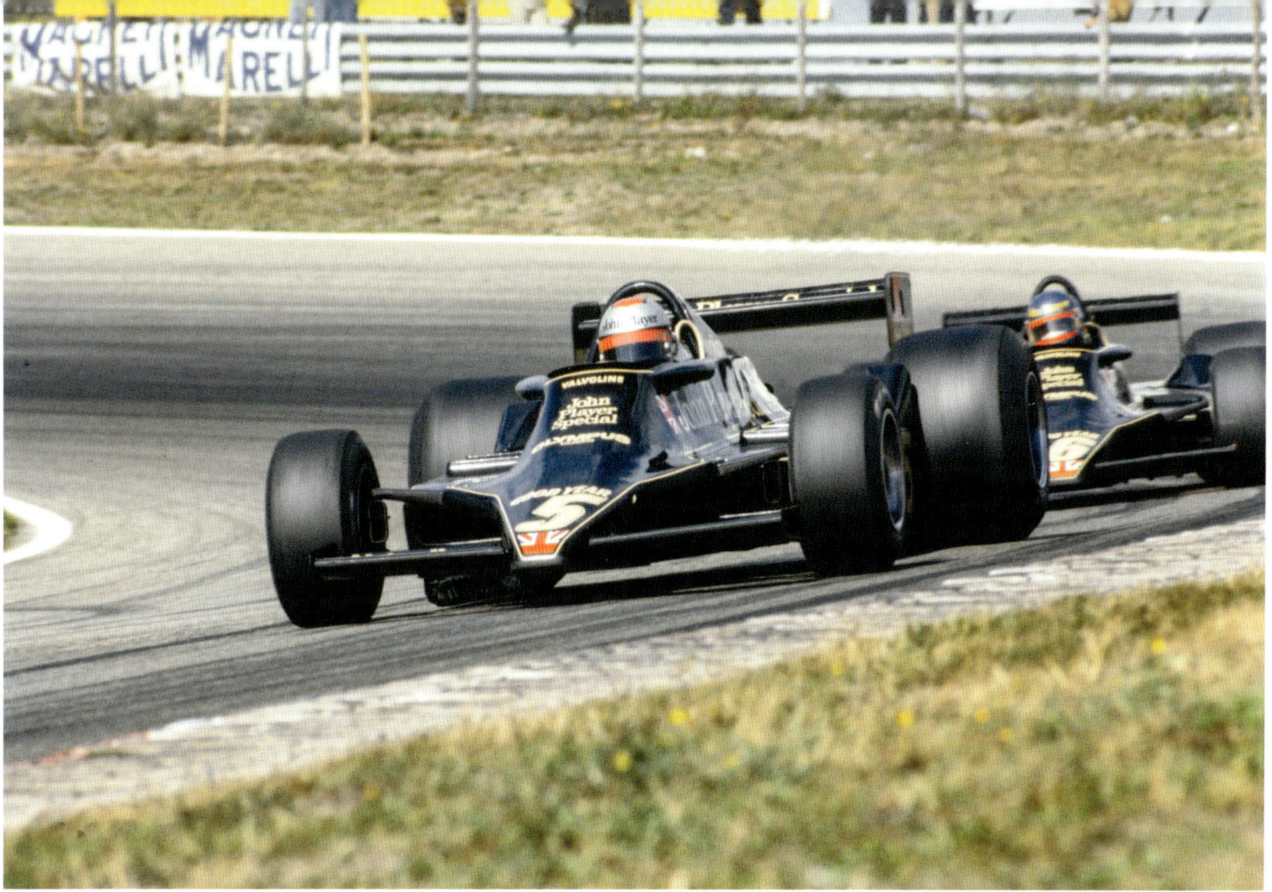

Fuji, Japanese GP, 1976.
James Hunt (McLaren M23
Ford) kicks up spray as he
drives down the main straight.
Photo: Ercole Colombo

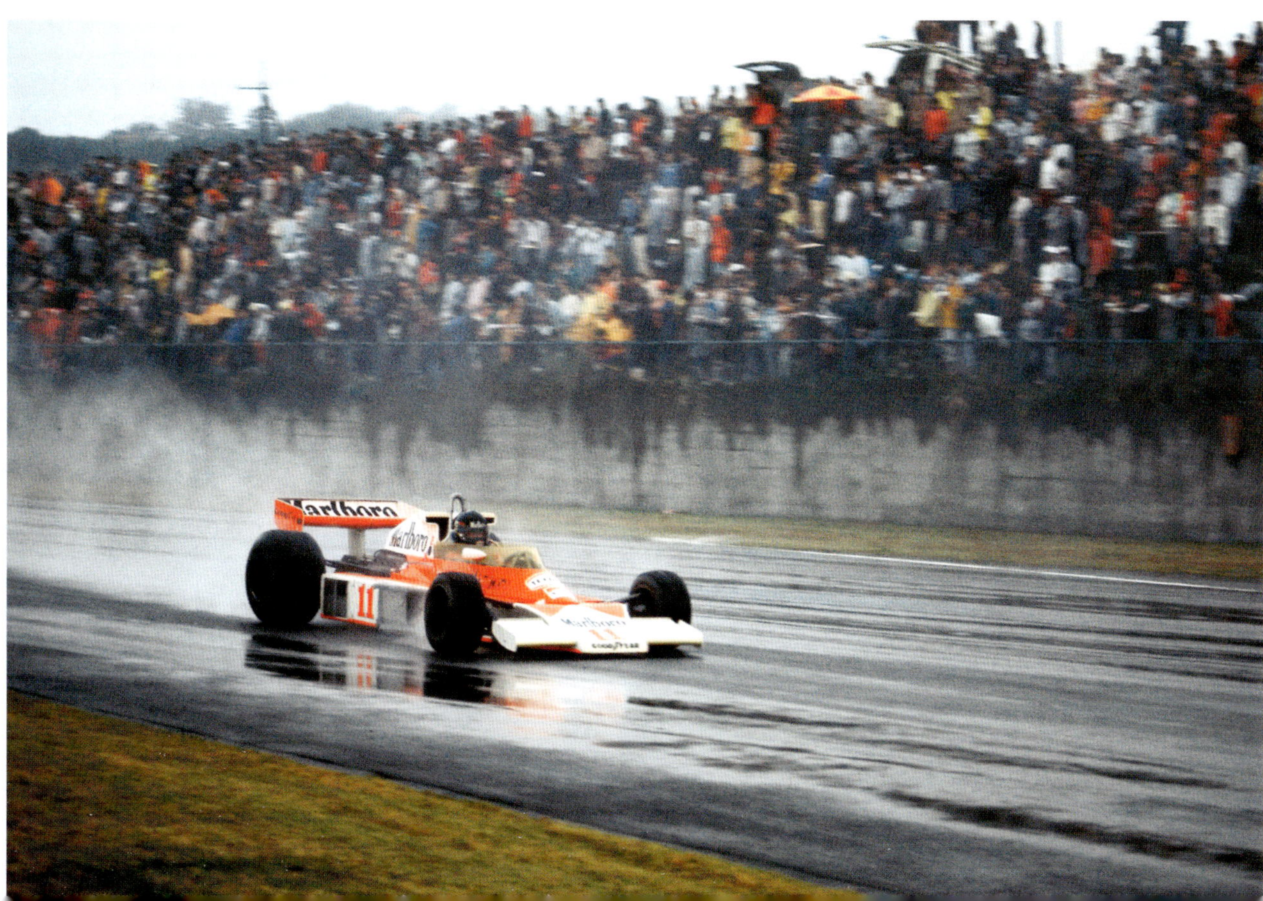

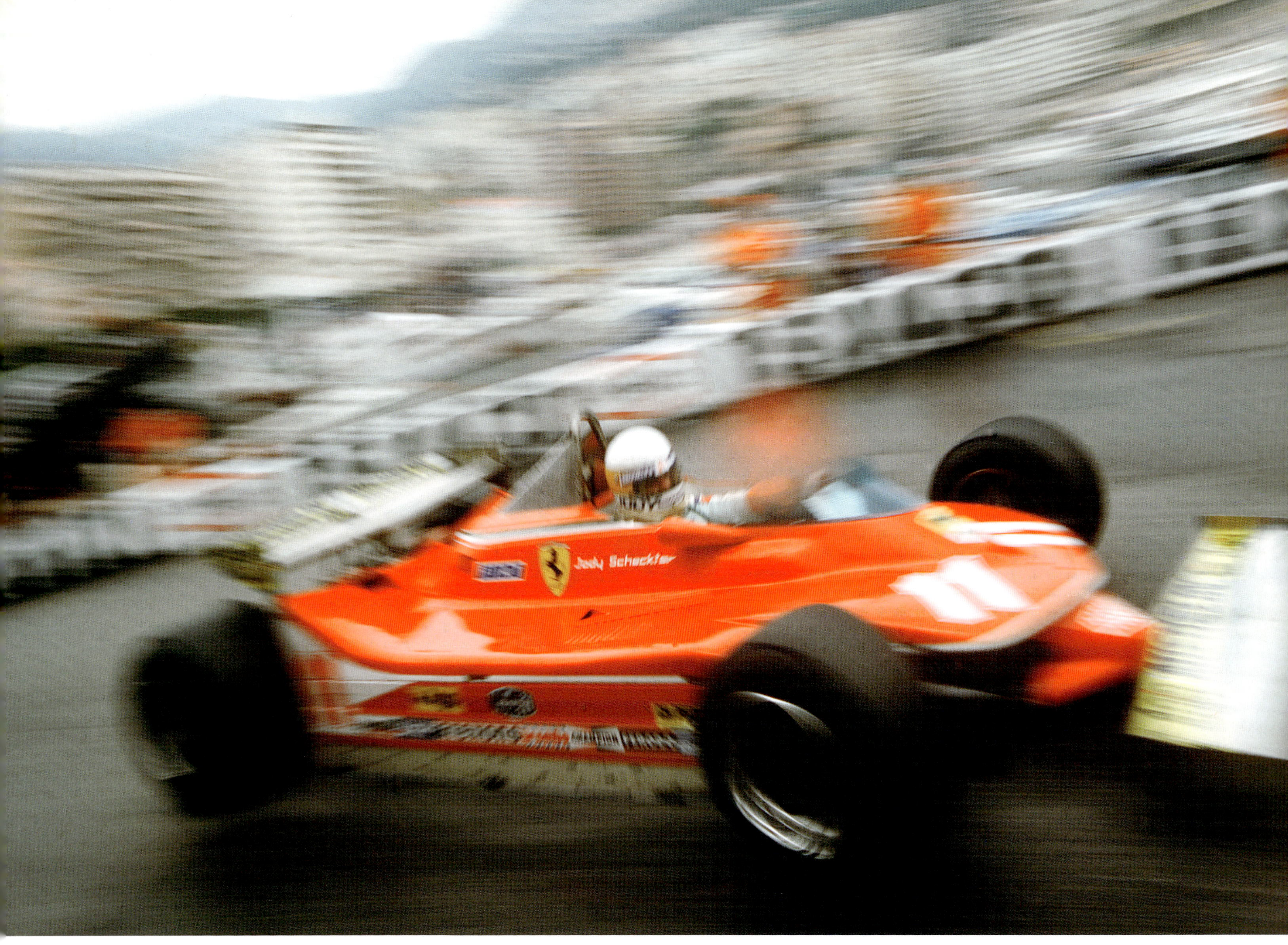

GP Monaco, 1979. Jody Scheckter (Ferrari) heads to victory. Photo: Ercole Colombo

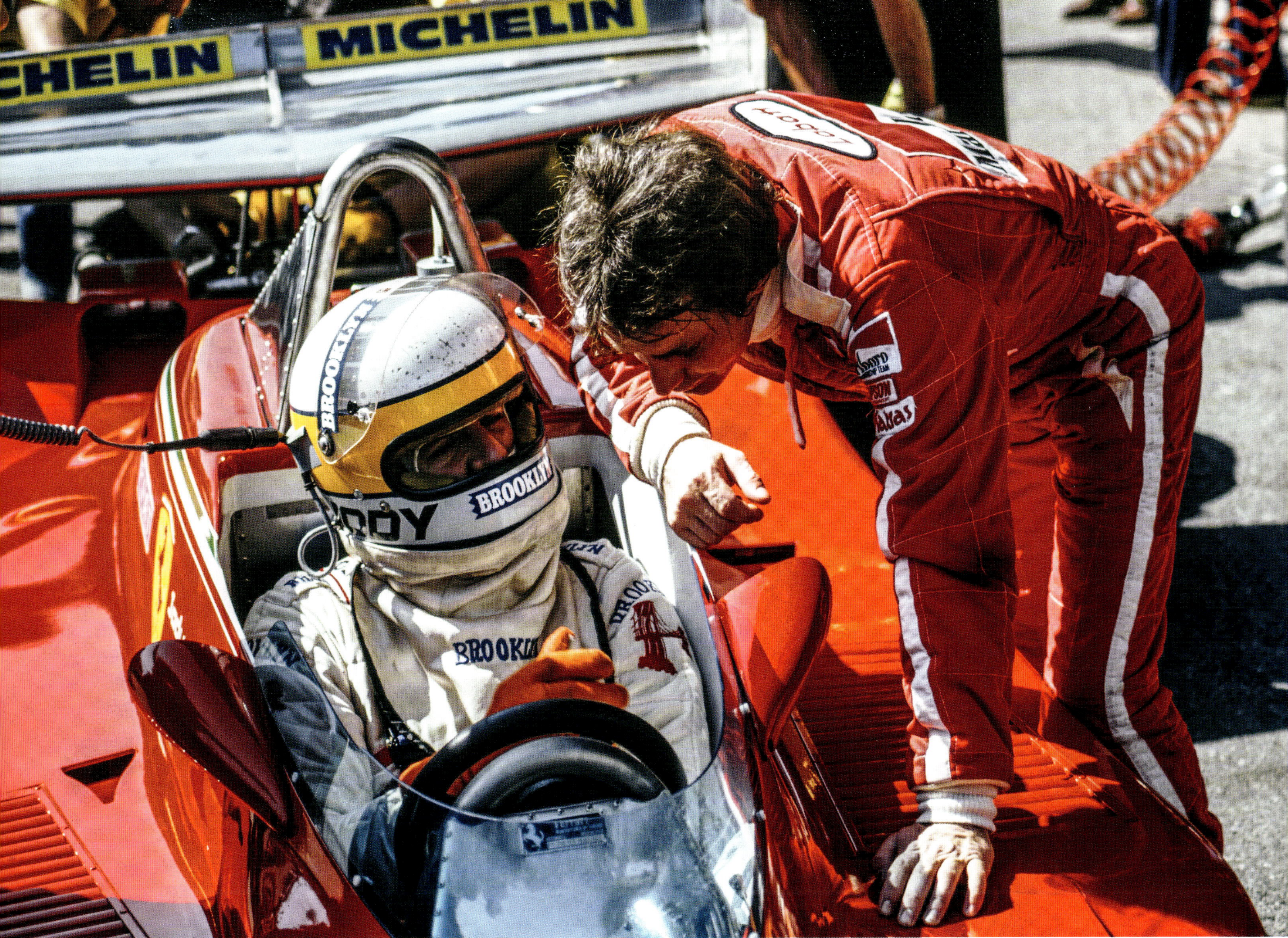

GP Monaco, 1979. Gilles Villeneuve talks with teammate Jody Scheckter, who is seated in his Ferrari 312T4. Photo: David Phipps

1980–1989
Astounding Duos

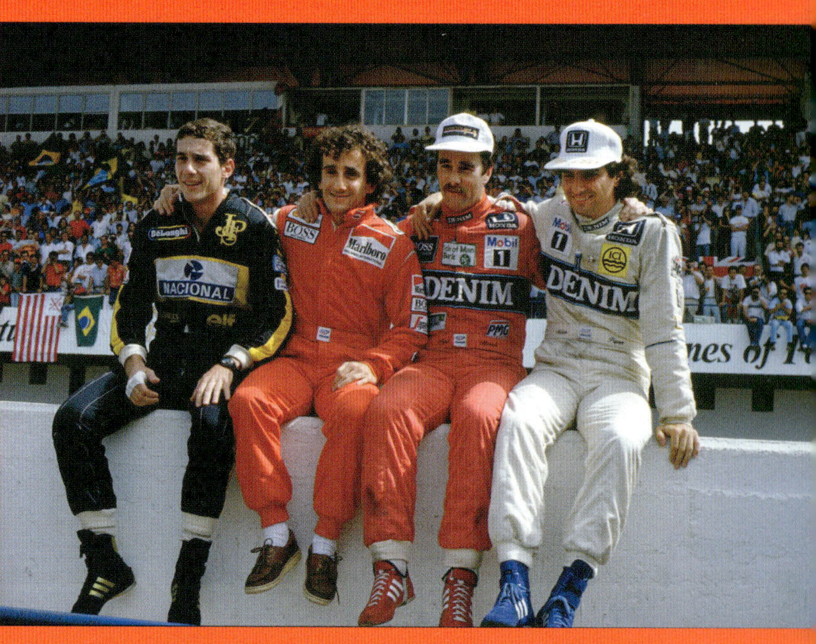

One decade, three teams: Williams, Brabham, McLaren. The turbocharged era was in full swing. Inaugurated by the victory of the Australian Alan Jones (1946), strong on the track, strong in body, not at all tactful. Coming up behind him, in 1980, were two drivers who encountered opposite fates: the Brazilian Nelson Piquet and his teammate, the Argentinian Carlos Reutemann. The former had an astounding career, the latter was consigned to the role of second driver despite his absolute skill for speed. Piquet was world champion three times, in 1981, 1983, and 1987. Born in Rio de Janeiro (1952), he was fast, extremely fast, on and off track. Two victories with Brabham, the team owned by Bernie Ecclestone, one with Williams. In 1981, Reutemann came in second; in 1983 it was Prost, with Renault; in 1987, Mansell, his teammate and bitter enemy. Great talents, great rivalries, the numbers of a decade full of adrenaline, marked by overpowered engines. Porsche, BMW, Renault, Ferrari. It is highly likely that the Maranello stable would have won both titles in 1982, but the year's color was black, not red. Gilles Villeneuve (1950–1982) died in Belgium on May 8, unsettled and offended by the internal rivalry with the French Didier Pironi (1957-1987), which had become full-blown at Imola two weeks earlier. Pironi was the victim of an extremely violent accident during the practice session of the German GP in Hockenheim, from

which he never fully recovered. Patrick Tambay, another Frenchman who had been called to replace Villeneuve, was blocked by a powerful inflammation of his neck tendons after the victory obtained in Germany. Ferrari also hired Mario Andretti, who immediately achieved pole position at Monza. Four drivers for a World Championship tainted by bad luck. The one to benefit from it was the Finnish Keke Rosberg (1948), world champion in 1982 with only one victory under his belt, in the Swiss GP that was held in France, in Dijon. Though present for only 10 of the 16 races, Pironi came in second, tied with John Watson, McLaren's driver. Ferrari had to make do with the Constructors' Championship. 1984 marked a sort of divide. McLaren deployed the pair Lauda-Prost to drive a vehicle designed by John Bernard, the first designer to use carbon fiber, the first to create the aerodynamic "Coke bottle styling" design that would become a feature of all vehicles from then on. Furthermore, McLaren installed the powerful Porsche turbocharged engine. The figures: the 1984 title conquered by Lauda (his third); the 1985 and 1986 titles won by Alain Prost. The French driver, born in 1955, who had come in second in the World Championship two times in a row (in 1983 and 1984), finally came to the fore. Threatened since 1984 by a young Brazilian driver on a steady rise: Ayrton Senna. The two were teammates at McLaren beginning in 1988, Senna having transferred from

Lotus, a team that made it possible for him to obtain his first F1 victories. Two in 1985, two in 1986, two in 1987, a season dominated by the Williams driven by the duo Piquet-Mansell in a frenzied, spectacular competition. Equally intense was the rivalry between Prost and Senna, which became full-blown at Imola, at the San Marino GP, the second date in the 1988 championship, a competition that was a display of performances of the highest level, as always happens when a champion faces an adversary who is equally talented and forces him to raise the level of his performance. Senna won the title in 1988; Prost was the champion in 1989, a championship with a very famous ending at Suzuka. Ayrton tried to overtake Alain, the two McLarens collided, Senna got a push from the marshals to restart his dead engine but skipped the chicane, worked his way up, and won the race, but was later disqualified. This was enough to make him imagine a plot hatched by Prost and the FIA President, Jean-Marie Balestre, who were both French. To the point that he plotted a terrible revenge, enacted on the same track one year later, at the dawn of the Nineties. Piquet and Mansell; Senna and Prost; Lauda's last win dated 1984. And then the five years spent with Ferrari by Michele Alboreto (1956–2001), a failed sprint for the title in 1985, when he came in second at the end of the season, with two victories, his last, for a man who had conquered five Grands

Prix. The scene was increasingly taken over by other young Italians: Riccardo Patrese, Andrea De Cesaris, and Elio De Angelis, Roman, cultured, courteous, winner in Austria in 1982 and in Imola in 1985 and Senna's teammate at Lotus. He transferred to Brabham in 1986 together with Patrese. He died in a practice session in Le Castellet, France, on May 15, when the rear wing of his car detached at high speed. Non long before, on September 1, 1985, a young German, Stefan Bellof, had been killed in an accident during a round of the World Endurance Championship. Another extraordinary talent, passed away too soon.

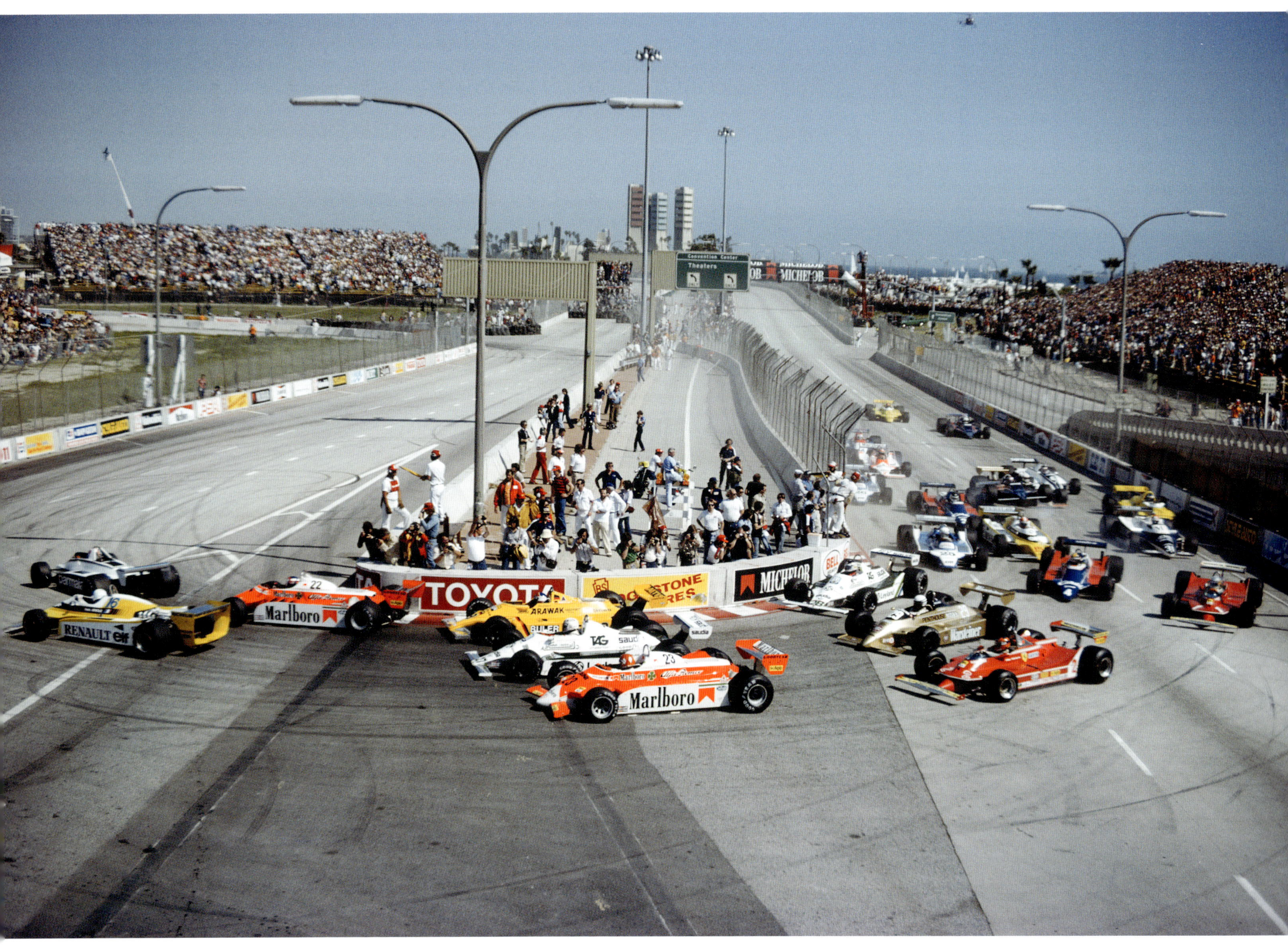

Long Beach, United States GP West, 1980. Nelson Piquet (Brabham BT49 Ford) leads from René Arnoux (Renault RE20), Patrick Depailler (Alfa Romeo 179), Jan Lammers (ATS D4 Ford), Alan Jones (Williams FW07B Ford), and Bruno Giacomelli (Alfa Romeo 179), at the start, while further back Mario Andretti (Lotus 81 Ford), and Jean-Pierre Jarier (Tyrrell 010 Ford) make contact. Photo: John Dumbar

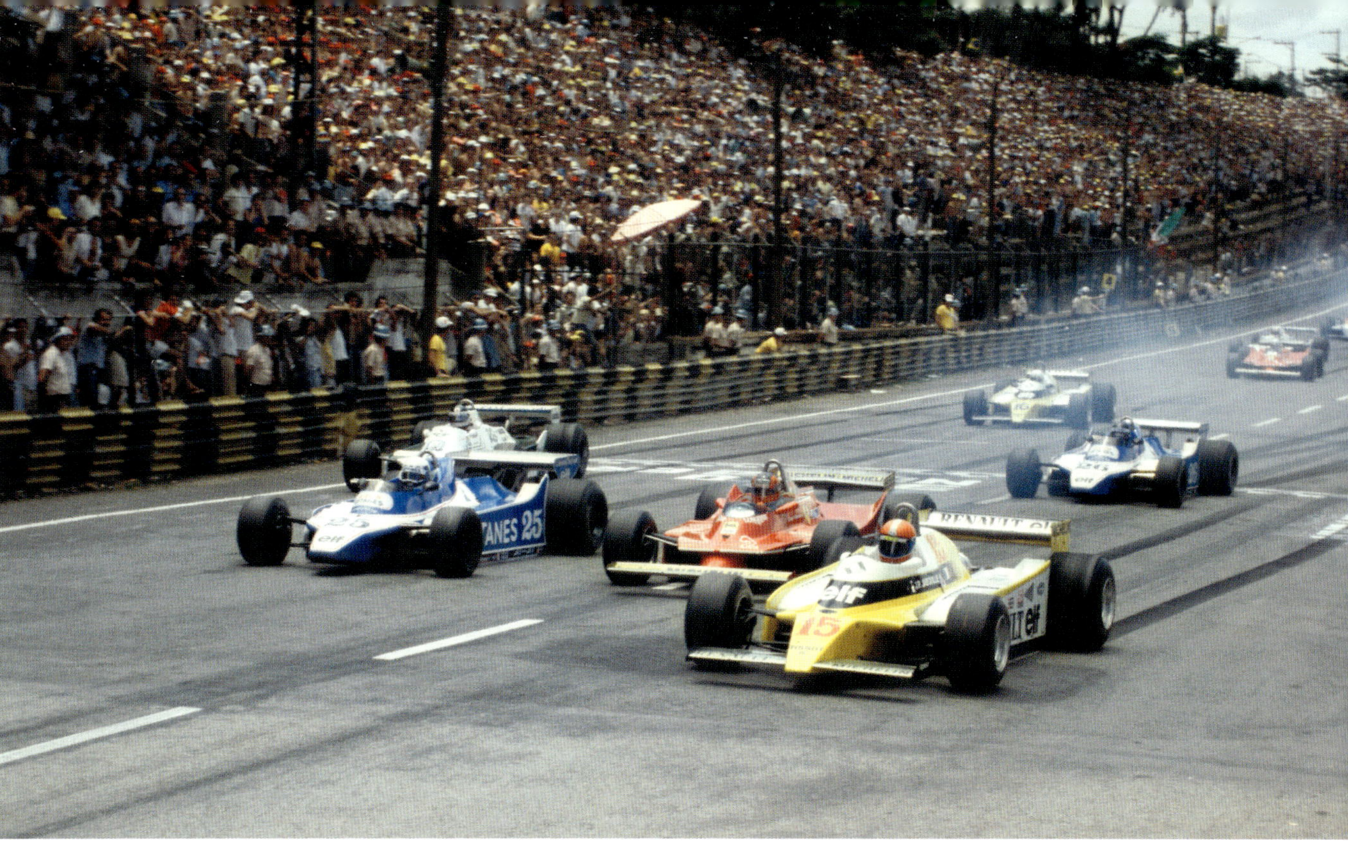

Brazilian GP, 1980. Jean-Pierre Jabouille (Renault RE20) with Gilles Villeneuve (Ferrari 312T5), and Didier Pironi (Ligier GS11/15) at the start. Photo: Ercole Colombo

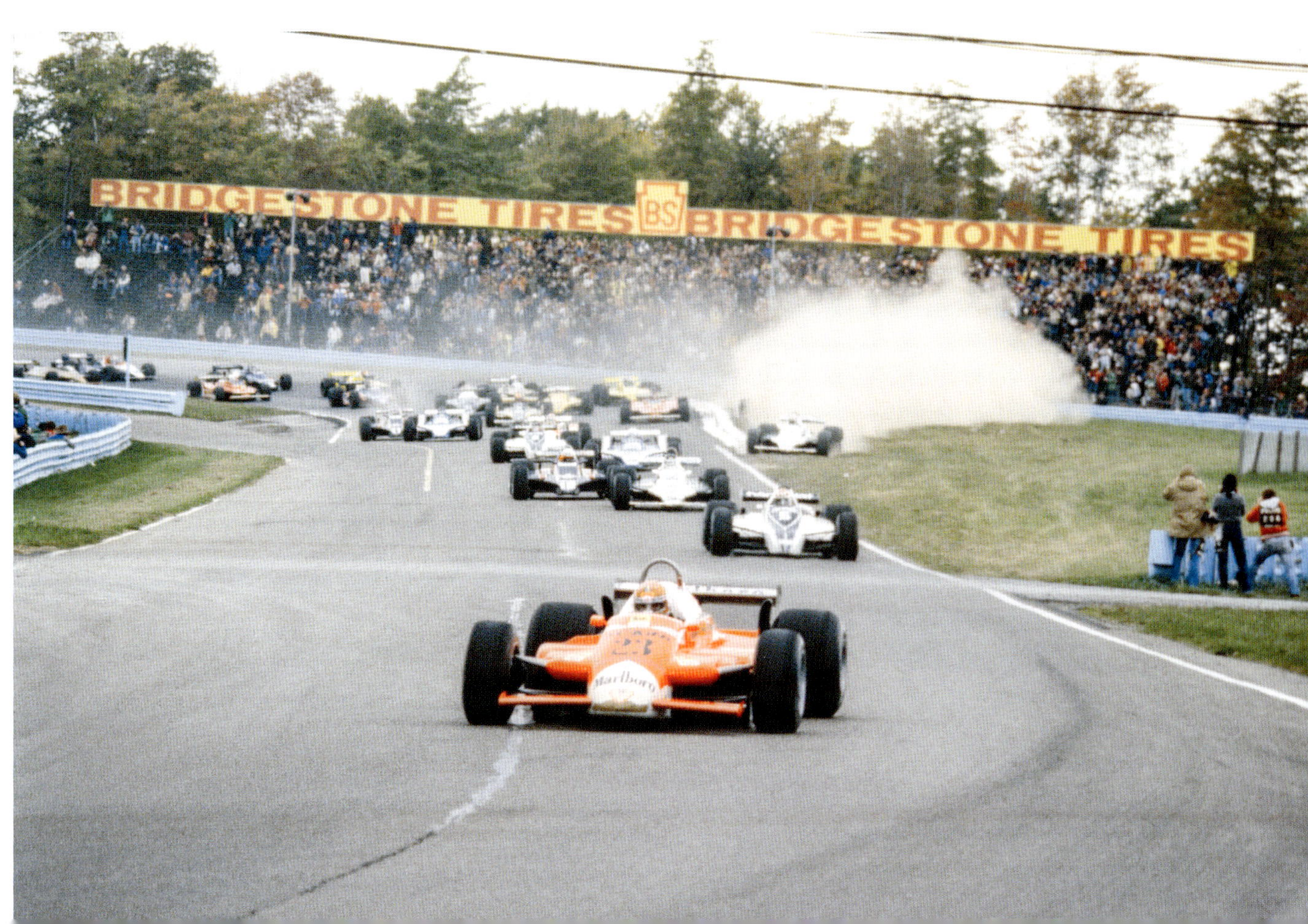

Watkins Glen, United States GP, 1980. Bruno Giacomelli (Alfa Romeo 179) leads Nelson Piquet (Brabham BT49 Ford), Carlos Reutemann (Williams FW07B Ford), and Elio De Angelis (Lotus 81 Ford), at the start. Further back, Alan Jones (Williams FW07B Ford) runs off the road at the first corner. Photo: LAT Images

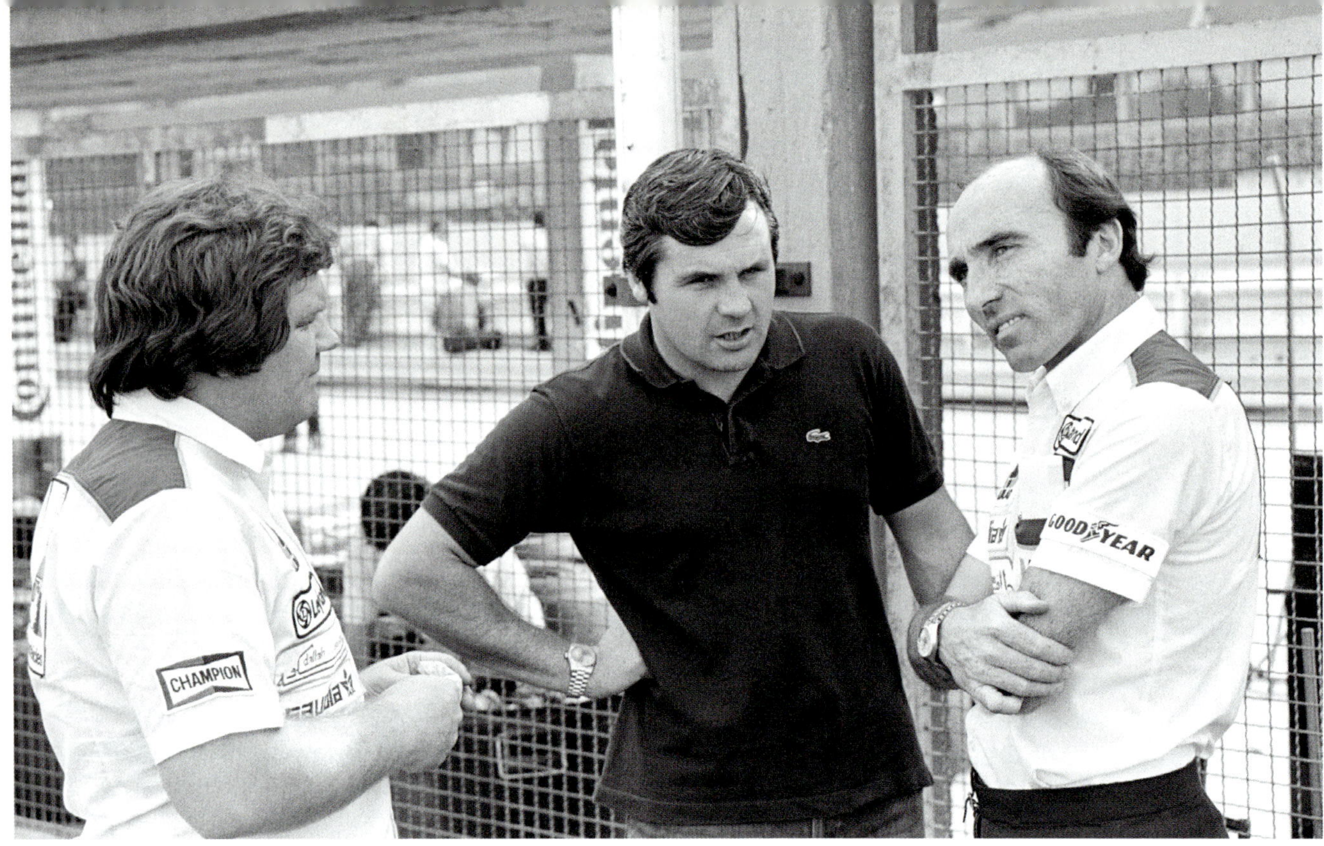

Hockenheim, German GP, 1980. Patrick Head and Frank Williams, co-founders of the Williams Grand Prix Engineering, with Alan Jones. The team and the Australian driver will win both World Championships at the end of the season. Photo: David Phipps

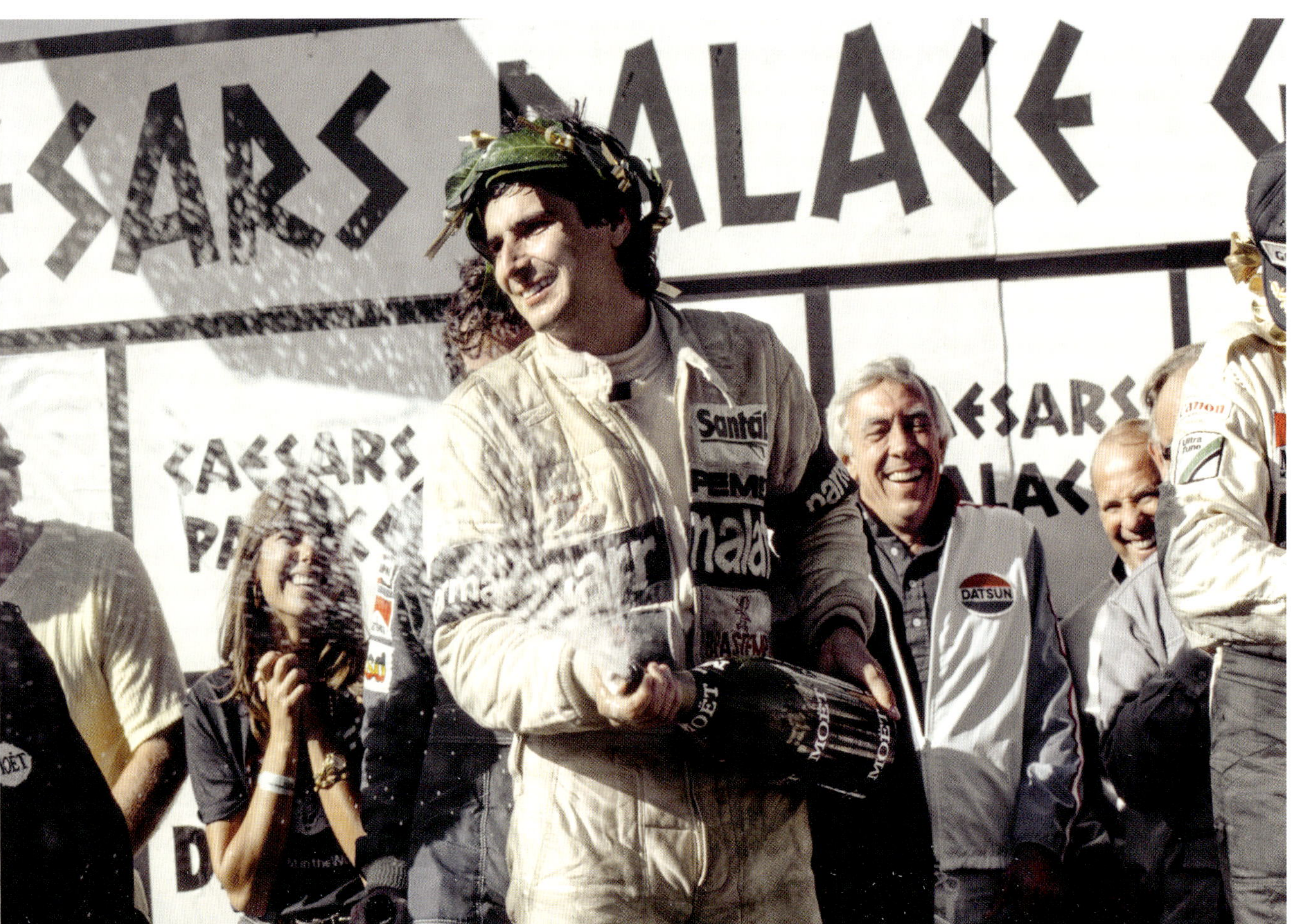

Las Vegas, Caesars Palace GP, 1981. Nelson Piquet celebrates on the podium after becoming world champion for the first time. Photo: David Phipps

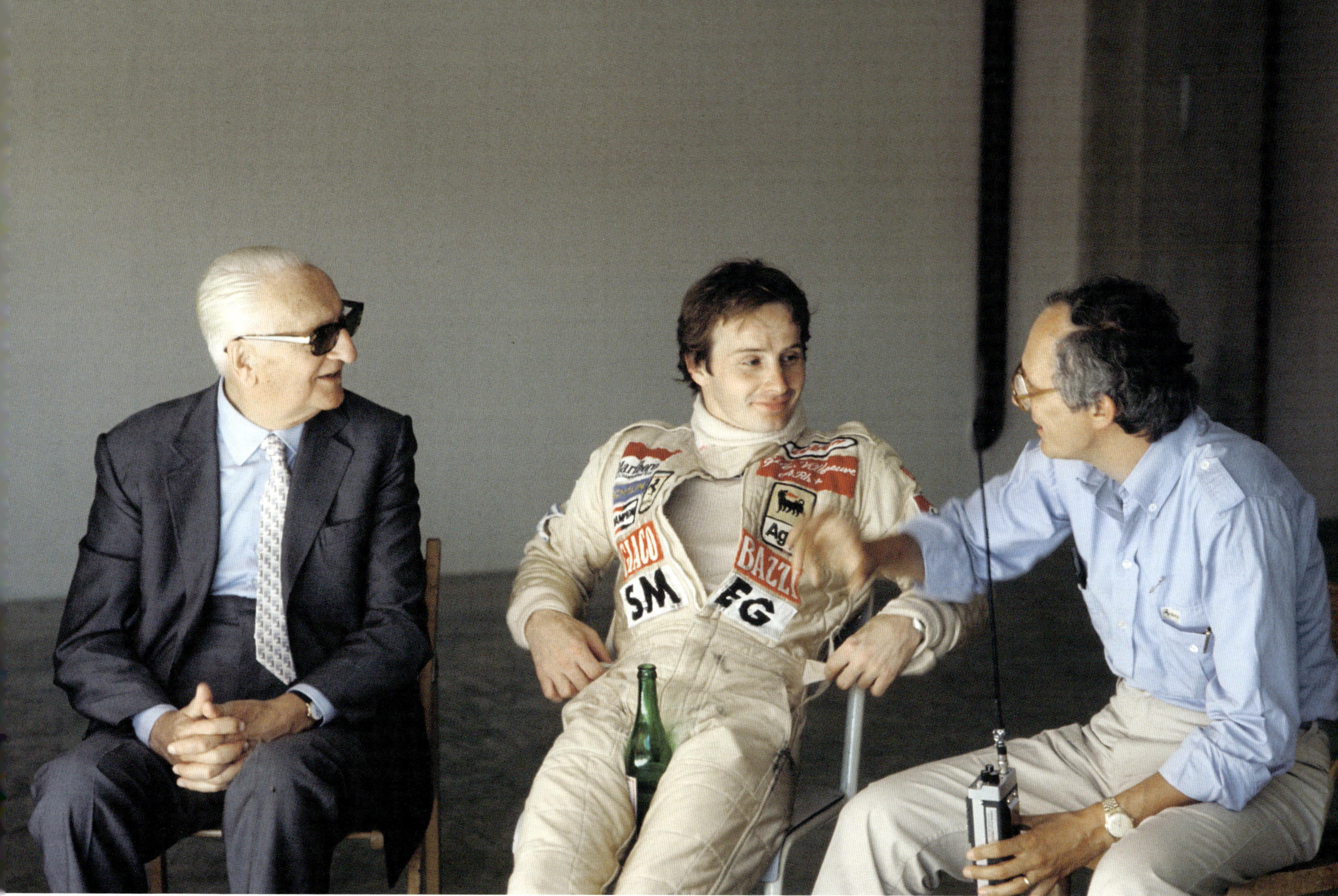

Imola Test, 1980. Enzo Ferrari with Gilles Villeneuve and Roberto Nosetto, manager of the circuit. Photo: Ercole Colombo

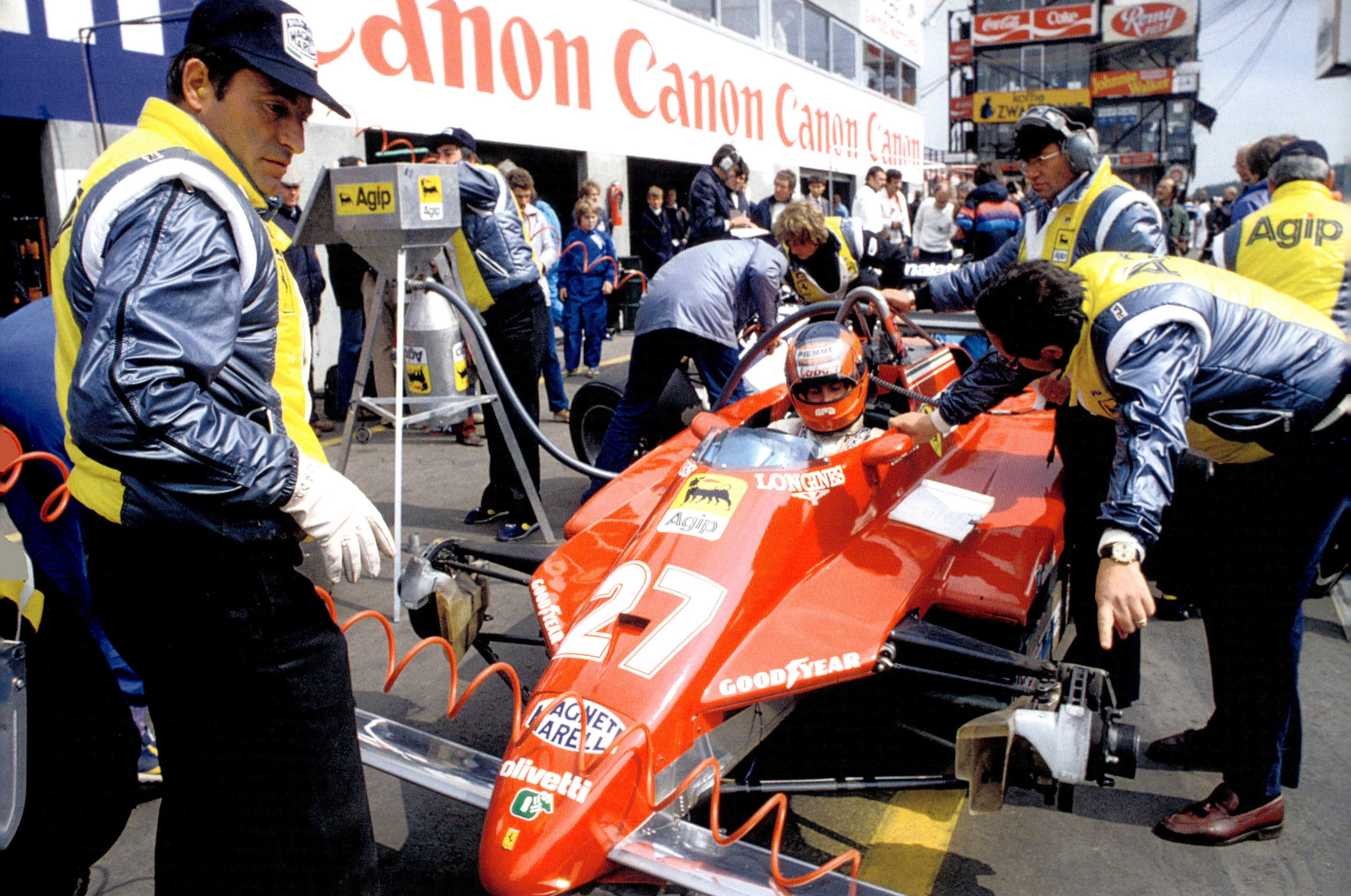

Zolder, Belgian GP, 1982. Gilles Villeneuve (Ferrari 126C2), in the pits, listens to Mauro Forghieri as mechanics work on his car during practice. Photo: Ercole Colombo

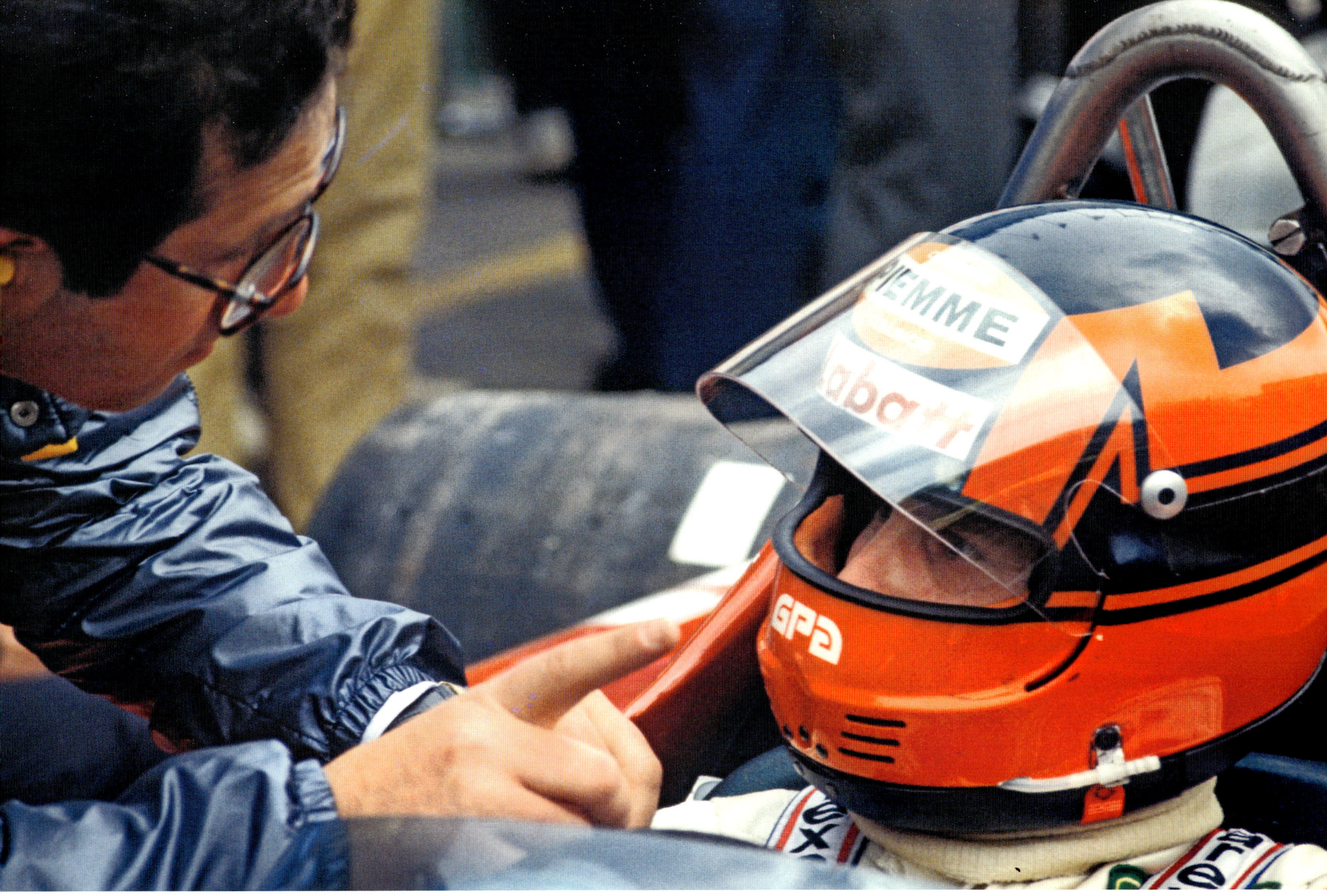

Spa-Francorchamps, Belgian GP, 1982. Gilles Villeneuve and Mauro Forghieri. The last conversation. Photo: Ercole Colombo

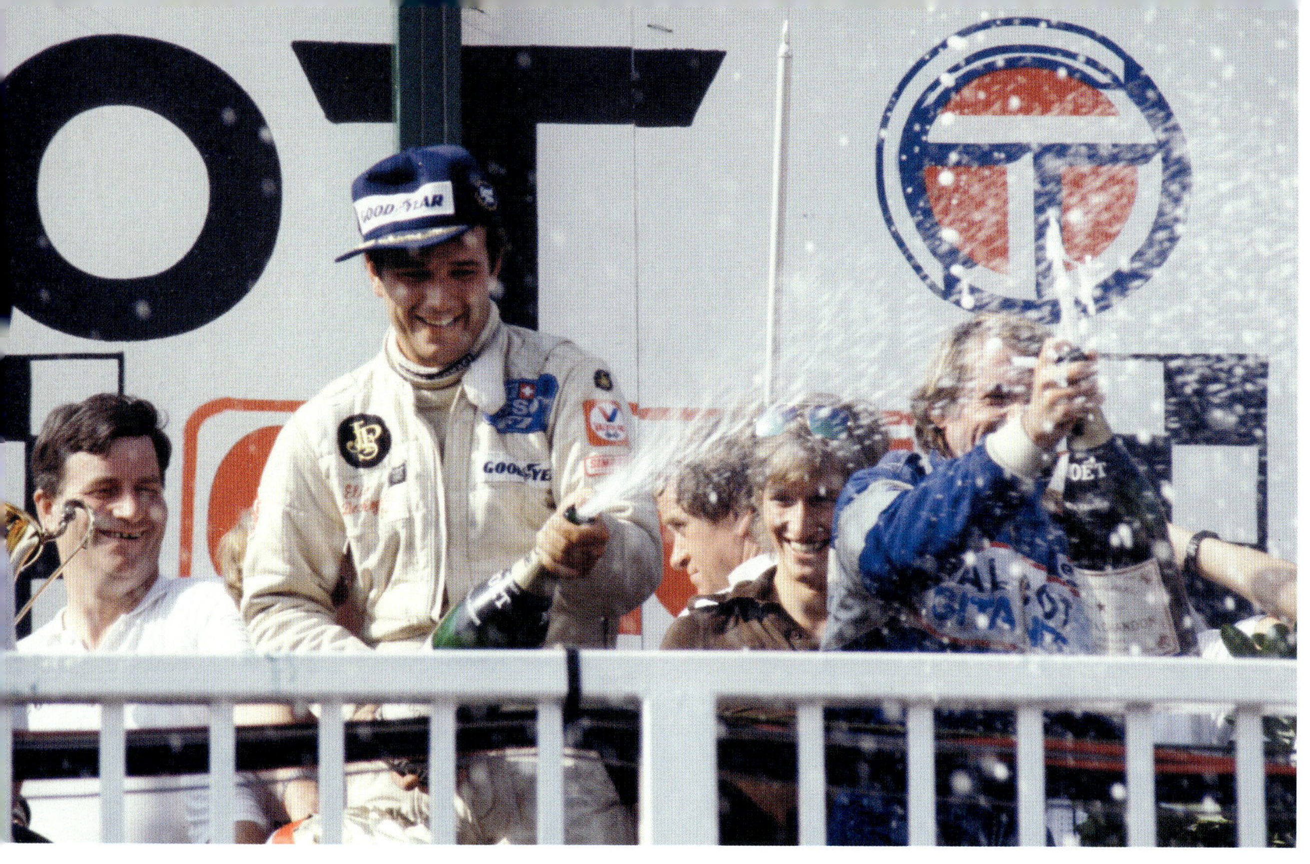

Zeltweg, Austrian GP, 1982.
De Angelis on the podium
with Jacques Laffite. Photo:
Ercole Colombo

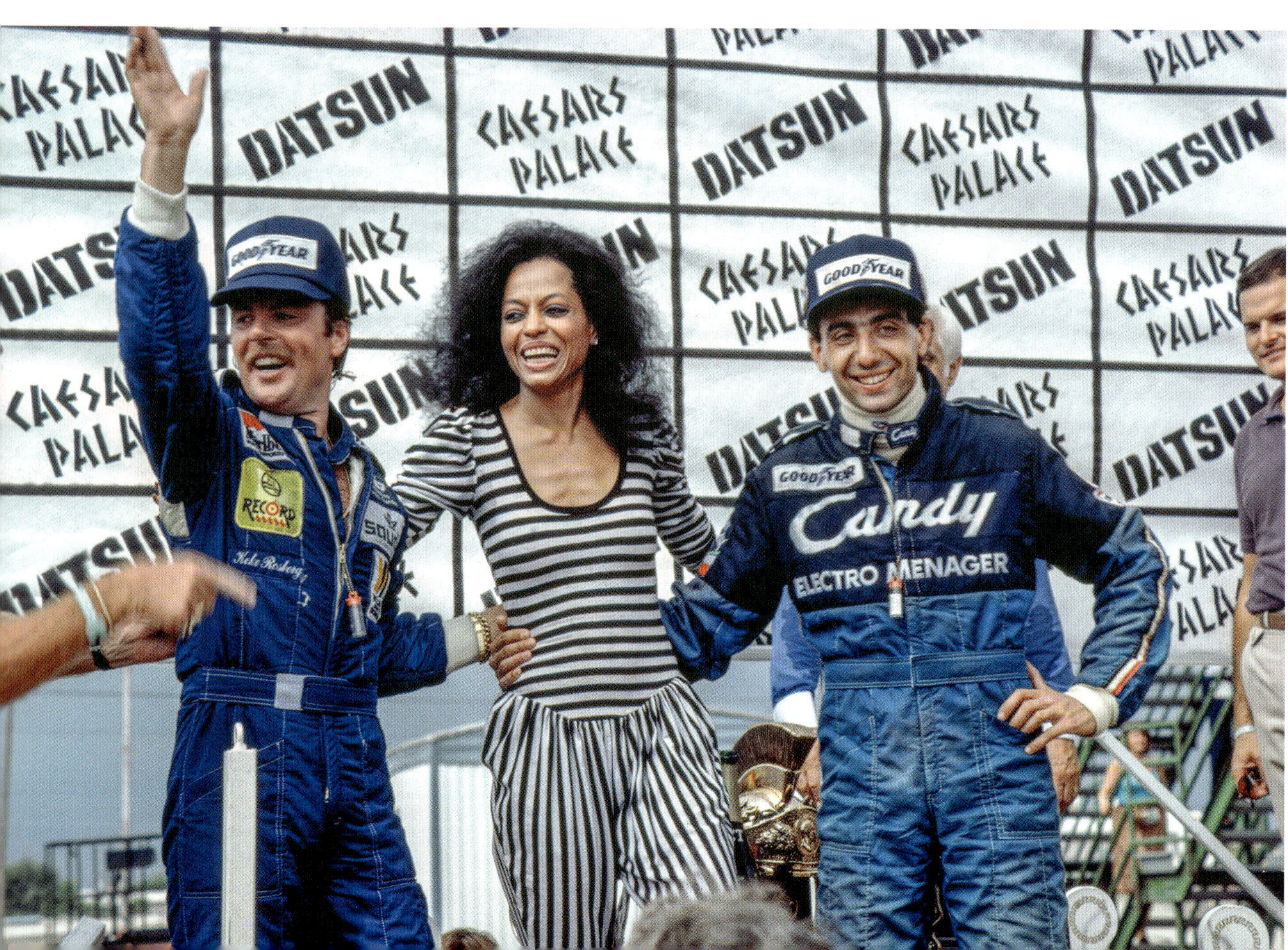

Las Vegas, Caesars palace GP,
1982. Newly-crowned world
champion Keke Rosberg, Diana
Ross, singer and actress, and
Michele Alboreto, winner of the
race, celebrate on the podium.
Photo: John Dunbar

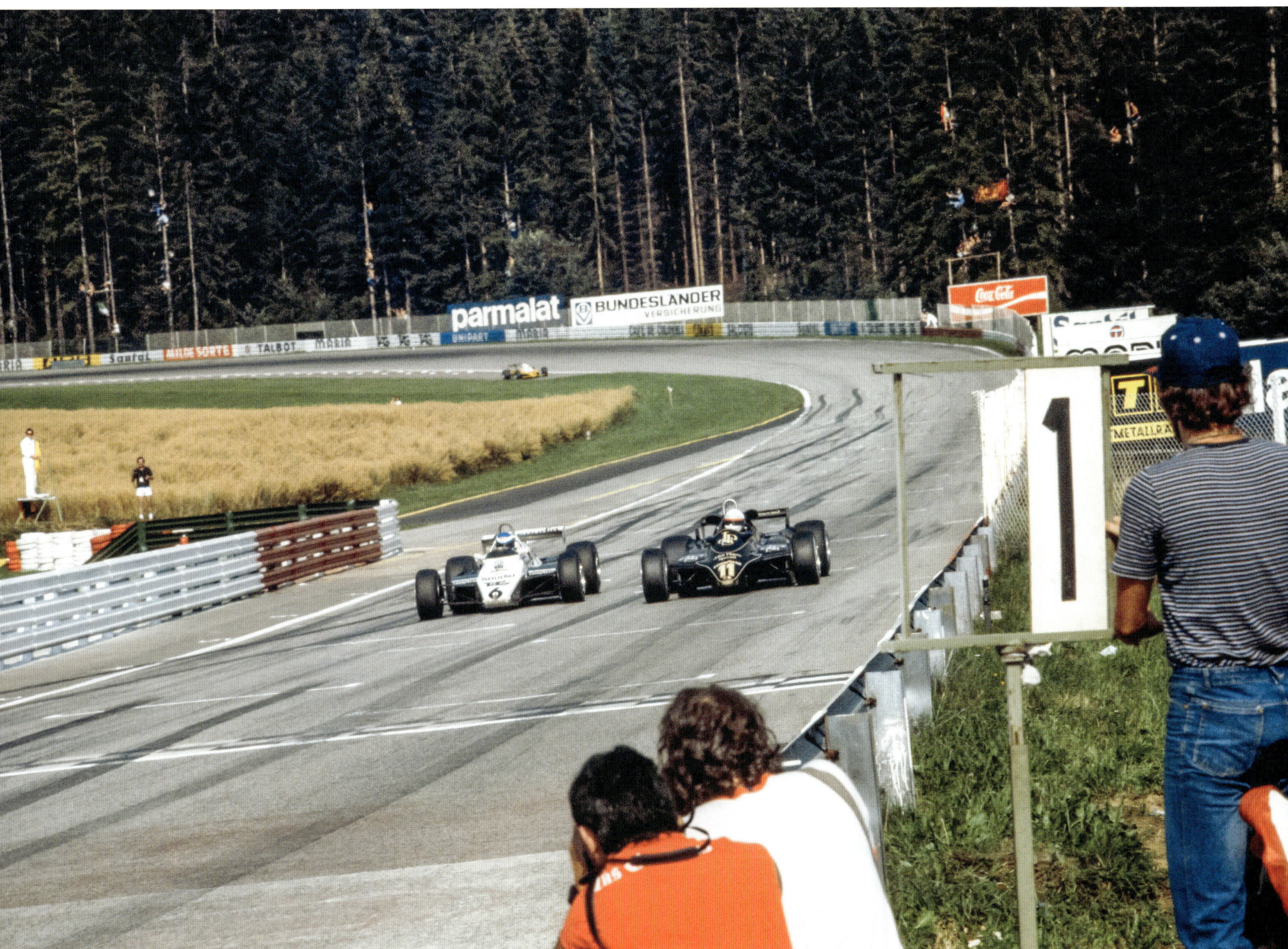

Zeltweg, Austrian GP, 1982. Elio De Angelis (Lotus 91 Ford) narrowly ahead of Keke Rosberg (Williams FW08 Ford) as they approach the finish line in one of Formula 1's closest-ever finishes. Photo: John Dunbar

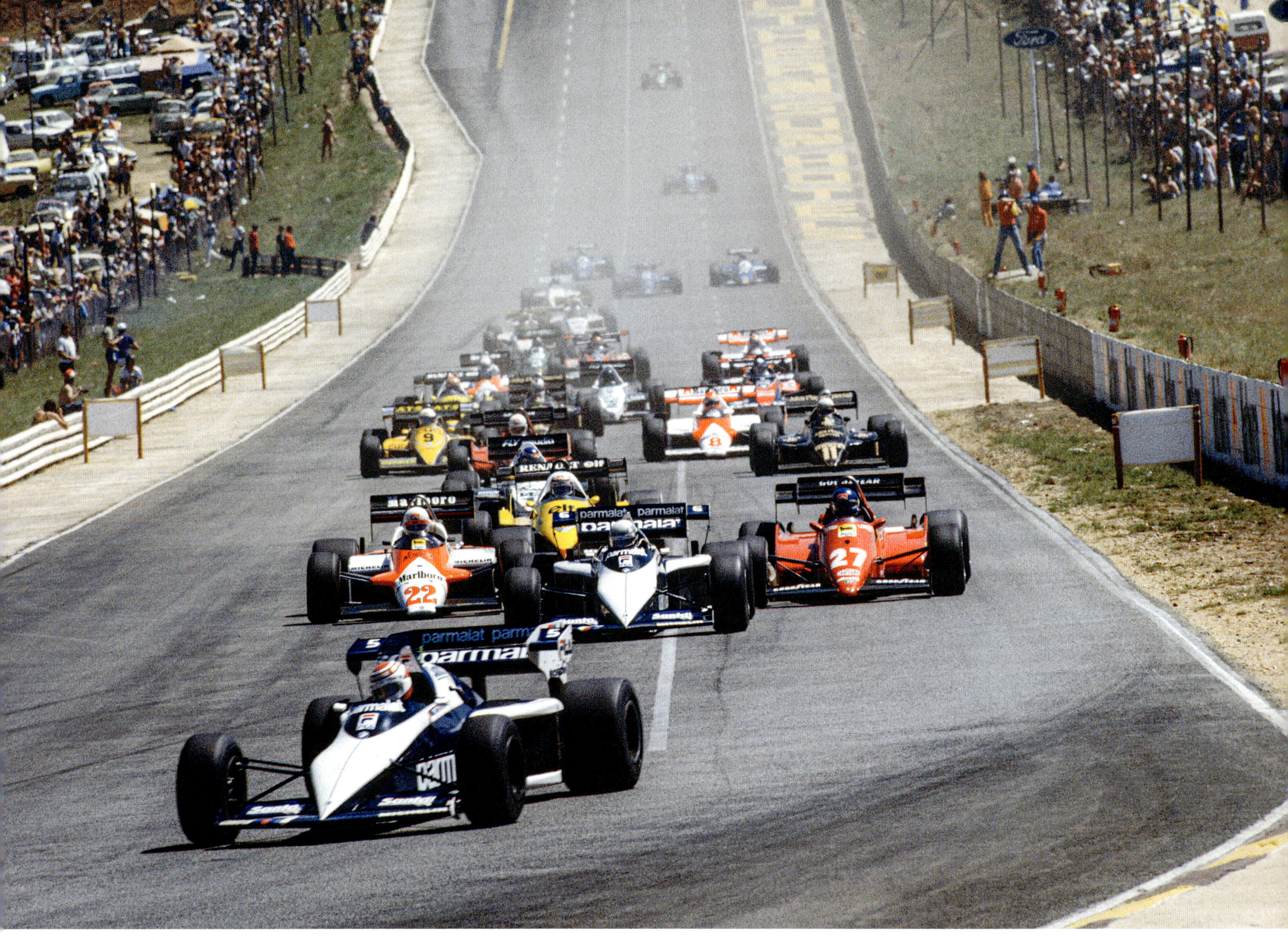

Kyalami, South African GP, 1983. Nelson Piquet (Brabham BT52B BMW) leads teammate Riccardo Patrese, Patrick Tambay (Ferrari 126C3), and Andrea De Cesaris (Alfa Romeo 183T). Photo: Steven Tee

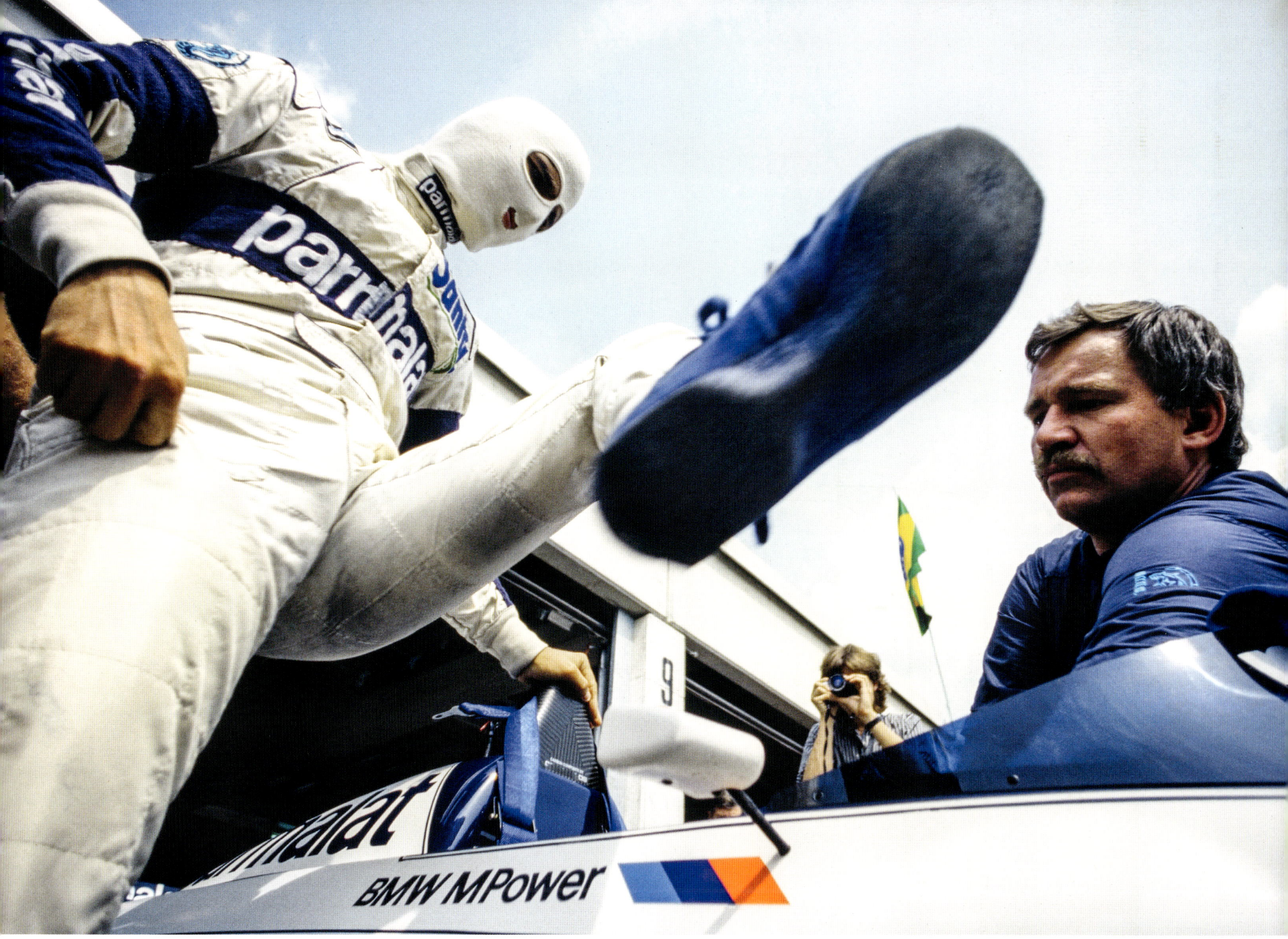

Zeltweg, Austrian GP, 1982. Nelson Piquet gets into his Brabham BT52B BMW. Photo: Ercole Colombo

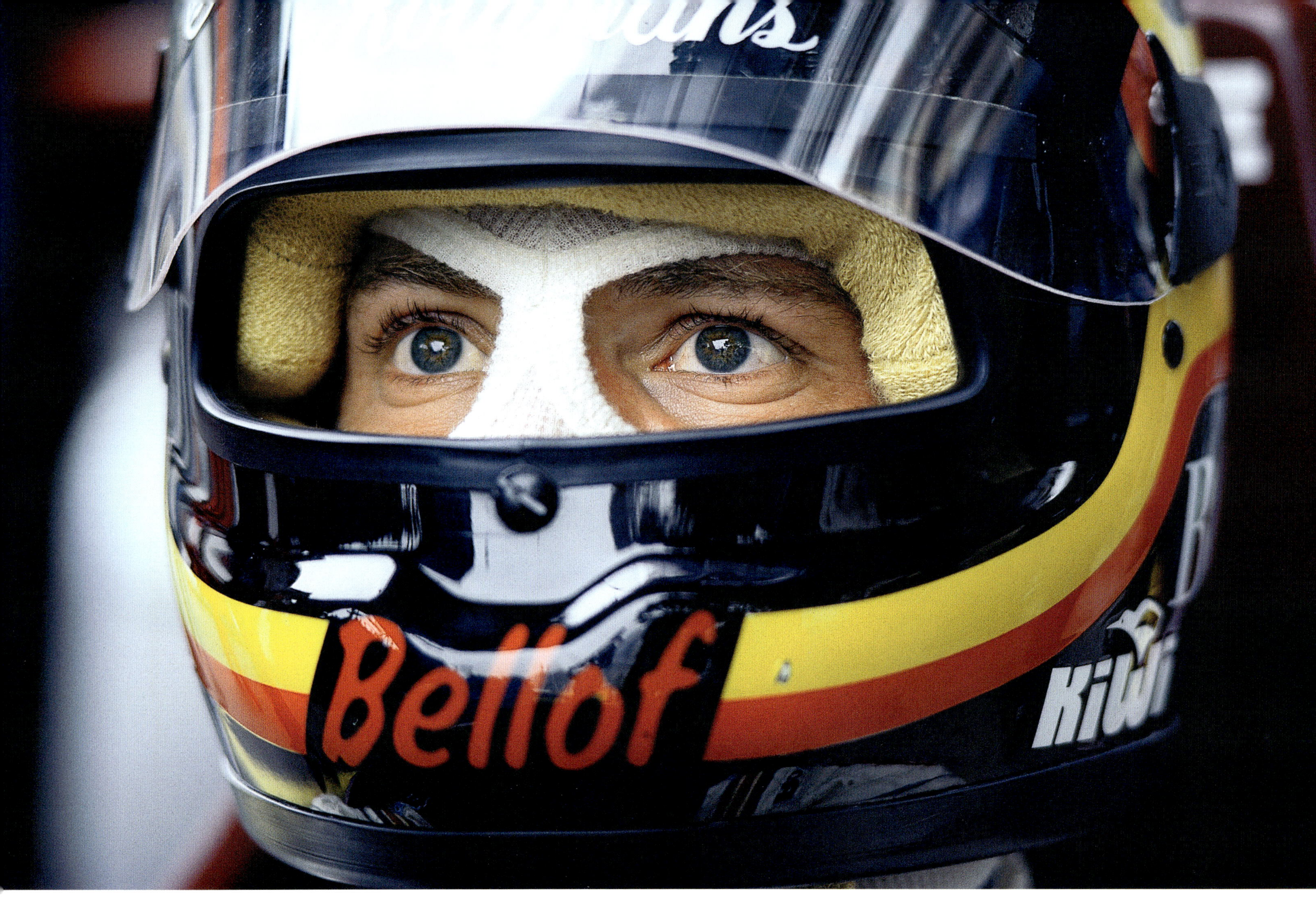

Monaco GP, 1984. Stefan Bellof. Photo: Rainer Schlegelmilch

Detroit, United States GP East,
1984. Niki Lauda sits looking
out across the river before the
race. Photo: Ercole Colombo

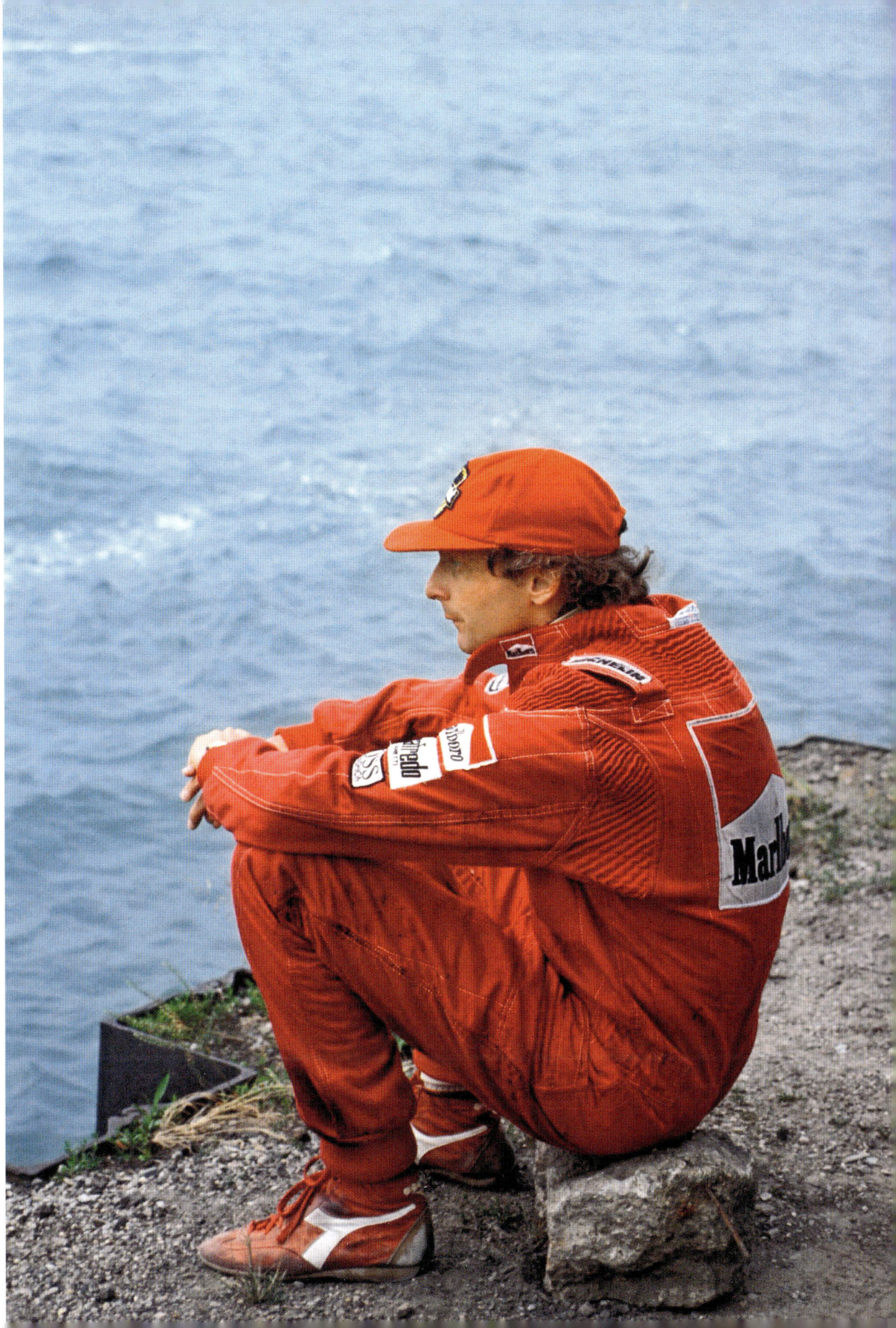

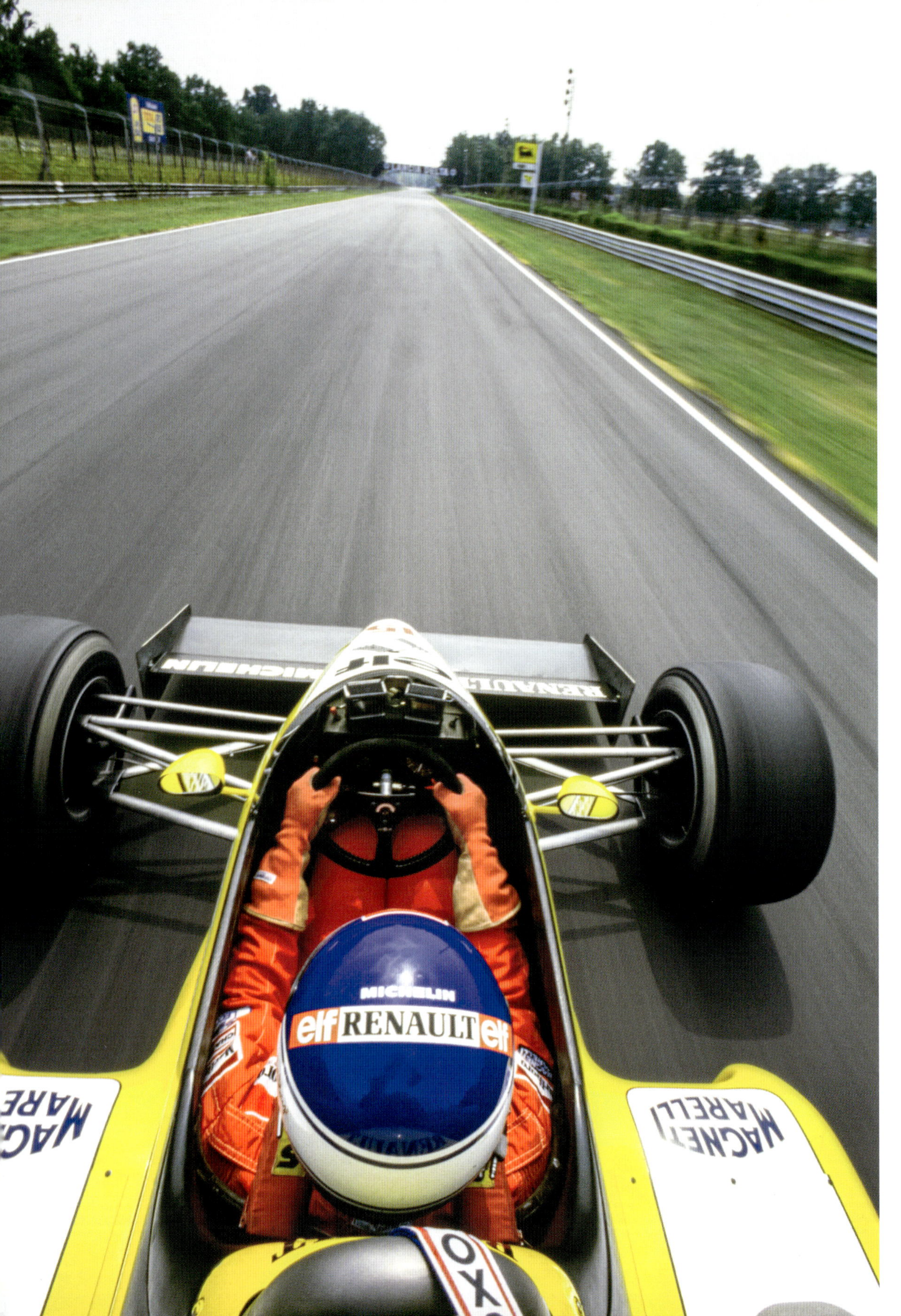

Monza Test, 1984.
Photographer Ercole Colombo
onboard with Patrick Tambay
(Renault RE50). Photo: Ercole
Colombo

Estoril, Portuguese GP, 1984.
Niki Lauda, newly-crowned
world champion, stands atop of
the podium with three fingers
showing for each title, alongside
Alain Prost and Ayrton Senna.
Photo: Ercole Colombo

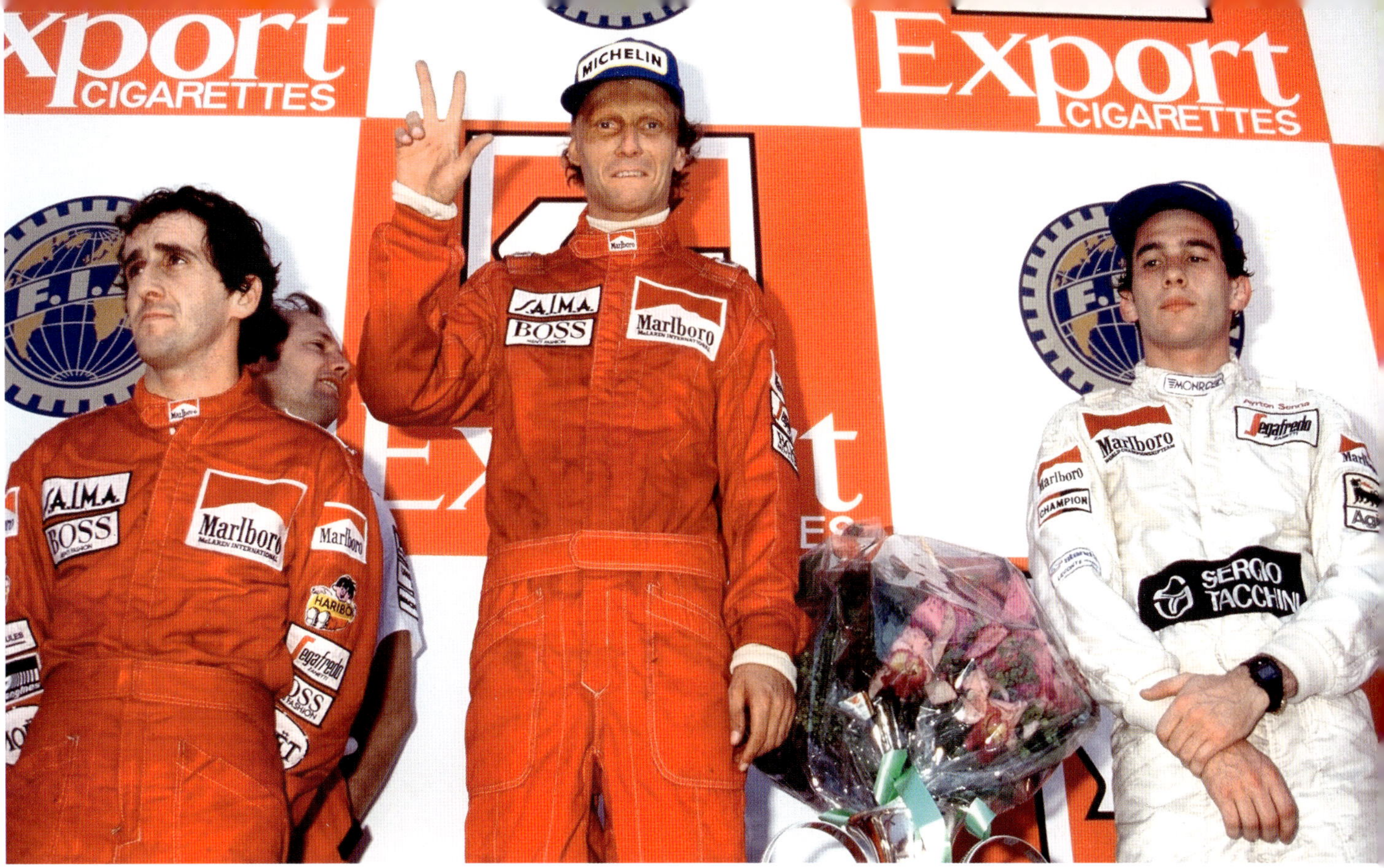

Estoril, Portuguese GP, 1985.
Ayrton Senna stands on
some rocks while watching
teammate Elio De Angelis
(Lotus 97T Renault) drive by.
Photo: Steven Tee

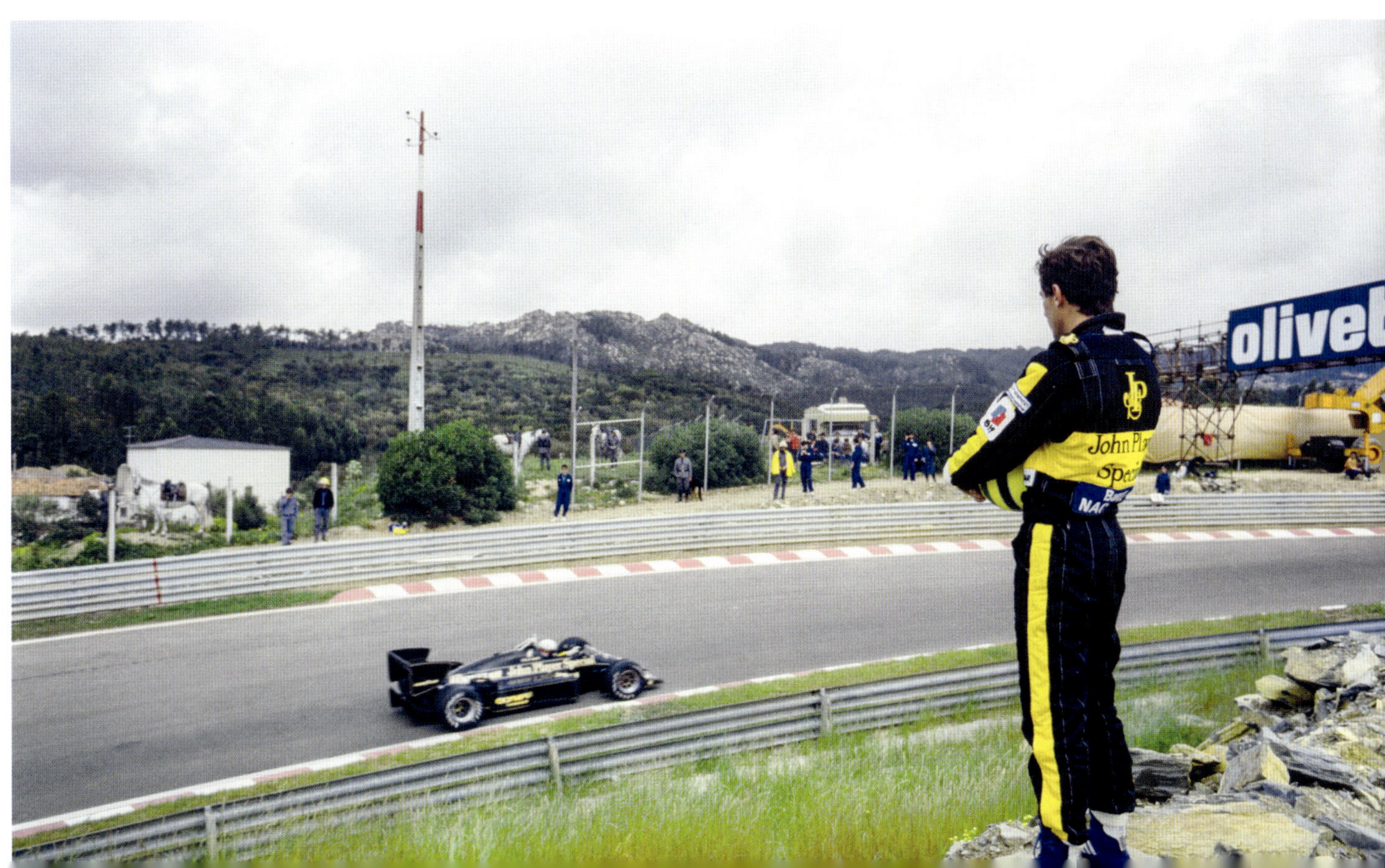

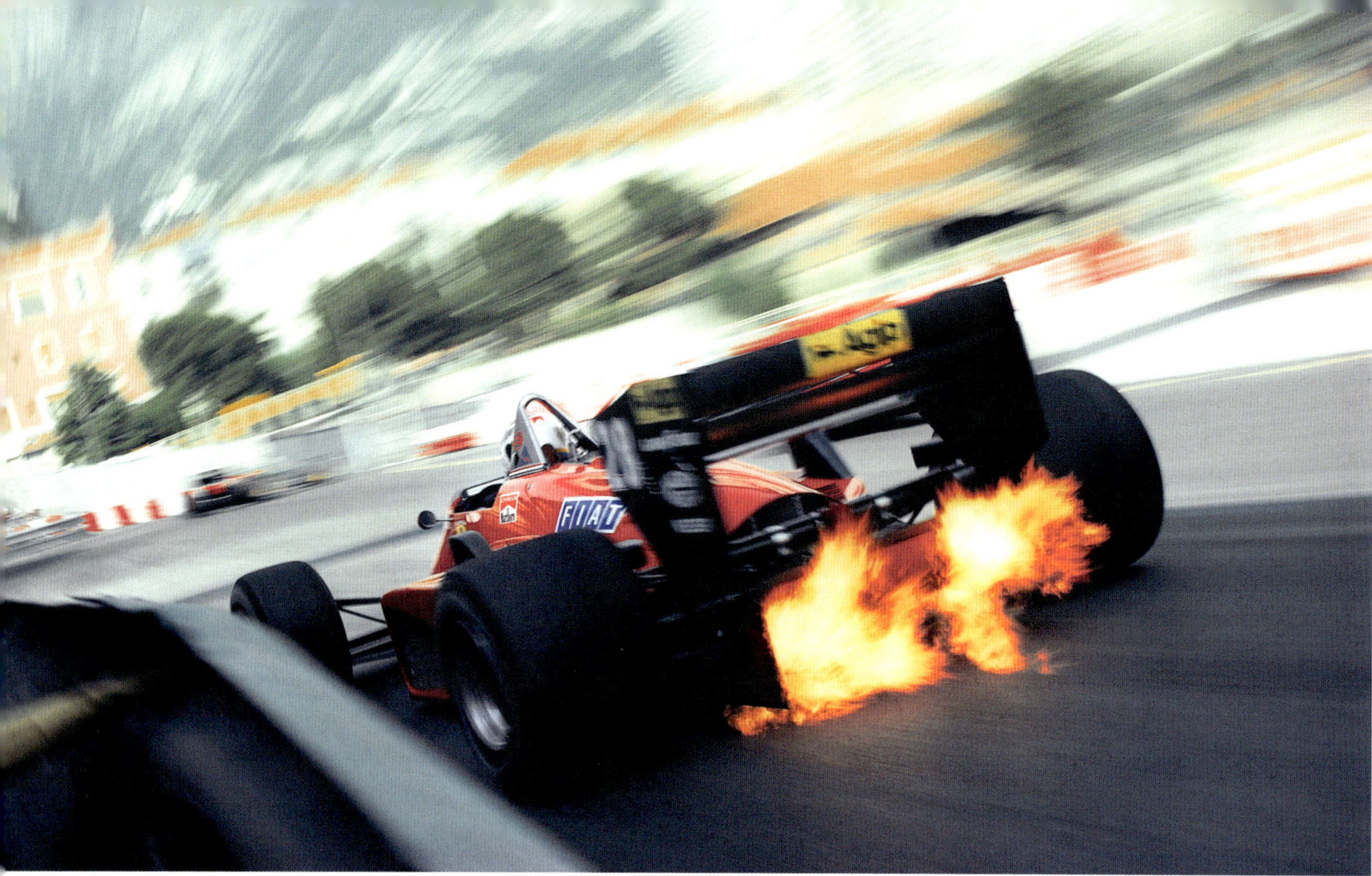

Monaco GP, 1985. Exhaust flames shoot up through the diffuser of Stefan Johansson's Ferrari 156/85 as he exits Rascasse corner. Photo: Rainer Schlegelmilch

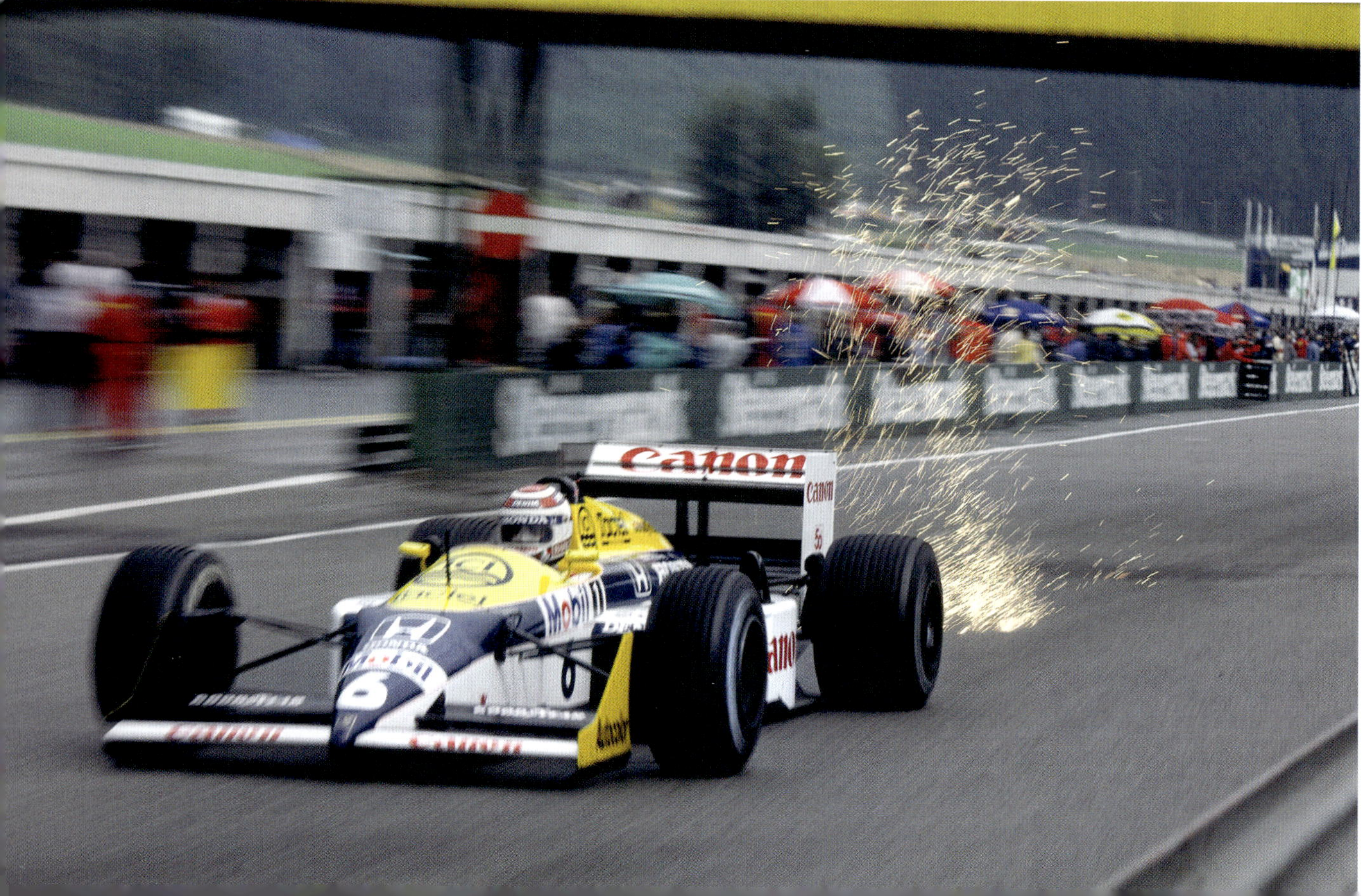

Zeltweg, Austrian GP, 1987. Nelson Piquet (Williams FW11B Honda) blasts down the home straight with sparks flying. Photo: Rainer Schlegelmilch

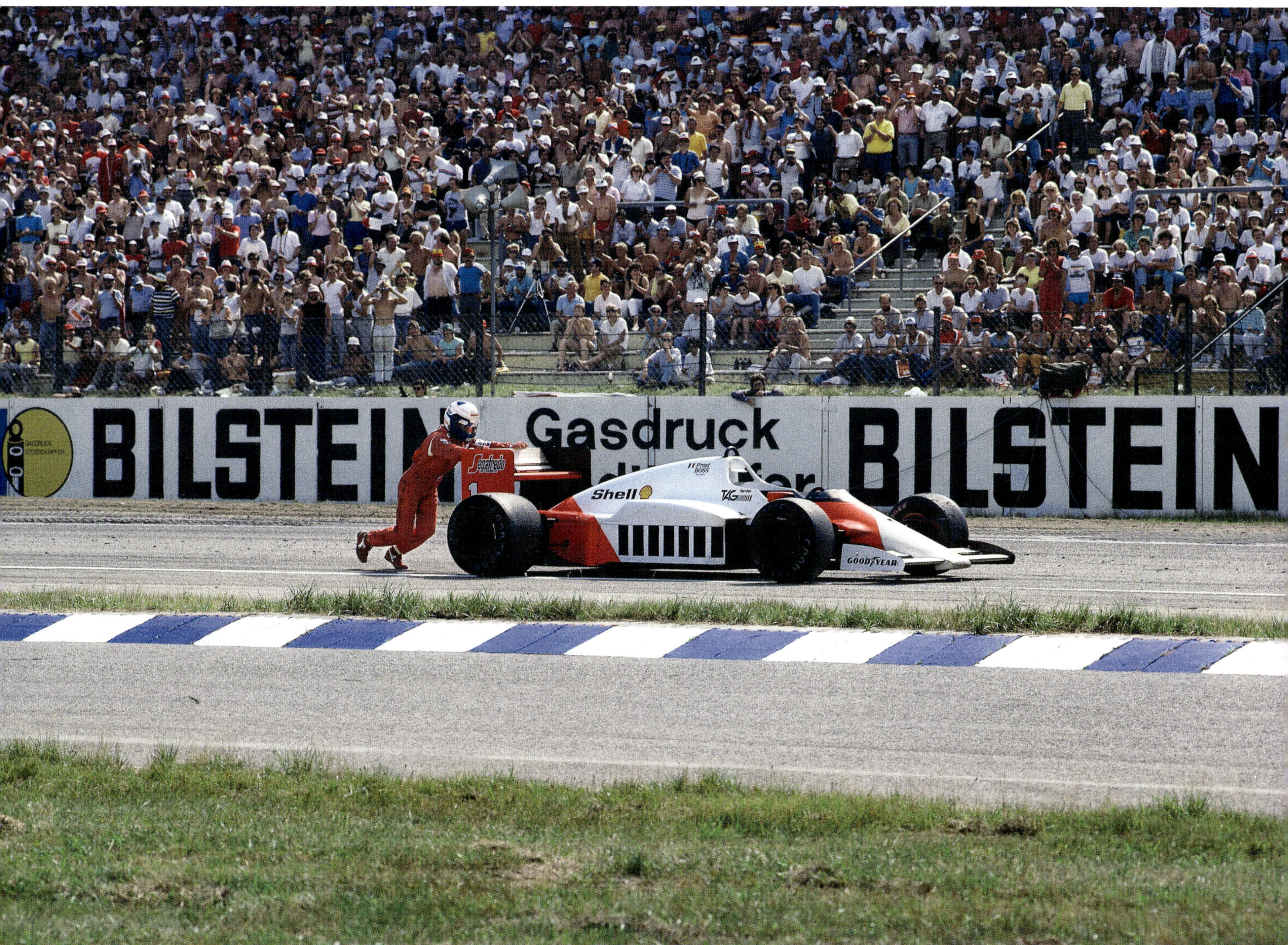

Hockenheim, German GP, 1986. Alain Prost pushes his McLaren MP4-2C TAG after running out of fuel on the last lap. Photo: Rainer Schlegelmilch

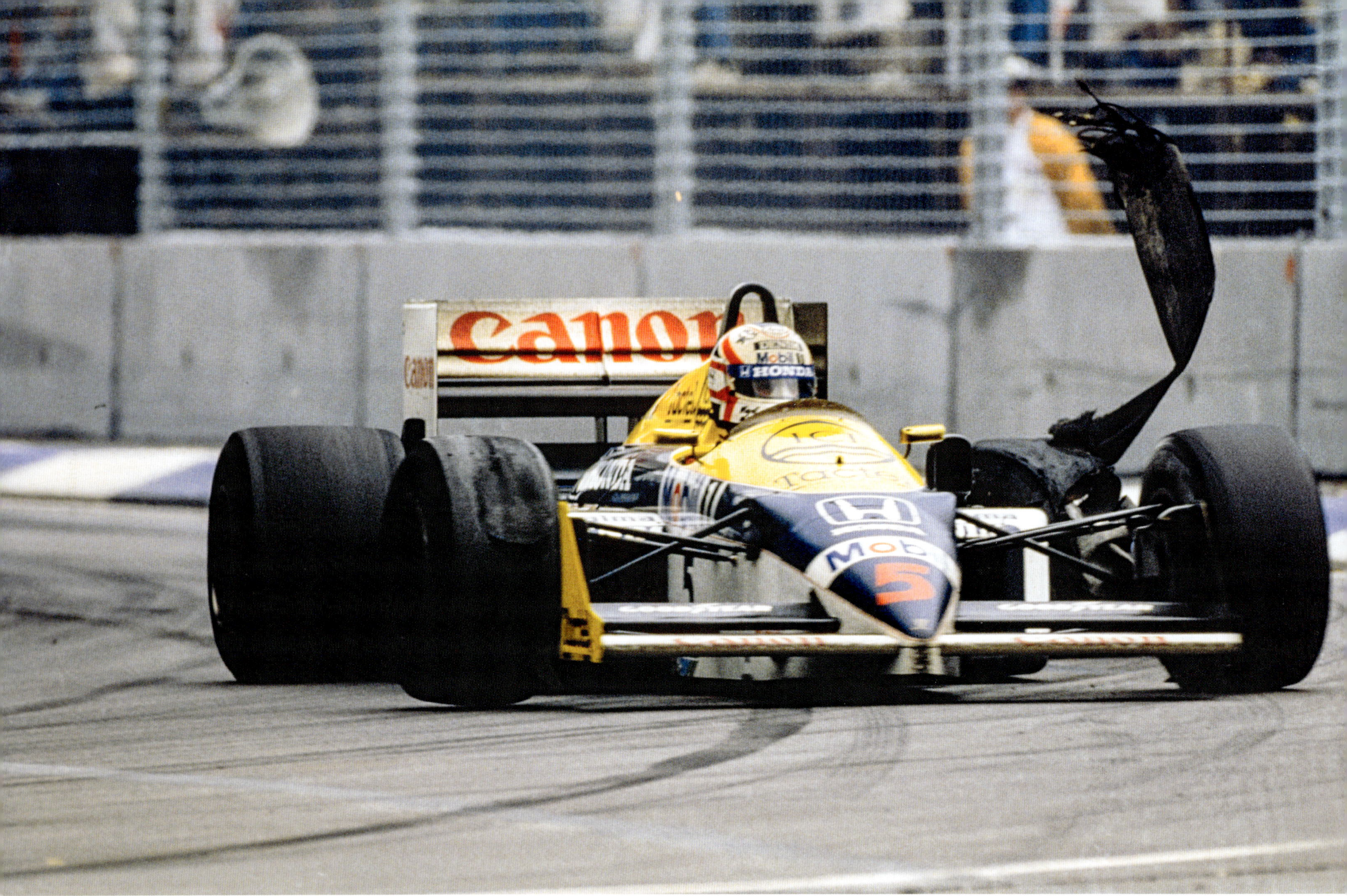

Adelaide, Australian GP, 1986. A burst tyre lets down Nigel Mansell (Williams FW11). Photo: Keith Sutton

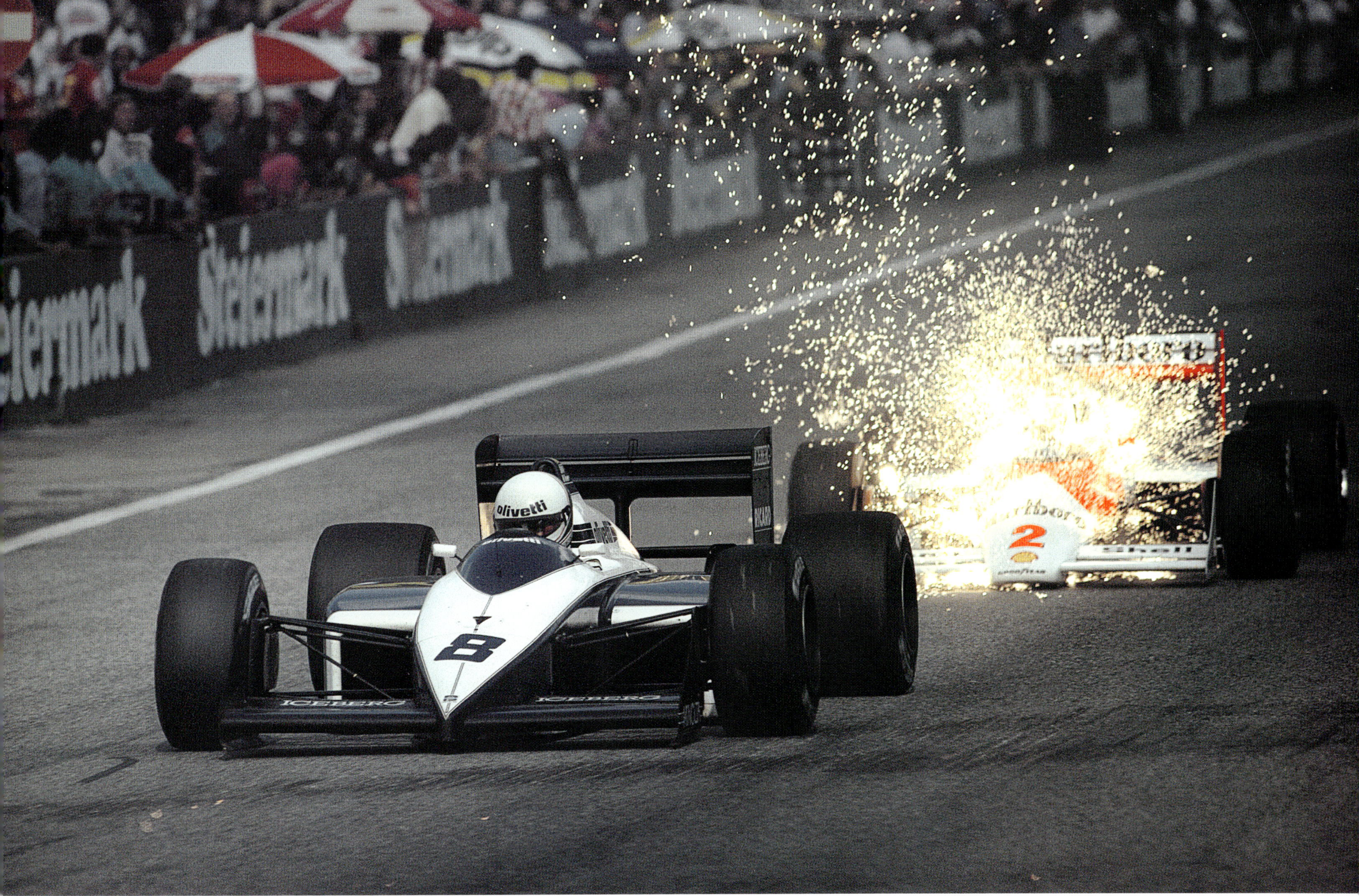

Zeltweg, Austrian GP, 1987. Stefan Johansson (McLaren MP4-3 TAG) is hit by a shower of sparks produced by the titanium skid blocks on Andrea De Cesaris's Brabham BT56 BMW. Photo: Rainer Schlegelmilch

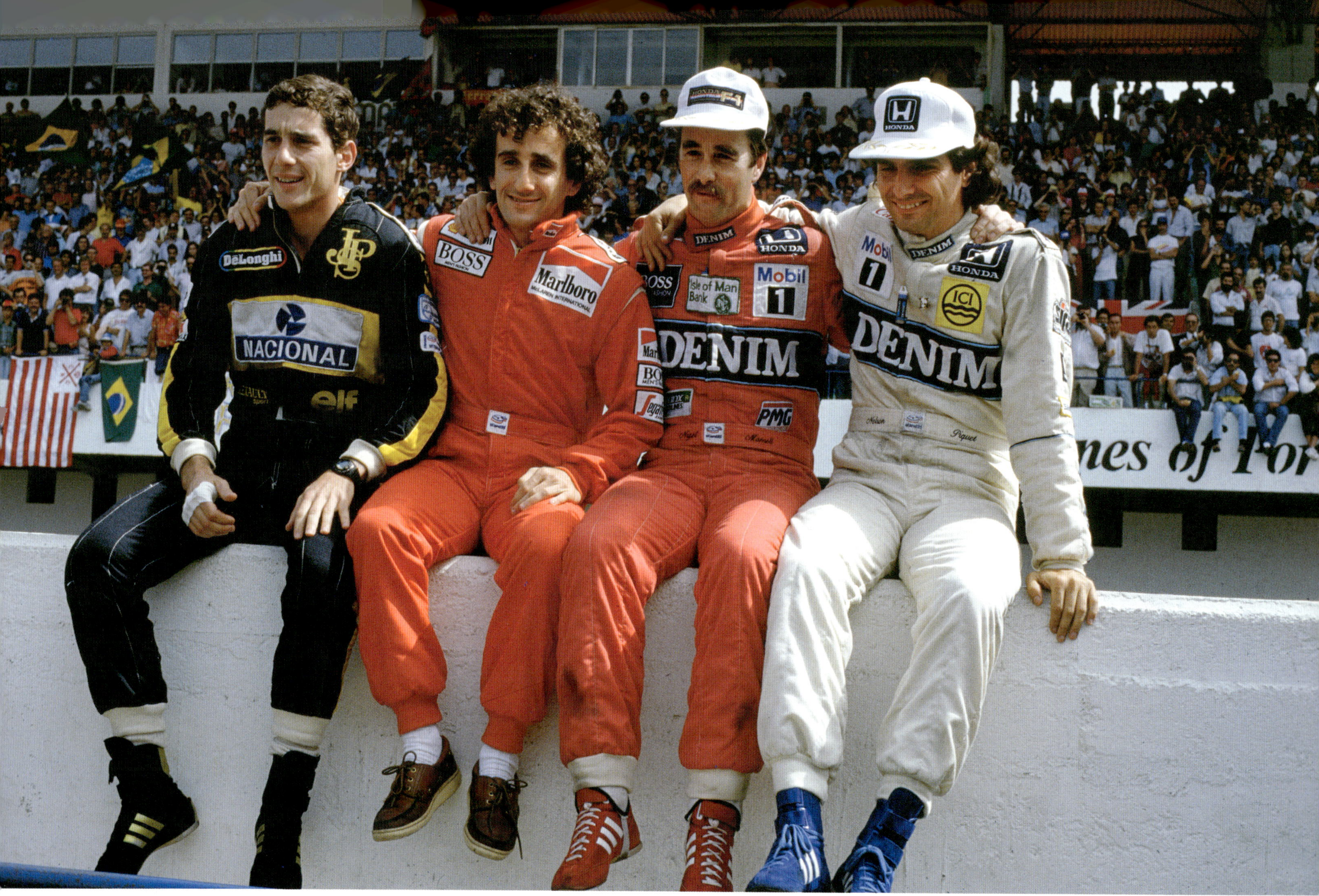

Estoril, Portuguese GP, 1986. Championship contenders Ayrton Senna, Alain Prost, Nigel Mansell, and Nelson Piquet sit on the pit wall. Photo: Steven Tee

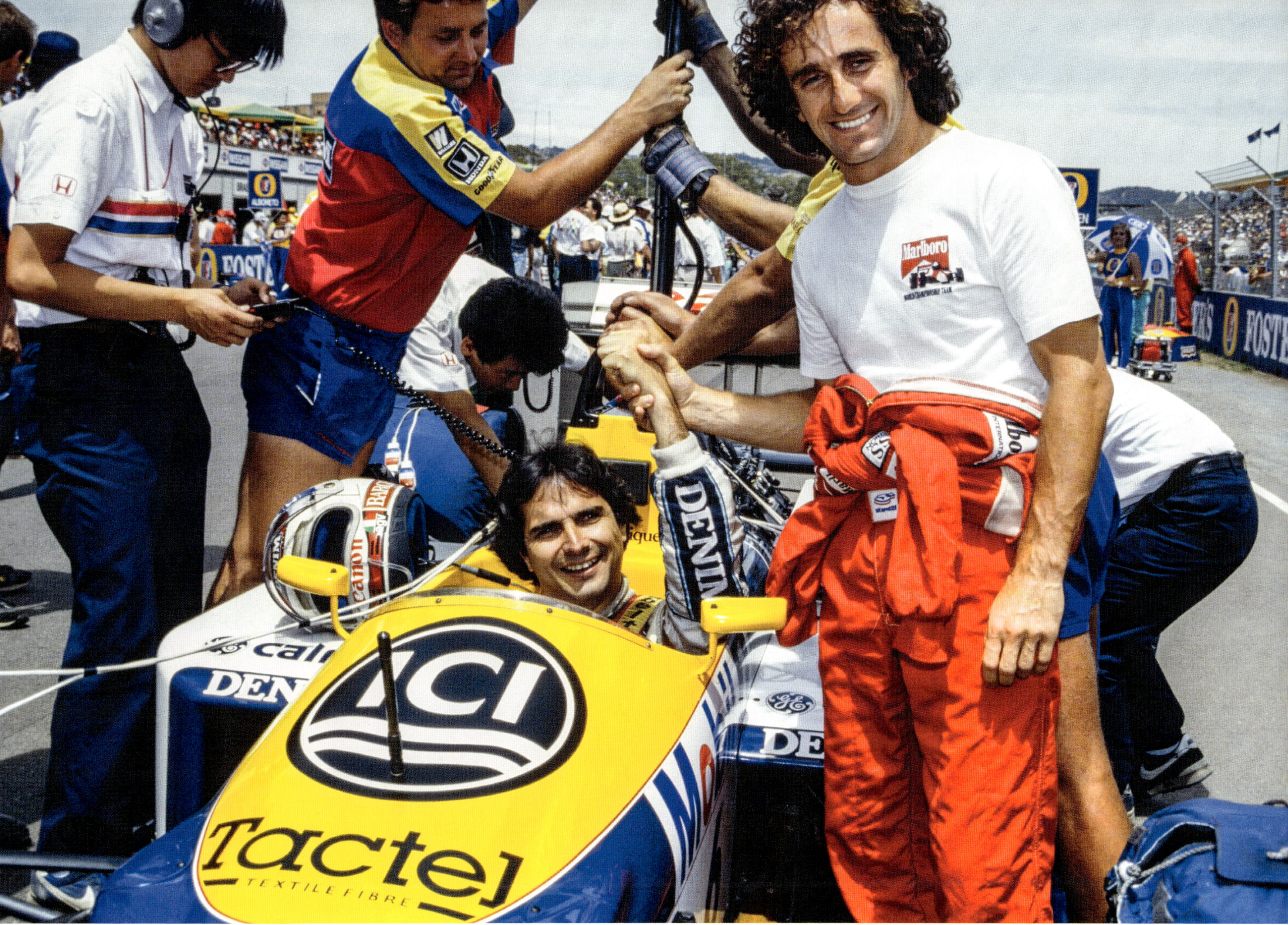

Adelaide, Australian GP, 1987. Alain Prost celebrates the world champion, Nelson Piquet. Photo: Ercole Colombo

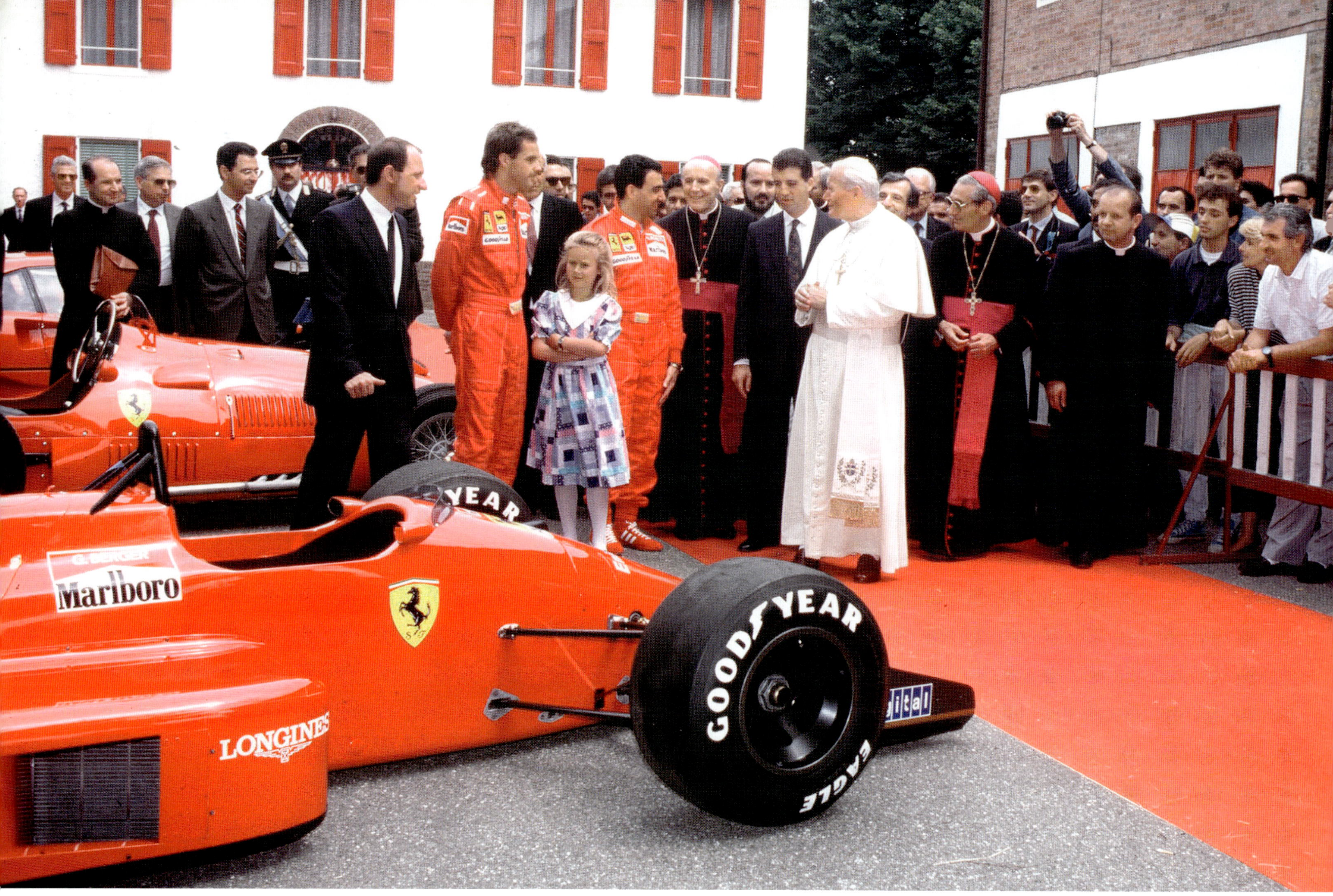

Fiorano, 1988. Pope John Paul II visits the Scuderia Ferrari and talks with Piero Ferrari, Michele Alboreto, Gerhard Berger, and Marco Piccinini. Photo: Ercole Colombo

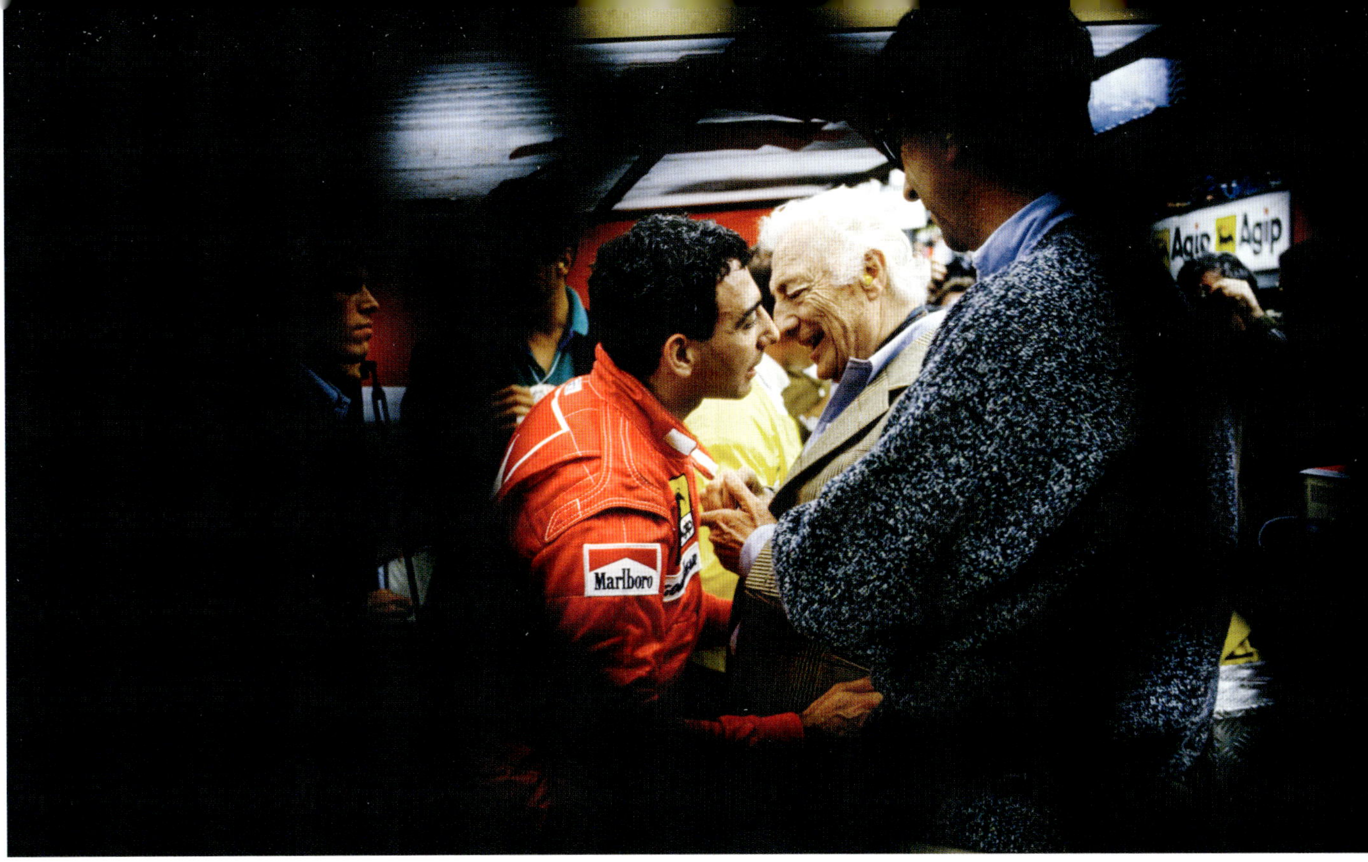

Monaco GP, 1988. Michele Alboreto (Ferrari) speaks to FIAT President Gianni Agnelli. Photo: Ercole Colombo

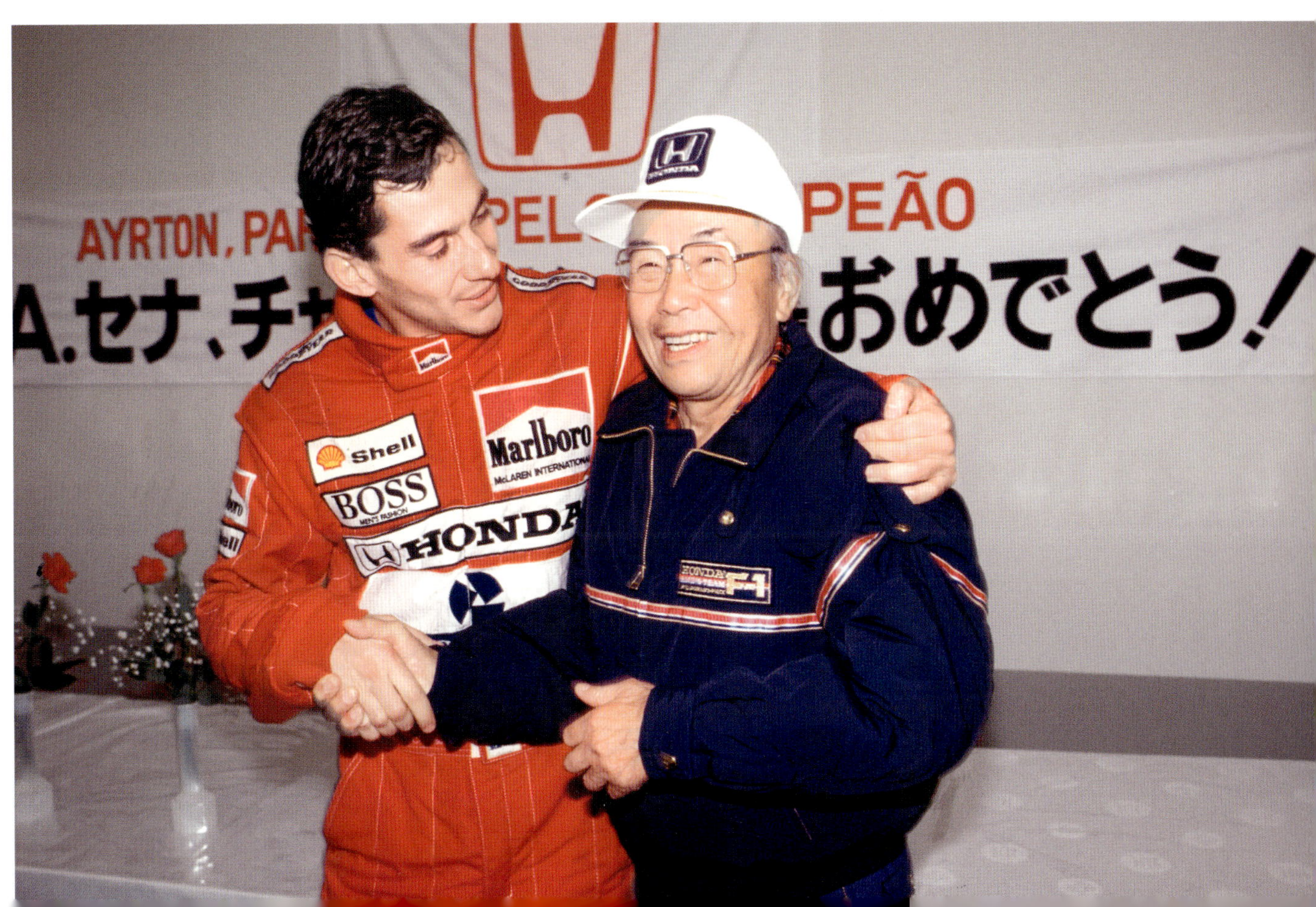

Suzuka, Japanese GP, 1988. Ayrton Senna shakes hands with Soichiro Honda, founder of Honda, after securing his first World Drivers' Championship. Photo: Ercole Colombo

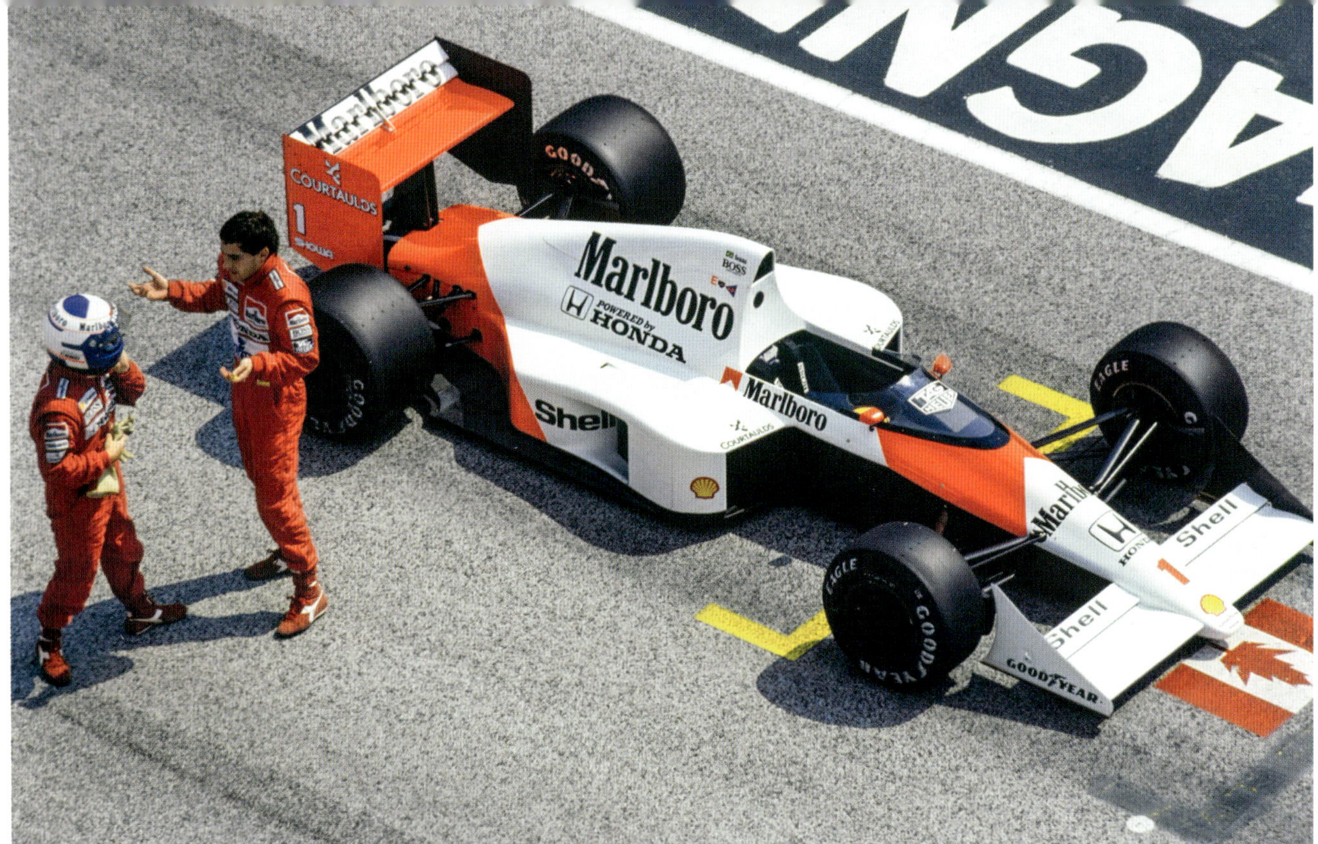

Imola, San Marino GP, 1989.
Alain Prost and Ayrton Senna
in discussion on the grid next
to Senna's McLaren MP4/5
Honda. Photo: Ercole Colombo

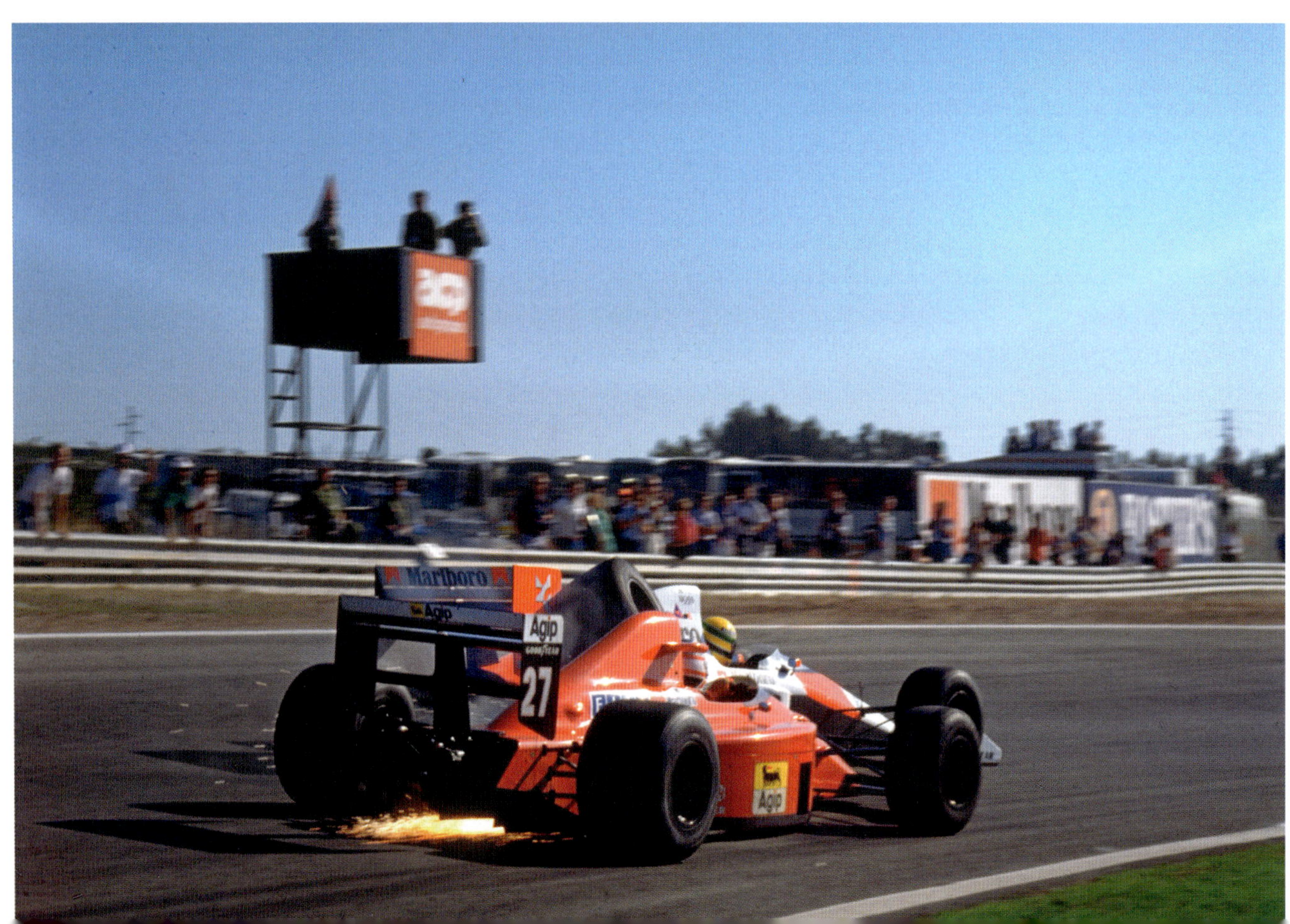

Estoril, Portuguese GP, 1989.
Collision between Ayrton
Senna (McLaren) and Nigel
Mansell (Ferrari). Photo: Ercole
Colombo

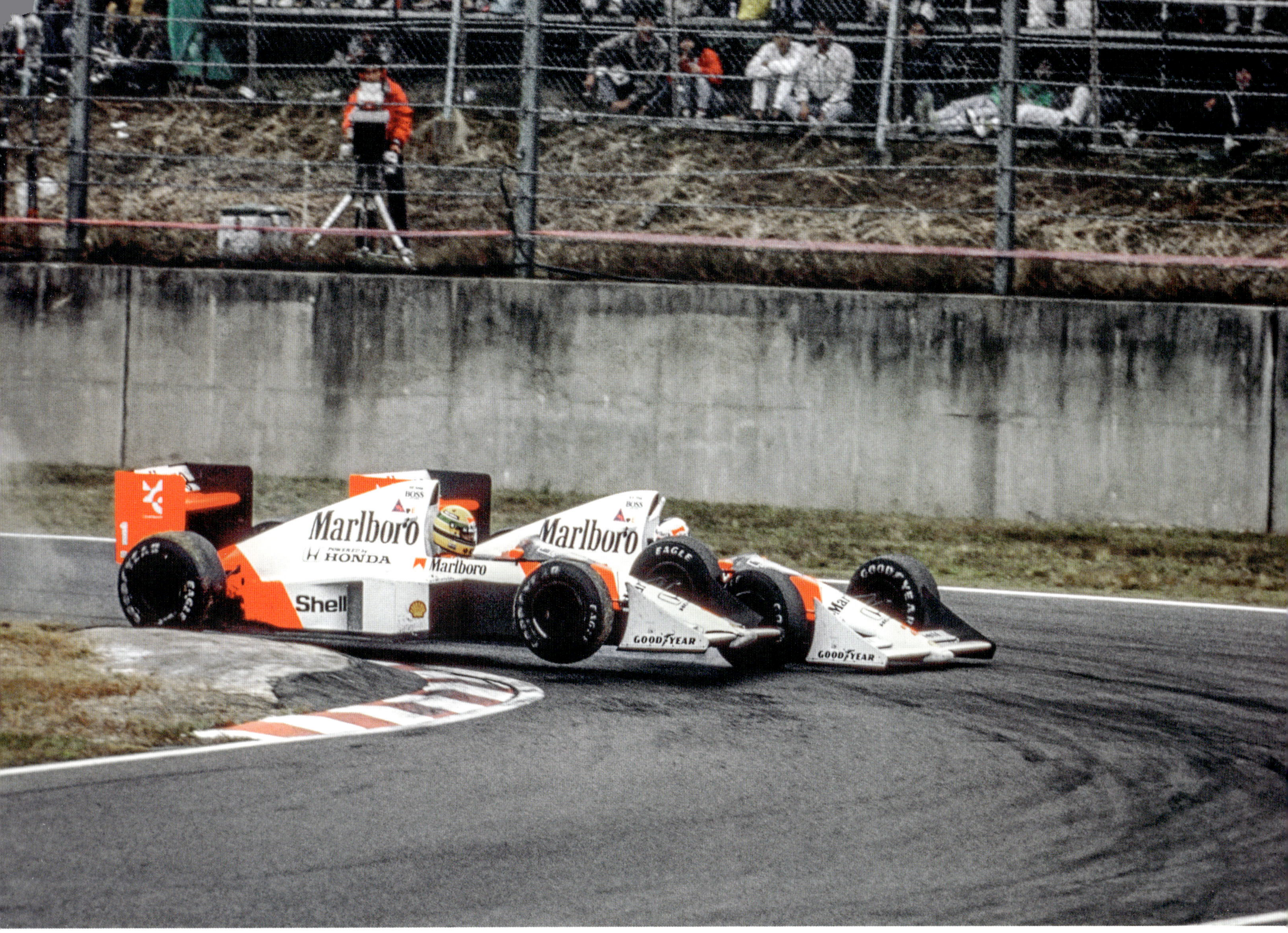

Suzuka, Japanese GP, 1989. Alain Prost (McLaren MP4-5 Honda) and Ayrton Senna (McLaren MP4-5 Honda) infamously clash at the chicane. Photo: Steven Tee

1990–1999
A Pain that Never Lessens

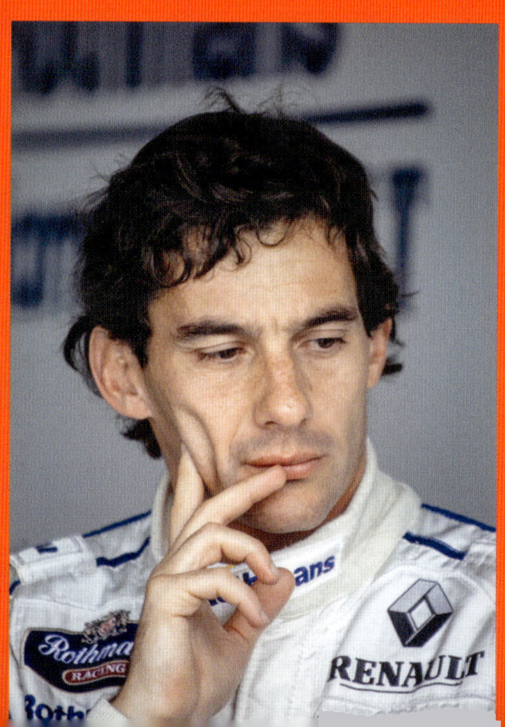

An extremely intense decade. Opened by Ayrton Senna's two consecutive victories, in 1990 and 1991, still with McLaren. Two new titles he could add to the World Championship conquered in 1988. His most debated title: the one attained in 1990, with his intentional collision at the opening round of the Japanese GP with Alain Prost, who in the meantime had transferred to Ferrari. A crazy maneuver, and extremely dangerous, which Ayrton always considered to be legitimate given the title he had lost the previous year in favor of his French rival. In 1991 it was an easier feat. With Berger, precious teammate and devoted friend, by his side. At the end of the season, Nigel Mansell, having returned to the Williams team after two years with Ferrari, came in second. Paving the way for the 1992 Championship, which he won with a long margin over Riccardo Patrese, his teammate at the British team powered by Renault. Mansell (1953), an Englishman from Upton-upon-Severn, was finally able to fulfill his dream, nearly at the end of a very brilliant and not always lucky career. He was much loved by enthusiasts of the sport for his grit, his brusque manners, and his competitive aggressiveness. He retired at the beginning of 1995 with a noteworthy scoresheet: 31 victories and 32 pole positions obtained in 187 World Championship races.
Alain Prost, fresh from a terrible experience with the Ferrari team that ended in a sensational and

specious layoff at the end of the 1991 Championship, was aware of the superiority of the Williams team's vehicle, designed by Adrian Newey and equipped with leading electronics. Prost dominated the season of 1993 with seven victories and won his fourth world title. All of this despite Senna's efforts driving a McLaren that was less competitive but didn't prevent him from achieving some memorable performances, such as his feat on the flooded tarmac in Donington, where he overtook four cars in the first lap and went on to win the European GP. Prost decided to retire at the end of the season: 199 World Championship races, 51 victories, 33 pole positions. A result that ranks him as one of the greatest drivers ever. Senna joined the Williams team in 1994. Meanwhile, the technical rules had changed (active suspension was no longer allowed), the vehicle itself had lost its sheen, and a new young protagonist had acquired international fame: Michael Schumacher, who debuted with Jordan in the Belgian GP in 1991 and was then immediately hired by the Benetton team, led by Flavio Briatore, where he obtained his first two victories (Belgium 1992 and Portugal 1993). Schumacher was leading the World Championship with a full score on the day before the third race, scheduled at Imola. That weekend has gone down as the most tragic in the history of modern motor sports. On Friday, young Barrichello was involved in a serious accident with his Jordan;

on Saturday, the debuting Austrian Roland Ratzenberger was killed in his Simtek; on Sunday there was a horrendous collision at the opening of the race. When it resumed, there was the crash at the Tamburello corner that cost Senna his life. A tragic end that touched the entire world. Ayrton was 34 years old. The cause of the accident: a steering column failure. With an ensuing long (and useless) trial. Schumacher. Just ahead of Senna in the World Championship, just behind him at the time of the accident at Imola. World champion for the first time in 1994, when he beat Damon Hill (1960), Senna's teammate at Williams, in the last race, with a questionable maneuver that caused both drivers to retire from the competition. World champion again in 1995, with a broad margin, once again over Hill. Michael was born in Hürth, Germany, on January 3, 1969. He grew up on the kart track managed by his father. His brother, Ralf, ran 180 GPs between 1997 and 2007 and achieved six victories.
The vitality of the Williams team returned in the heart of this decade. Two victories in a row. With Hill, in 1996, 28 years after the last title conquered by his father Graham; with Jacques Villeneuve in 1997. Jacques, too, was born into the art. Gilles' son, fresh from a triumphal career in the United States, where he won the CART Championship and the Indy 500 in 1995, was the protagonist of an unforgettable action in Jerez, when he attempted to overtake Schumacher,

driving for the Ferrari team since 1996. A daring and timely overtake that forced Michael to turn in on him, an irregular and useless maneuver, punished by FIA with disqualification from the World Championship. Even the Ferrari-Schumacher partnership seemed to be in distress. The last world title obtained by a red-clad driver dated back to 1979 (Scheckter) and against all expectations Ferrari was forced to wait until the end of the decade. In 1998 and 1999 the world champion was Mika Häkkinen (1968), Finnish, the aggressive, extremely fast McLaren driver. Schumacher: second in 1998, the victim of a serious accident at Silverstone in 1999, year in which Eddie Irvine, the Irish second driver for the Ferrari team, was left to fight for the title until the last race, in Japan. The ending? Fantastic and still mysterious. With Ferrari first having been disqualified and then later re-admitted after the race won by Irvine in Malaysia, while the Irishman was completely disoriented during the last act at Suzuka.
A long time before, at the end of 1993, Riccardo Patrese (1954), had ended a brilliant career, begun in 1977, that counted 256 GPs, six victories and eight pole positions.

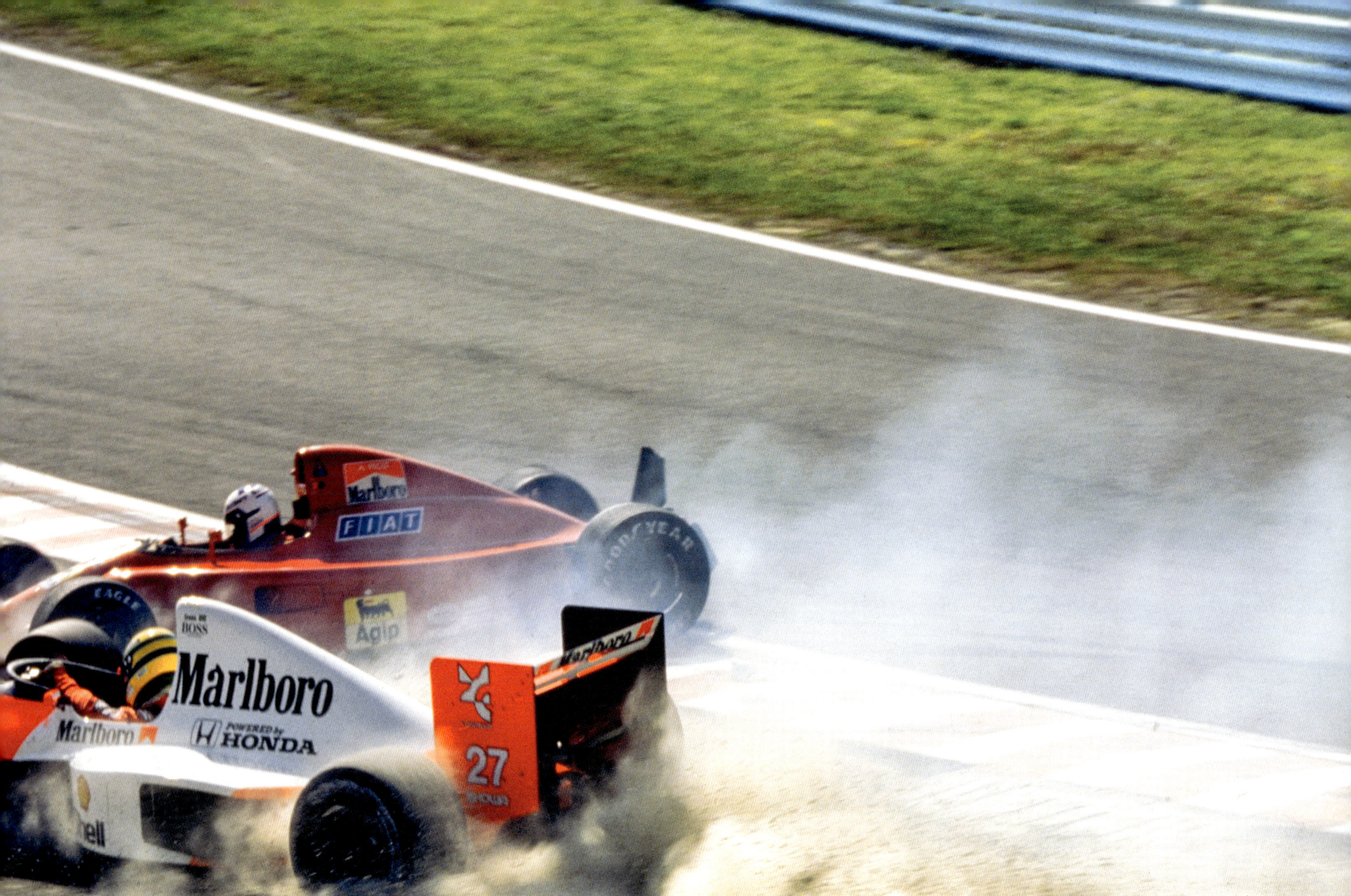

Suzuka, Japanese GP, 1990. Ayrton Senna (McLaren MP4/5B Honda) and Alain Prost (Ferrari 641) collide at the first corner, settling the World Championship in the Brazilian's favor. Photo: Keith Sutton

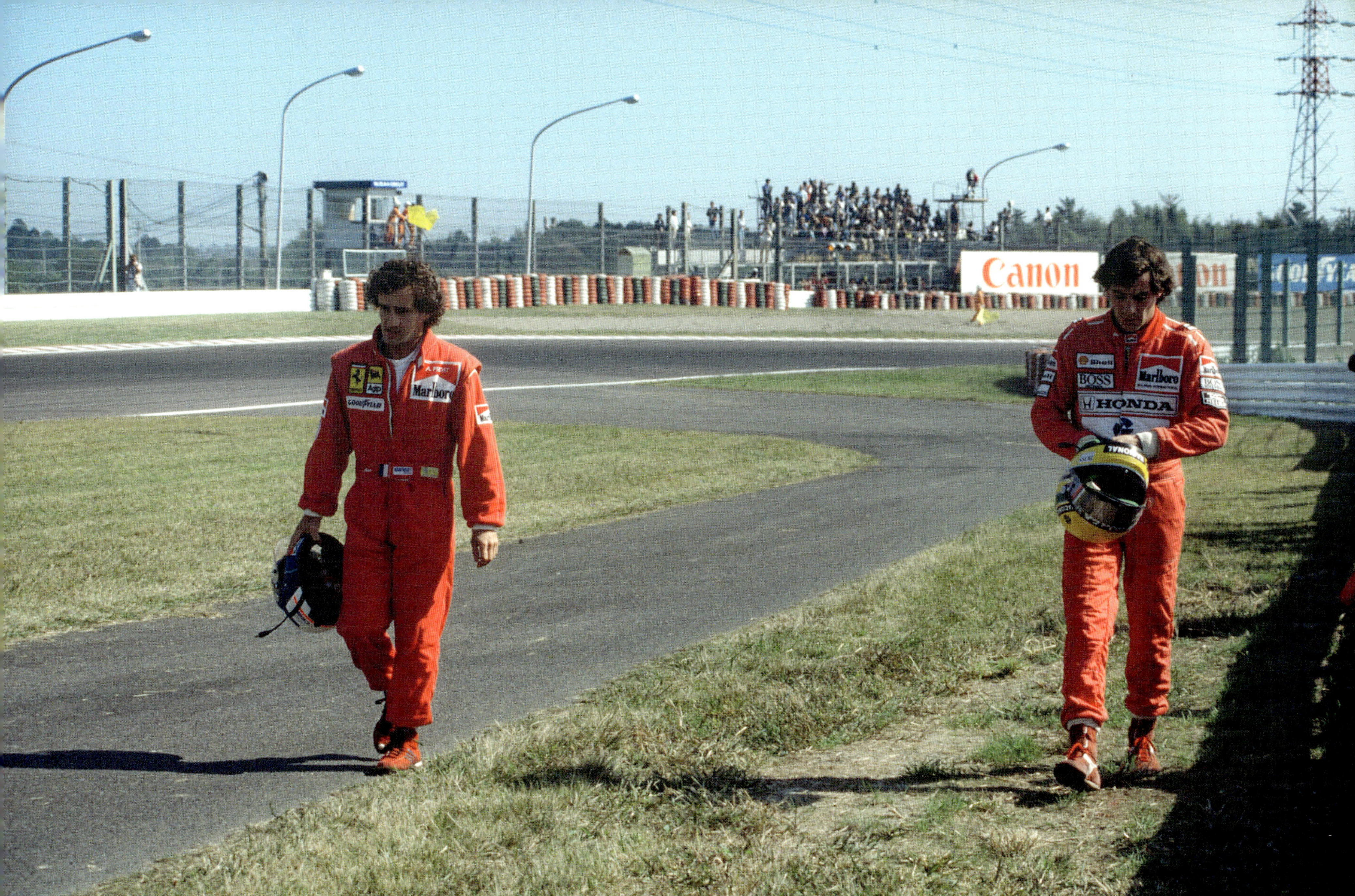

Suzuka, Japanese GP, 1990. Alain Prost and Ayrton Senna walk away following their collision at the start of the race. Photo: Ercole Colombo

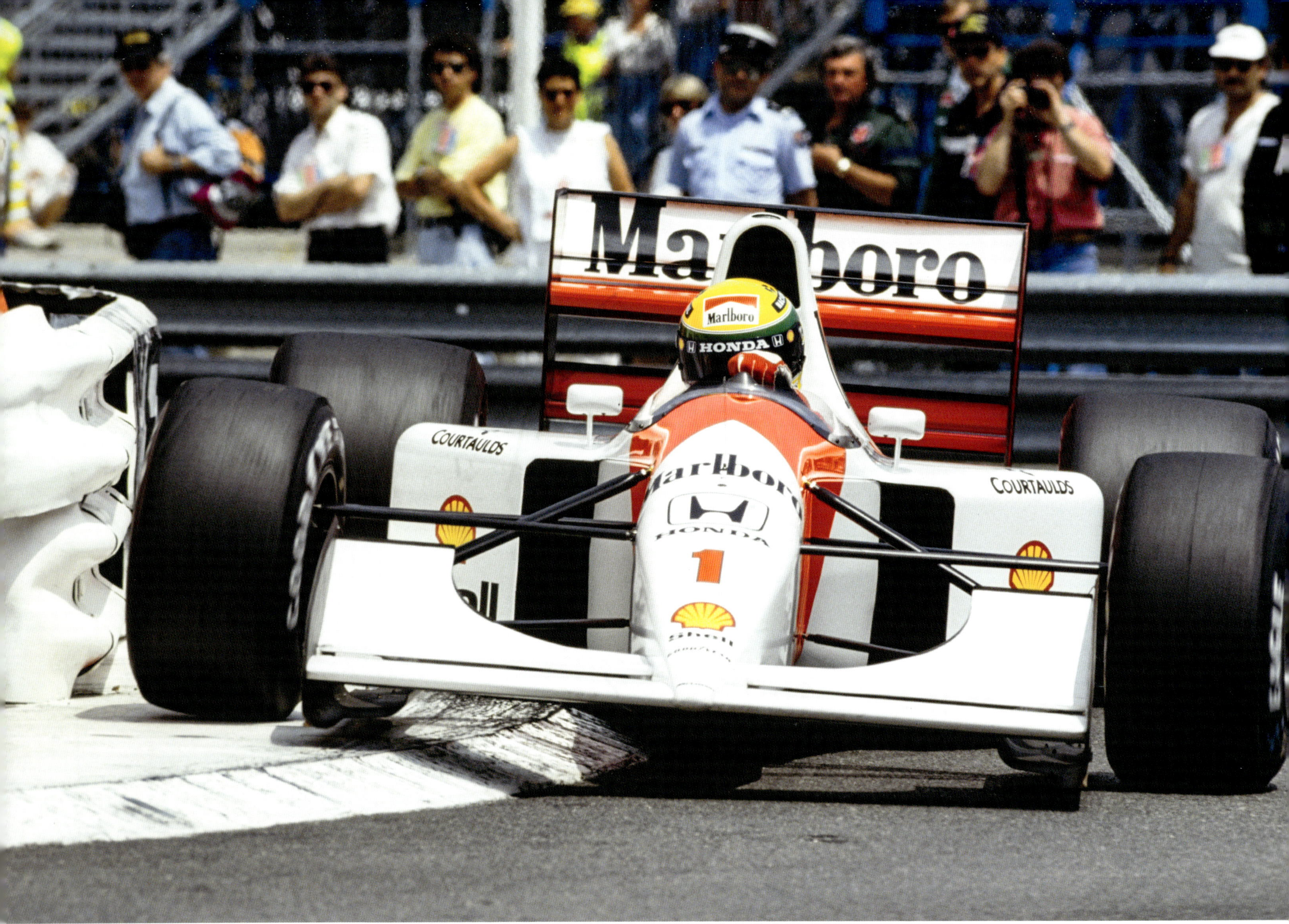

Monaco GP, 1992. Ayrton Senna (McLaren MP4-7A Honda). Photo: Ercole Colombo

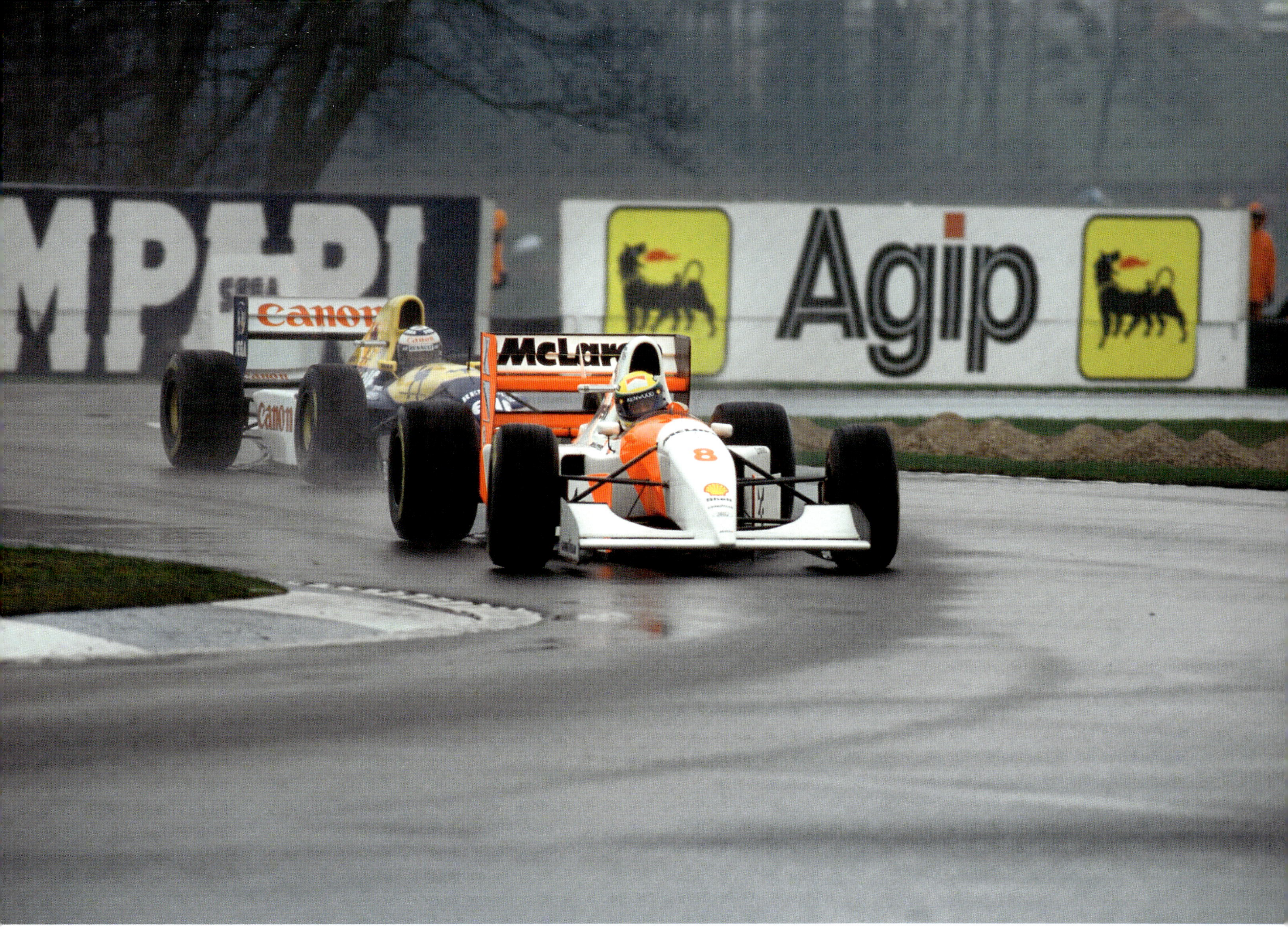

Donington Park, European GP, 1993. Ayrton Senna (McLaren MP4-8 Ford) leads Alain Prost (Williams FW15C Renault). Photo: Ercole Colombo

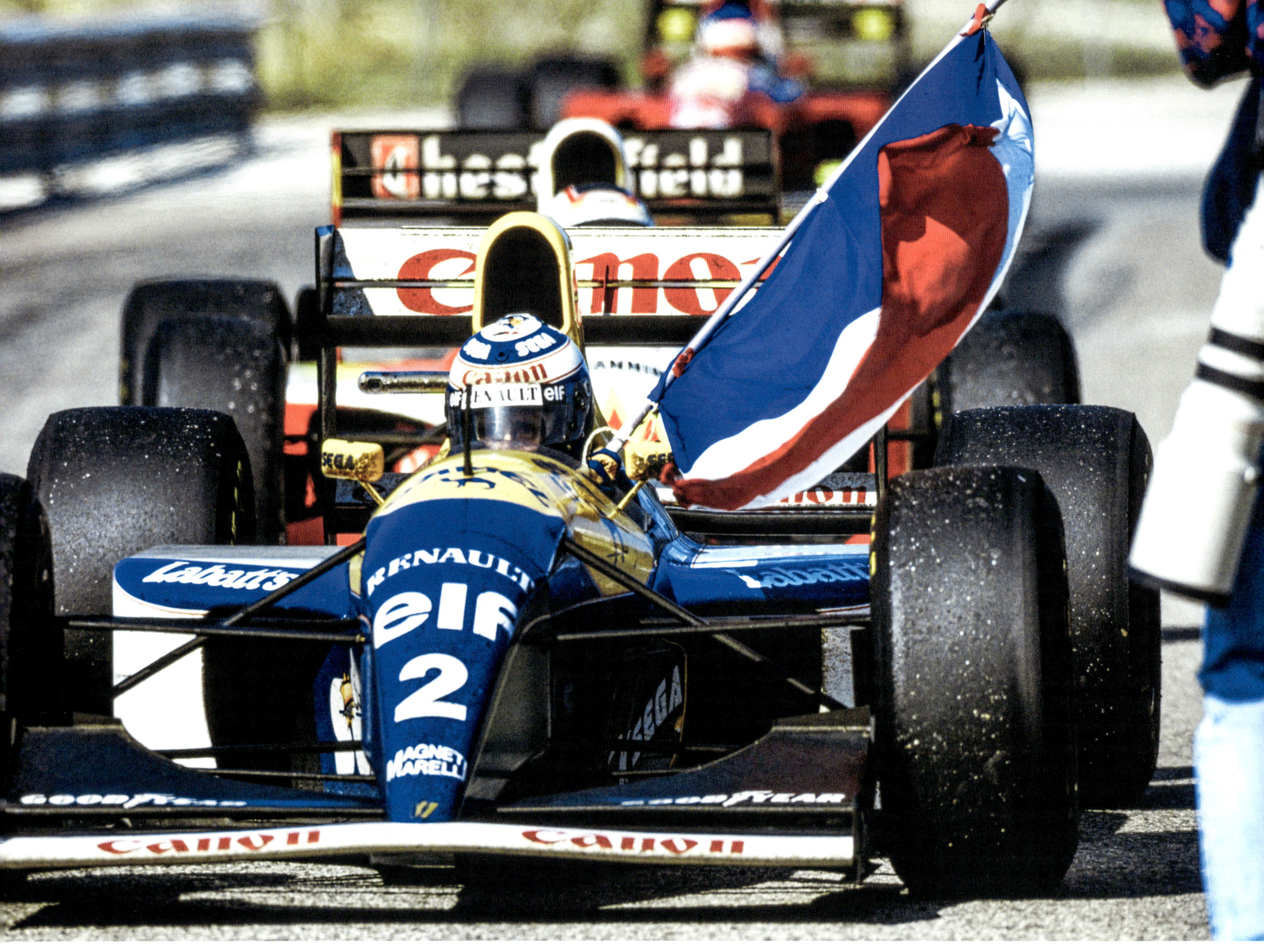

Estoril, Portuguese GP, 1993. Alain Prost (Williams FW15C Renault) holds a French flag after winning his fourth and final world title. Photo: Steven Tee

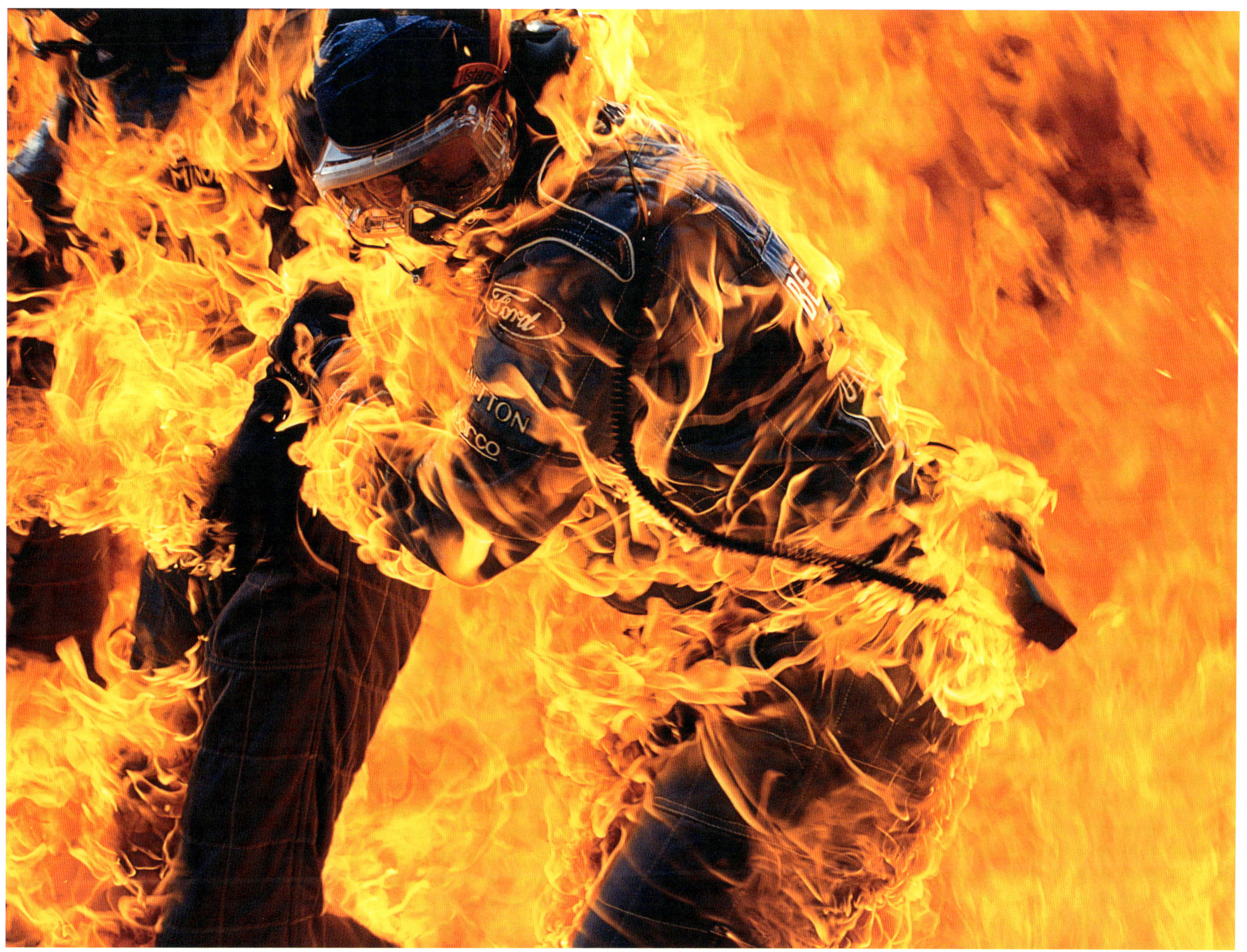

Hockenheim, German GP, 1994. Fire during the refueling of Jos Verstappen's Benetton B194 Ford. Photo: Steven Tee

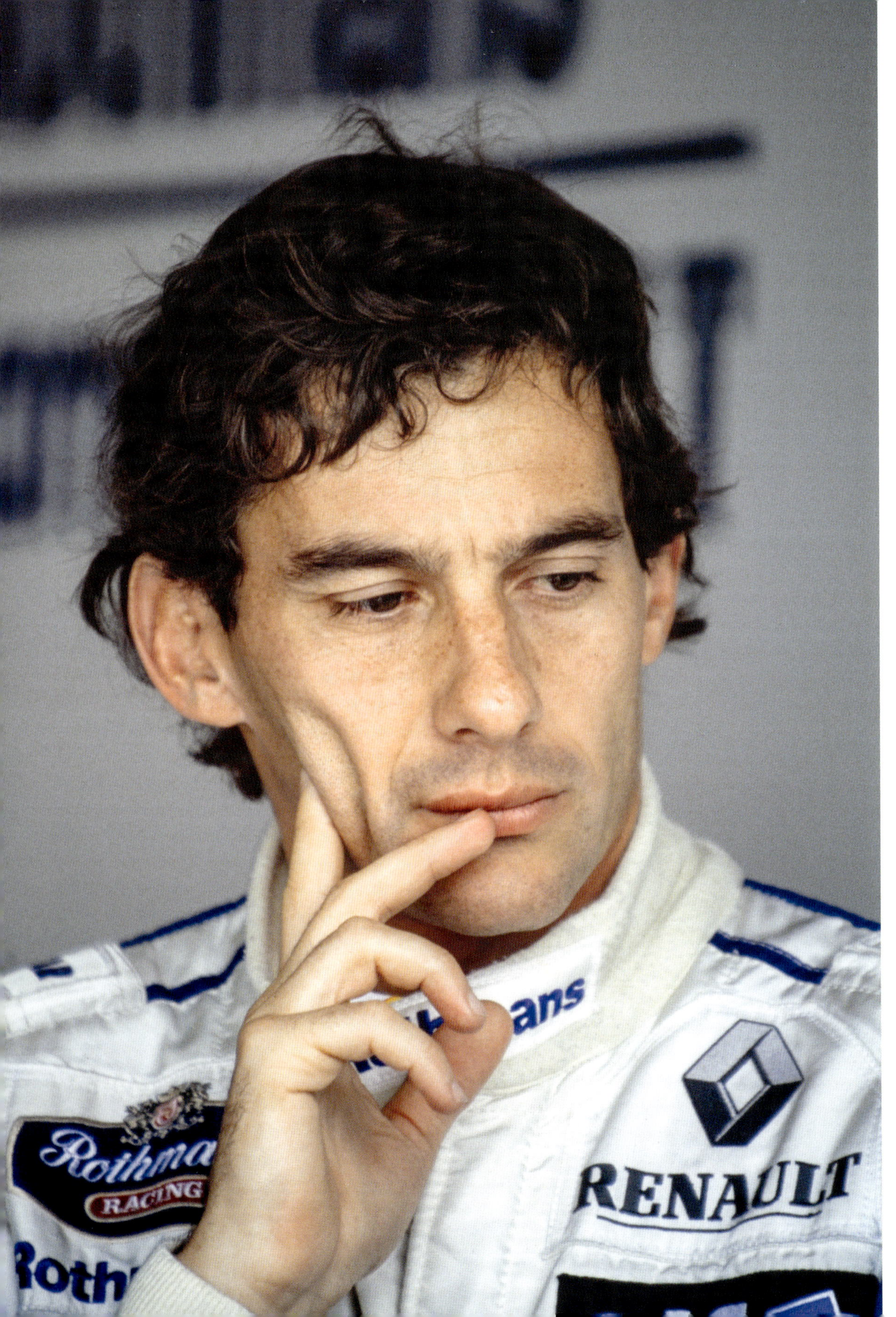

Imola, San Marino GP, 1994.
Ayrton Senna in the Williams
garage before the start. Photo:
Ercole Colombo

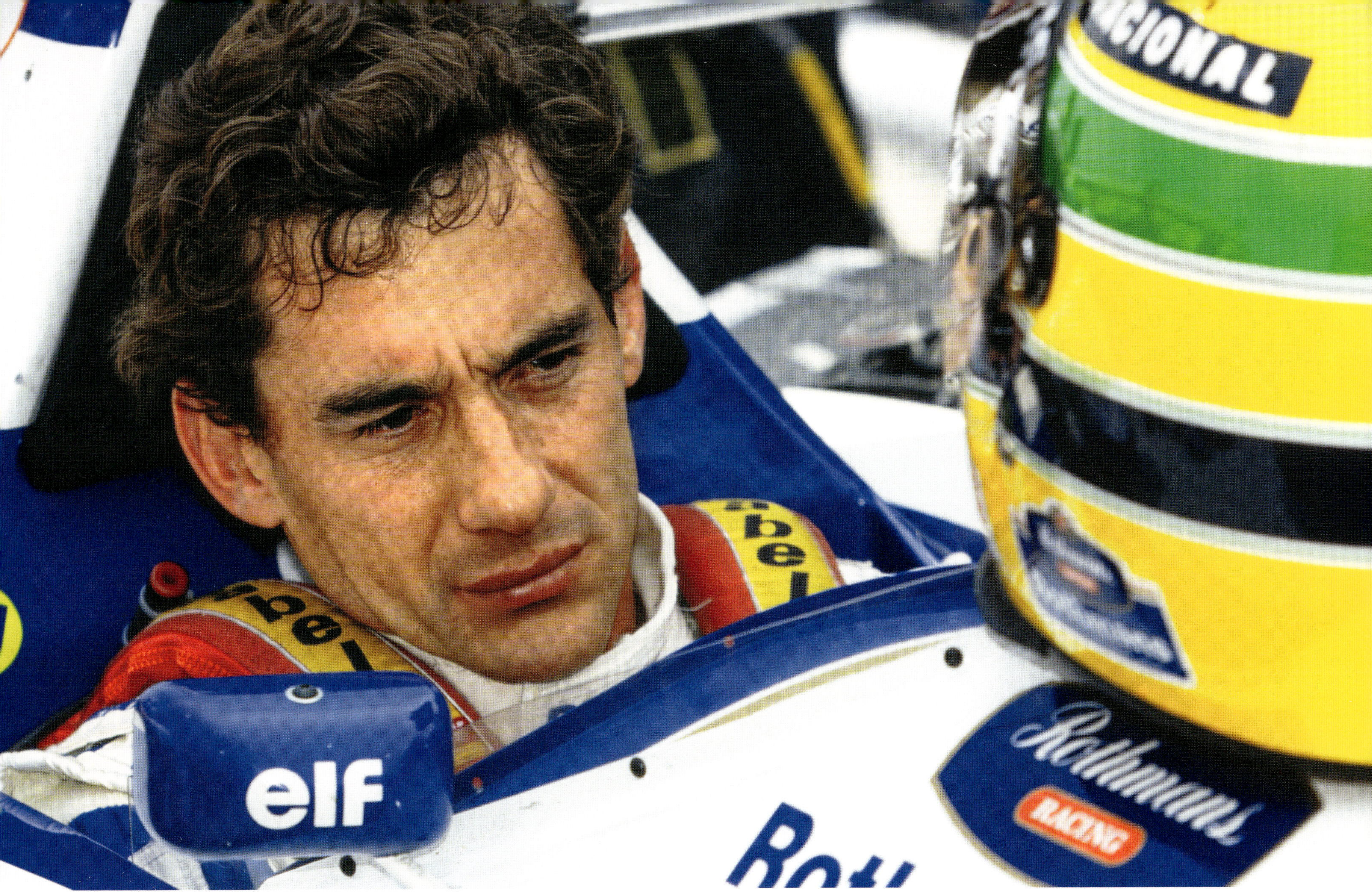

Imola, San Marino GP, 1994. Ayrton Senna sits in his Williams FW16 Renault on the grid before his tragic final race. Photo: Ercole Colombo

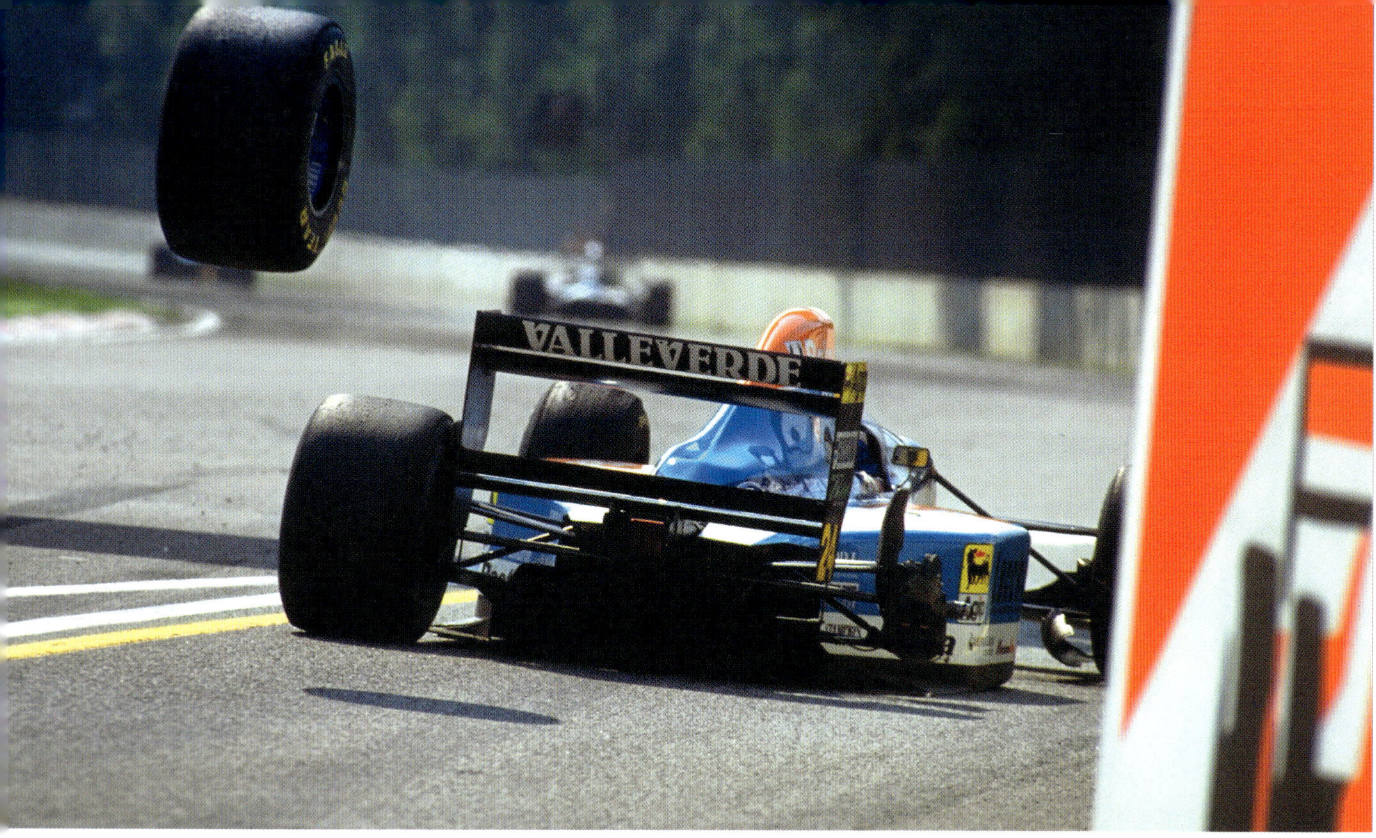

Imola, San Marino GP, 1994. Michele Alboreto (Minardi M193B) loses his rear right wheel at the pit lane exit. Photo: Ercole Colombo

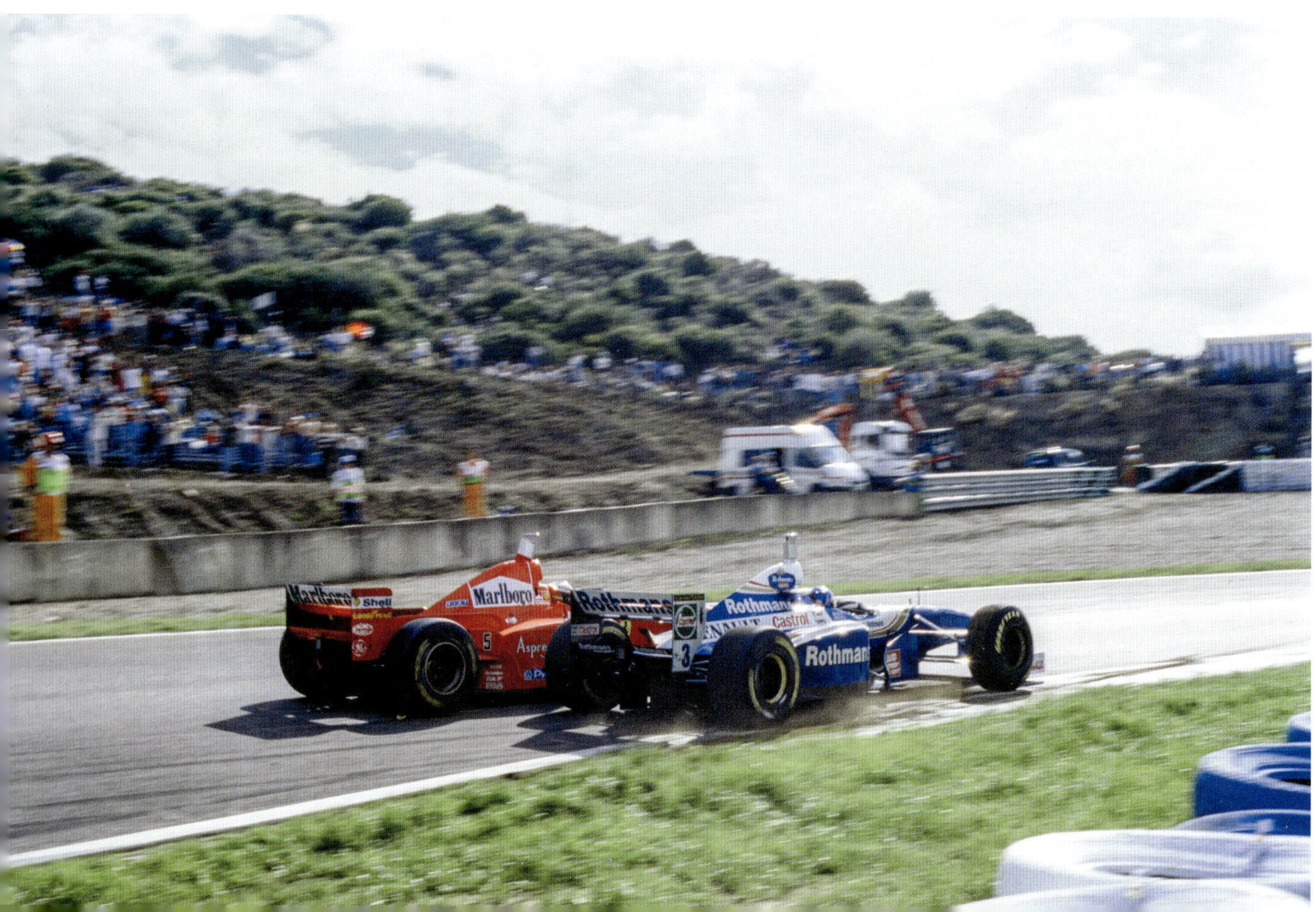

Jerez, European GP, 1997. The controversial collision between Michael Schumacher (Ferrari F310B) and Jacques Villeneuve (Williams FW19 Renault) into the Curva Dry Sack. Photo: Steven Tee

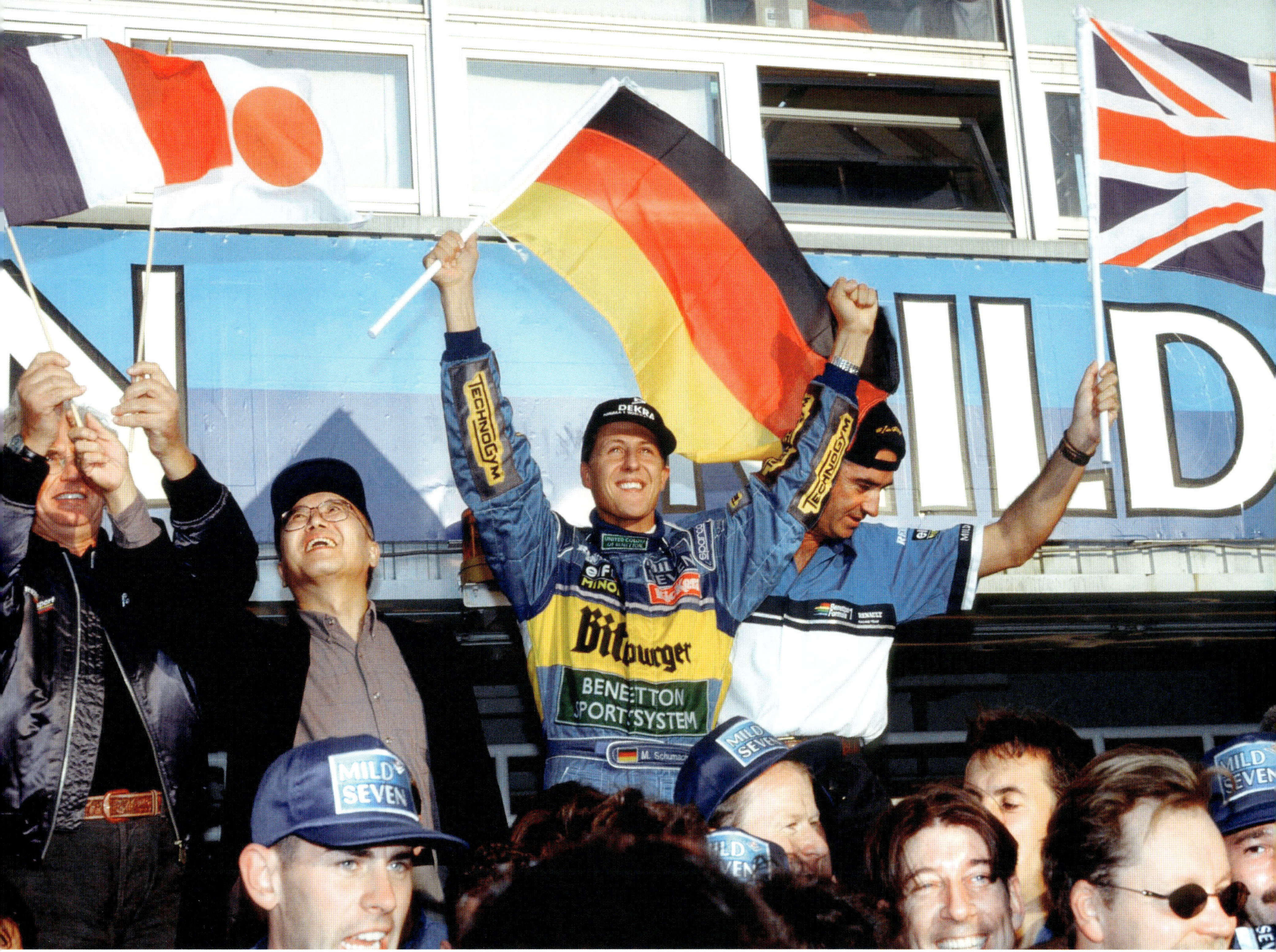

Aida, Pacific GP, 1995. Michael Schumacher waves the German flag after his victory that clinched his second World Championship. Photo: Ercole Colombo

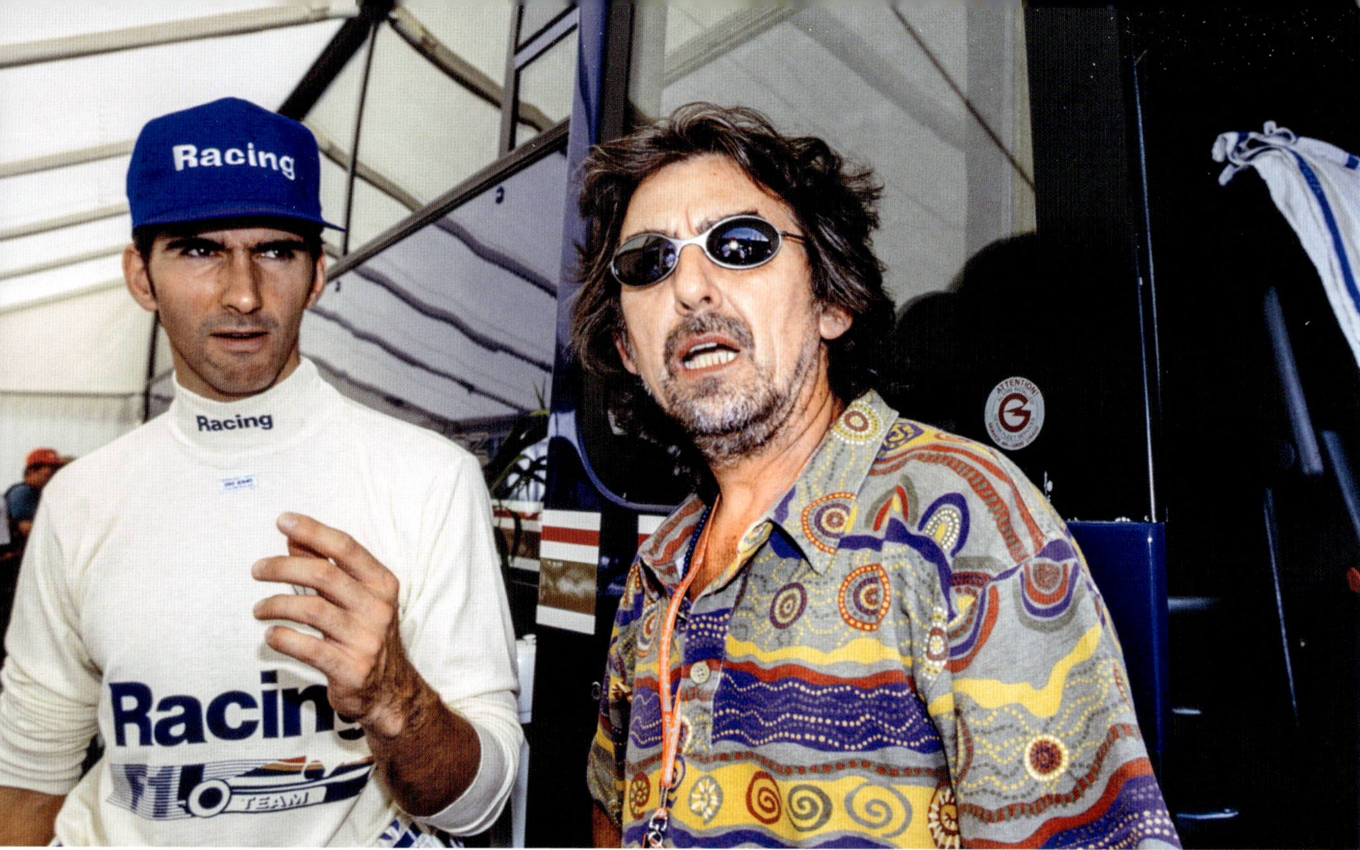

Hockenheim, German GP, 1994. Ex Beatle George Harrison talks with Damon Hill (Williams), on the left. Photo: Sutton Images

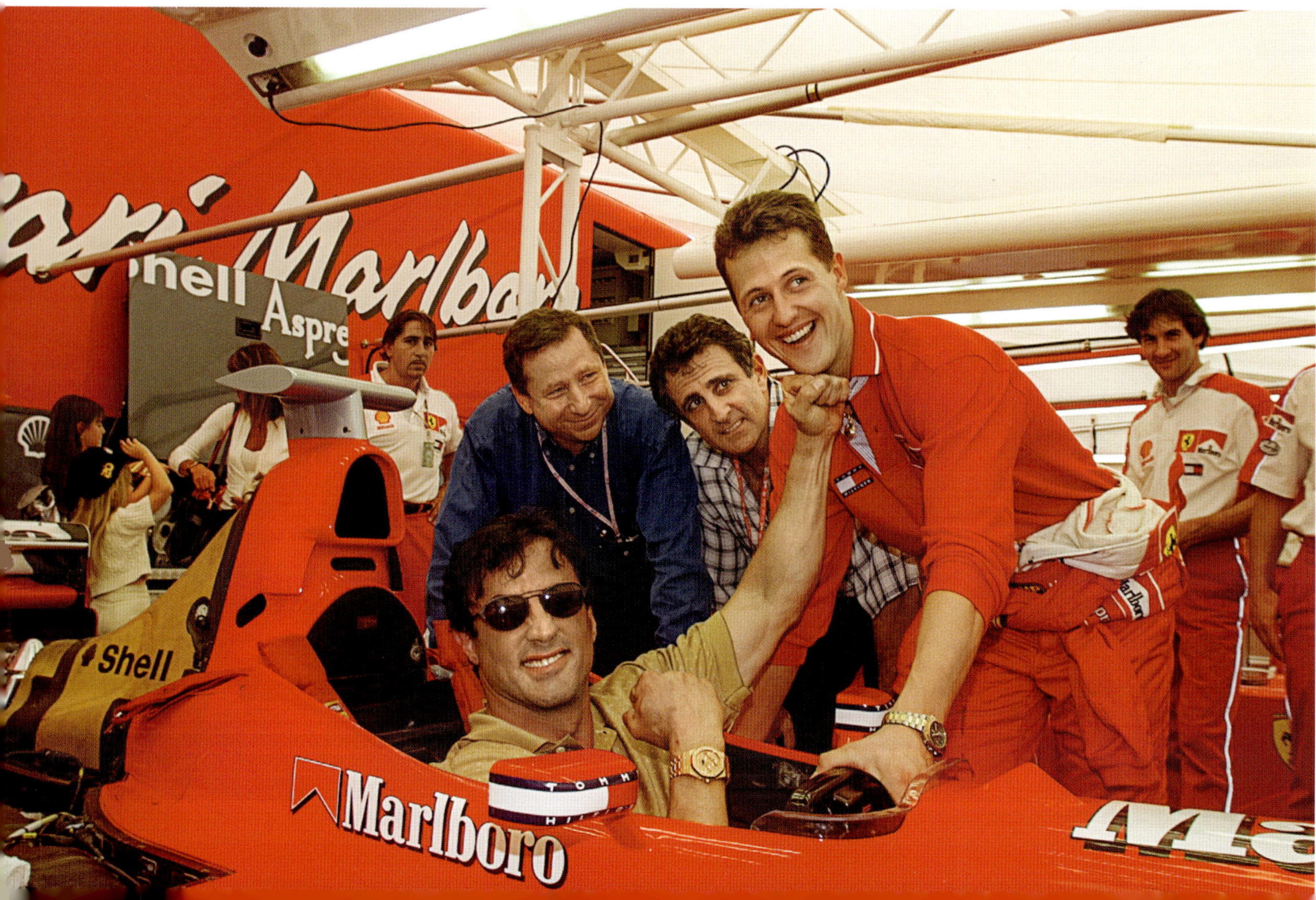

Monaco GP, 1988. Silvester Stallone and Michael Schumacher. Photo: Ercole Colombo

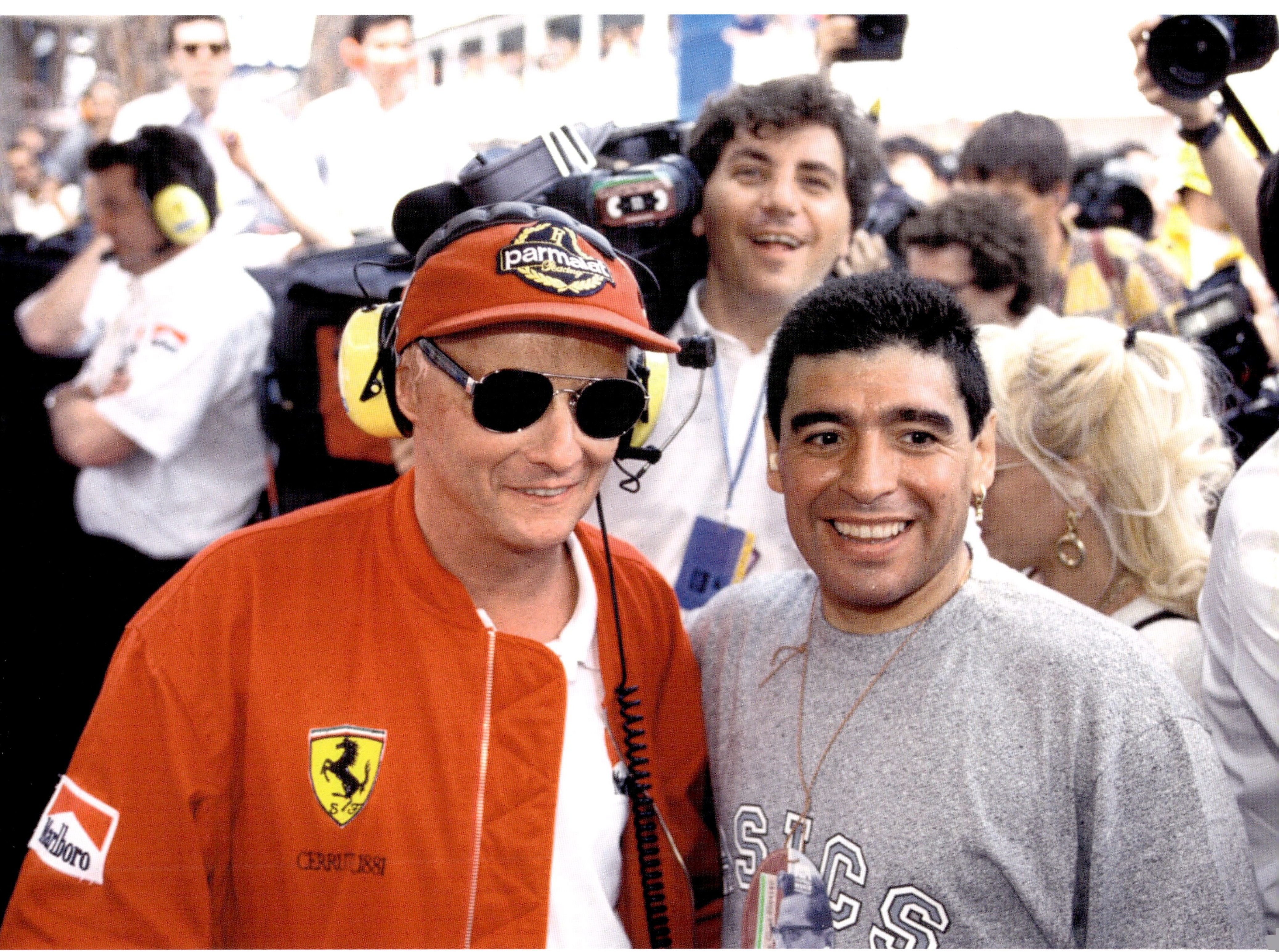

Monaco GP, 1995. Niki Lauda and Diego Maradona. Photo: Ercole Colombo

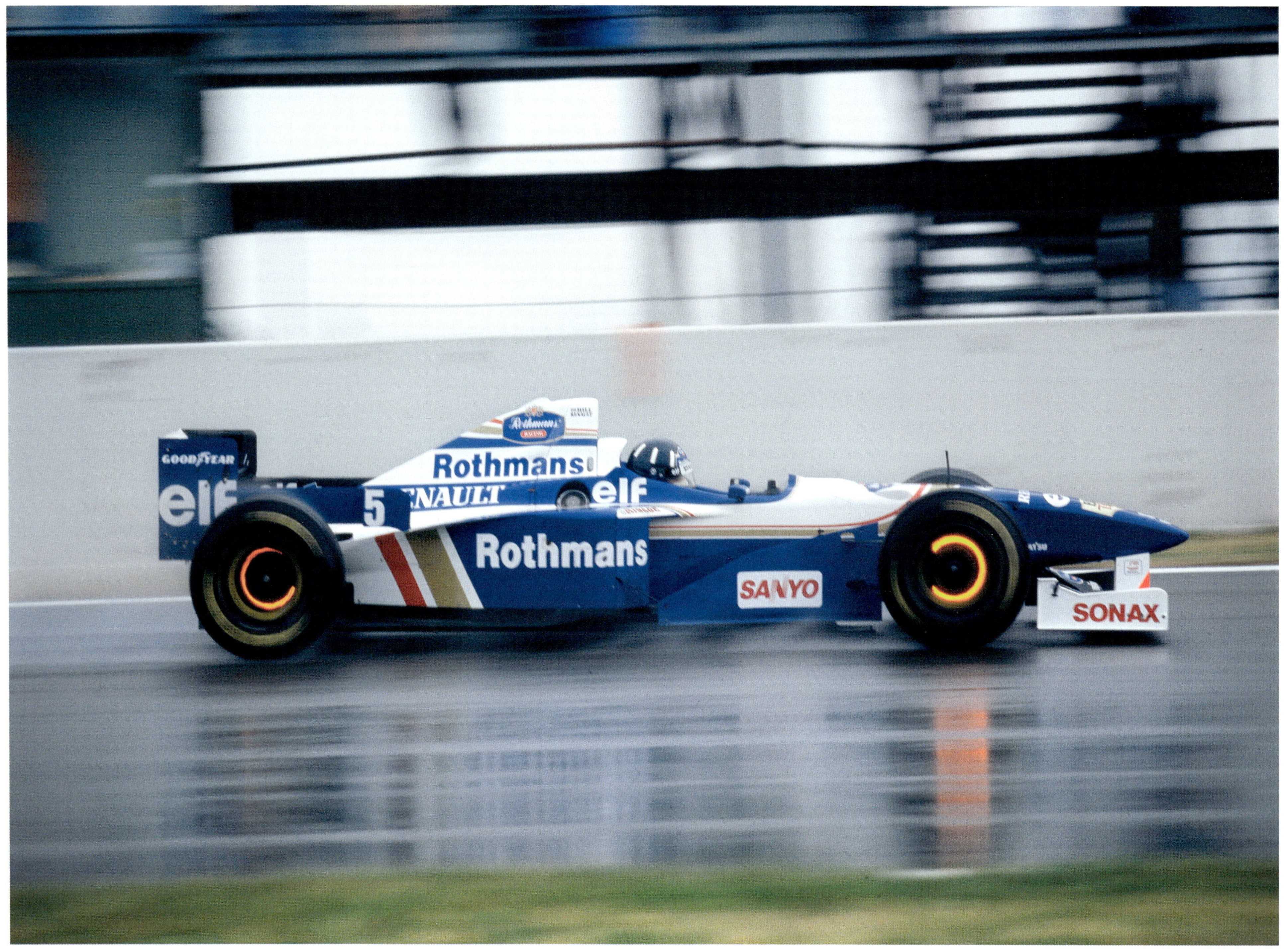

Barcelona, Spanish GP, 1996. Damon Hill (Williams FW18 Renault). Photo: Rainer Schlegelmilch

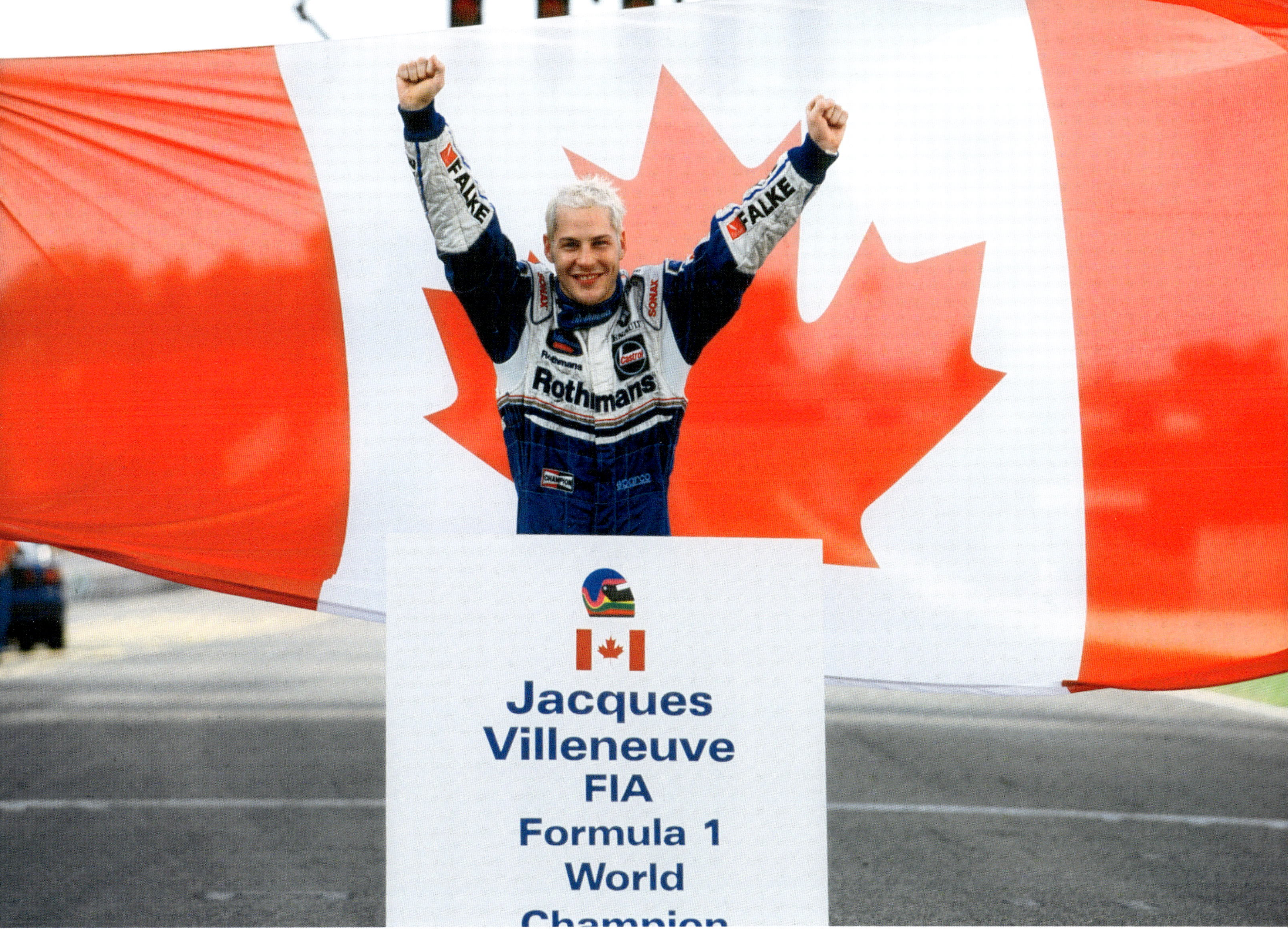

Jerez, European GP, 1997. Third placed Jacques Villeneuve (Williams) celebrates becoming the world champion. Photo: Mark Sutton

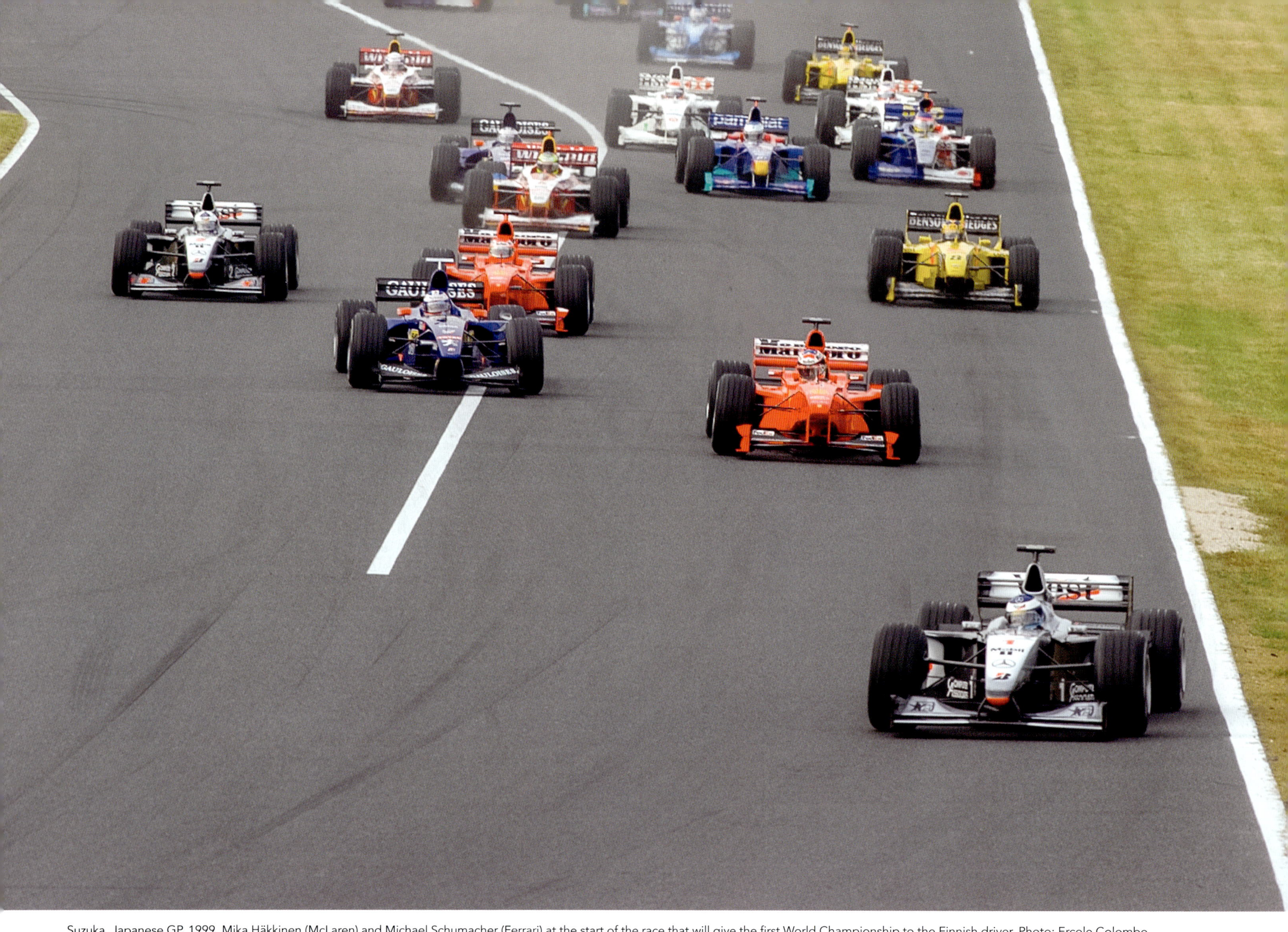

Suzuka, Japanese GP, 1999. Mika Häkkinen (McLaren) and Michael Schumacher (Ferrari) at the start of the race that will give the first World Championship to the Finnish driver. Photo: Ercole Colombo

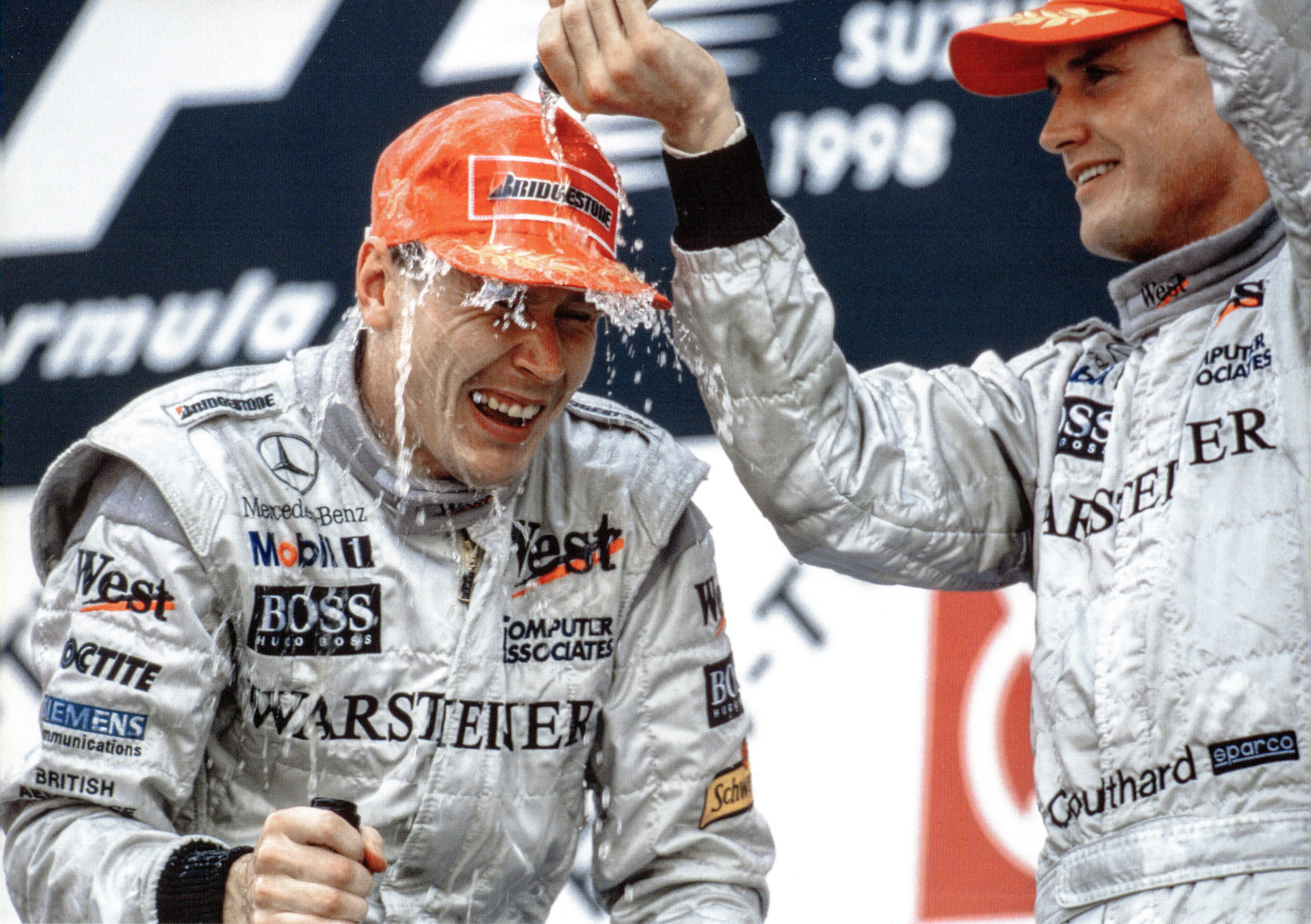

Nürburgring, Luxenbourg GP, 1988. Mika Häkkinen celebrates on the podium with David Coulthard. Photo: Steven Tee

2000–2009
Schumy Red

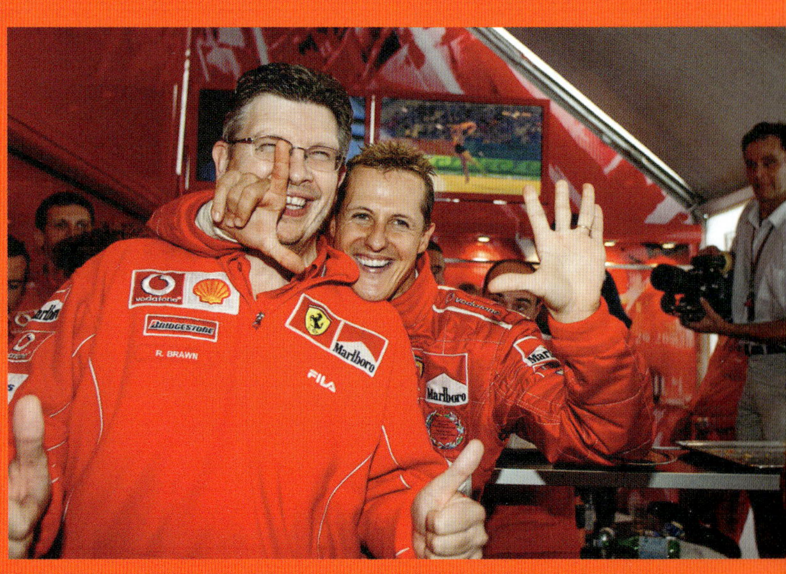

The new century was monochromatically red. Five titles for Ferrari. Five World Championships won by Michael Schumacher who thus accomplished seven world titles, two more than Juan Manuel Fangio. His records seemed unsurpassable. First win in the year 2000, the fifth in 2004, in a string that marked a joyful and unforgettable time for Ferrari fans. Schumacher became Schumy, the Brazilian Rubens Barrichello always by his side, fast but not as practical, determined, capable of holding his own, of behaving like a real leader in a team that was strong from every point of view. Luca di Montezemolo, President; Jean Todt at the helm of the Racing Division, a pool of inspired technicians that included Rory Byrne and Ross Brawn, in charge of design, and Paolo Martinelli, in charge of the engine. Stefano Domenicali directed everything and everyone with an extraordinary verve. And there were many brilliant young men—such as Luca Baldisserri and Mattia Binotto—born and raised within the Ferrari team.

The figures speak for themselves: Schumacher won nine races in 2000, the same number in 2001, 11 GPs in 2002, seven in 2003, and an astounding 13 in 2004. Basically a monopoly. With Barrichello inevitably forced into the role of second, with many consolation prizes: nine victories for him, too, over the five years dominated by his formidable captain. The defeated. Many and distinguished. Häkkinen and Coulthard with the

two McLarens closed the 2000 World Championship just behind Schumacher; Coulthard and Barrichello were on the podium for the 2001 Championship. In 2002 the Ferrari duo was followed by Juan Pablo Montoya, the Williams team's Colombian driver. The young and extremely fast Kimi Räikkönen and his McLaren came in second in 2003, only two lengths from the world champion, while Montoya came in third once again. In 2004, Schumy and Barrichello preceded the Briton Jenson Button and the Spaniard Fernando Alonso. The former driver for the BAR team powered by Honda, the latter for Renault.

Alonso, a Spaniard, was born in Oviedo on July 29, 1981. He was tremendously gifted and debuted in F1 in 2001 with Minardi. It was he who broke the red circle. Two titles in a row, in 2005 and 2006. The first conquered over Räikkönen, who came in second once again with McLaren, and Schumacher, who won only one race, in the United States. The second achieved at the end of a drawn-out neck and neck with the German champion: 134 points to 121. The Brazilian Felipe Massa, who had replaced Barrichello in Ferrari, came in third with 80 points.

Schumy quit. Ferrari hired Kimi Räikkönen. Alonso transferred to McLaren, where he found a very talented young man at his debut, Lewis Hamilton, groomed by his father Anthony and by the boss of the British team, Ron Dennis. It was a hectic year, marked by a sensational spy story:

a huge number of documents and designs smuggled out of Maranello and intended for a McLaren designer. The aberration was macroscopic, it was self-evident. The British team was punished with the annulment of the scores achieved that season. Not only: the rivalry between Alonso and Hamilton led to repeated conflicts and tensions at McLaren. While he struggled with his teammate and with Räikkönen for the title, Alonso announced he would be leaving the team at the end of the season. Which led to a pacey epilogue in Brazil. Räikkönen won, world champion with a single point over both Hamilton and Alonso.

Another neck and neck marked the 2008 Championship. Disputing the title were Massa for Ferrari and Hamilton for McLaren, while Alonso went back to driving—and suffering—for Renault. Once again, it was all decided in São Paulo, during the last race. Massa won the GP, but in the last yards Hamilton regained enough ground to come in fifth, overtaking Timo Glock's Toyota on the damp track. It was enough for him to become world champion with a single point over the Brazilian. Another scandal marked this season. Renault was the protagonist. Nelsinho Piquet, Nelson's son, the team's second driver, intentionally crashed his car to favor his teammate Alonso's victory in the Singapore GP. This maneuver put technician Pat Symonds and Flavio Briatore on the stand; the latter was expelled from the Federation and later reinstated by the Parisian court.

The last act of the decade was also marked by shadows and controversy. Ross Brawn, outstanding Benetton and Ferrari designer, took over the Honda team and gave it his name. He created a vehicle powered by Mercedes, designed for the duo Button-Barrichello. Its performance: irresistible. Thanks to an aerodynamic tweak of the body considered irregular by everyone except for the FIA. The team achieved 8 victories in 17 races and won the Constructors' Championship, while Button was consecrated 2009 world champion ahead of a very young Sebastian Vettel (Red Bull) and Barrichello. At the end of the season, the team was taken over by Mercedes, determined to reenter F1, 55 years after its last participation.

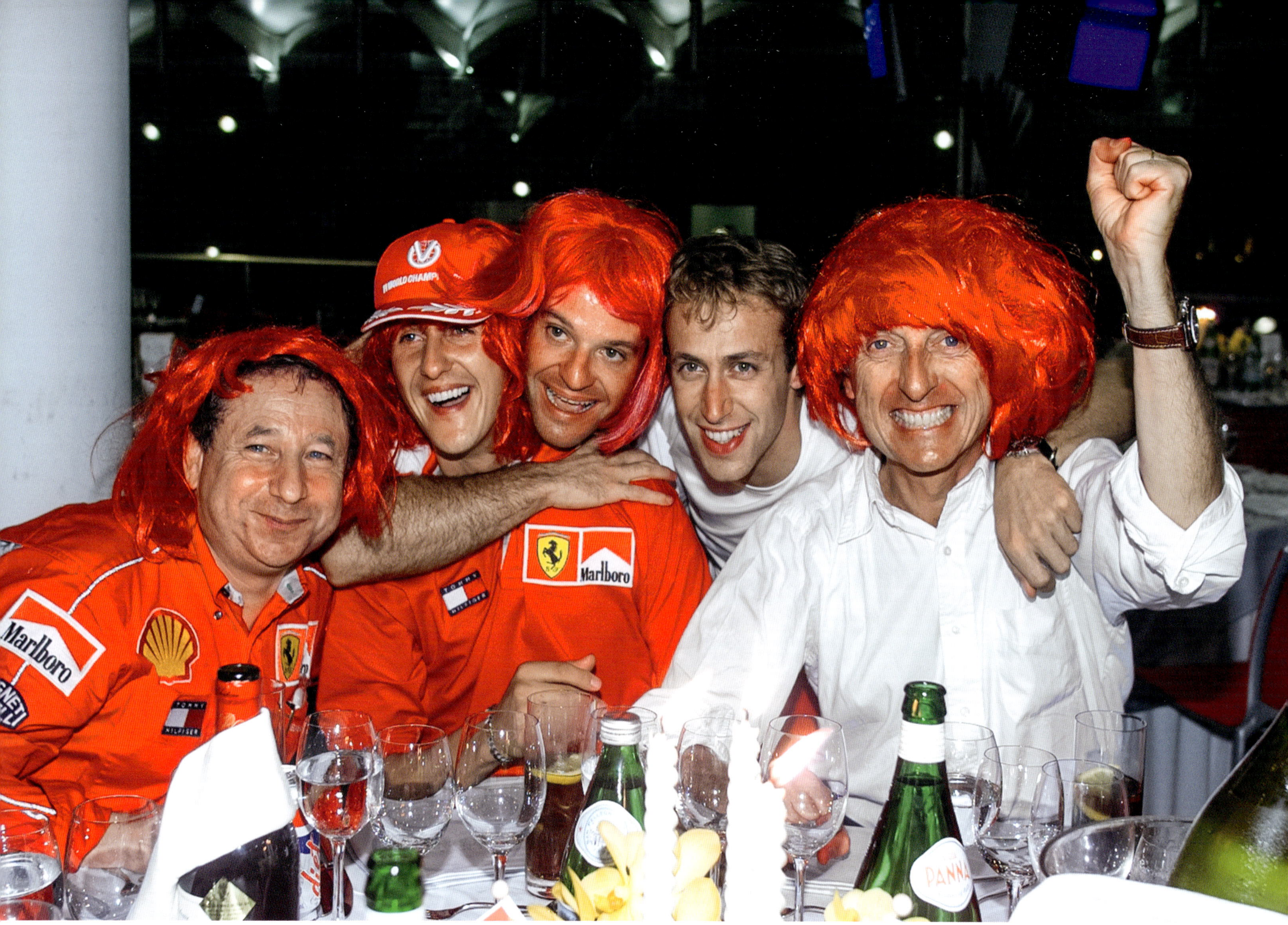

Sepang, Malaysian GP, 2000. Jean Todt, Michael Schumacher, Rubens Barrichello, Luca Badoer, and President Luca di Montezemolo, happy after the victory of the World Constructors' Championship. Photo: Ercole Colombo

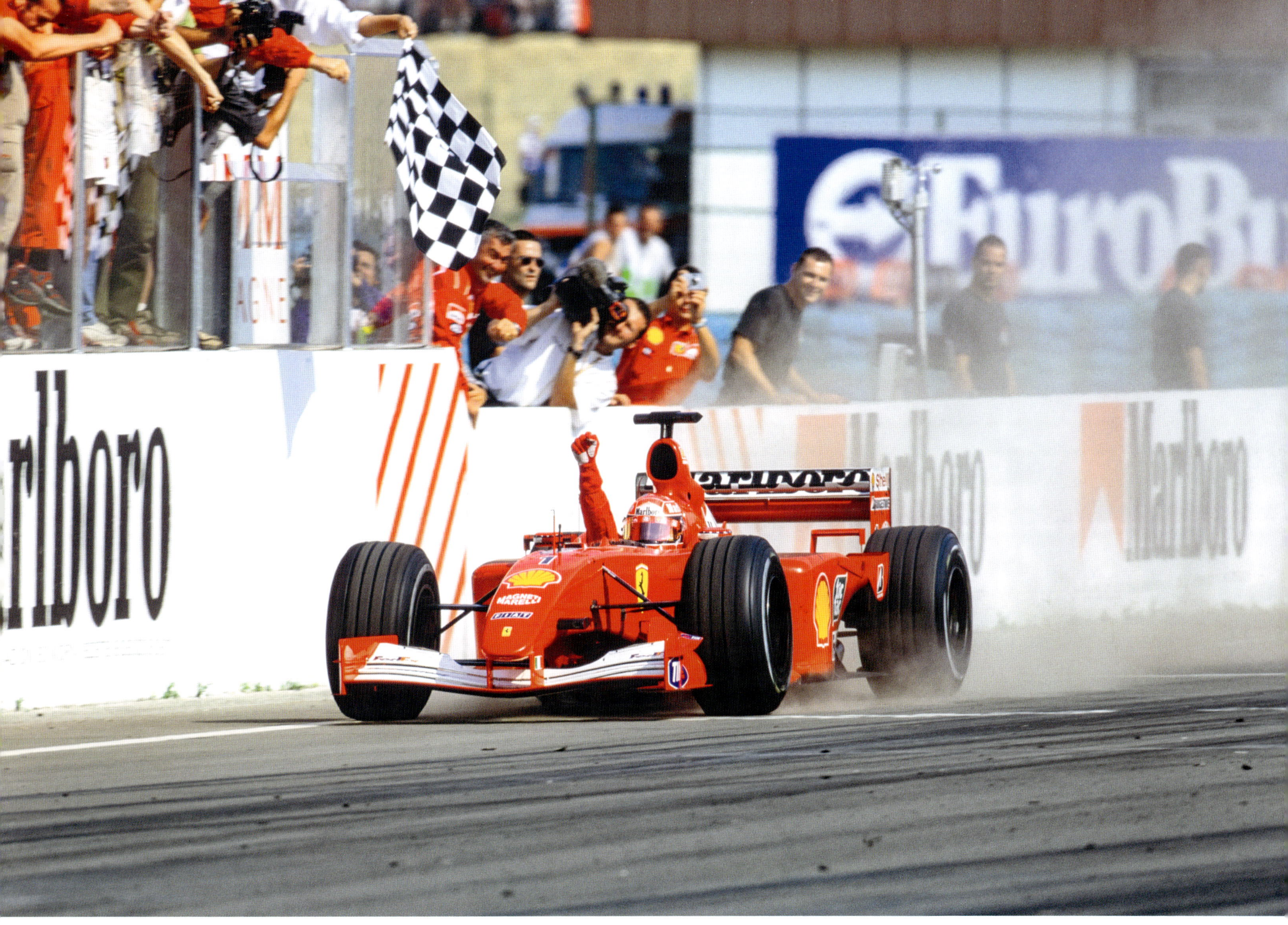

Budapest, Hungarian GP, 2001. Michael Schumacher (Ferrari F2001) crosses the finish line to win his fourth World Championship. Photo: Mark Sutton

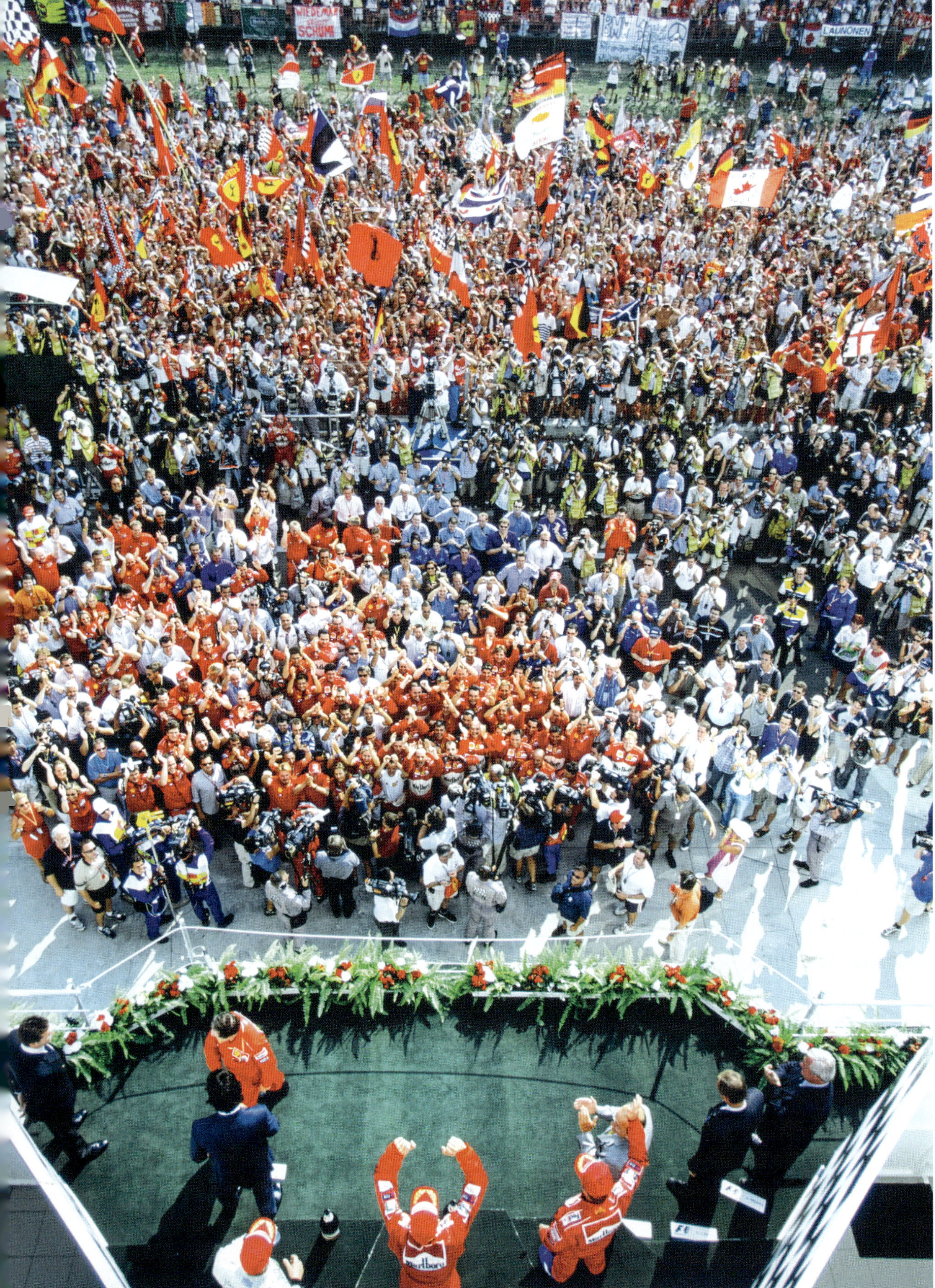

Budapest, Hungarian GP, 2001. Michael Schumacher celebrates winning his fourth World Championship alongside Rubens Barrichello and David Coulthard. Photo: Mark Sutton

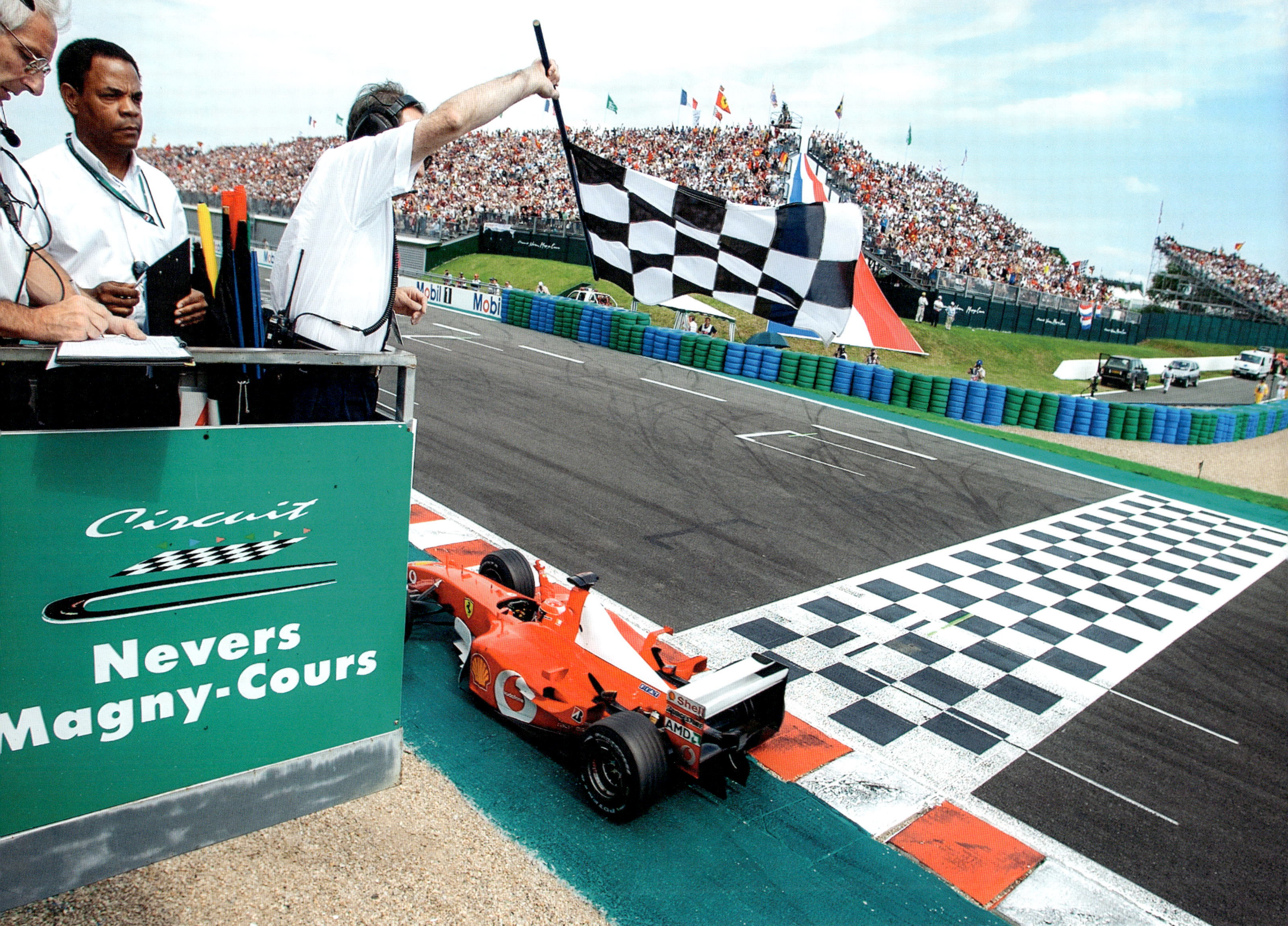

Magny-Cours, French GP, 2002. Michael Schumacher wins his fifth world title. Photo: Ercole Colombo

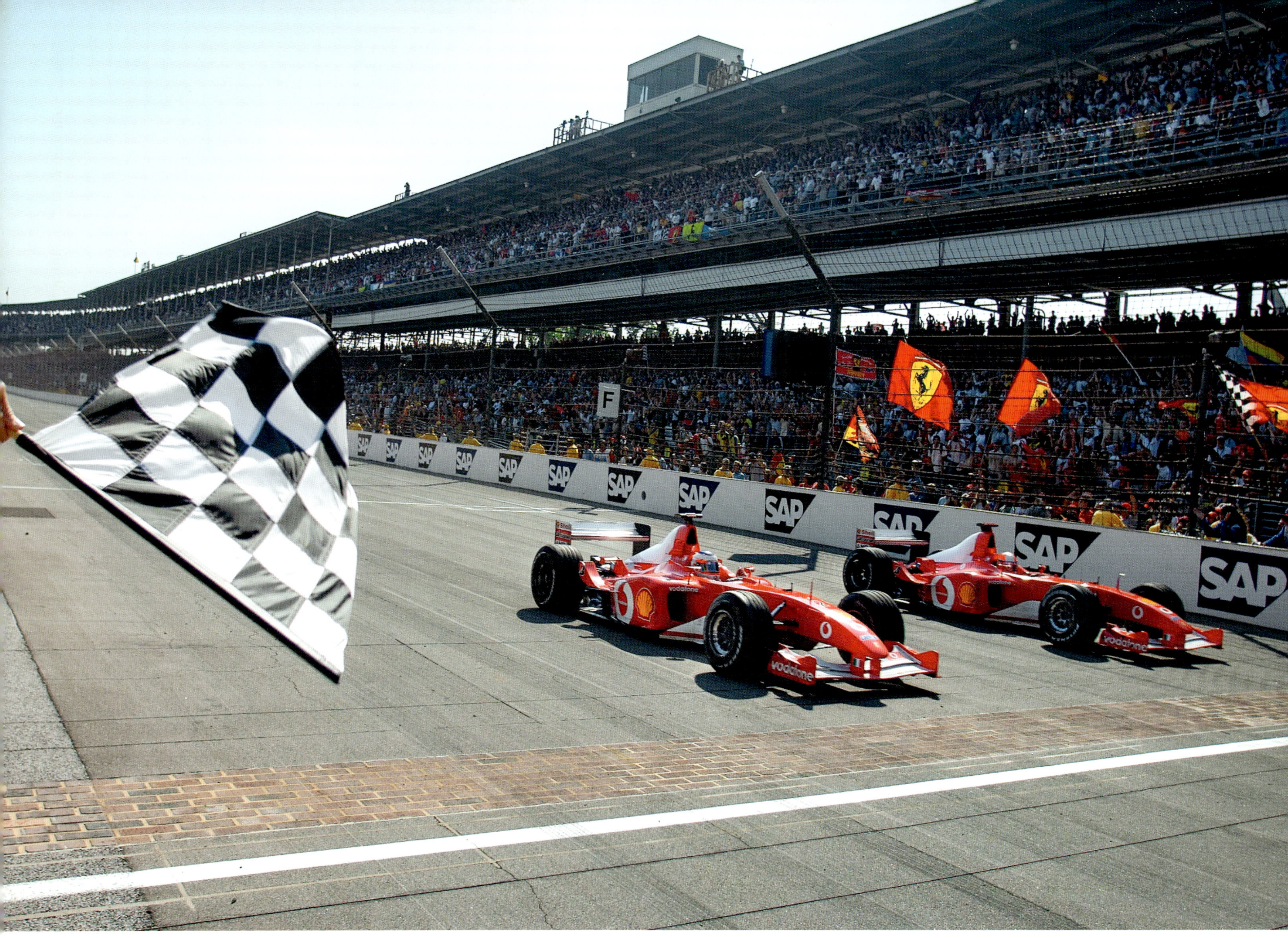

Indianapolis, United States GP, 2002. Ferrari driver Rubens Barrichello wins the race in front of his teammate Michael Schumacher. Photo: Ercole Colombo

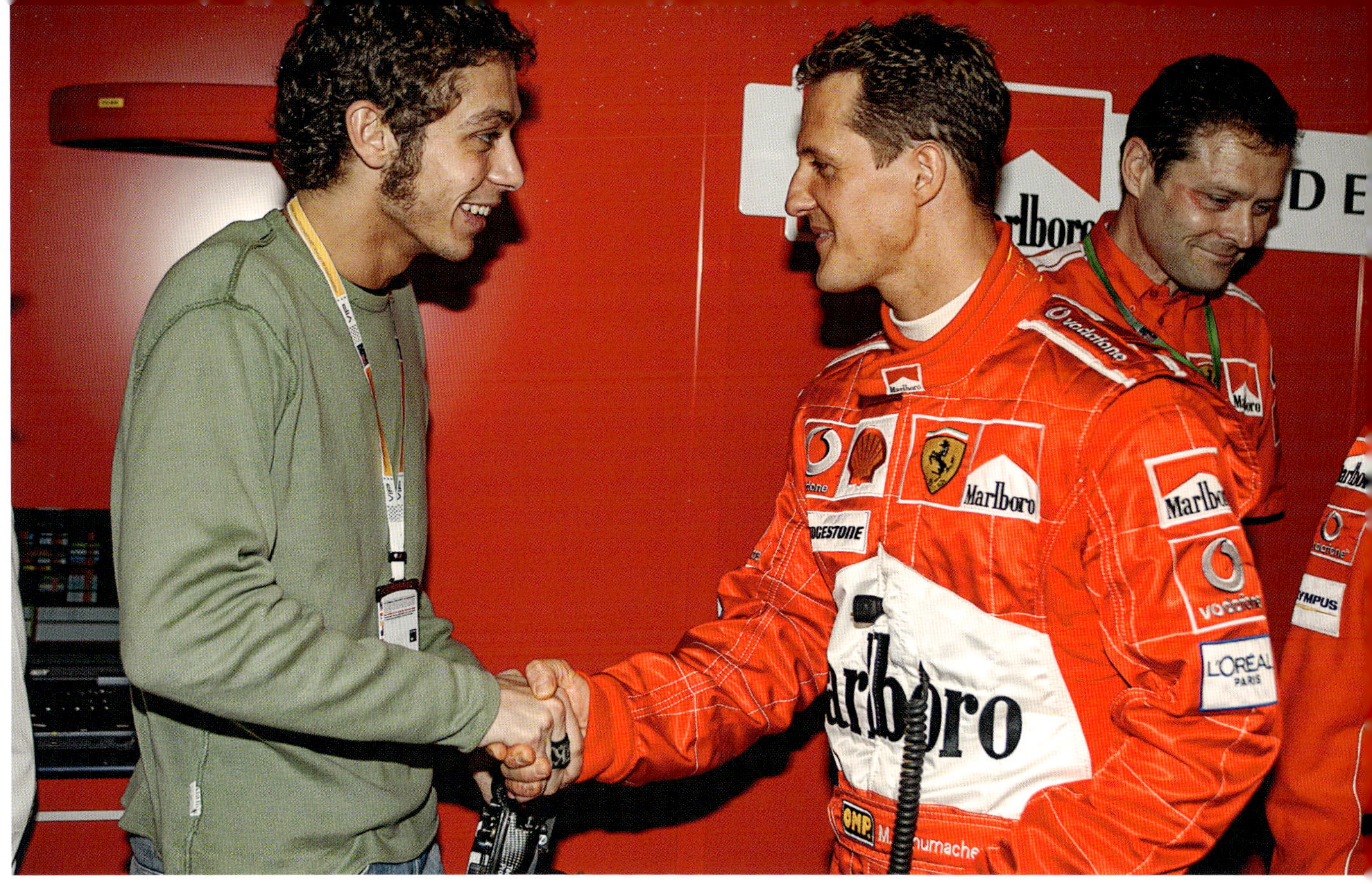

Melbourne, Australian GP, 2004. Valentino Rossi and Michael Schumacher. Photo: Ercole Colombo

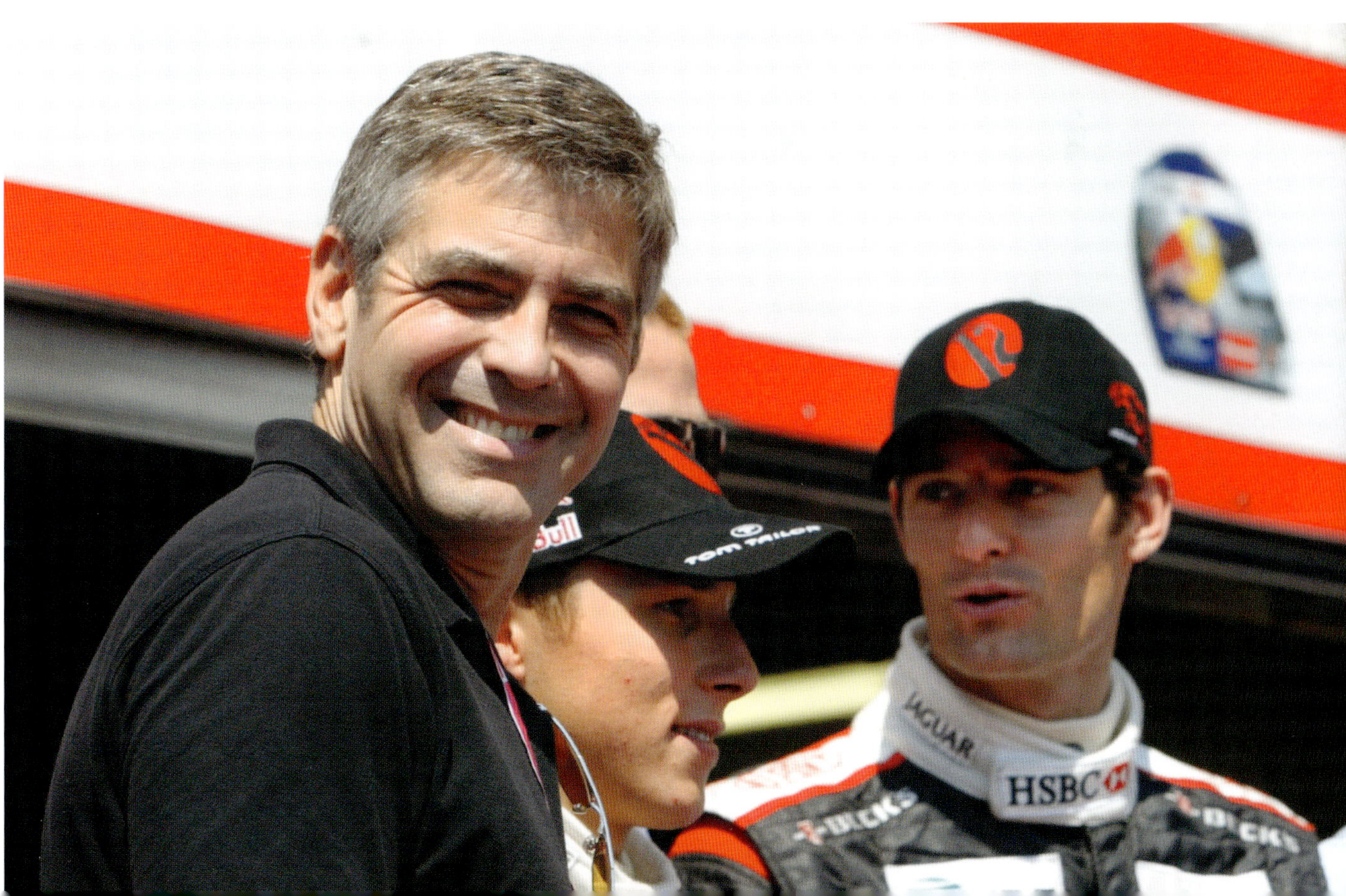

Monaco GP, 2004. George Clooney promotes his film *Ocean's Twelve* with the Jaguar team. Photo: Sutton Images

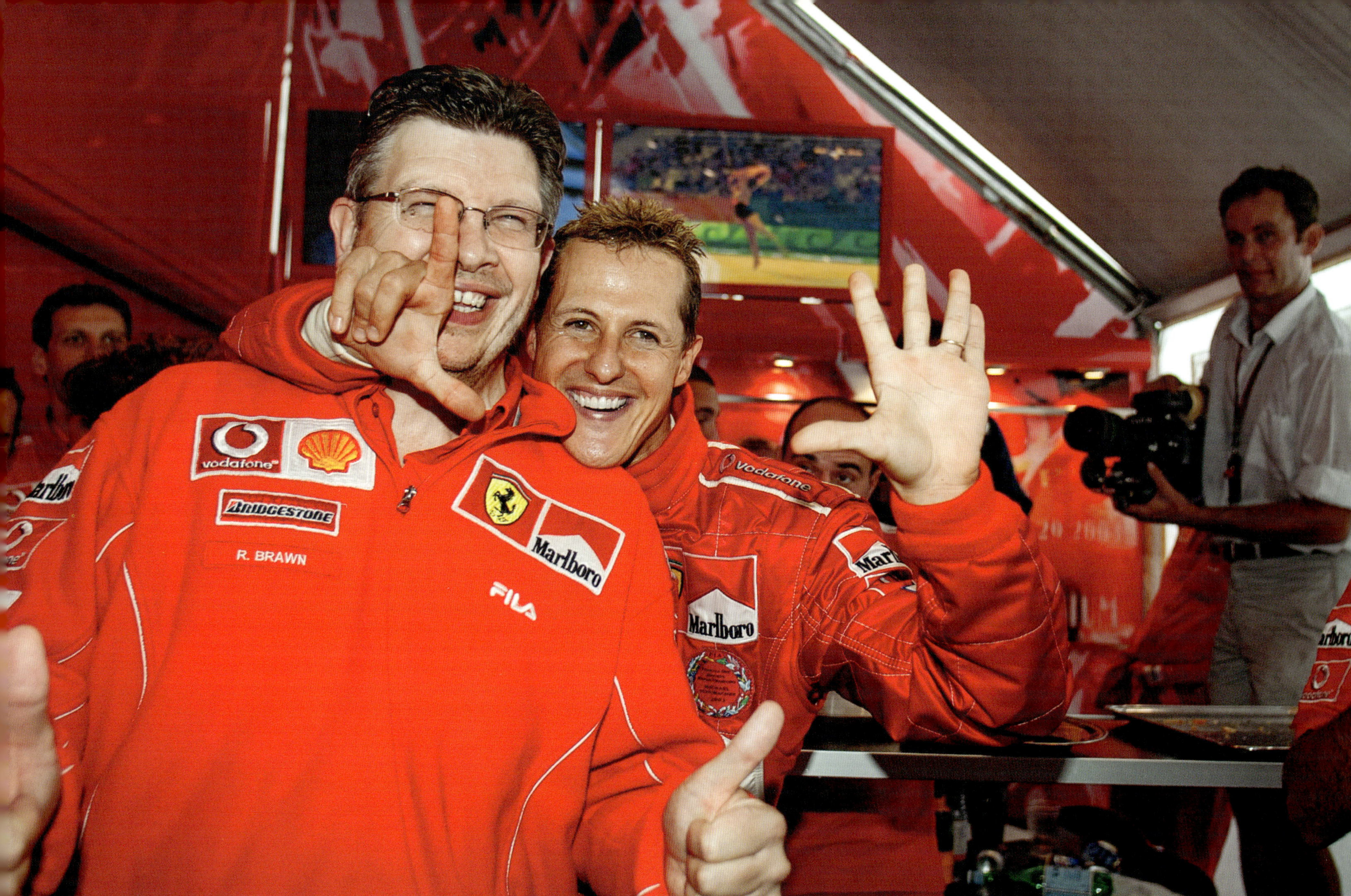

Spa-Francorchamps, Belgian GP, 2004. Michael Schumacher and Ross Brawn celebrate the seven World Championship wins. Photo: Ercole Colombo

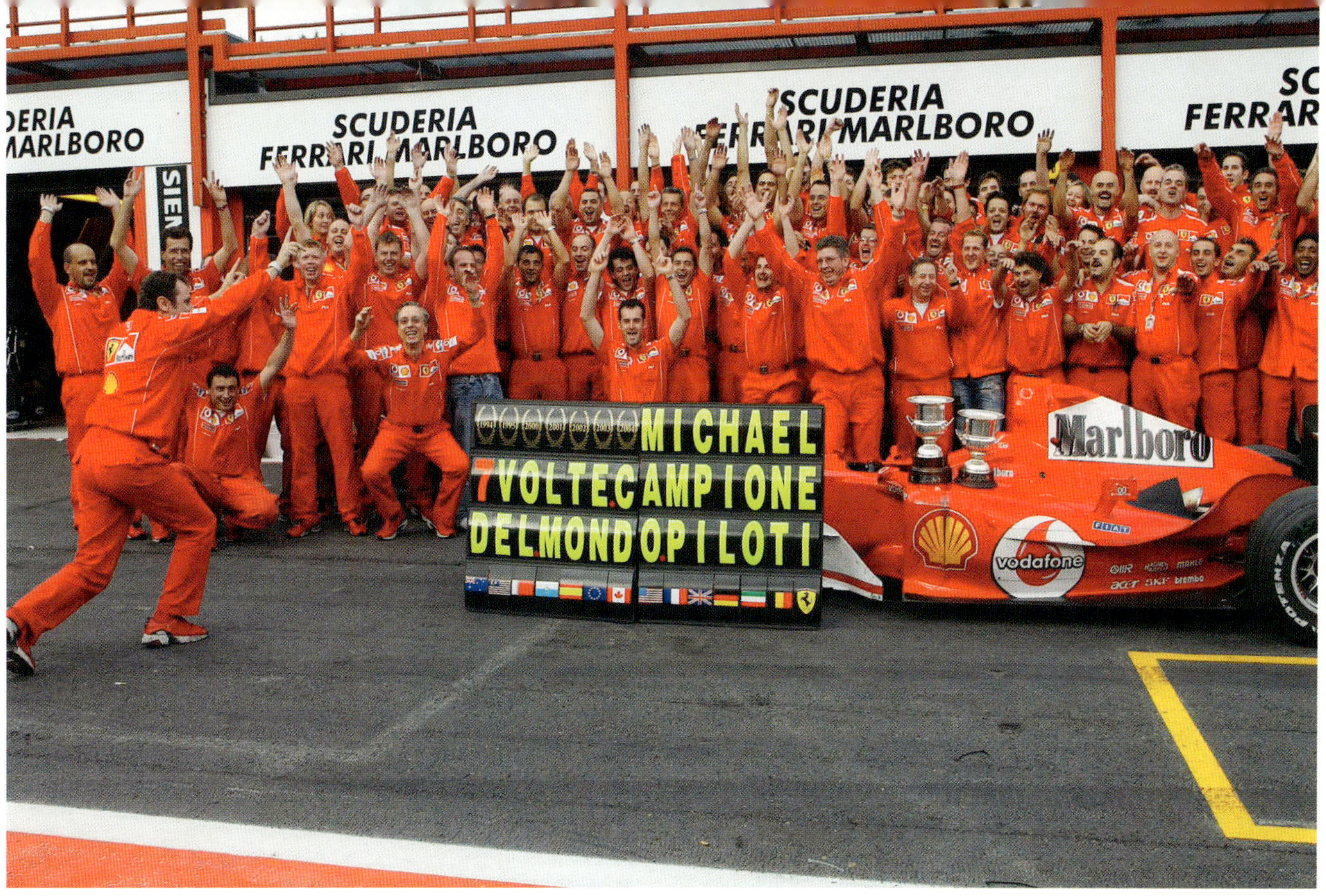

Spa-Francorchamps, Belgian GP, 2004. Ferrari's team celebrate Michael Schumacher, seven times world champion. Photo: Ercole Colombo

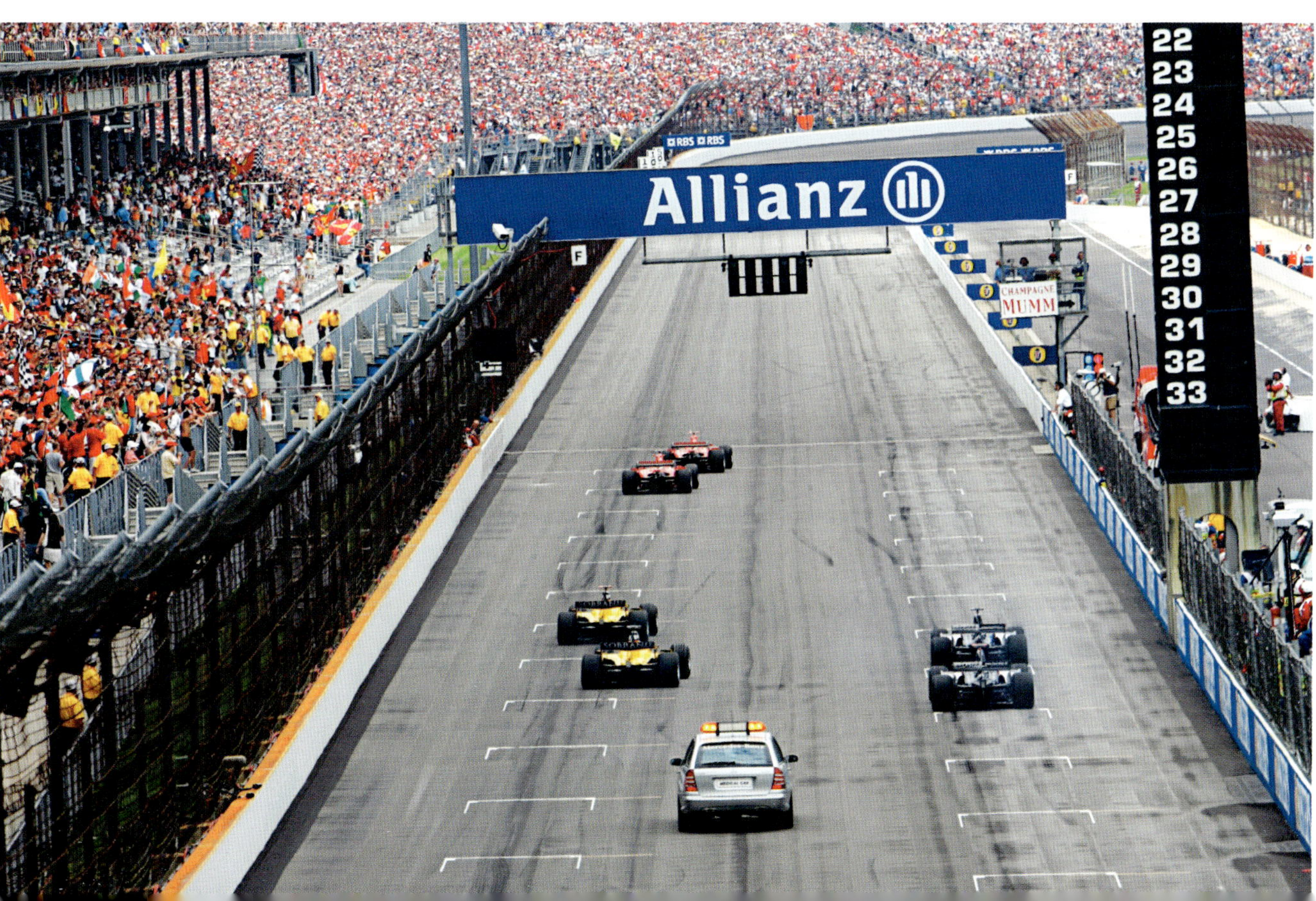

Indianapolis, United States GP, 2005. The start of the race with only six cars. Photo: Steve Swope

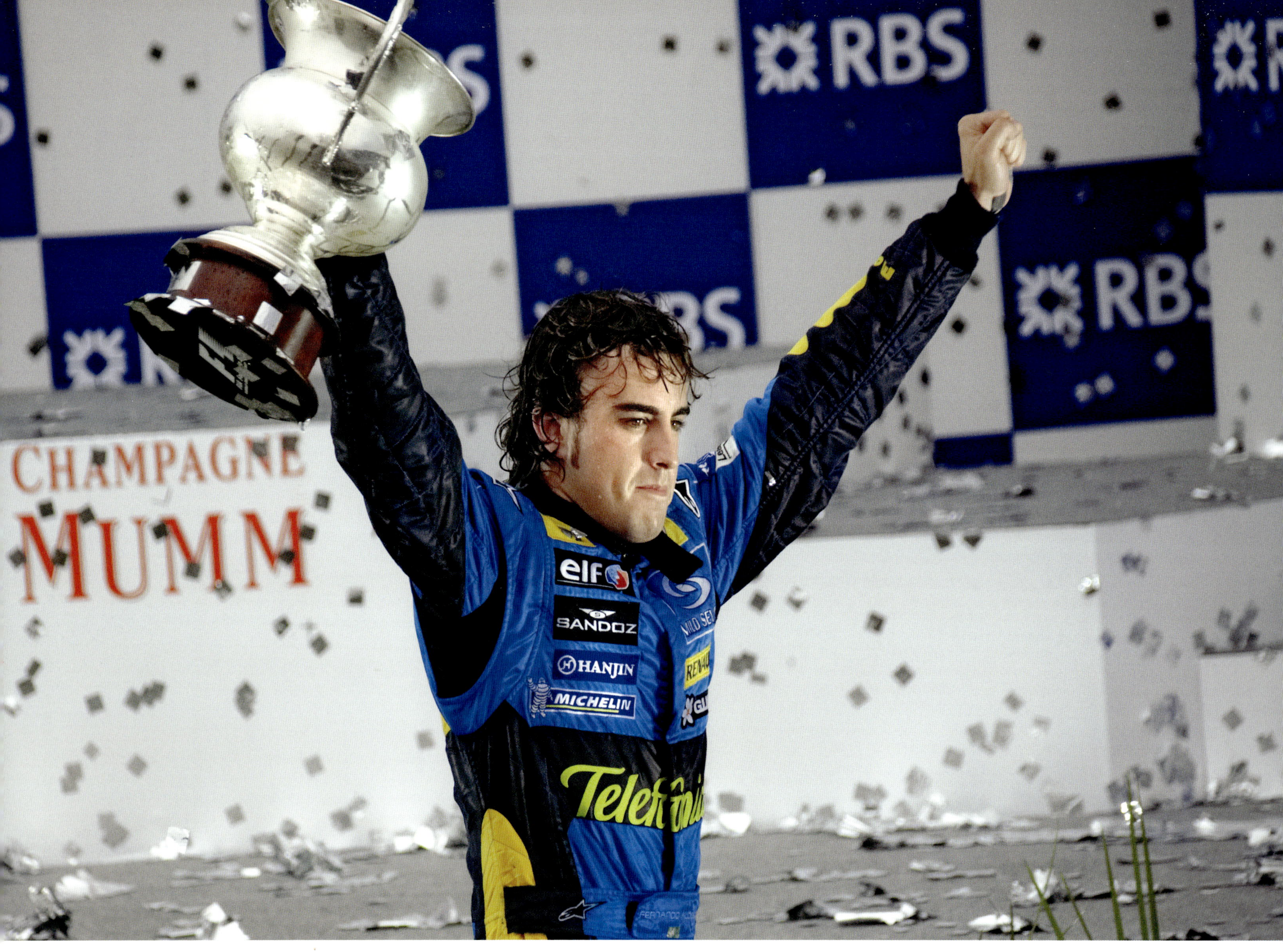

Interlagos, Brazilian GP, 2005. Fernando Alonso celebrates clinching his first World Championship title on the podium. Photo: Rainer Schlegelmilch

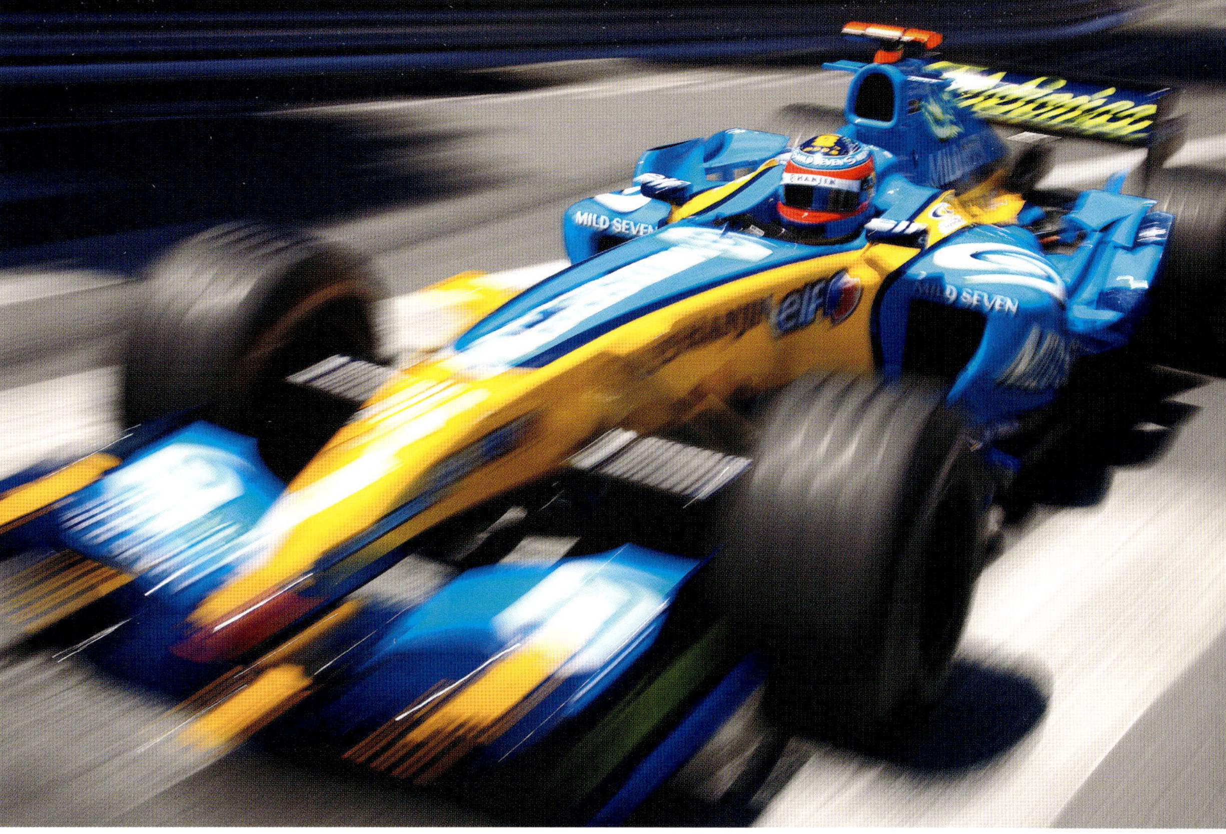

Monaco GP, 2005. Fernando Alonso (Renault R25) gets oversteer on the exit of Mirabeau. Photo: Rainer Schlegelmilch

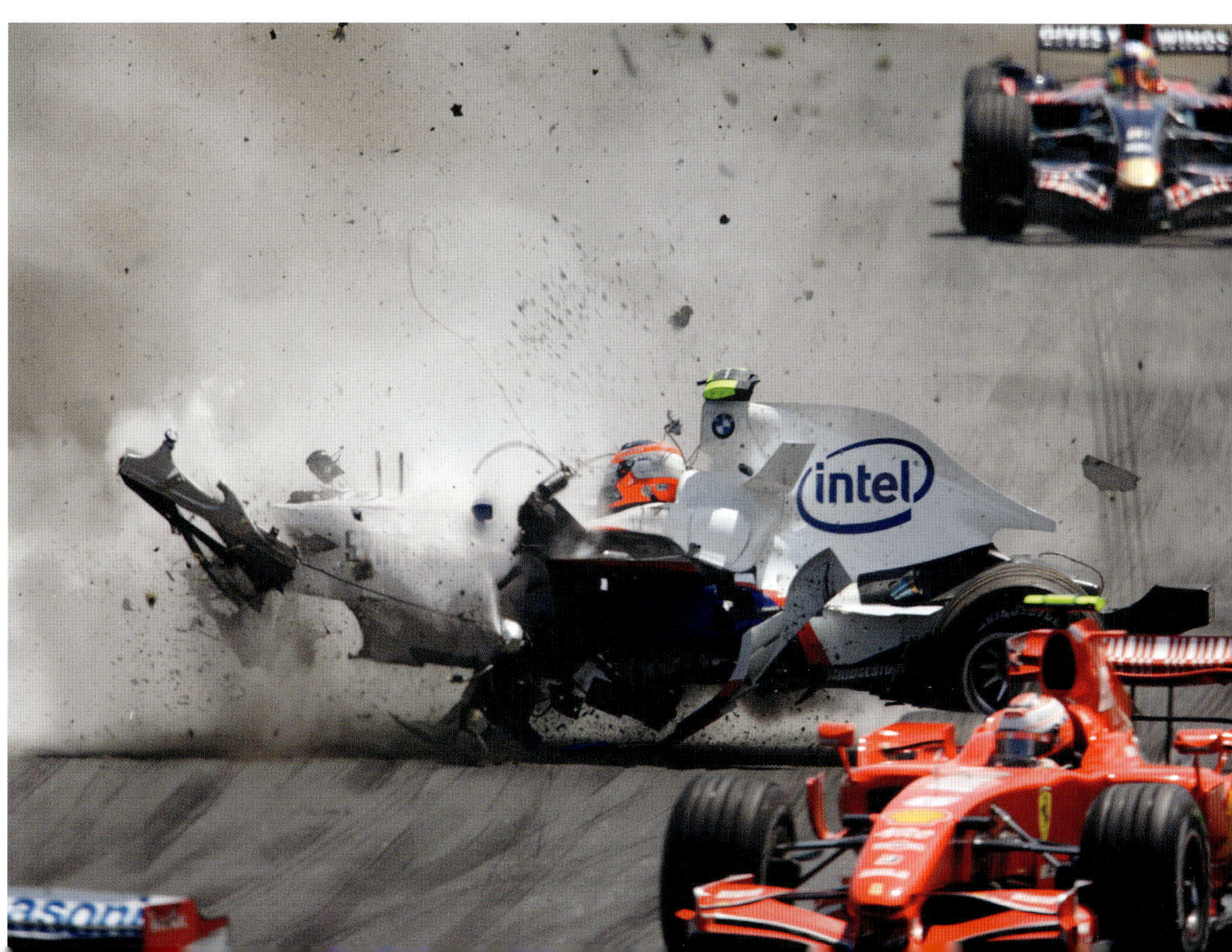

Montreal, Canadian GP, 2007. Robert Kubica (BMW Sauber F1 07) crashes heavily into a concrete wall, injuring his foot. Photo: Andrew Ferraro

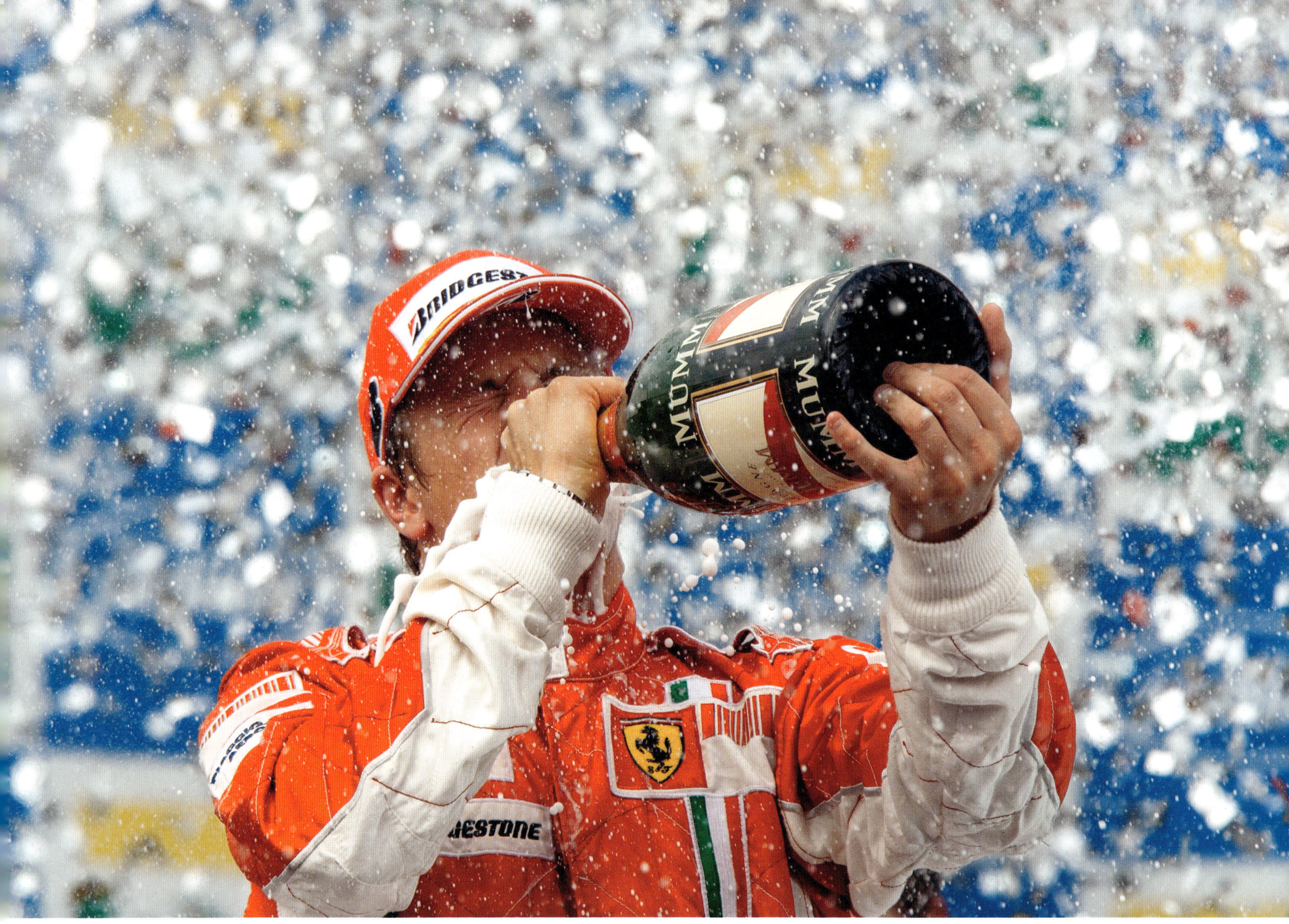

Interlagos, Brazilian GP, 2007. Kimi Räikkönen (Ferrari) becomes world champion. Photo: Ercole Colombo

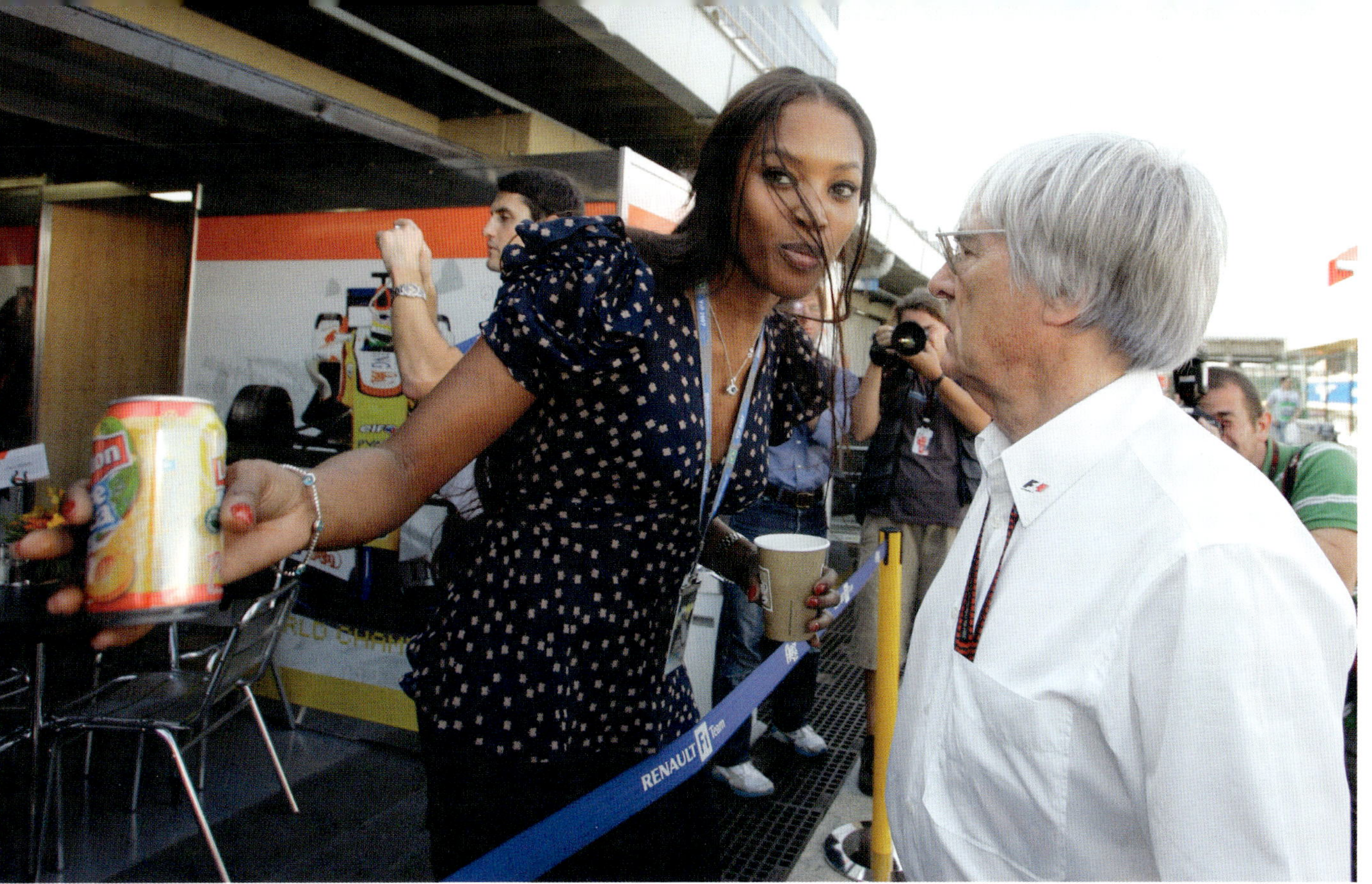

Interlagos, Brazilian GP, 2007. Supermodel Naomi Campbell with Bernie Ecclestone. Photo: Mark Sutton

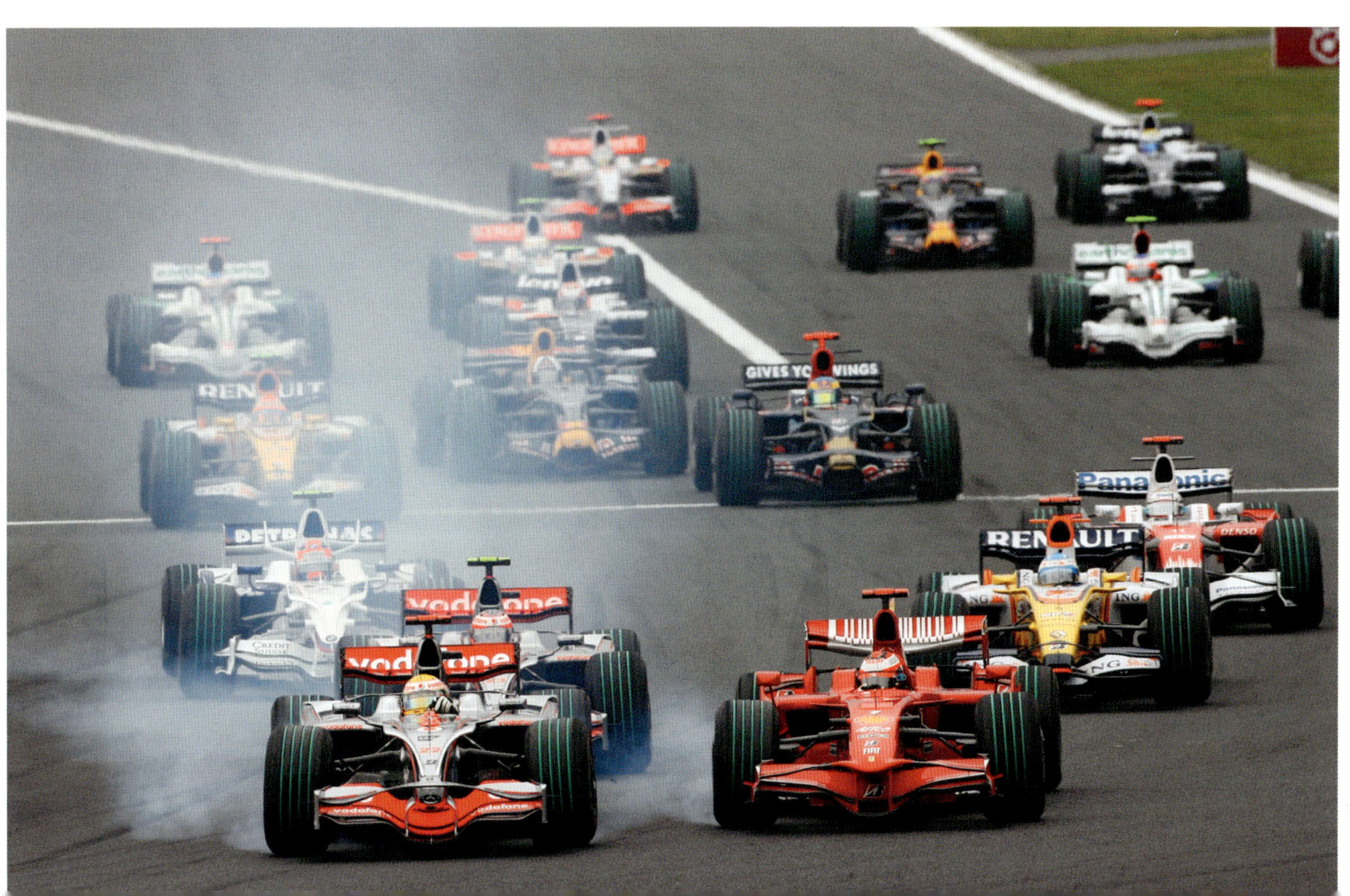

Suzuka, Japanese GP, 2008. Lewis Hamilton (McLaren MP4-23 Mercedes) locks up heavily into the first corner and forces himself and Kimi Räikkönen (Ferrari F2008) wide at the start. Photo: James Moy

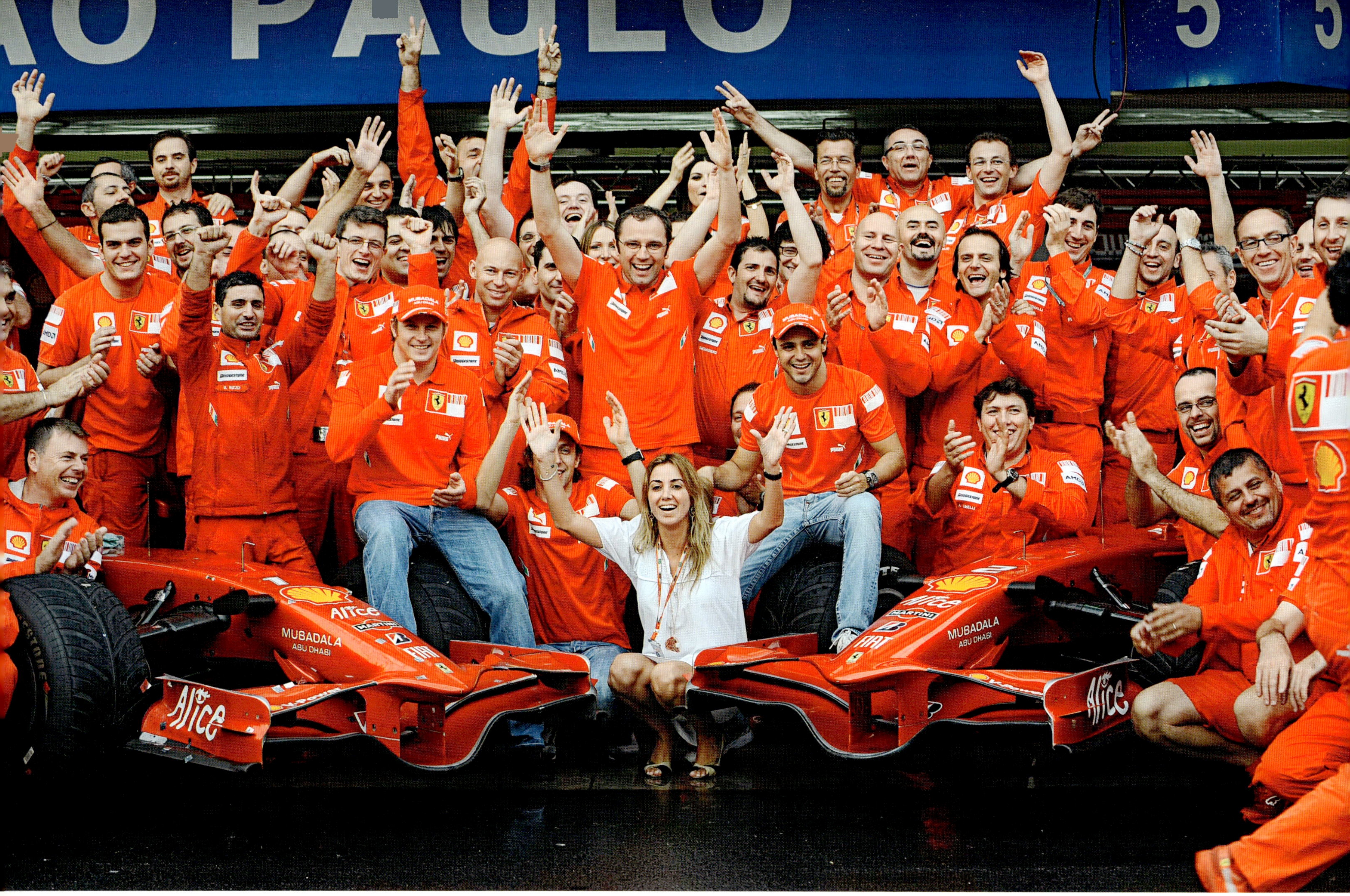

Interlagos, Brazilian GP, 2008. Scuderia Ferrari celebrates the World Constructor's Champioship victory. Photo: Ercole Colombo

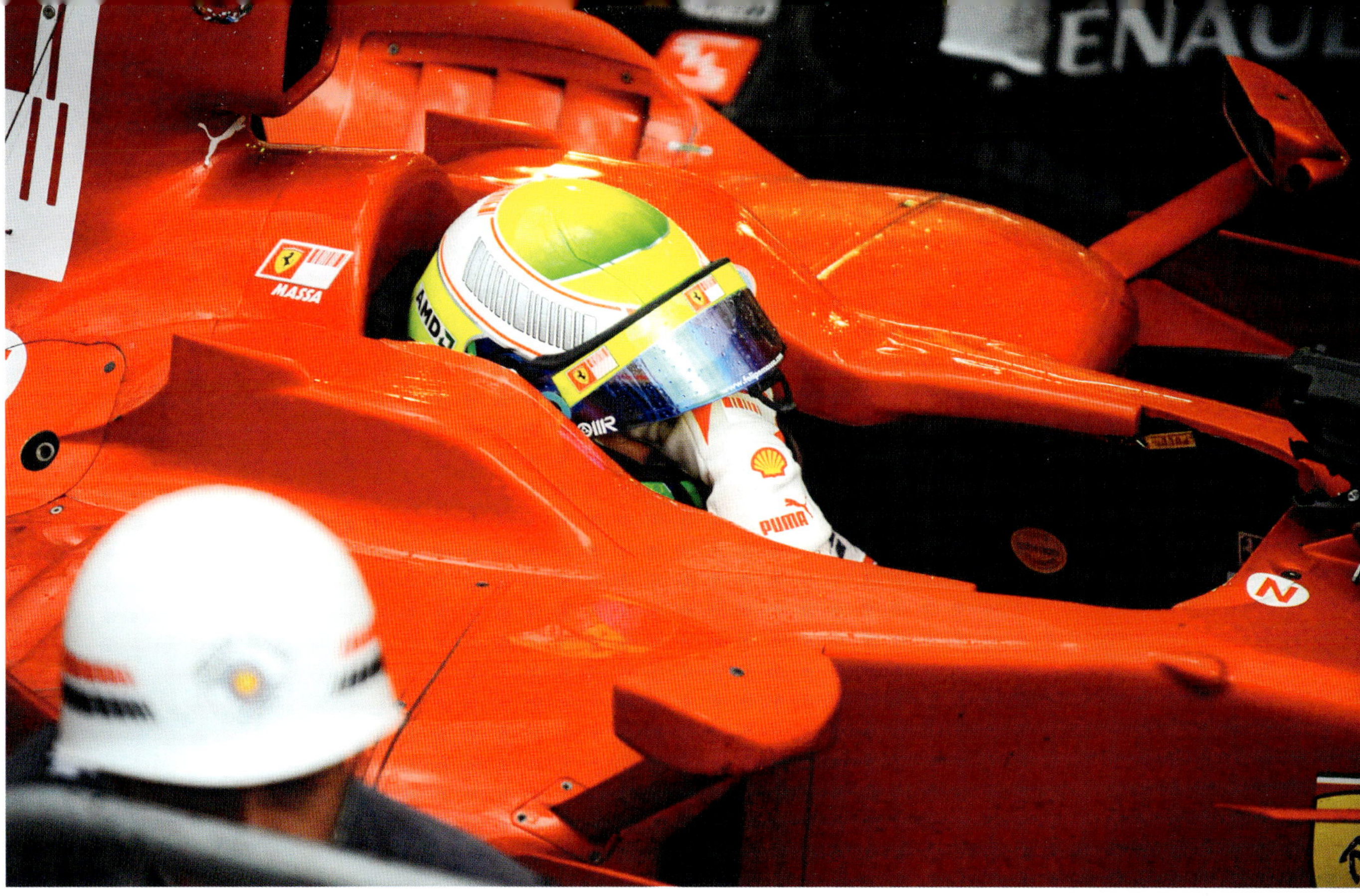

Interlagos, Brazilian GP, 2008.
Felipe Massa crying. He won
the race but lost the title by
one point. Lewis Hamilton is
the new champion. Photo:
Ercole Colombo

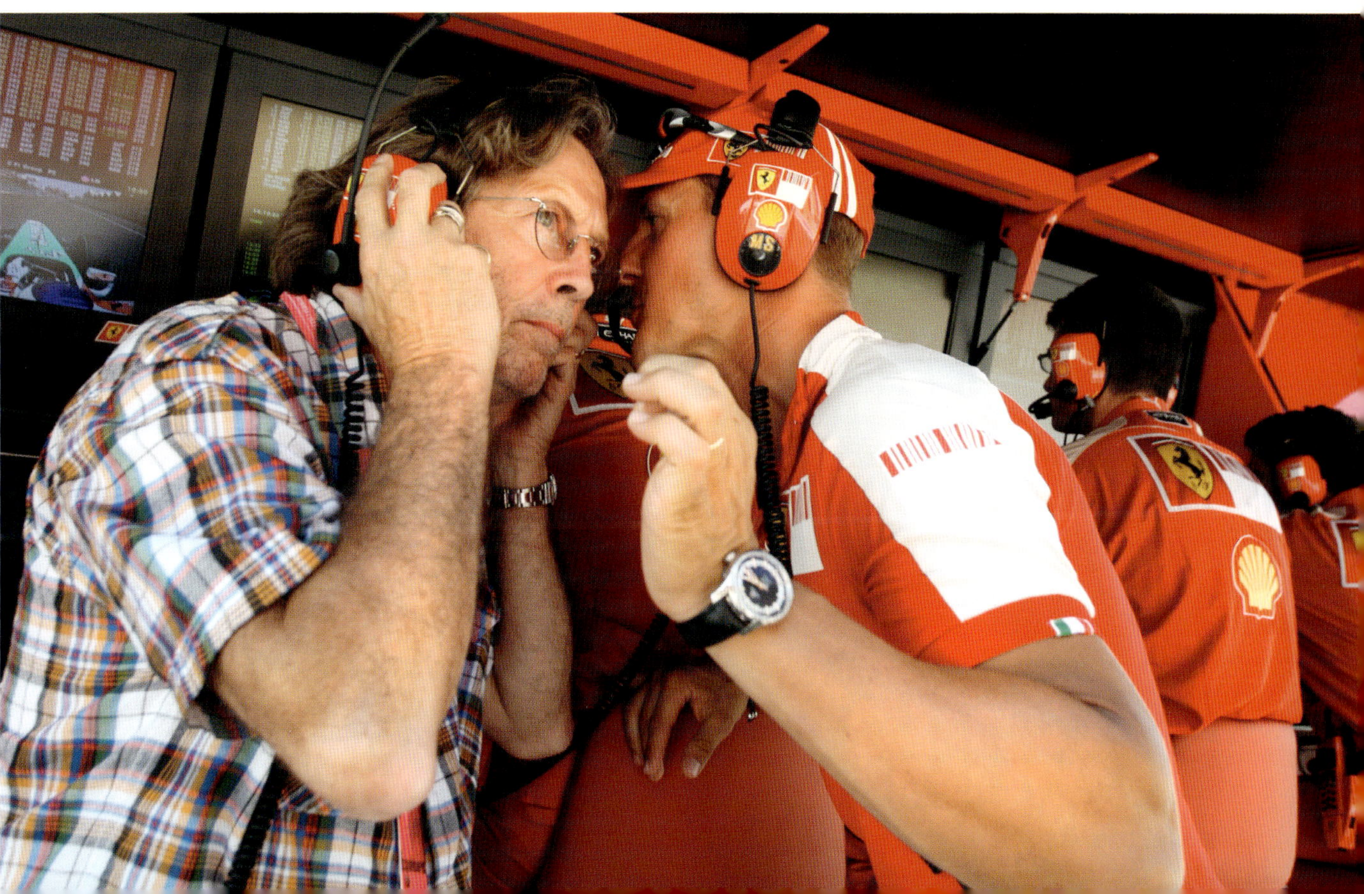

Valencia, European GP, 2009.
Rock legend Eric Clapton with
Michael Schumacher. Photo:
Mark Sutton

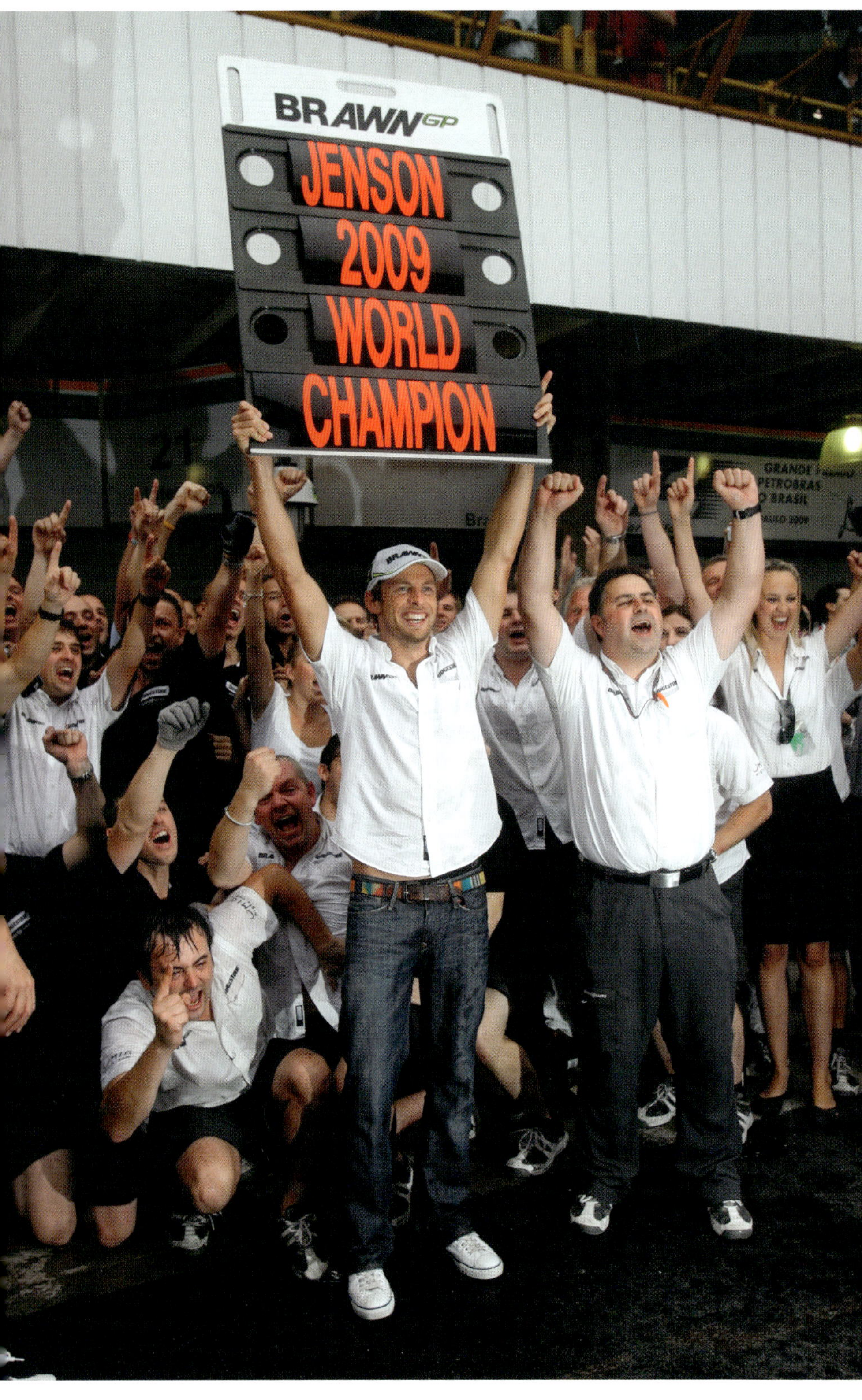

Interlagos, Brazilian GP, 2009.
Jenson Button celebrates his Drivers'
World Championship title. Photo:
Rainer Schlegelmilch

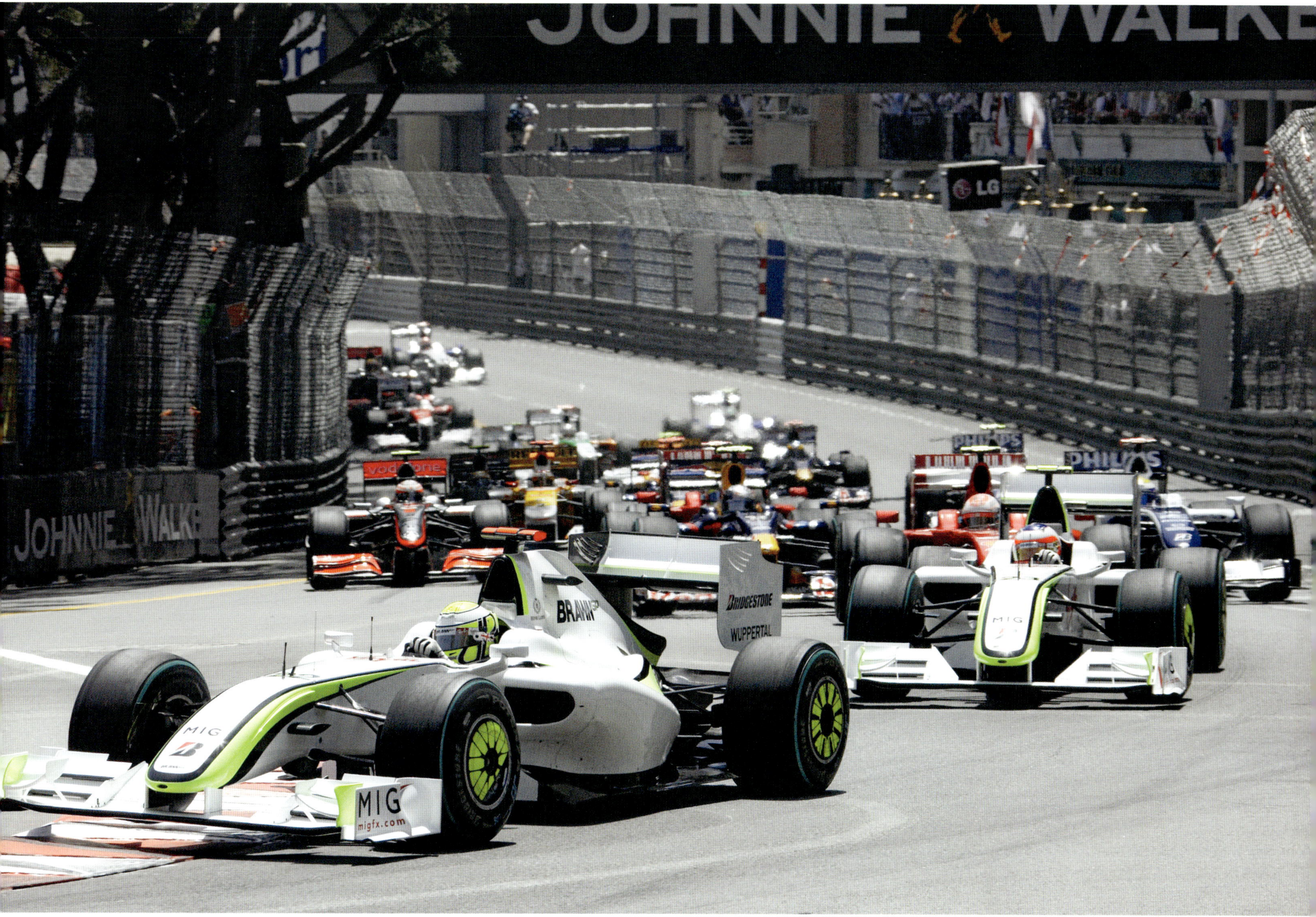

Monaco GP, 2009. Jenson Button (Brawn BGP 001 Mercedes) leads Rubens Barrichello and Kimi Räikkönen (Ferrari F60). Photo: Rainer Schlegelmilch

2010–2019
The Blond King and the Black King

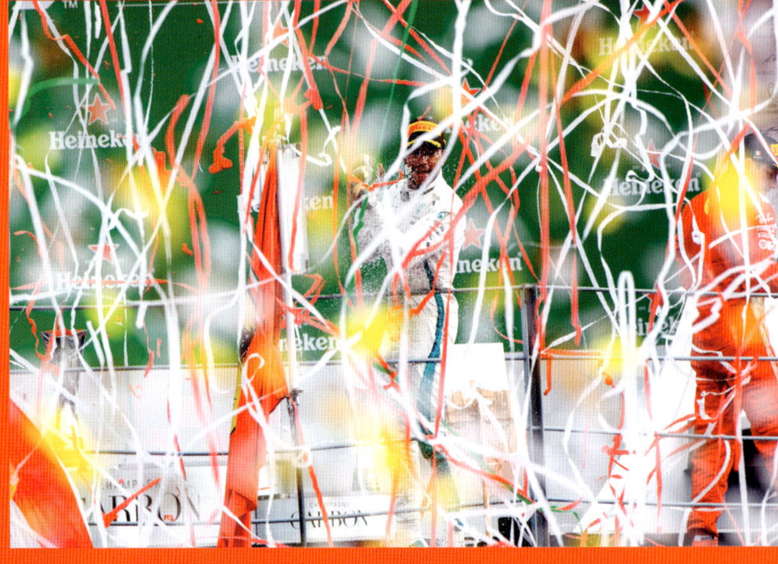

A couple and a third wheel. The hall of fame for the decade 2010–2019 reads as an anomaly: it is far too simple. Four times in a row it bears the name of Sebastian Vettel, five that of Lewis Hamilton's. Only one exception: Nico Rosberg, winner of the title in 2016. If you browse the list of the winning teams, the issue becomes increasingly peculiar: four victories for Red Bull with Renault engines, six for Mercedes. Thus, two double monologues, two distinct phases. The first, from 2010 to 2013, was marked by the extraordinary aerodynamic efficiency of the single-seaters created by Adrian Newey for the Austrian team, combined with Vettel's talent. Born in Happenheim, in Germany, on July 3, 1987, he grew up racing karts. He made his debut in F1 in 2007, in the United States GP, with Sauber, when he substituted Robert Kubica, victim of a horrendous accident in Canada. Vettel was soon hired by the Toro Rosso team (formerly Minardi), with whom he won the Italian GP at Monza in 2008 under a veritable deluge. He transferred to Red Bull in 2009 and the following year, at the age of 23, he became the youngest world champion in F1 history. The final, decisive act was played out in Abu Dhabi. And the result of the race was heavily influenced by a tremendous mess caused by Ferrari's strategist, which cost Fernando Alonso, finally on the Maranello team, the victory and the title. The rivalry between Vettel and Alonso lasted four long years, with exceedingly severe consequences for the Spaniard, who often found himself competing

in a Ferrari that was inferior to the Red Bull, but still capable of offering an extraordinary performance. The final ranking in 2010 showed Vettel with 256 points against Alonso's 252, Mark Webber's 242 (the other Red Bull driver), and Hamilton's 240 (McLaren), all competing for the title until the last race. In 2011, Vettel's race for the world title was less complicated, very tense his sprint for the title in 2012. Curtain call in Brazil, with the German surviving a crash at the beginning of the race miraculously unscathed. Sebastian came in sixth, Alonso second, after Button. Thus once again losing the competition and the crown by a handful of points. Then came 2013 and Vettel's fourth confirmation, with Alonso vice-champion once again, but quite a way behind Sebastian's Red Bull. In the meantime, Hamilton had transferred to Mercedes, along with Nico Rosberg, son of Keke, world champion in 1982. Lewis took the place of Michael Schumacher, who in 2010 had resumed racing with the three-pointed star team and was determined to finally close his career at the end of the 2012 championship with a tremendous scoresheet: seven world titles, 91 victories, 68 pole positions. A terrible chapter opened for Schumacher on December 29, 2013. A skiing accident in Méribel, France, left him with extensive brain damage and led to a very critical recovery, managed with extraordinary care (and reserve) by his family, followed with sadness and regret by millions of baffled fans. A cruel trick of destiny, when Michael had

decided to put an end to his racing days and the risks they entailed. A technical novelty brought about a veritable revolution in 2014, when power units made their first appearance. These extremely sophisticated engines employed a double turbocharger as well as electric power to generate a hybrid propulsion. This was the beginning of Mercedes' supremacy, which continued uninterrupted throughout the ensuing decade. Between 2014 and 2019, the struggle for the world title was fought exclusively between the drivers of this formidable and very well-equipped team that could rely on enormous resources. Hamilton immediately obtained his second title, and achieved the third in 2015, when he beat Rosberg by a long call, though the latter was capable of making the Englishman's life difficult on several occasions. Theirs was a profound rivalry, born many years prior, when they both raced karts, made deeper by their personal backgrounds: Nico's more well-to-do, Lewis's less comfortable. Rosberg used every ounce of energy to achieve the title in 2016, when Hamilton made a few too many errors, and likely underestimated his teammate and rival, who thus obtained a well-deserved albeit arduous victory. It was not by chance that Nico announced his retirement from the competition right after winning the World Championship. In 2017, Mercedes chose a less difficult teammate for Hamilton: the Finn Valtteri Bottas. Lewis achieved another three consecutive victories, closing the decade with a total of six world titles. His new

rival was Vettel, hired by the Ferrari team in 2015. Their antagonism put a strain above all on the German champion, who committed some mistakes in moments that were most favorable to Ferrari, especially during the 2018 championship, when the red car seemed to be offering a higher performance than the Mercedes. After leaving the Ferrari team in 2014, Alonso transferred to McLaren, which was experiencing a serious technical decline. Sergio Marchionne took Luca di Montezemolo's place as Ferrari President on October 13, 2014, a position he held until his death on July 25, 2018. His role at the helm of Ferrari was taken up by John Elkann. At the beginning of the decade, F1 lost Robert Kubica, an exquisitely talented Polish driver and winner of the 2008 Canadian GP, victim of a very serious accident during a rally in Liguria that led to an unending series of operations. In 2019, Kubica managed to return to F1 with the Williams team, despite a serious impairment to his right arm. On July 17, 2015 Jules Bianchi, a promising young French pilot trained by Ferrari, died. The previous year, during the Japanese GP, he had been the victim of a tragic accident when his Marussia crashed into a tractor in one of the escape roads. Bianchi had been the mentor and tutor of a very talented young man from Monaco, Charles Leclerc, who debuted in F1 in 2018 with Sauber. Three years earlier, another very young and particularly talented driver had made his debut with Toro Rosso, the Dutchman Max Verstappen.

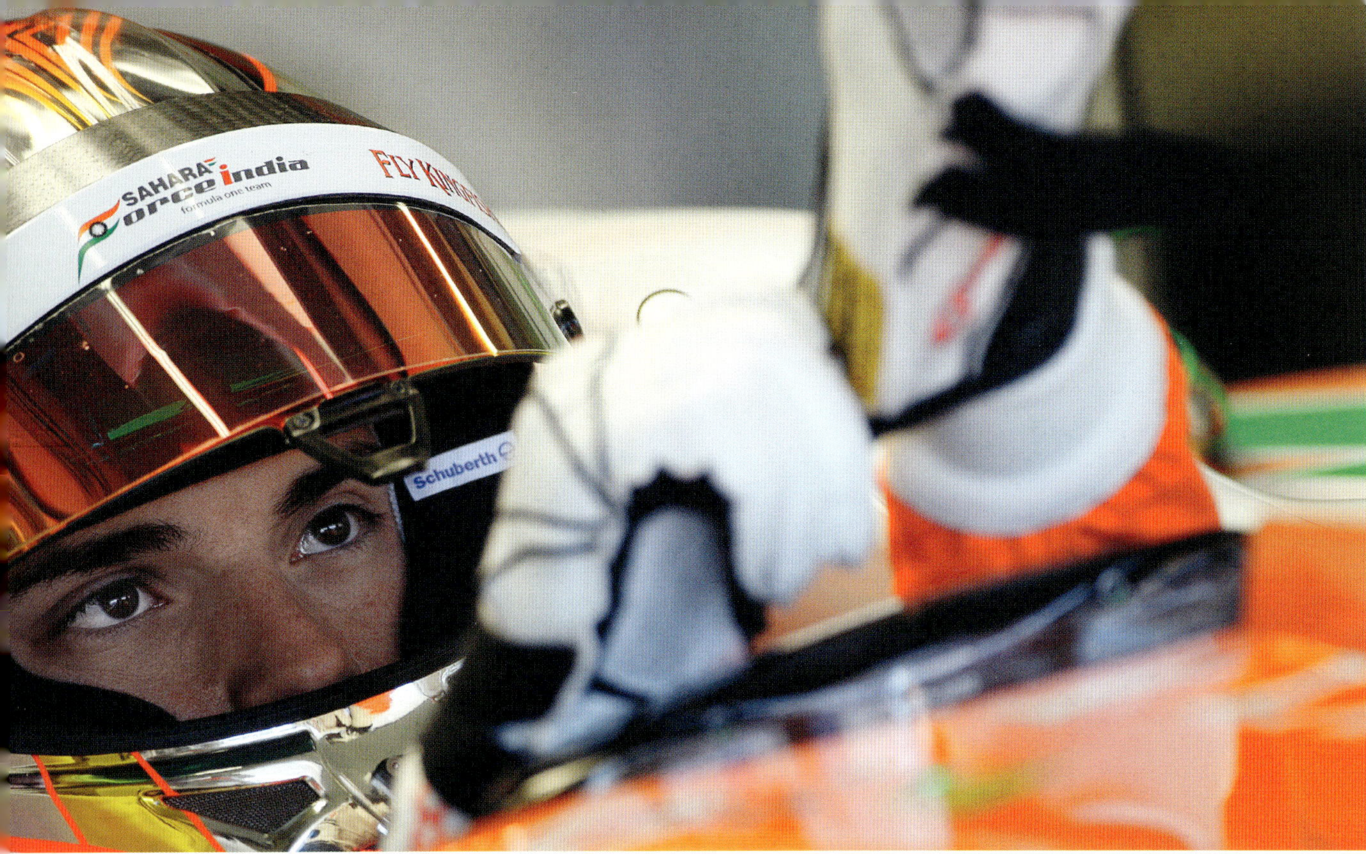

Jerez, Spain Test, 2012. Jules Bianchi (Force India F1 Team VJM05). Photo: Emily Davenport

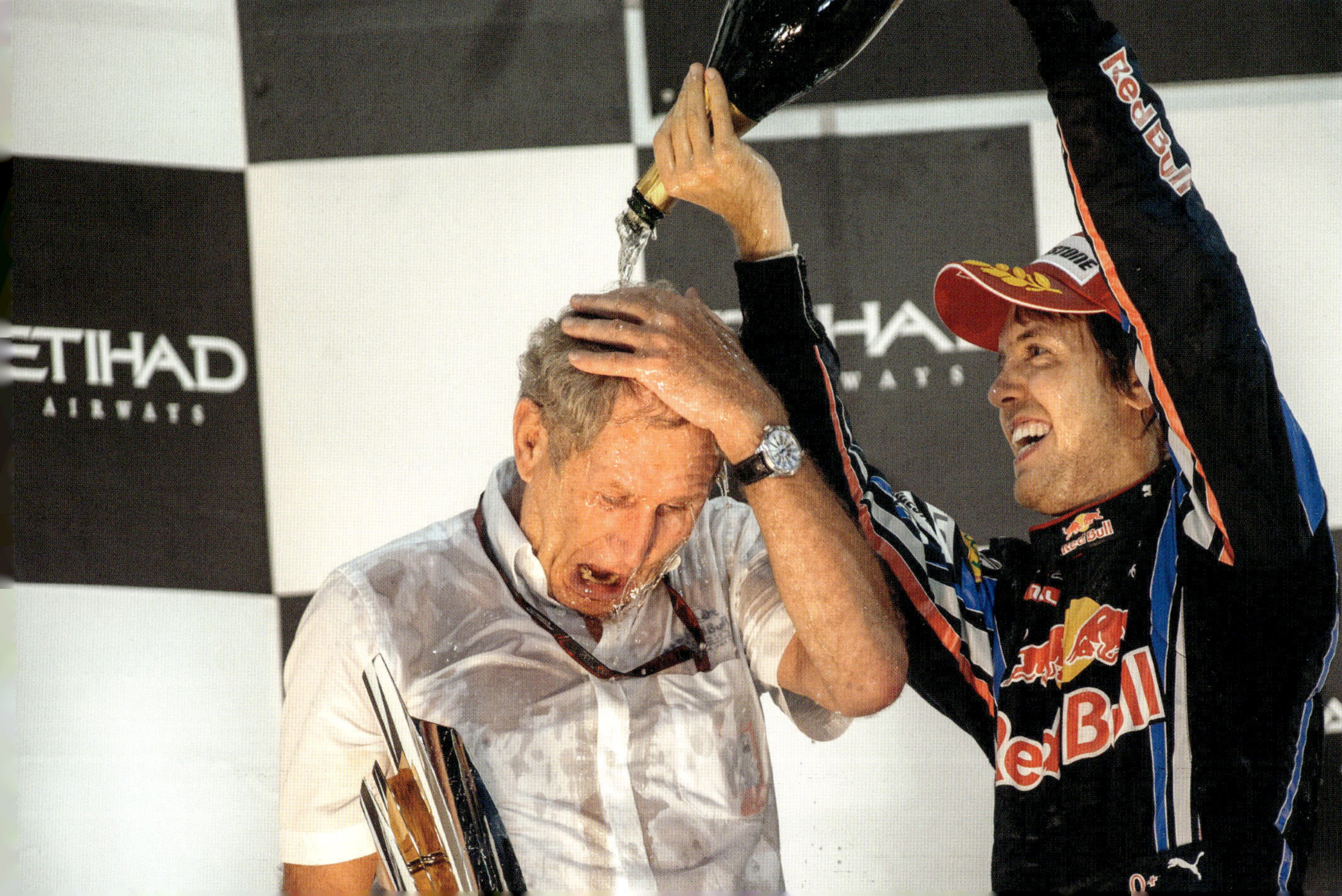

Abu Dhabi GP, 2010. Helmut Marko and Sebastian Vettel (Red Bull) on the podium after clinching the Drivers' World Championship. Photo: Ercole Colombo

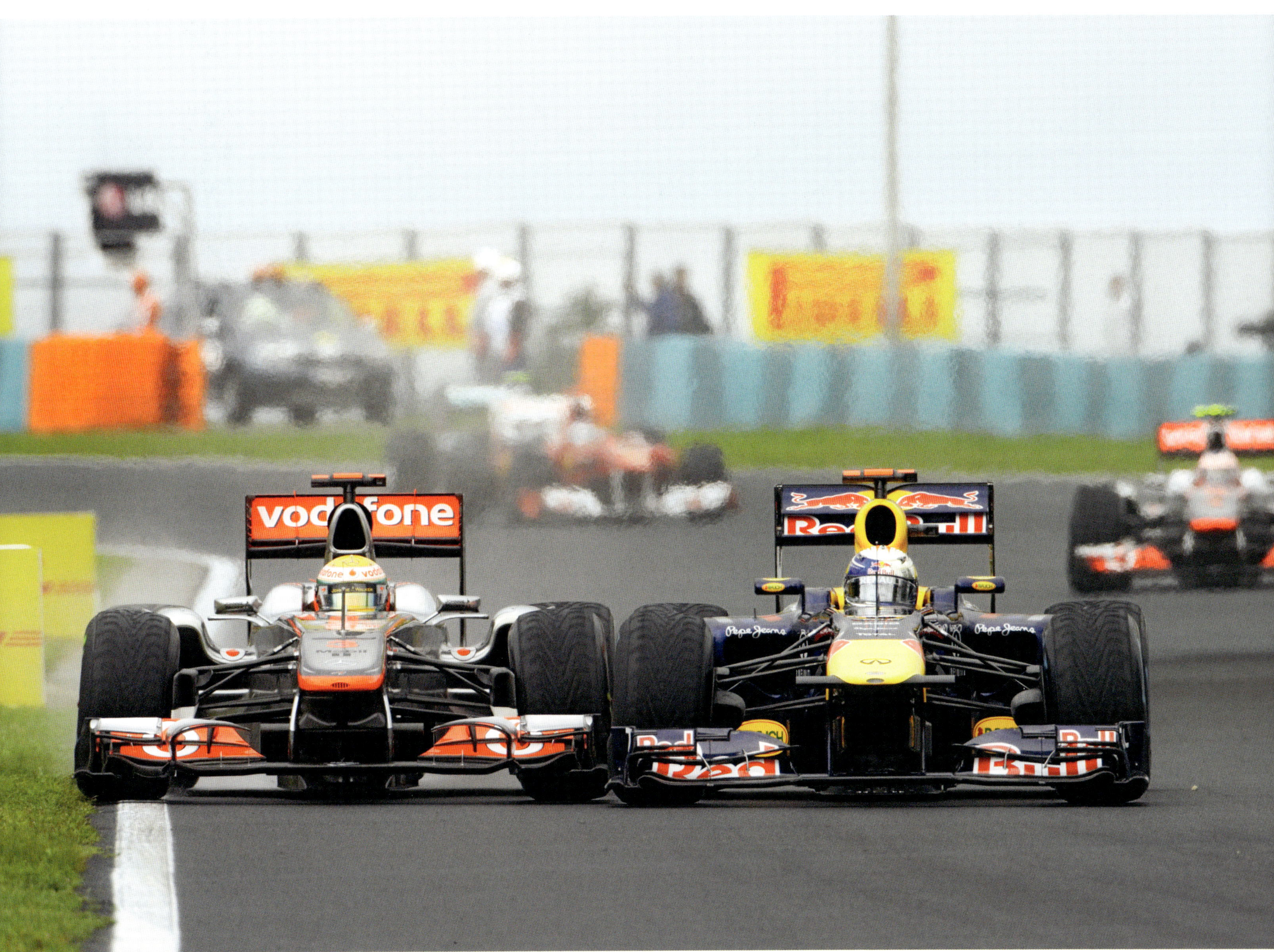

Budapest, Hungarian GP, 2011. Sebastian Vettel (Red Bull RB7 Renault) battles hard with Lewis Hamilton (McLaren MP4-26 Mercedes). Photo: Rainer Schlegelmilch

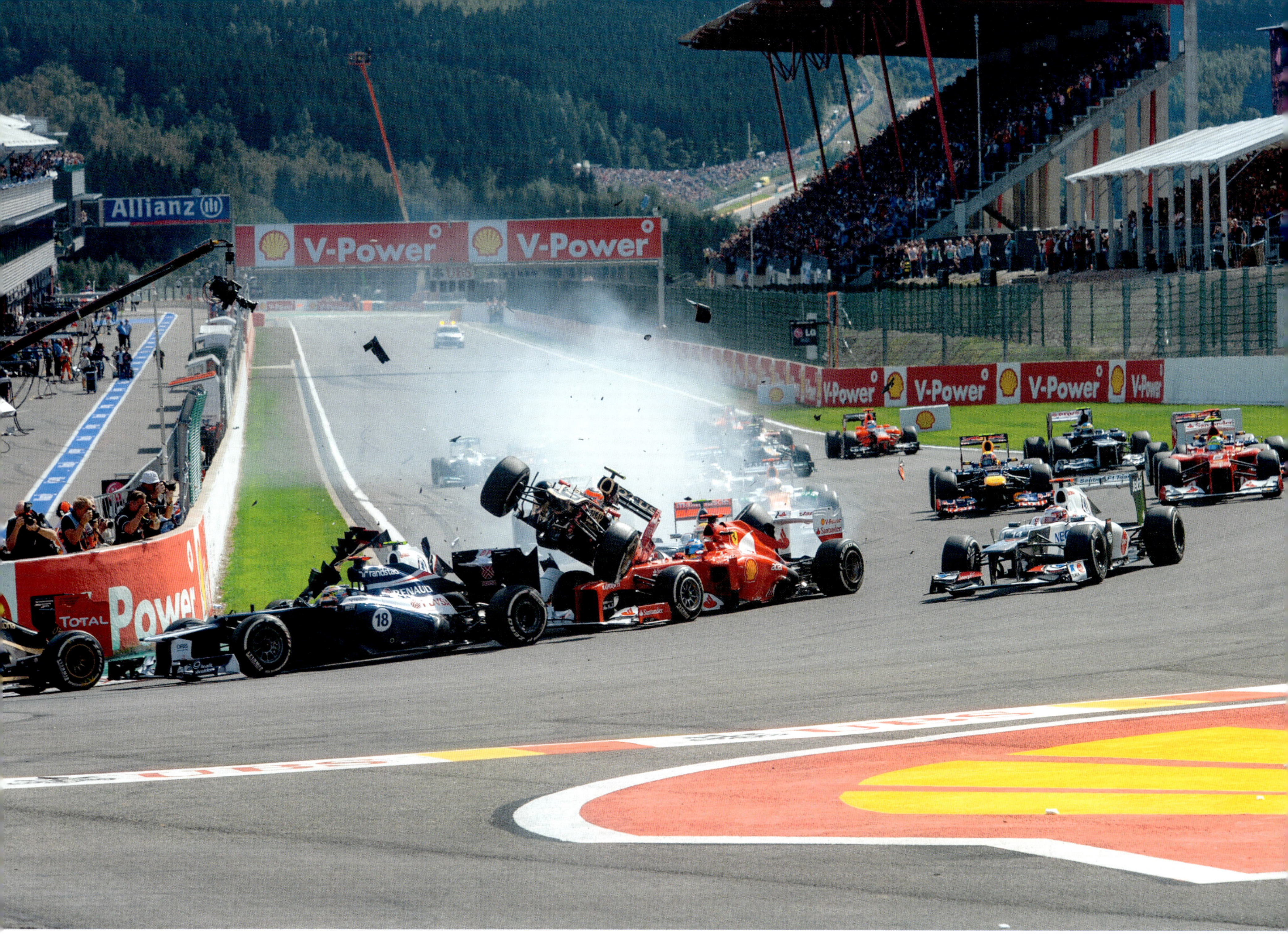

Spa-Francorchamps, Belgian GP, 2012. Romain Grosjean (Lotus) is launched over the top of Fernando Alonso (Ferrari). Photo: Alberto Crippa

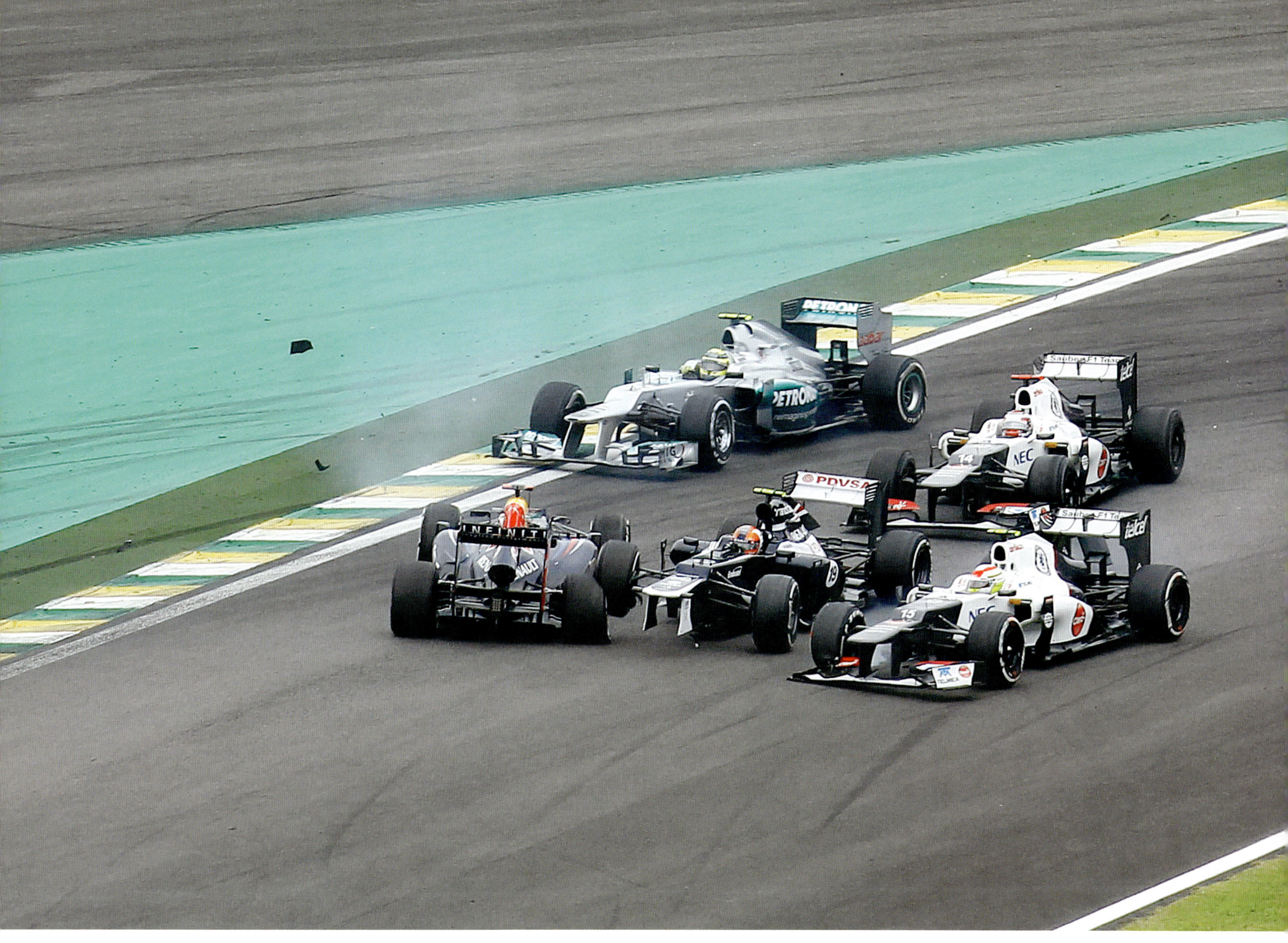

Interlagos, Brazilian GP, 2012. The crash in the opening corner involving Bruno Senna (Williams FW34 Renault), Sebastian Vettel (Red Bull RB8 Renault), and Sergio Perez (Sauber C31 Ferrari). Photo: Steven Tee

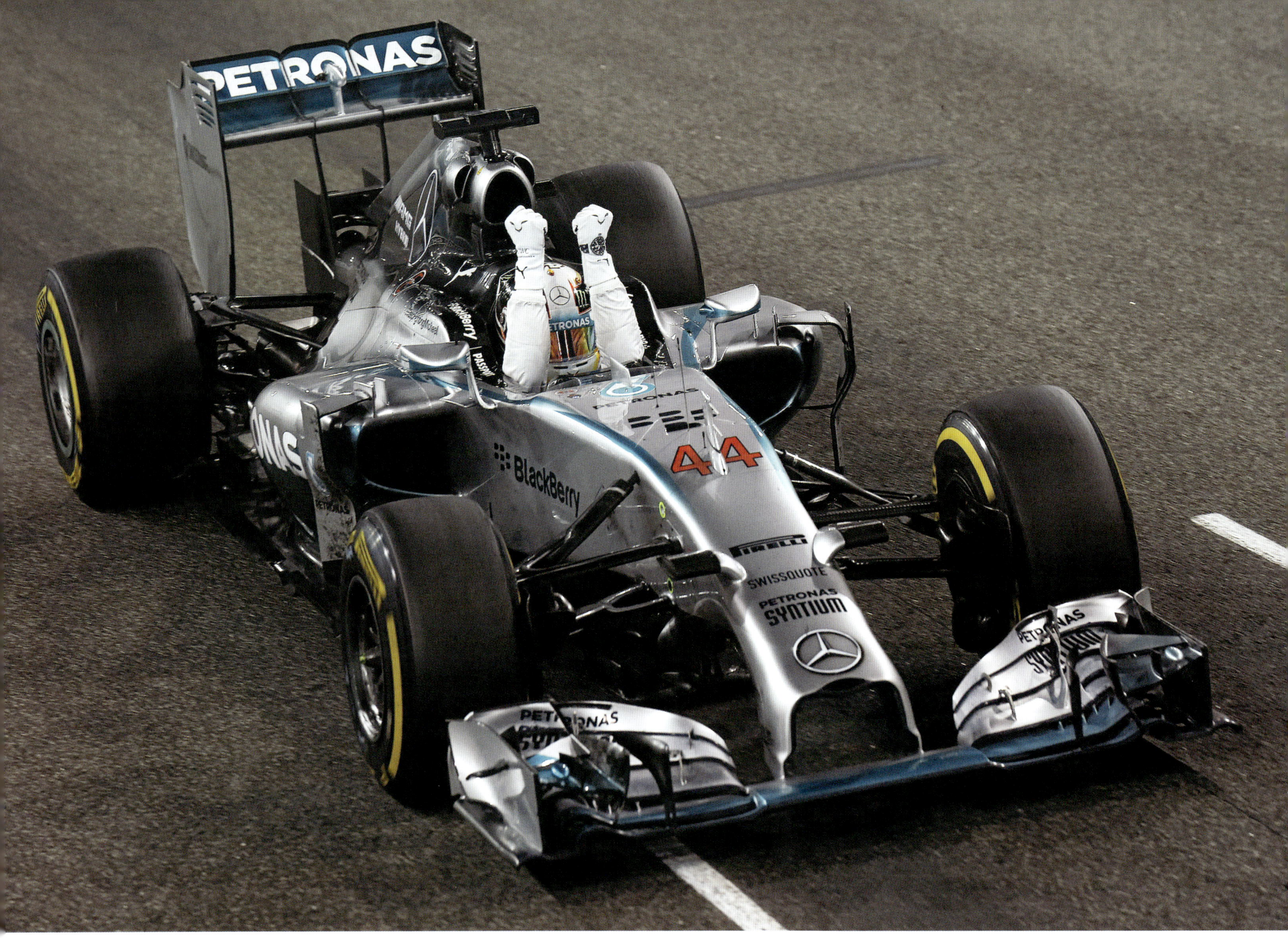

Abu Dhabi GP, 2014. Lewis Hamilton (Mercedes F1 W05) celebrates becoming world champion for the second time. Photo: Steven Tee

Abu Dhabi GP, 2016. Nico
Rosberg (Mercedes F1 W07)
celebrates as he jumps from
his car after winning the
World Championship. Photo:
Glenn Dunbar

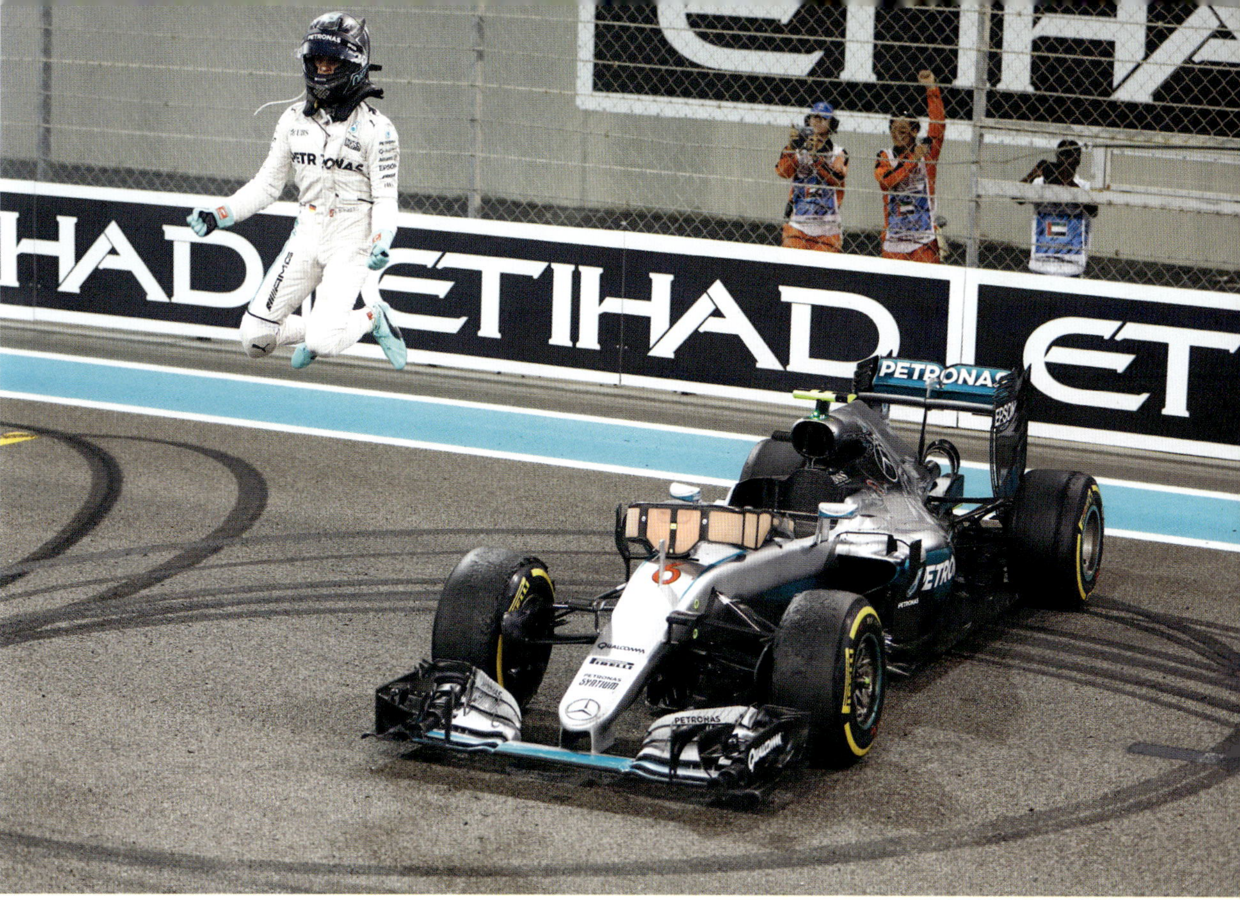

Barcelona, Spanish GP, 2016.
Lewis Hamilton and Nico
Rosberg (Mercedes F1 W07)
collide while battling for the
lead on the opening lap of the
race. Photo: Zak Mauger

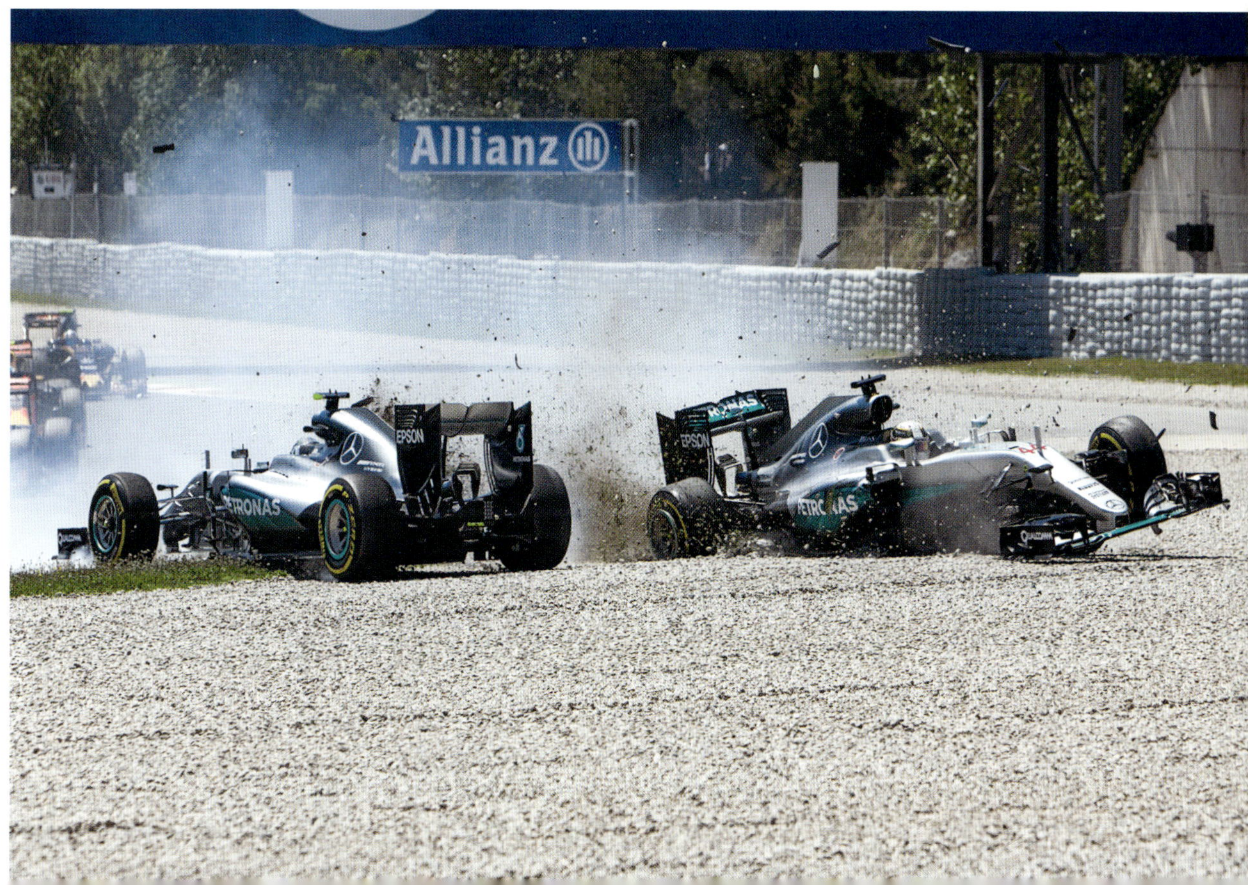

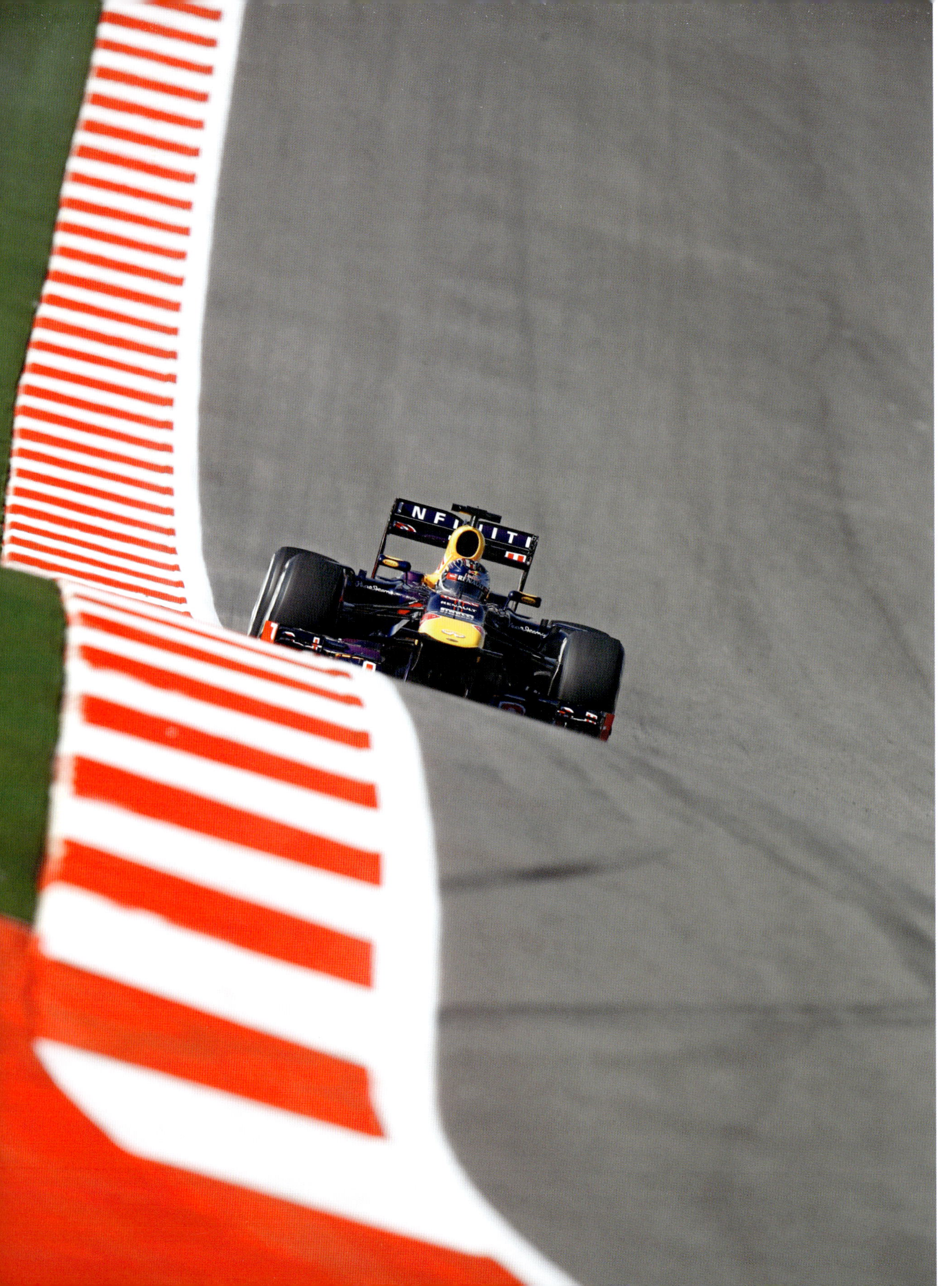

Austin, United States GP, 2013.
Sebastian Vettel (Red Bull
RB9 Renault) climbs the hill
towards the first corner. Photo:
Steven Tee

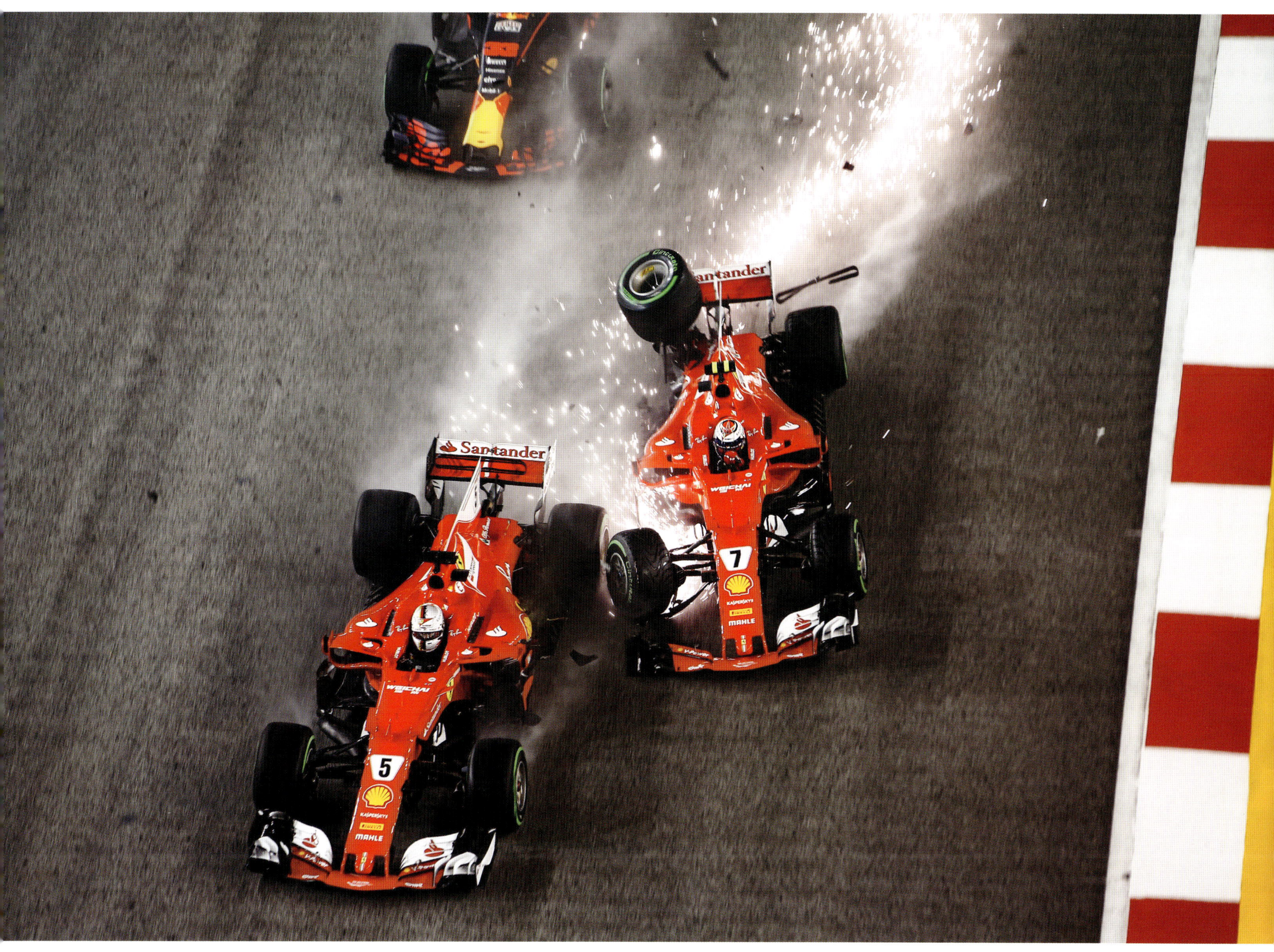

Singapore GP, 2017. Sebastian Vettel (Ferrari SF70H), Max Verstappen (Red Bull RB13), and Kimi Räikkönen (Ferrari) crash out at the start of the race. Photo: Andrew Hone

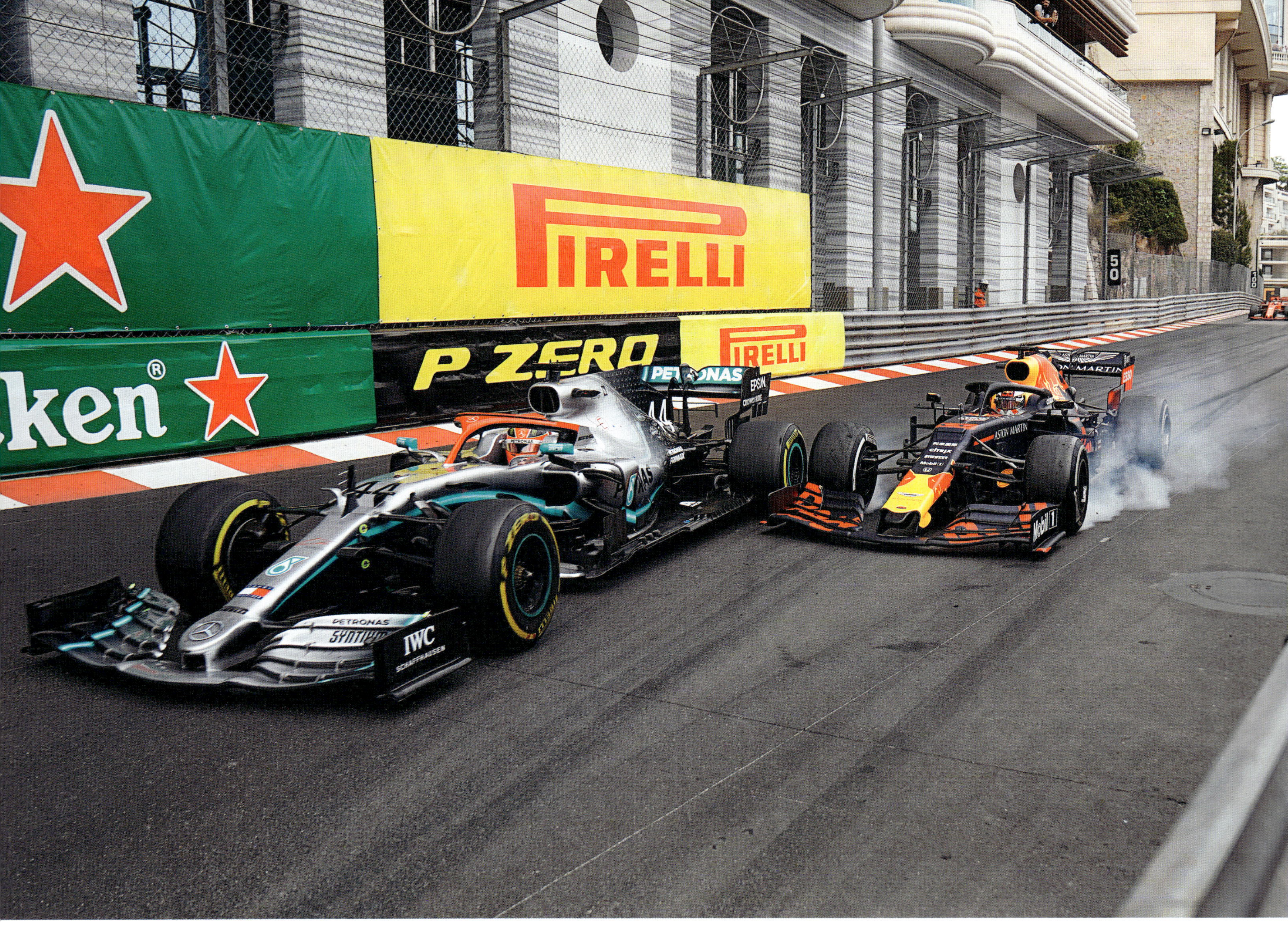

Monaco GP, 2019. Max Verstappen (Red Bull Honda) makes contact with leader Lewis Hamilton (Mercedes AMG F1 W10) into the Nouvelle Chicane, in the closing stages of the race. Photo: Hasan Bratic

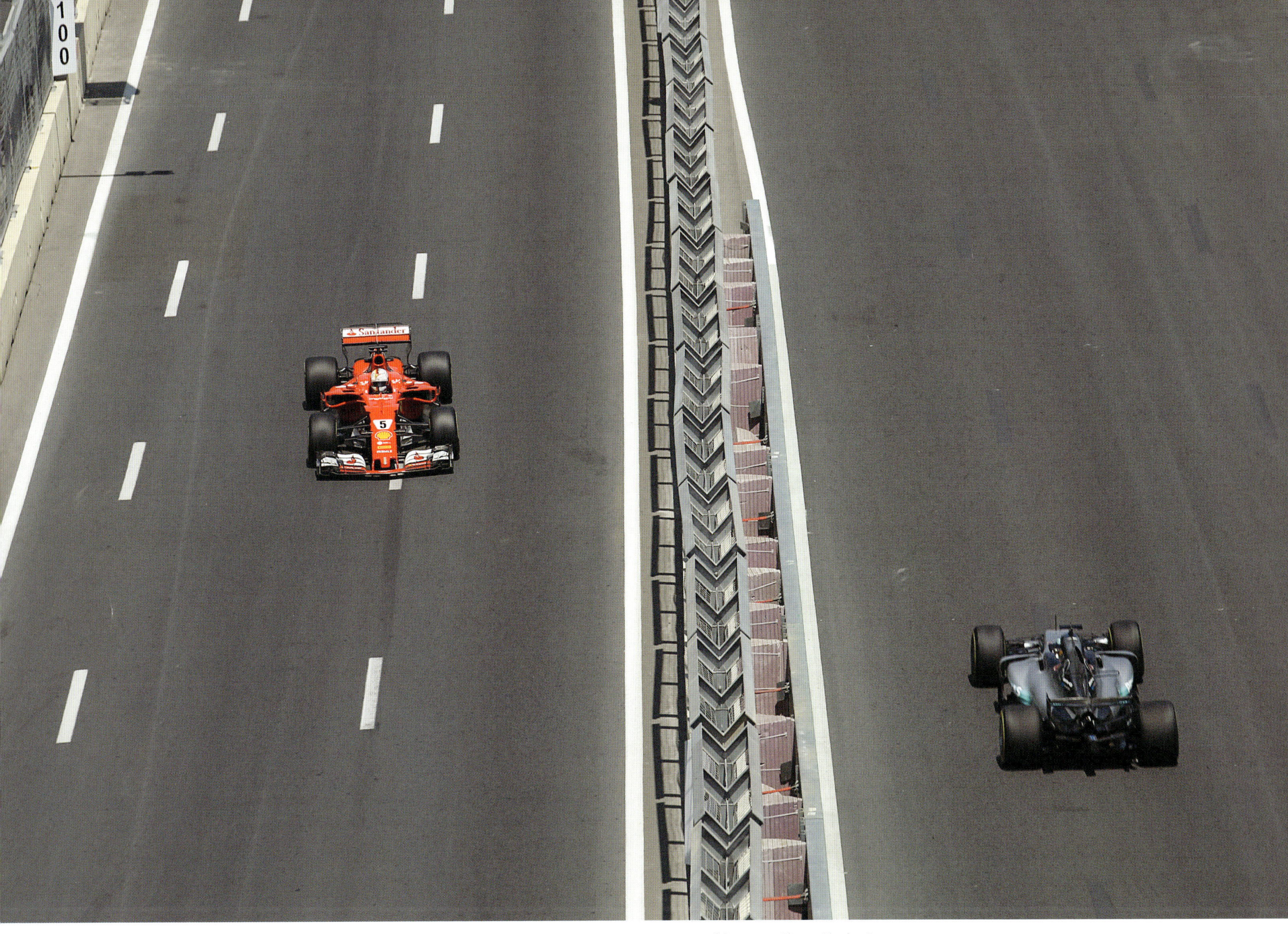

Baku, Azerbaijan GP, 2017. Sebastian Vettel (Ferrari SF70H) and Lewis Hamilton (Mercedes F1 W08) on opposite sections of the circuit. Photo: Charles Coates

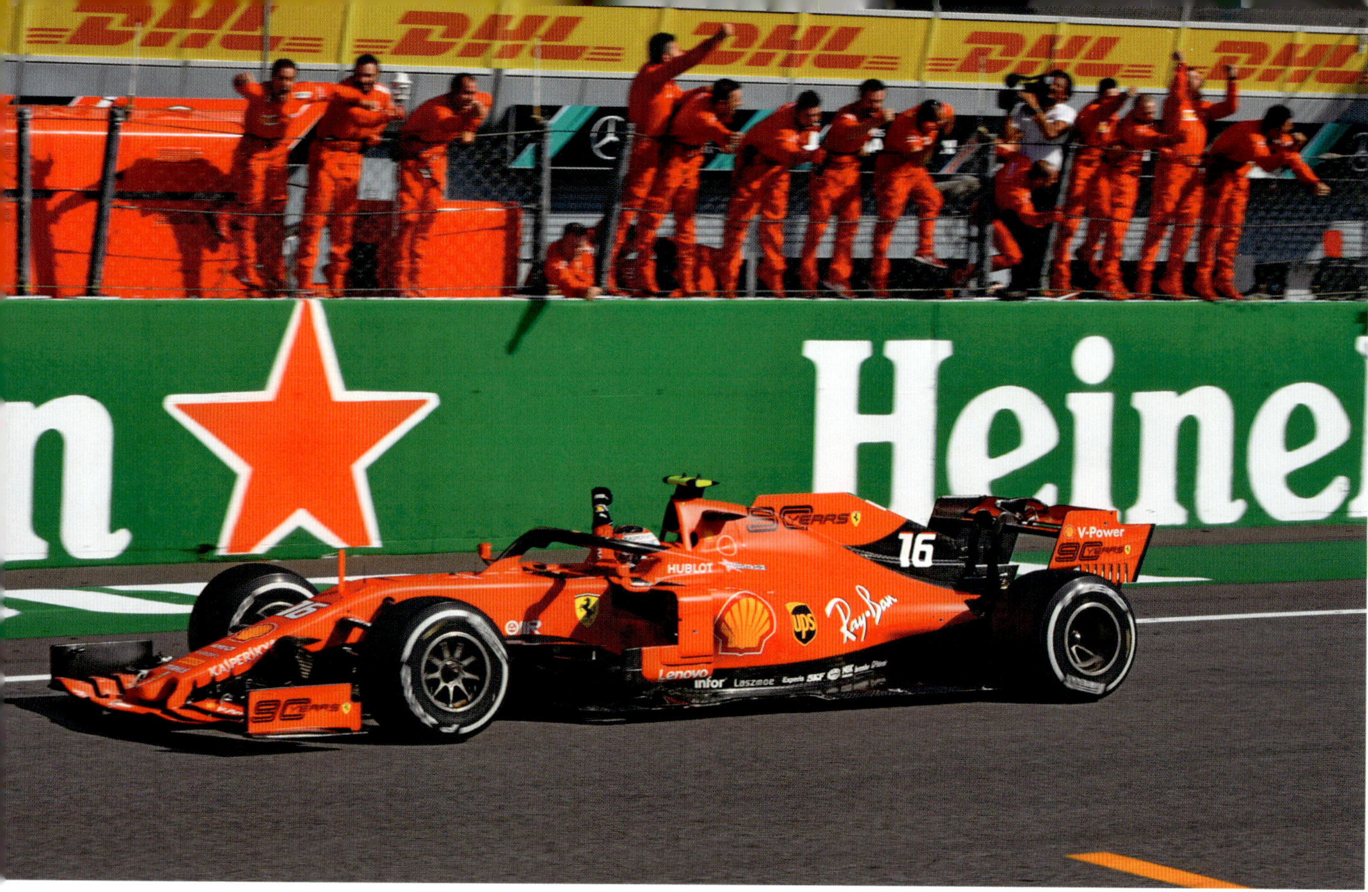

Monza, Italian GP, 2019.
Charles Leclerc (Ferrari SF90)
takes victory to the delight of
his team. Photo: Mark Sutton

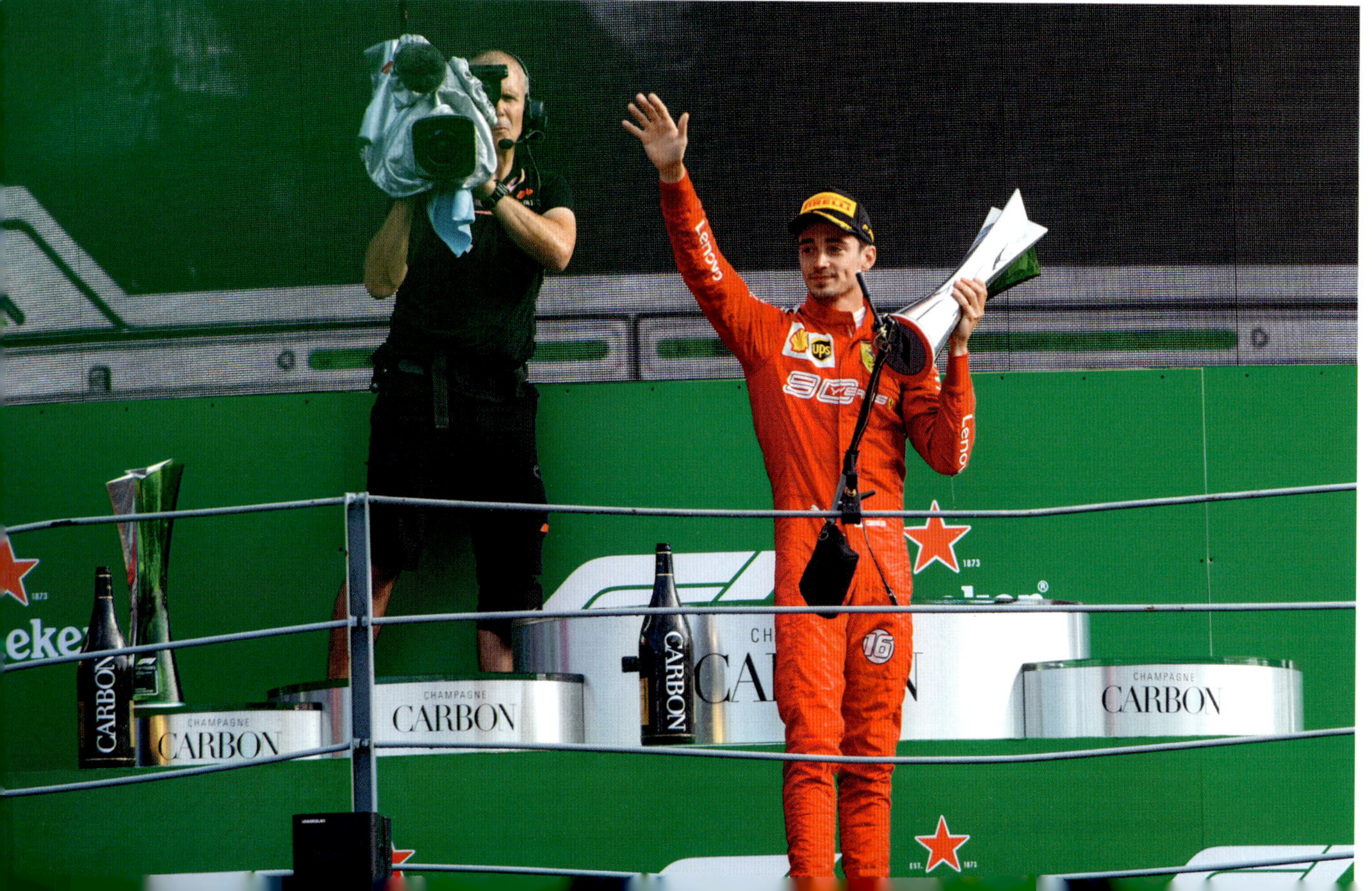

Monza, Italian GP, 2019.
Charles Leclerc (Ferrari SF90)
after his first victory in F1.
Photo: Ercole Colombo

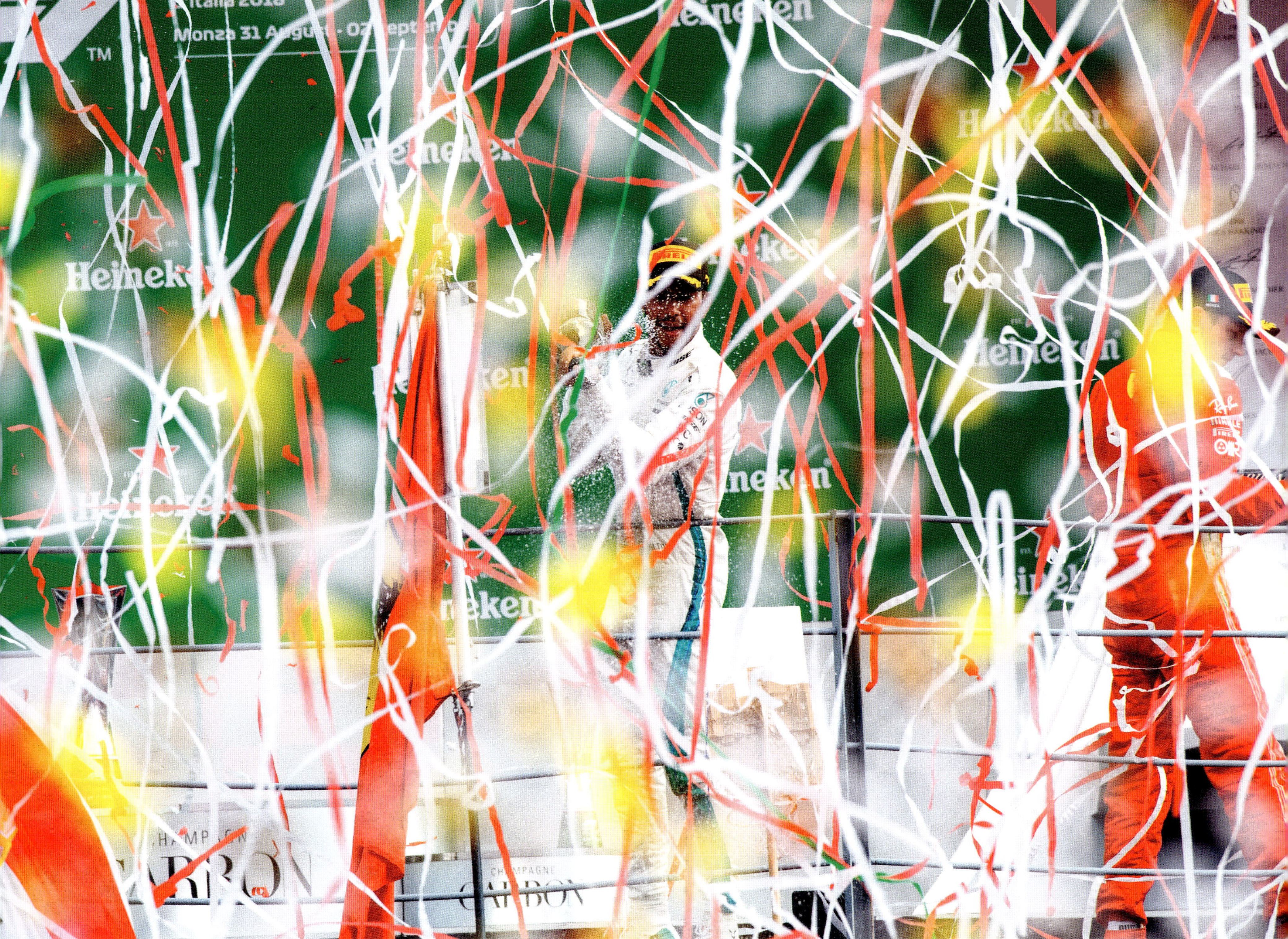

Monza, Italian GP, 2018. The winner Lewis Hamilton on the podium. Photo: Ercole Colombo

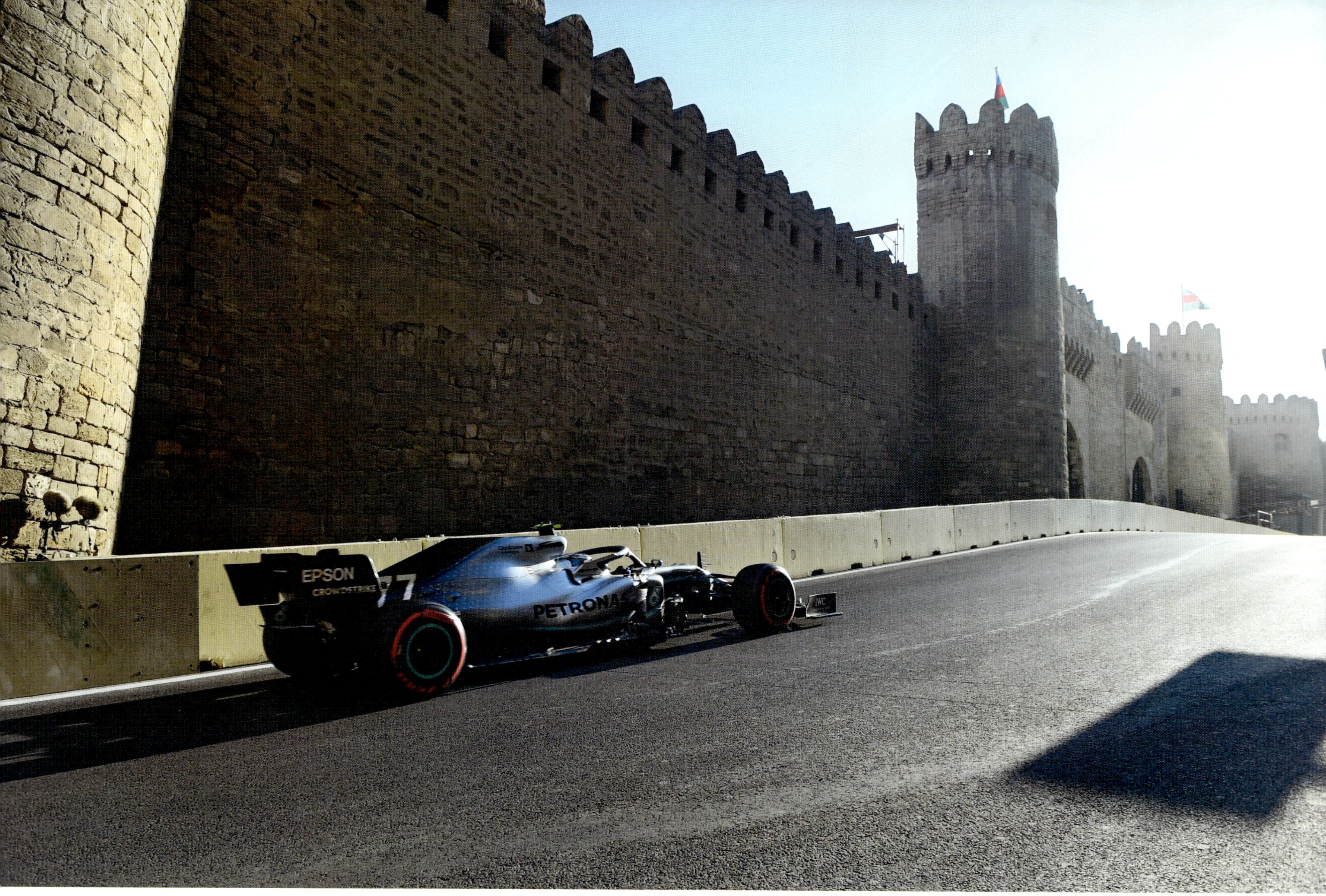

Baku, Azerbaijan GP, 2019. Valtteri Bottas (Mercedes F1w10). Photo: Alberto Crippa

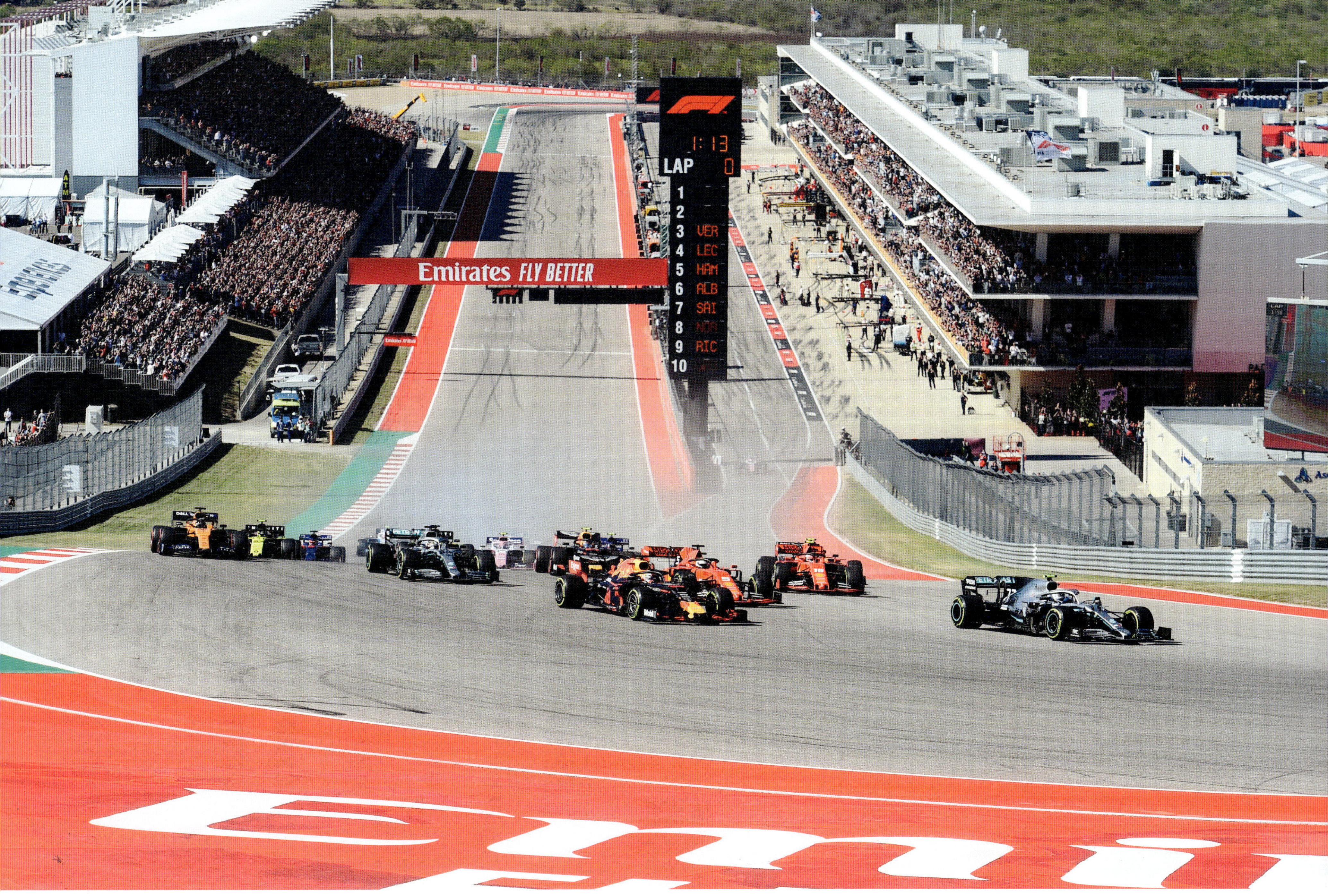

Austin, United States GP, 2019. Valtteri Bottas (Mercedes F1w10) leads just after the start. Photo: Alberto Crippa

2020...
Heirs to the Throne

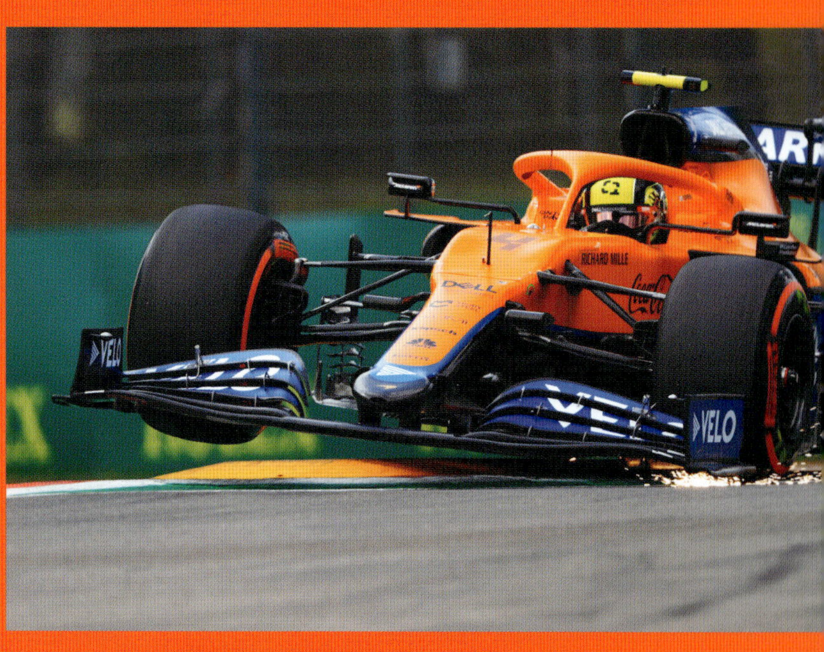

Lewis Hamilton still dominates the scene. He was born in Stevenage, a town north of London, on January 7, 1985. In 2020 he conquered his seventh world title, matching Michael Schumacher's record, having collected in the meantime an impressive series of records of his own. His intention: to continue to compete and win as no one before in F1. By virtue of his skills and extraordinary mental strength, combined with his experience. Hamilton is well acquainted with the various media and he uses them with great ability, winning over admirers of all ages, even the very young, to whom he speaks in terms they can understand, referring to images and ideas from an entire universe of activities and interests that span from the world of music to fashion. Not only: he has become the most incisive and acknowledged supporter of the fight against racism, modifying the procedures of each Grand Prix and involving his colleagues, the institutions, and many other athletes. So much so that he has changed the public's perception of the role of a sport's champion which, with him and thanks to him, is now to bear witness to his times, to be always present, careful, and modern. Thus, he is not just the driver who has won the most in history, but a transversal symbol, a role which he interprets with great skill. Lewis shows himself, he extends invitations, his declarations have a very broad following, and at the same time he manages to protect his private life.

At first sight, we know everything about him. In truth, we know very little, in line with a communication strategy that offers much and thus avoids exposing what belongs to the more private, deeper sphere of his feelings. On the track, he is spectacularly efficient, also thanks to Mercedes' technical excellence. Only marginally threatened by a narrow circle of young talents destined to carry on the legacy of King Lewis, with a timing and manner that are yet to be defined. For years now, people who are capable of recognizing and judging the talent of a driver have been talking about Max Verstappen and Charles Leclerc as possible, probable heirs. Verstappen slightly ahead of the game. He is the son of Jos, a driver who never excelled, former teammate of Schumacher's at the Benetton team. He was raised with great severity by his father and displayed a superior talent from a very young age. Max was born in Hasselt on September 30, 1997. He too set some impressive records very early on: his first miles in F1 with Toro Rosso in 2014, three days after he had turned 17; the Australian GP, 2015, when he still hadn't turned 18; his first victory in 2016, when he debuted with the Red Bull team, achieved in Barcelona when he was 18 years, seven months, and 15 days old. He is consistent, aggressive, extremely popular, with a huge following of Dutch fans. He has established a lasting relationship with Red Bull, and now, in 2021, for the first time he is in the position to challenge

Hamilton for the title, driving a vehicle that is competitive anywhere. Leclerc, born in the Principality of Monaco on October 16, 1997, fatherless, brought up through the Ferrari Driver Academy, is a young man endowed with unique grace and ferocity. Hired as a driver for the Ferrari team in 2019, he immediately achieved astounding feats: two victories and seven pole positions in his first year in red. A performance that caused the relationship between Ferrari and Vettel to become increasingly strained, the latter being let go by the Maranello team at the end of the 2020 season, replaced by the young Spaniard Carlos Sainz, born in 1994, the son of Carlos Senior, a former world rally champion. Leclerc's class, grit, and speed are not up for debate. Driving a car that isn't a winner—with a multi-year contract— often leads him to push things a little further than necessary. As he awaits the year 2022, which will mark a new, profound change in technical regulations, and a concrete opportunity for those who have at length suffered the excessive power of Mercedes. Hamilton, Verstappen, Leclerc: these are the figures who more than others bring value to the F1 of the present and of the near future. Though they don't stand entirely alone. Lando Norris (1999), a McLaren driver, and George Russell (1998)—a driver "lent" by Mercedes to the Williams team, brilliant substitute for Hamilton in Bahrain in 2020 when Lewis was forced to stop because he had contracted

the coronavirus—both seem destined to exciting careers, provided they will have the opportunity to drive top-notch cars. Still awaiting consecration is Daniel Ricciardo (1989), an Australian from Perth of Sicilian origins, Norris's teammate at McLaren, very fast but still in search of a winning car. Aiming to make a return is Vettel, now with Aston Martin, a team brought back to life by the rich and ambitions Canadian manager Lawrence Stroll. Seeking a second youth is Fernando Alonso who, after two years of absence in which he won the 24 Hours of Le Mans twice, nearly won the Indy 500, and took part in the Dakar Rally, has returned to F1 with Renault, which in the meantime has taken on the name Alpine. Mick Schumacher, Michael's son, born in 1999, made his debut in F1 at the beginning of the 2021 World Championship driving an underperforming Haas. His manners and style are admirable, and he carries such a heavy name into the race with pride, and the intention to grow without pushing things too hard, without suffering the pressure that has been put on him since his first kart races, run with father Michael by his side.

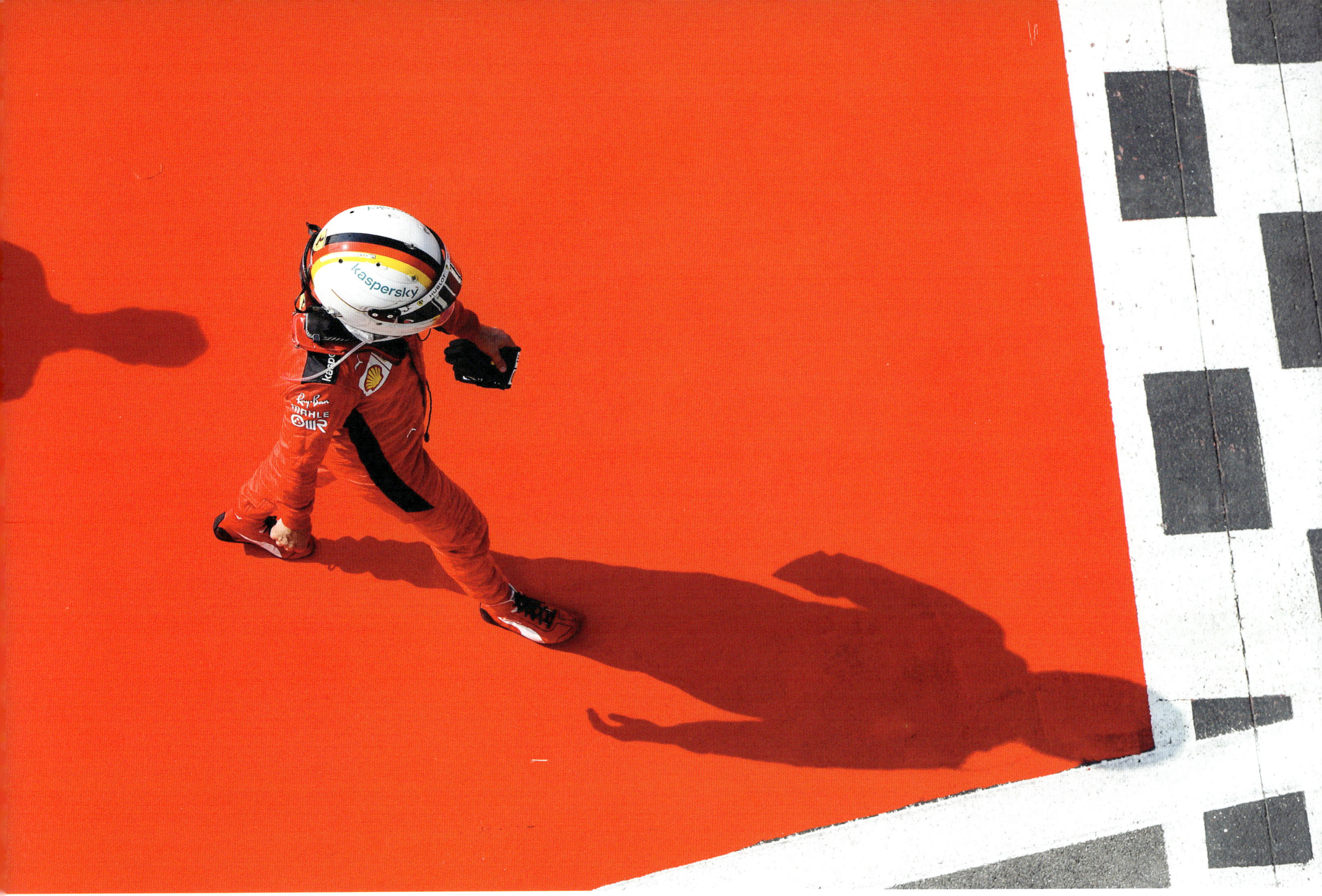

Silverstone, 70th Anniversary GP, 2020. Sebastian Vettel (Ferrari). Photo: Charles Coates

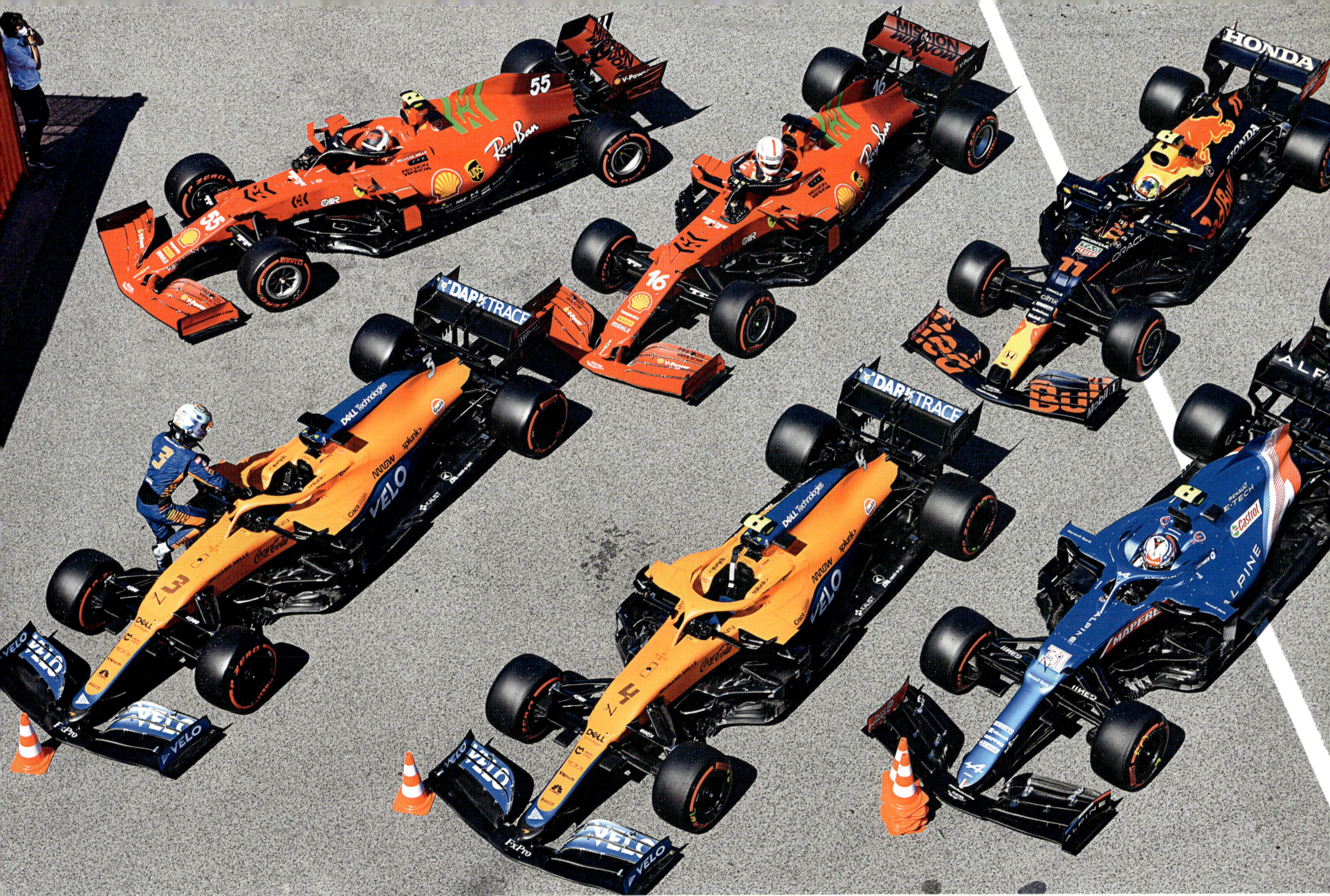

Barcelona, Spanish GP, 2021. The cars of Daniel Ricciardo (McLaren MCL35M), Lando Norris (McLaren MCL35M), Esteban Ocon (Alpine A521), Carlos Sainz (Ferrari SF21), Charles Leclerc (Ferrari SF21), Sergio Perez (Red Bull Racing RB16B), and Fernando Alonso (Alpine A521) in Parc Fermé after qualifying. Photo: Mark Sutton

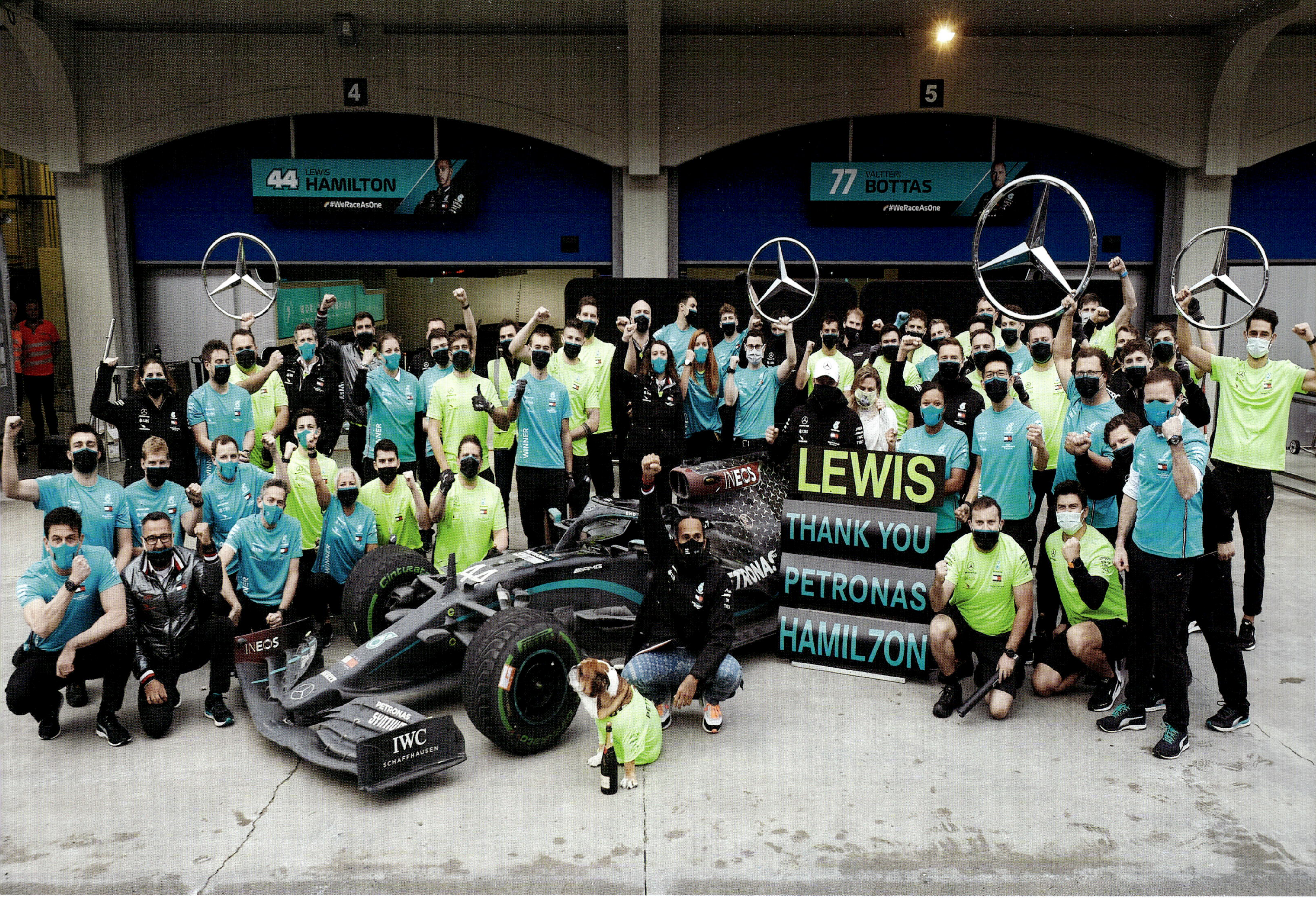

Istanbul, Turkish GP, 2020. Lewis Hamilton celebrates a record-equalling seventh World Championship alongside his Mercedes-AMG F1 M11, with teammate Valtteri Bottas. Photo: Steve Etherington

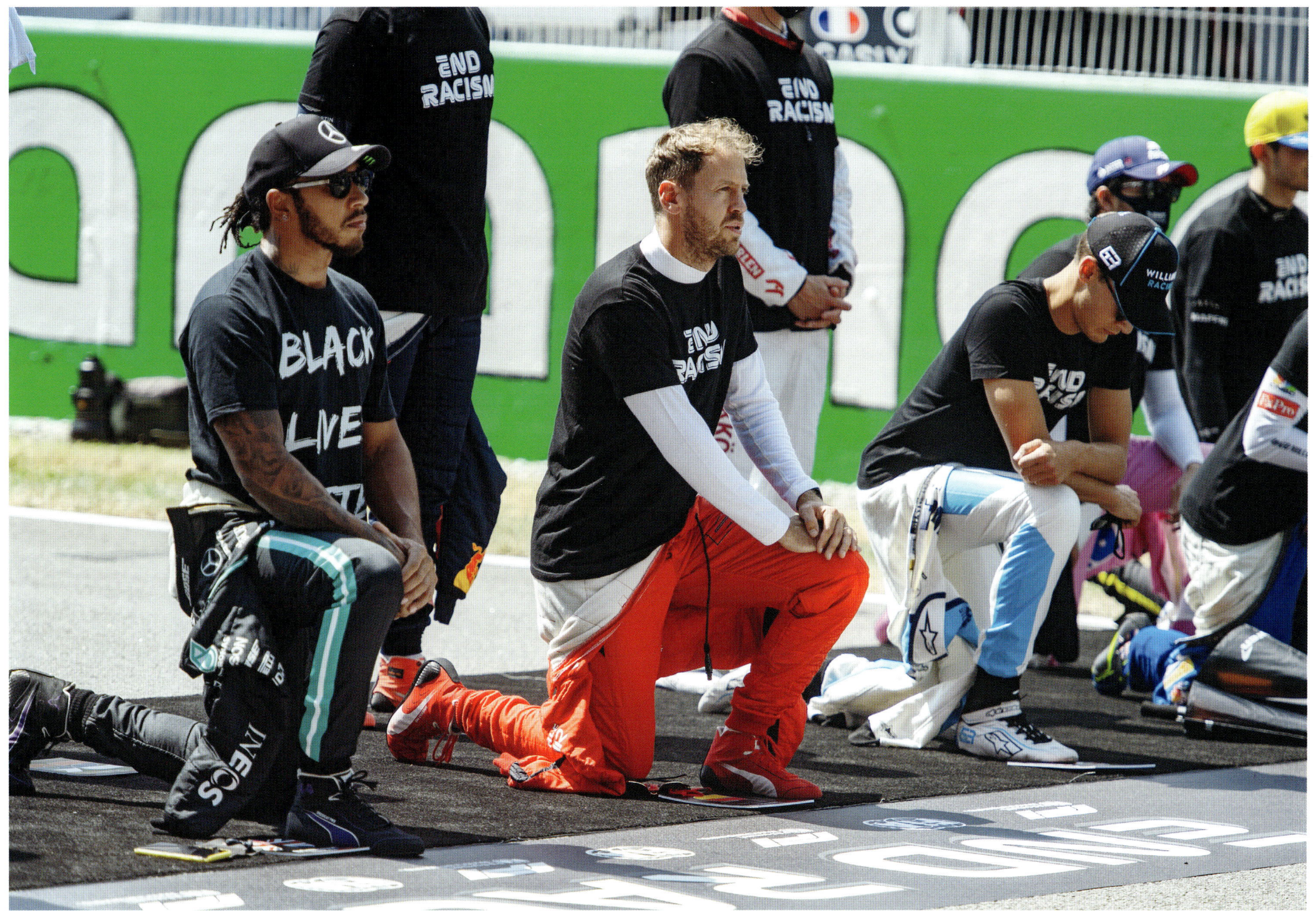

Barcelona, Spanish GP, 2020. Lewis Hamilton, Sebastian Vettel, and George Russell. Photo: Alberto Crippa

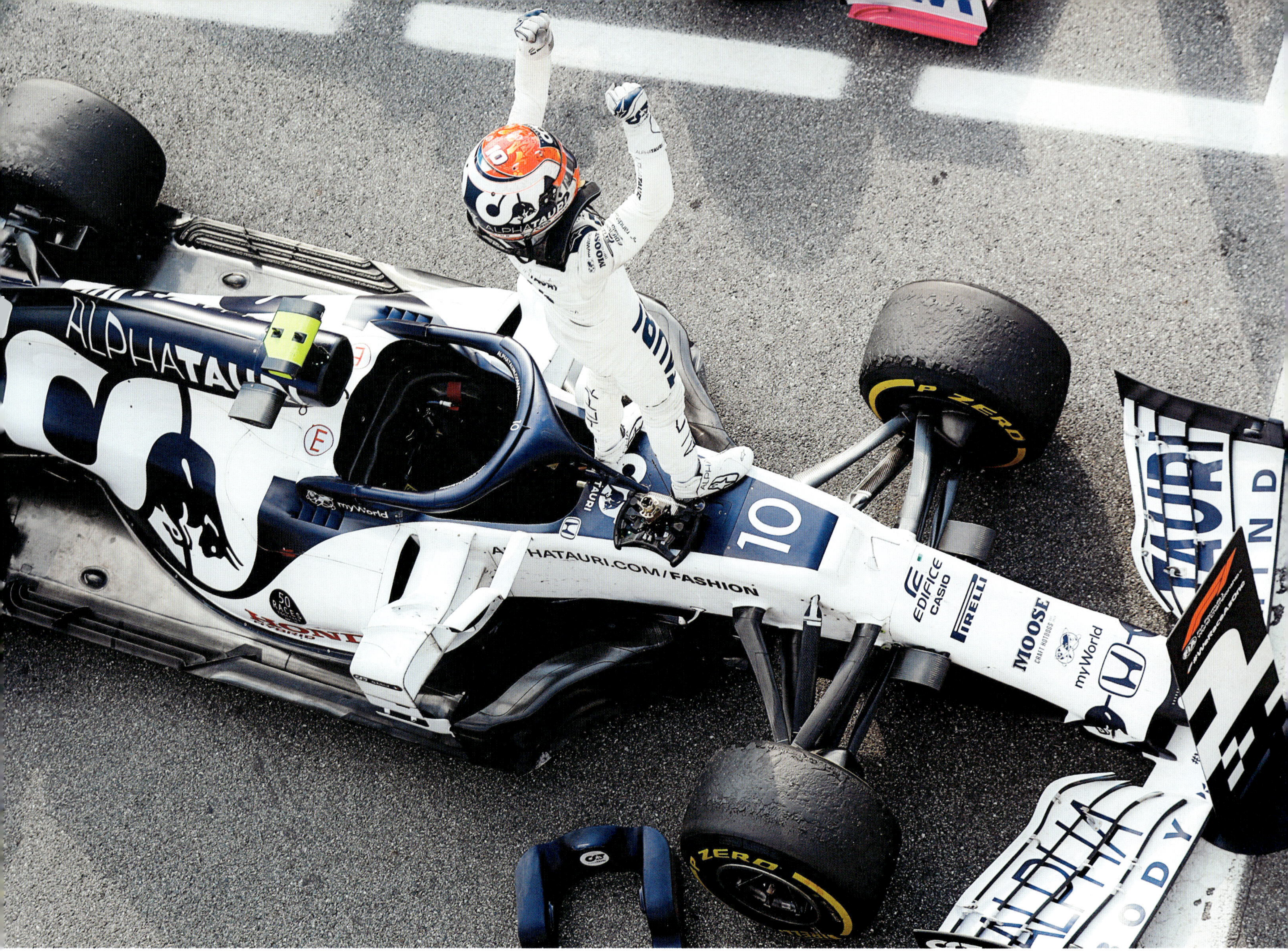

Monza, Italian GP, 2020. Pierre Gasly stands on top of his AlphaTauri AT01 Honda as he celebrates his maiden victory. Photo: Steven Tee

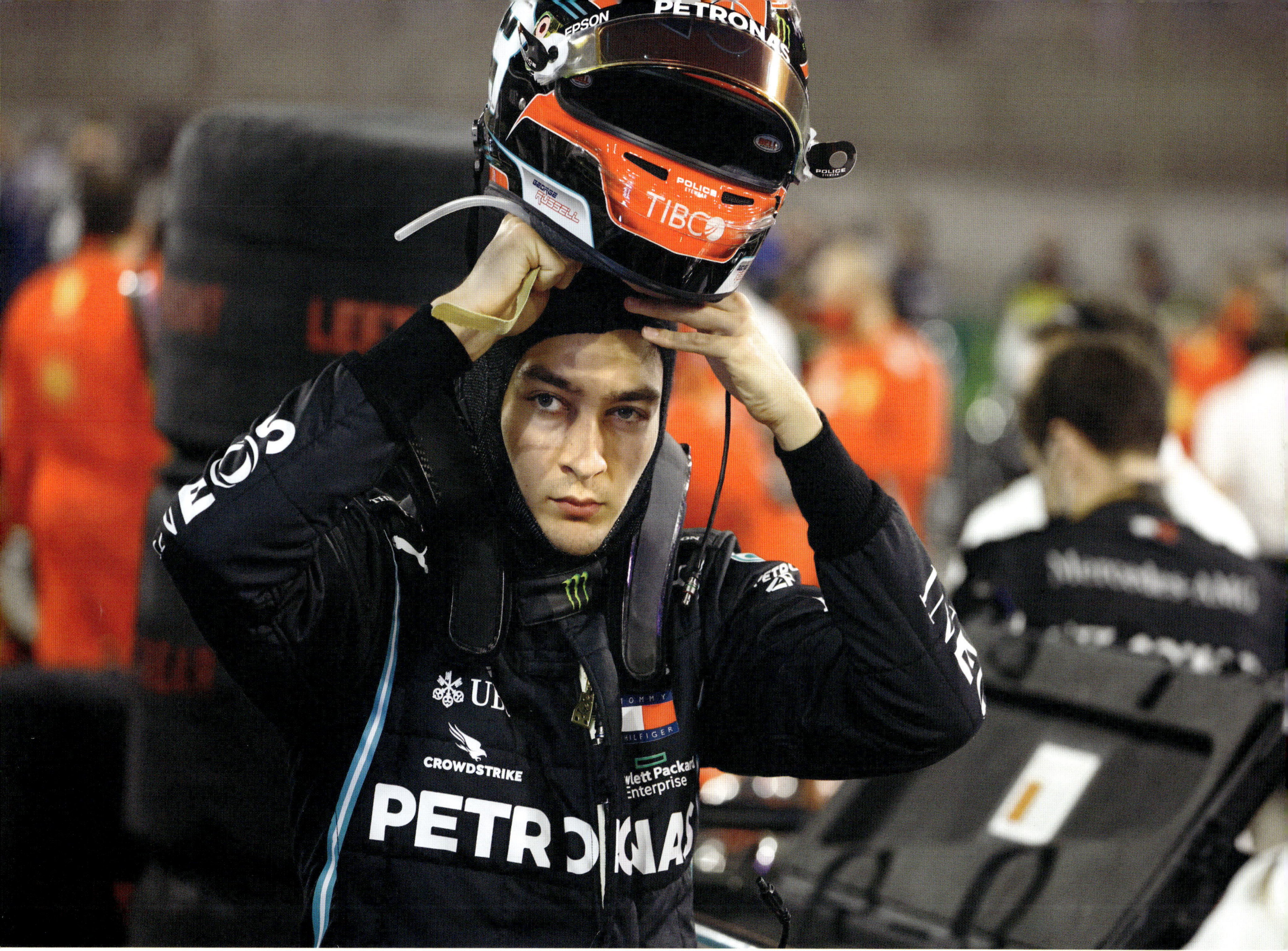

Bahrain, Sakhir GP, 2020. George Russell removes his helmet as he reflects on missing out at a chance of victory on his debut with Mercedes. Photo: Glenn Dunbar

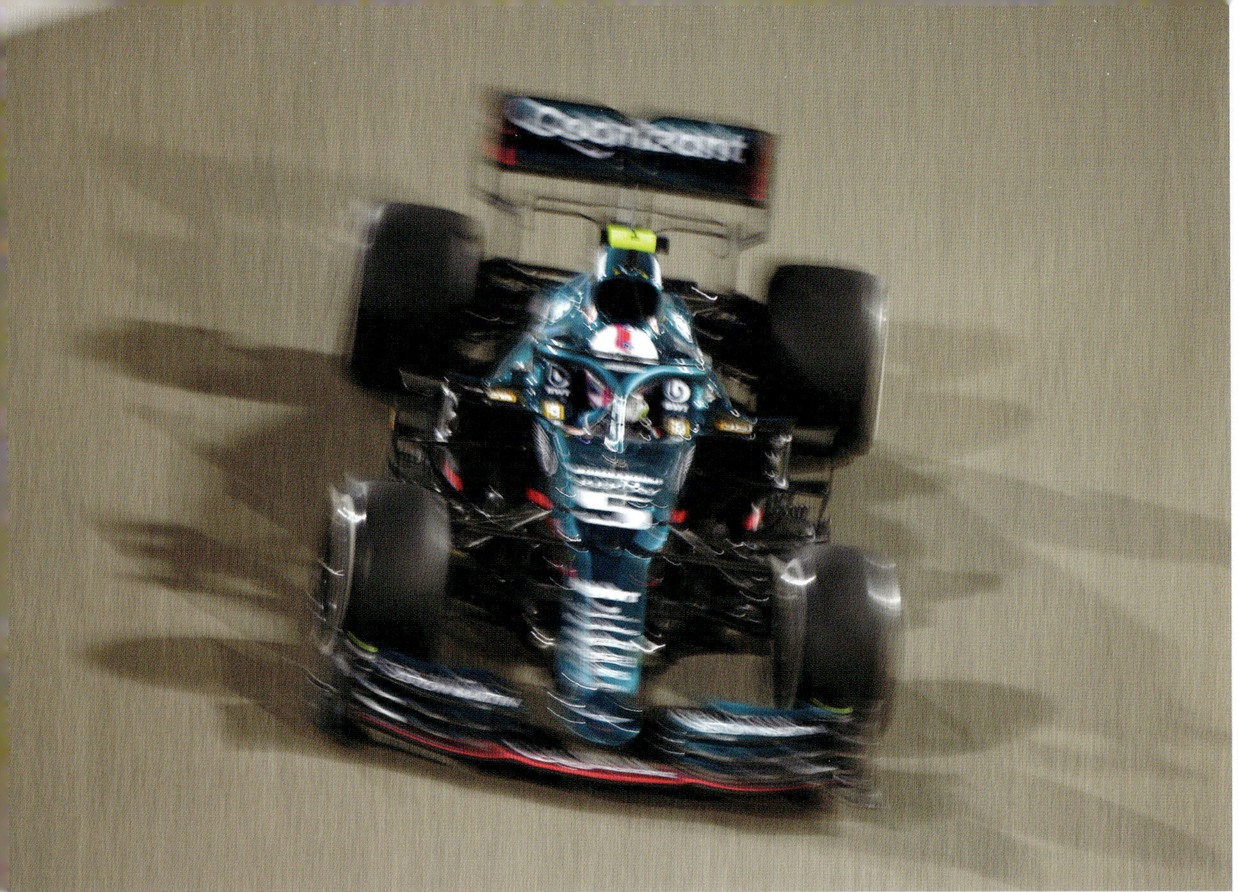

Bahrain GP, 2021. Sebastian Vettel (Aston Martin AMR21 Mercedes) on his race debut for the team. Photo: Andrew Hone

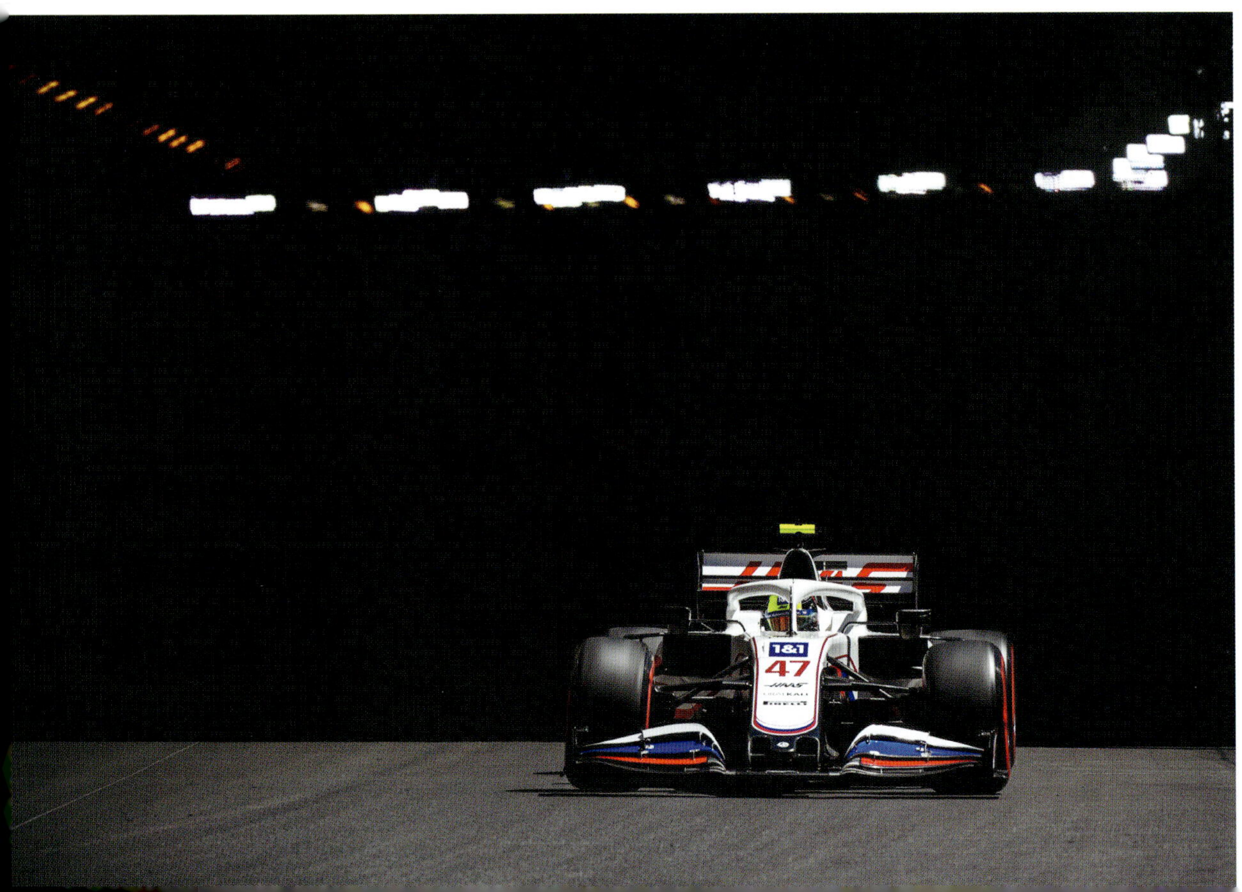

Monaco GP, 2021. Mick Schumacher (Haas VF-21 Ferrari) at the exit of the Tunnel. Photo: Steven Tee

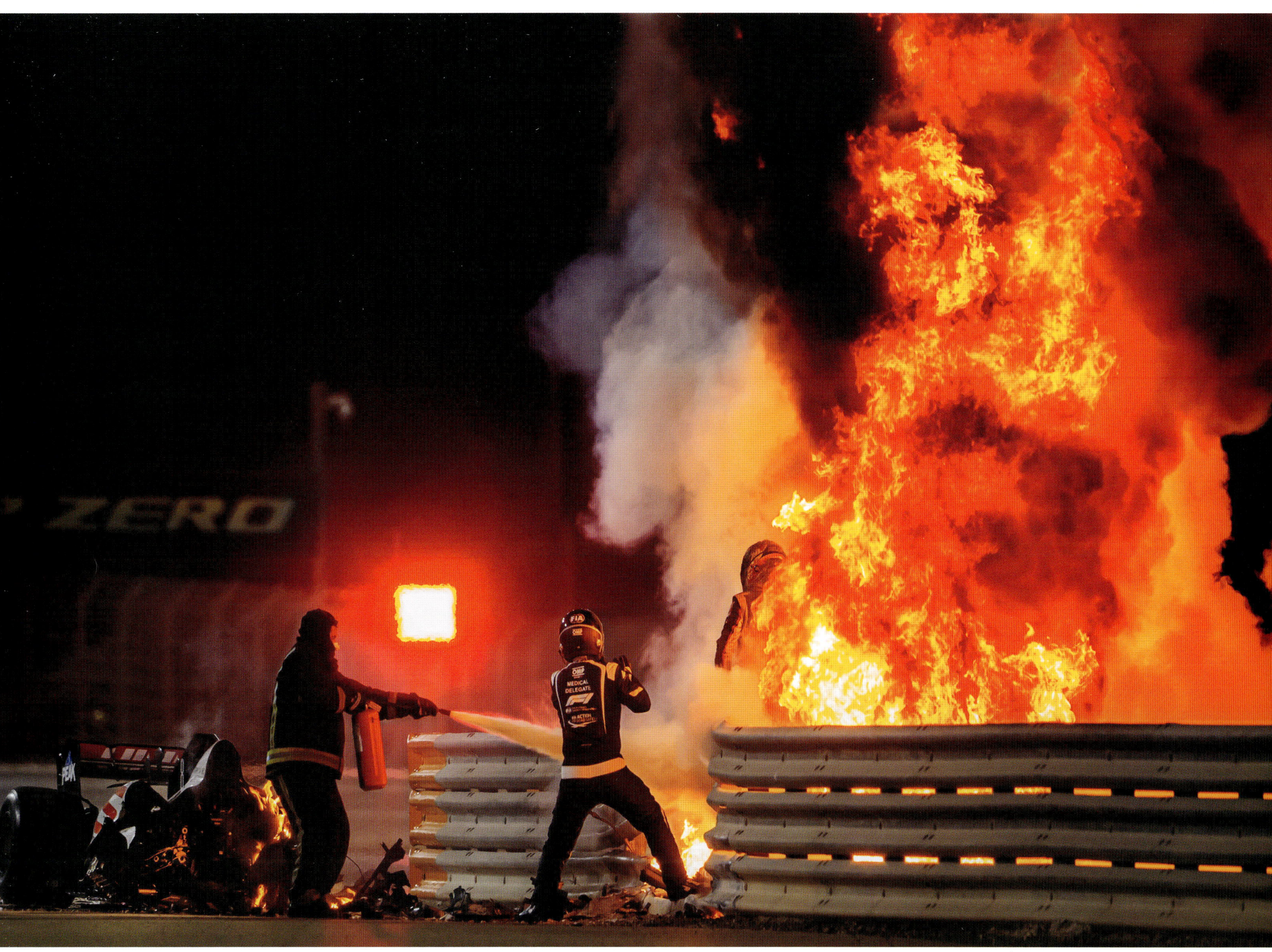

Bahrain GP, 2020. Romain Grosjean (Haas VF-20 Ferrari) emerges from flames after a horrific accident on the opening lap of the race. Photo: Andrew Hone

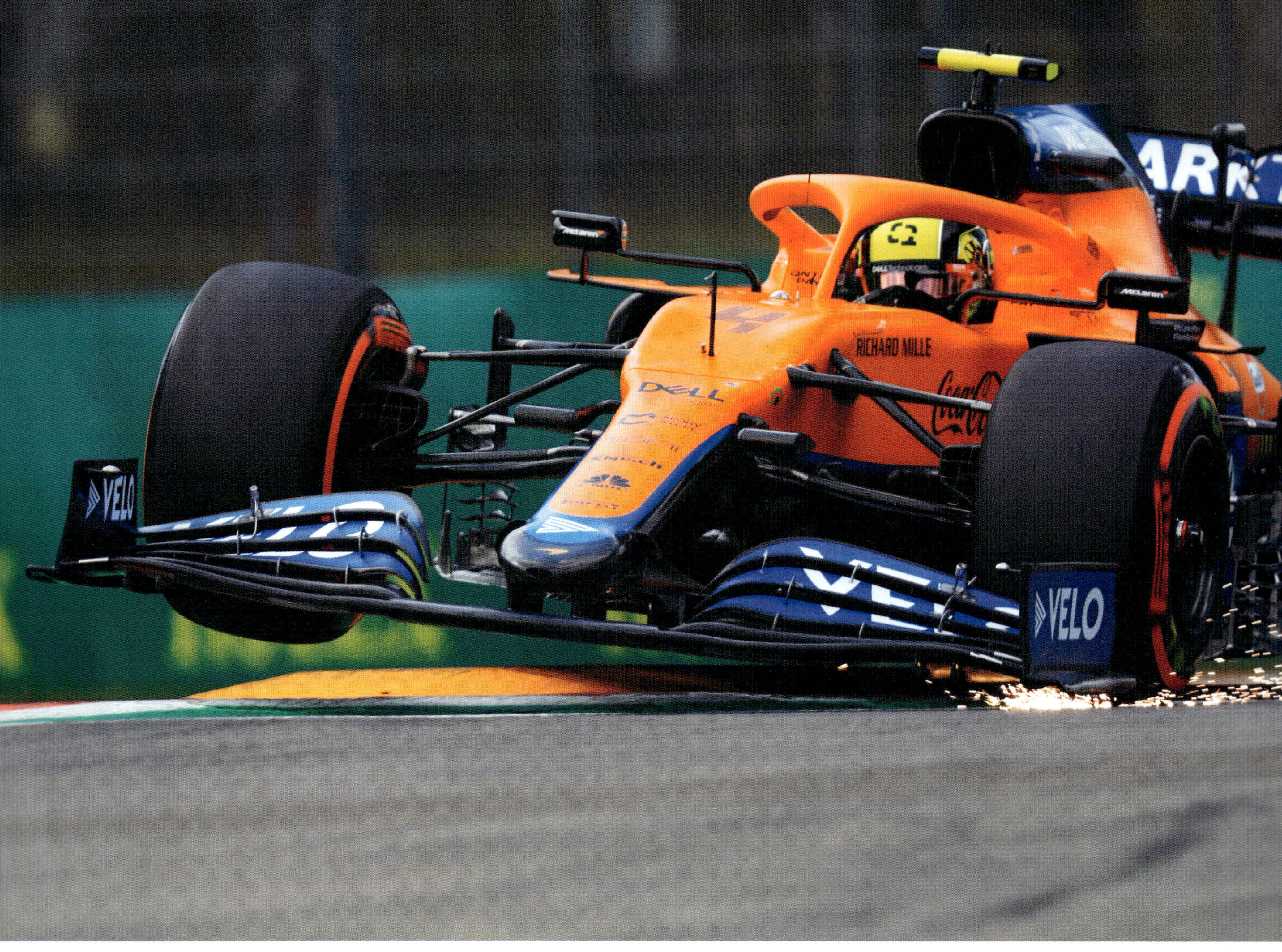

Imola, Emilia Romagna GP, 2021. Lando Norris (McLaren MCL35M Mercedes) clatters the kerb at Variante Alta. Photo: Charles Coates

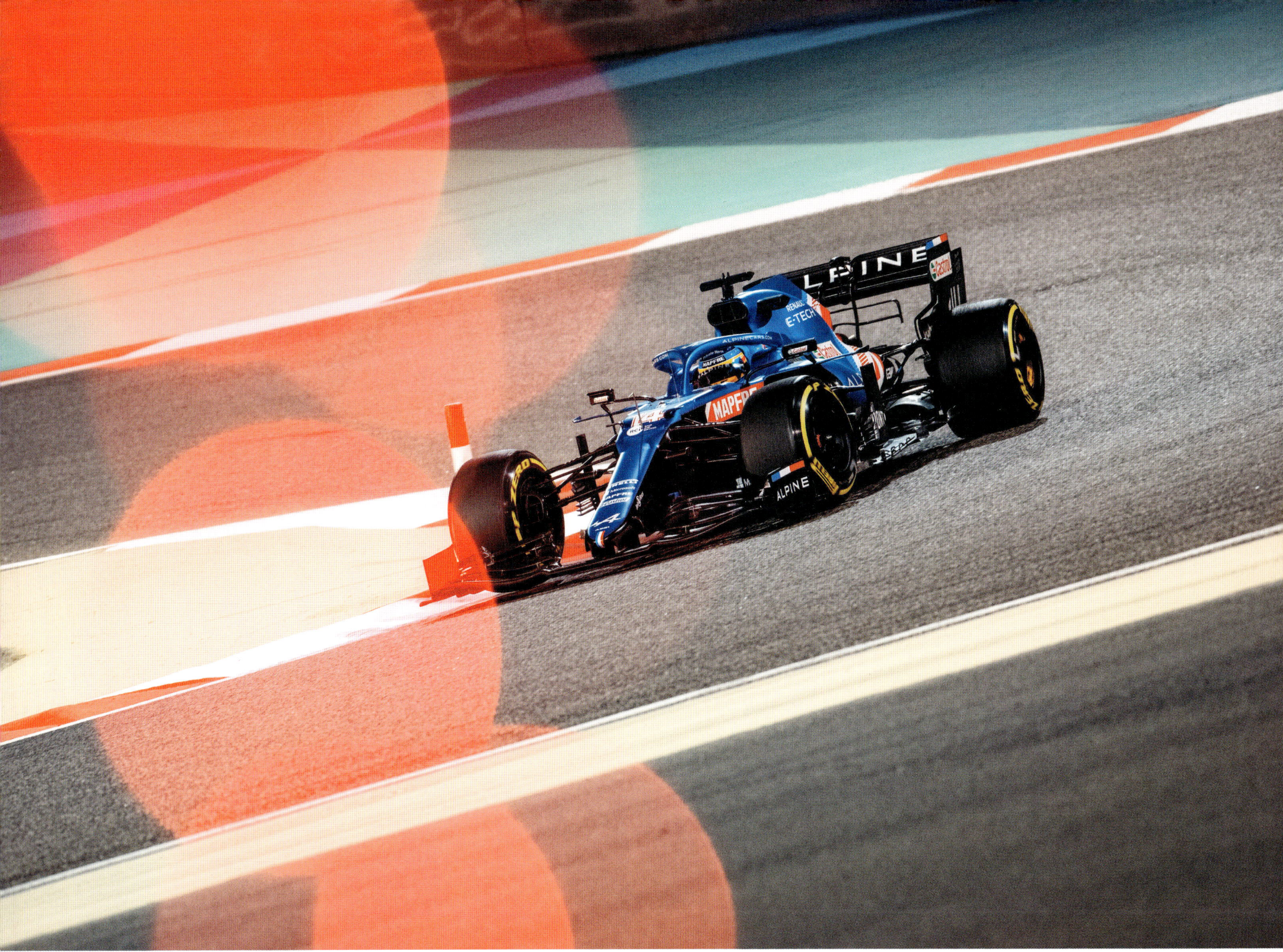

Bahrain GP, 2021. Fernando Alonso (Alpine A521 Renault) on his Formula 1 return. Photo: Alberto Crippa

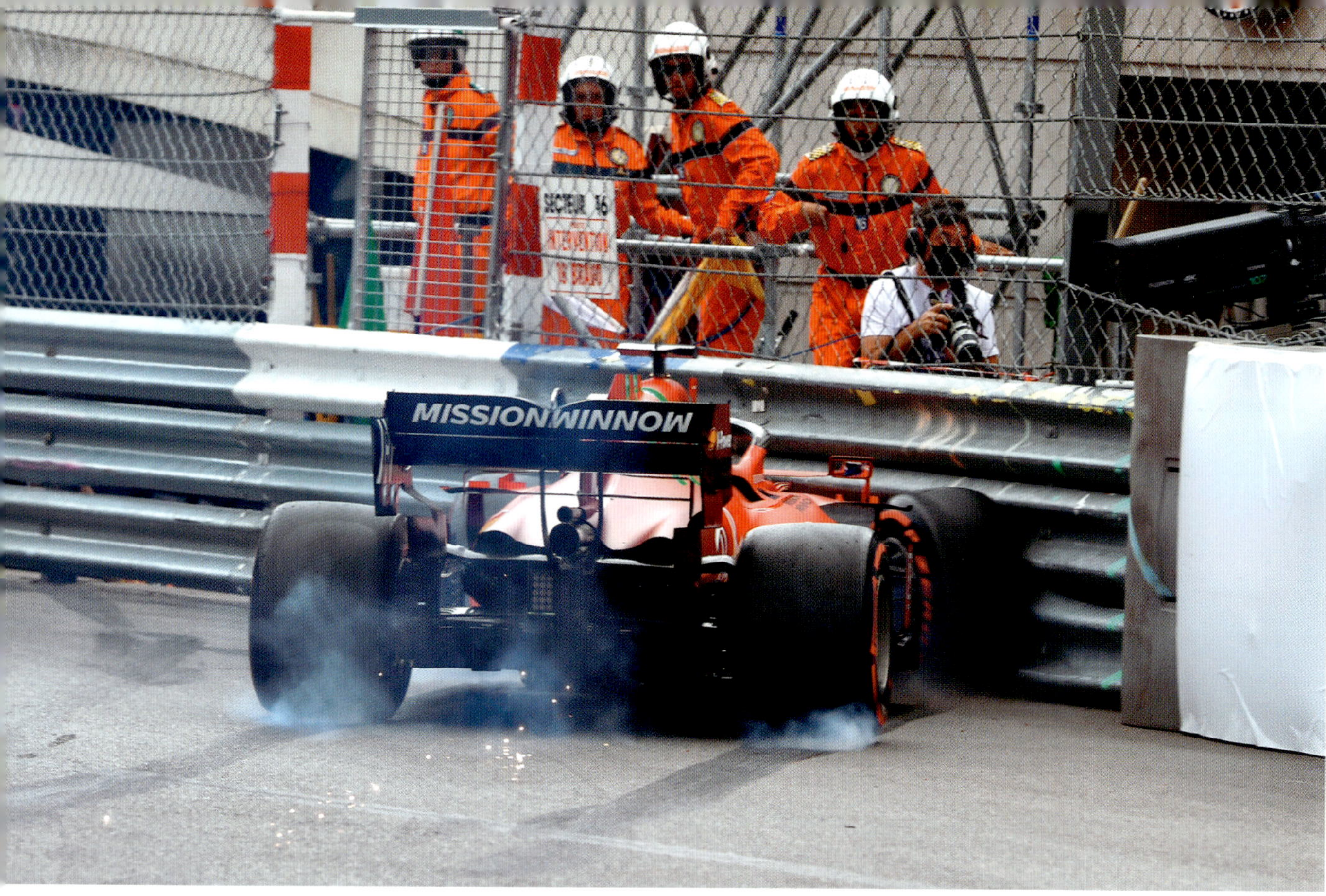

Monaco GP, 2021. Charles Leclerc (Ferrari SF21) clinches pole position as he crashes out towards the end of qualifying. Photo: Jean Petin

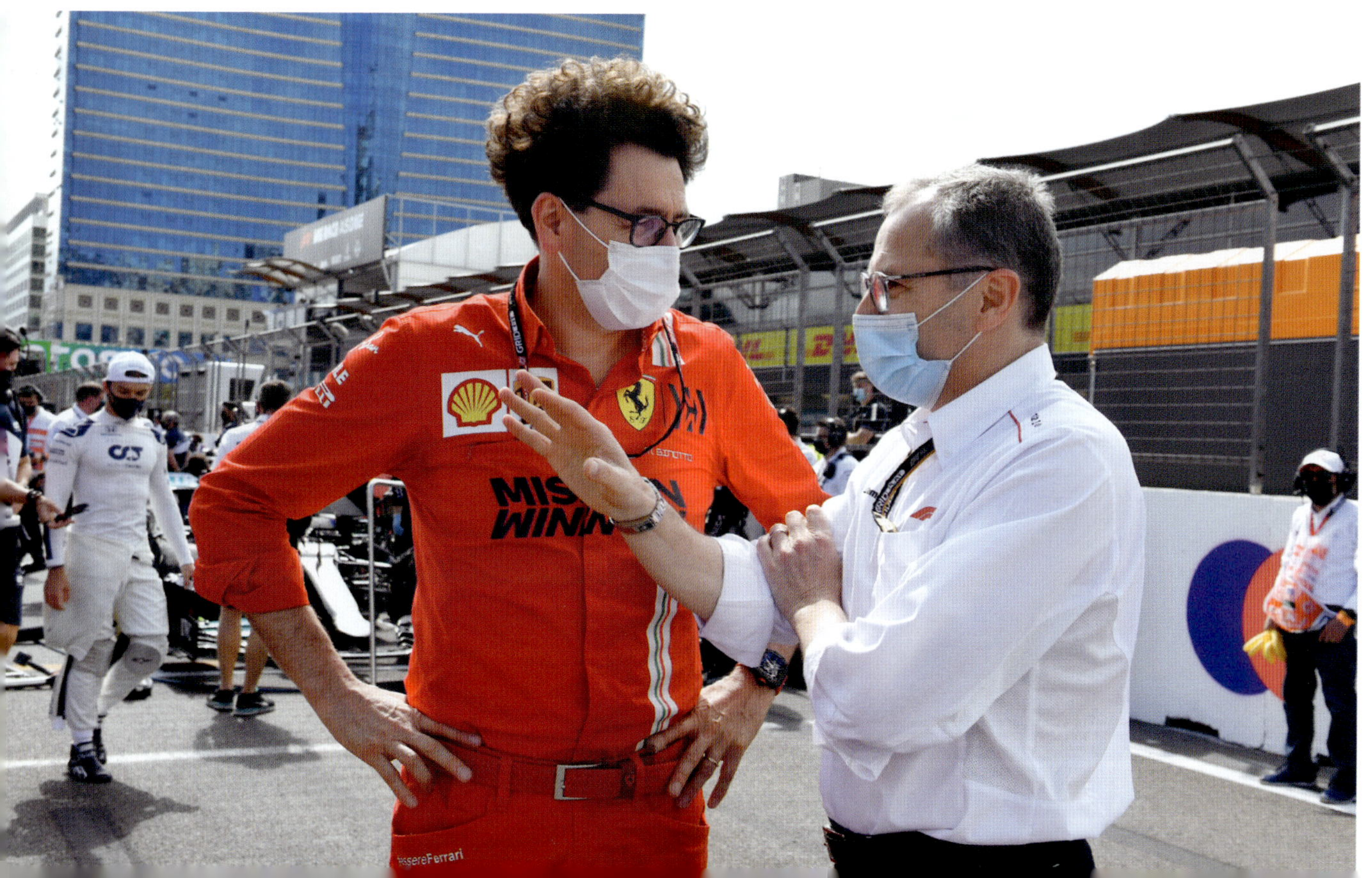

Baku, Azerbaijan GP, 2021. Mattia Binotto (Team Principal, Ferrari) and Stefano Domenicali (Formula 1 President and CEO). Photo: Mark Sutton

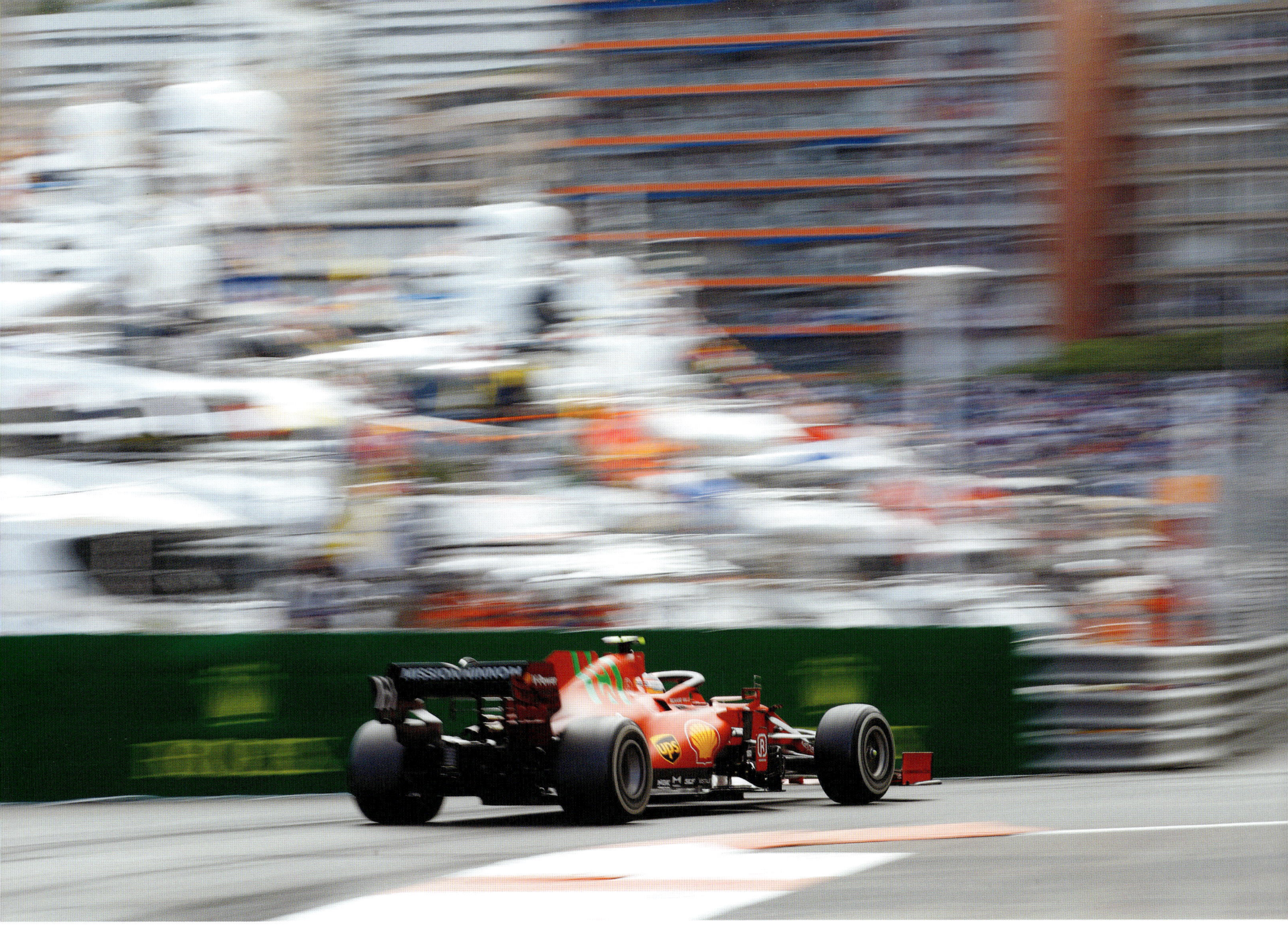

Monaco GP, 2021. Carlos Sainz (Ferrari SF21) on the exit of the Nouvelle Chicane. Photo: Zak Mauger

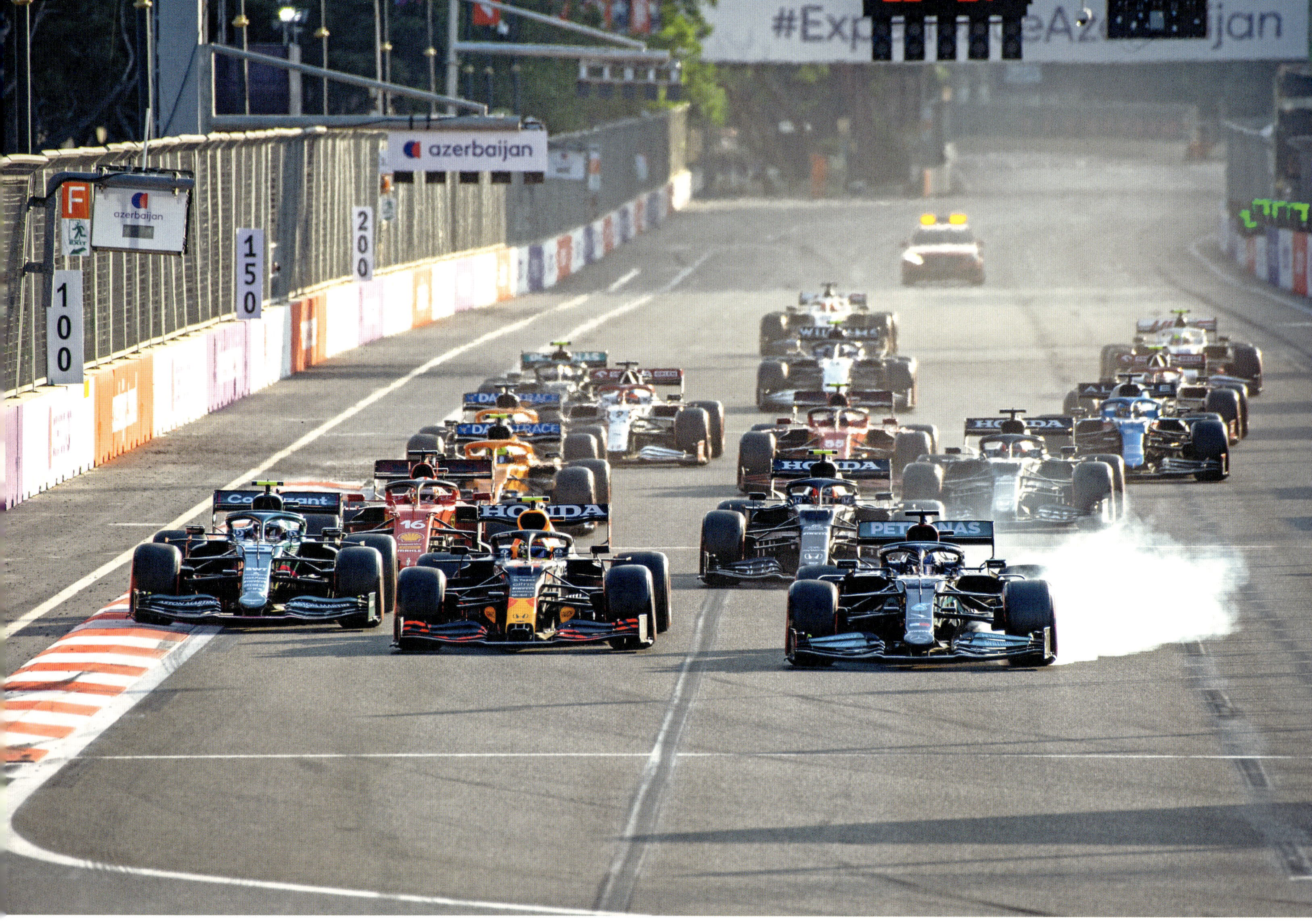

Baku, Azerbaijan GP, 2021. Lewis Hamilton locks his front brakes at the second start. Photo: Alberto Vimercati

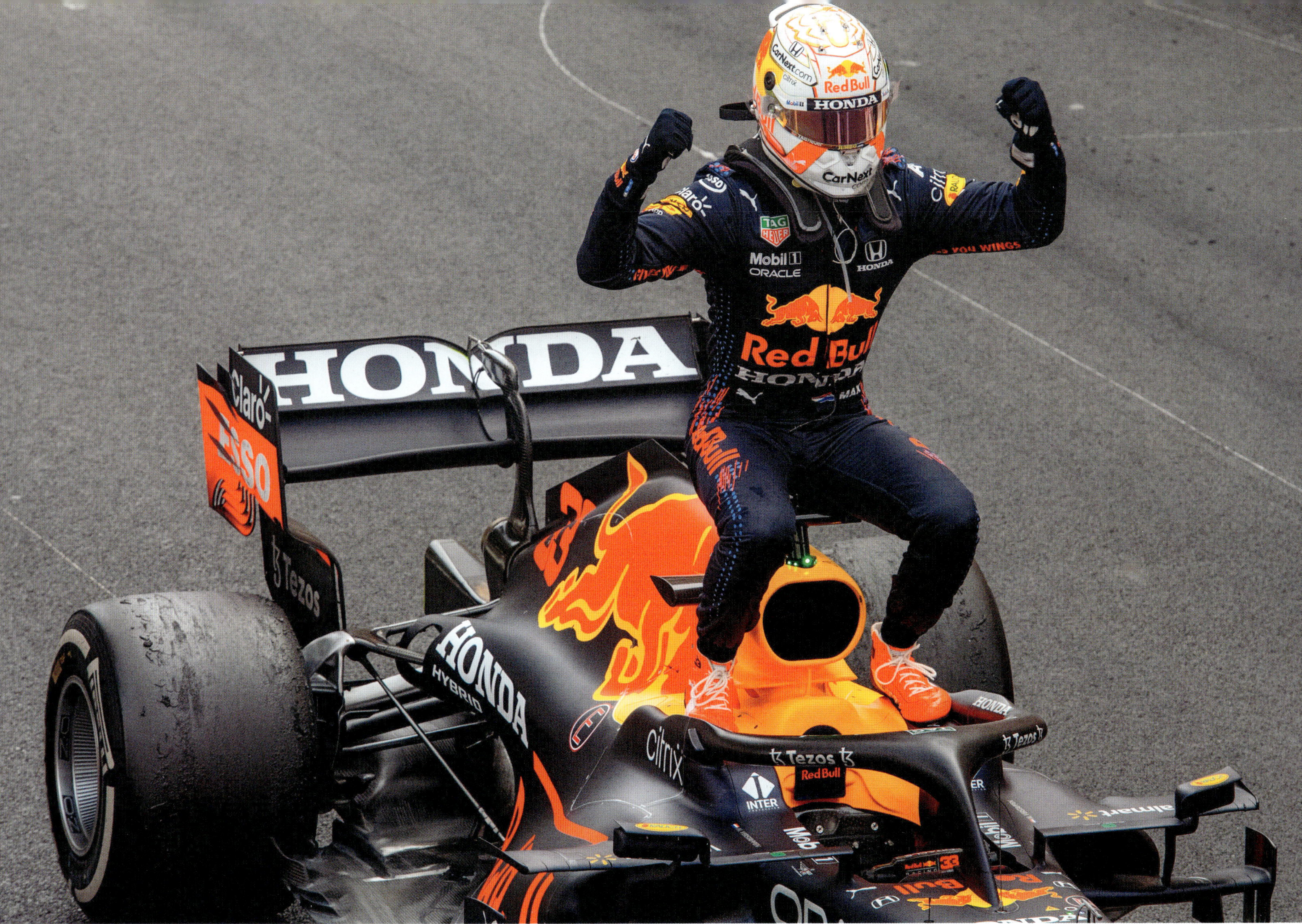

Monaco GP, 2021. Max Verstappen celebrates his first position. Photo: Alberto Crippa

Timeless
Heroes

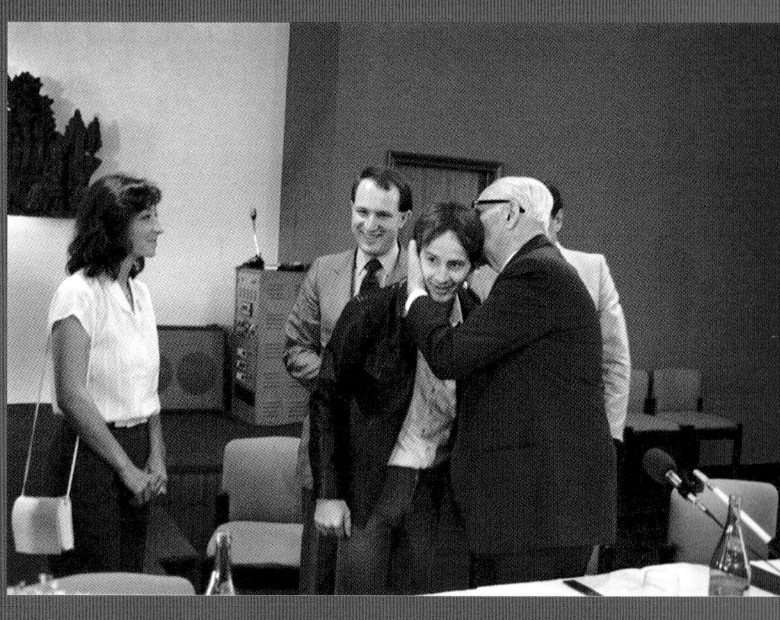

Sports expose character and inclinations. They reveal the souls of those who race, who fight, who offer themselves up. A display of humanity that creates unique ties, intimate, independent from any and all ranking. The reason is simple: witnessing excellence triggers admiration and respect, but also offers a unique opportunity. Something that lets you see a curious, precious similarity. A feeling of belonging that ends up determining a choice. Thus, in our own personal halls of fame there might be room for figures who don't necessarily appear in the official rankings. Absolute champions, identified by passion, by something that escapes rationality and statistics, the recipients of a peculiar and very profound gratitude.

The generosity, the courage, and even a certain, deliberate devilry, leave lasting marks on the tarmac. Traces that become impressed in the memories of spectators. That soar through the firmament thanks to the sentiments that generated them. Ayrton Senna is emblematic in this sense, he lives on in the memories of older enthusiasts, but also in the perception of young people born after his demise. The reason lies in the words and the emotions that he was capable of transmitting, as a person among the others, willing to expose the nodes of his existence. Something that counts more, today, than the most extraordinary victories achieved on the track. Gilles Villeneuve didn't become a world champion. And yet, he is an unparalleled prodigy for an enormous number of yesterday's and today's spectators, intrigued by his deliberate, overwhelming, and even destructive exuberance.

The list of timeless heroes is long and highly subjective. It includes Stirling Moss and his unlucky chases, Ronnie Peterson and his unforgettable displays of speed, the generosity and irony of Clay Ragazzoni, Alex Zanardi, stronger than any misfortune; and then Jean Alesi's incredible enthusiasm, the congeniality and intelligence of Gerhard Berger, Daniel Ricciardo's cheerfulness. And even more than these. This list could be endless. For here rankings don't count. Rather, what counts is our sympathies, and our affection. Thus, someone is always missing and always will be. The images, exactly those, are hung in every room, and in every heart, priceless souvenirs.

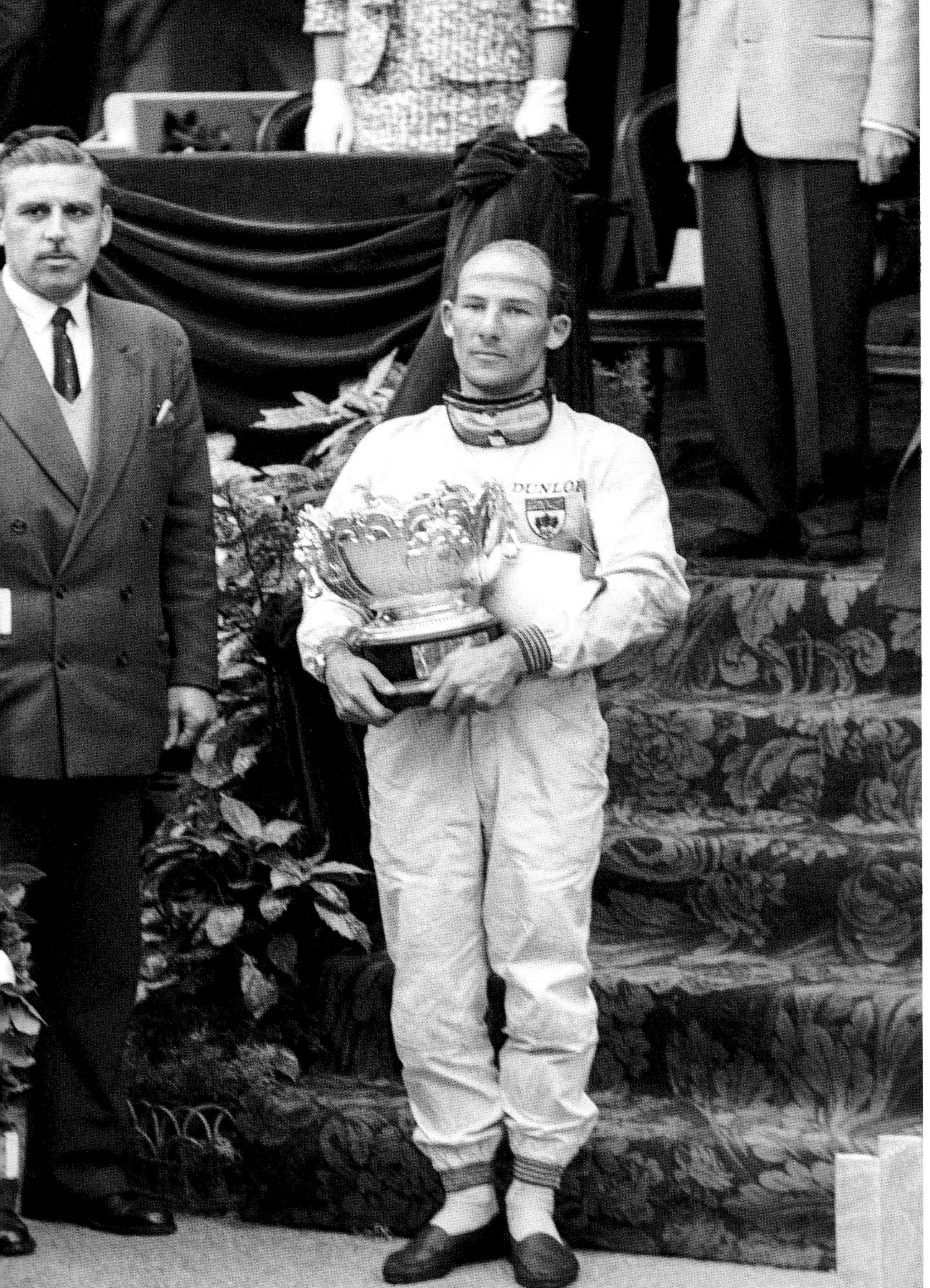

Monaco GP, 1961. Stirling Moss, the winner, with his trophy by the Royal Box. Photo: David Phipps

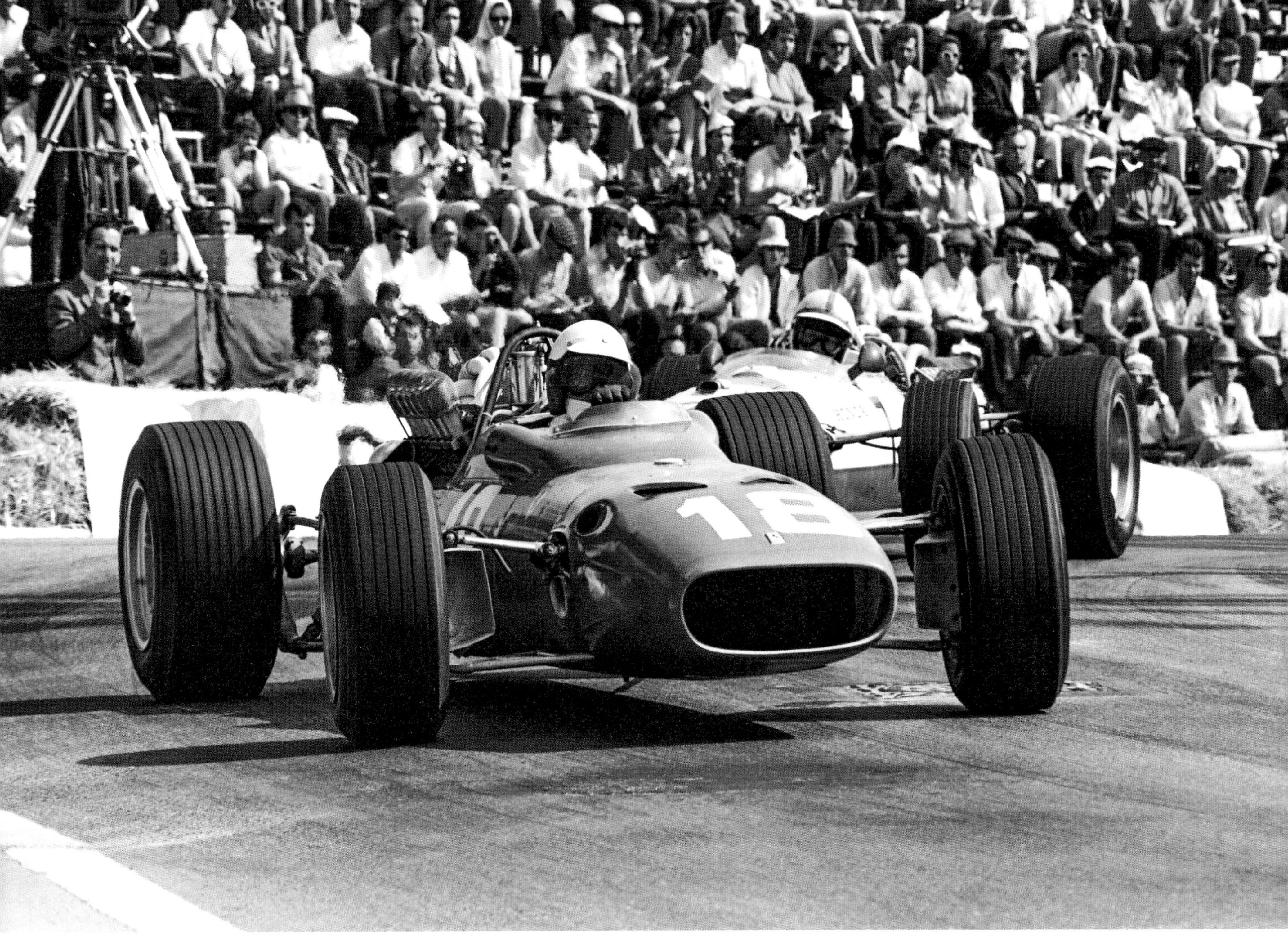

Monaco GP, 1967. Lorenzo Bandini (Ferrari 312), at his tragical last race, leads John Surtees (Honda RA273) out of the Station Hairpin. Photo: Michael Tee

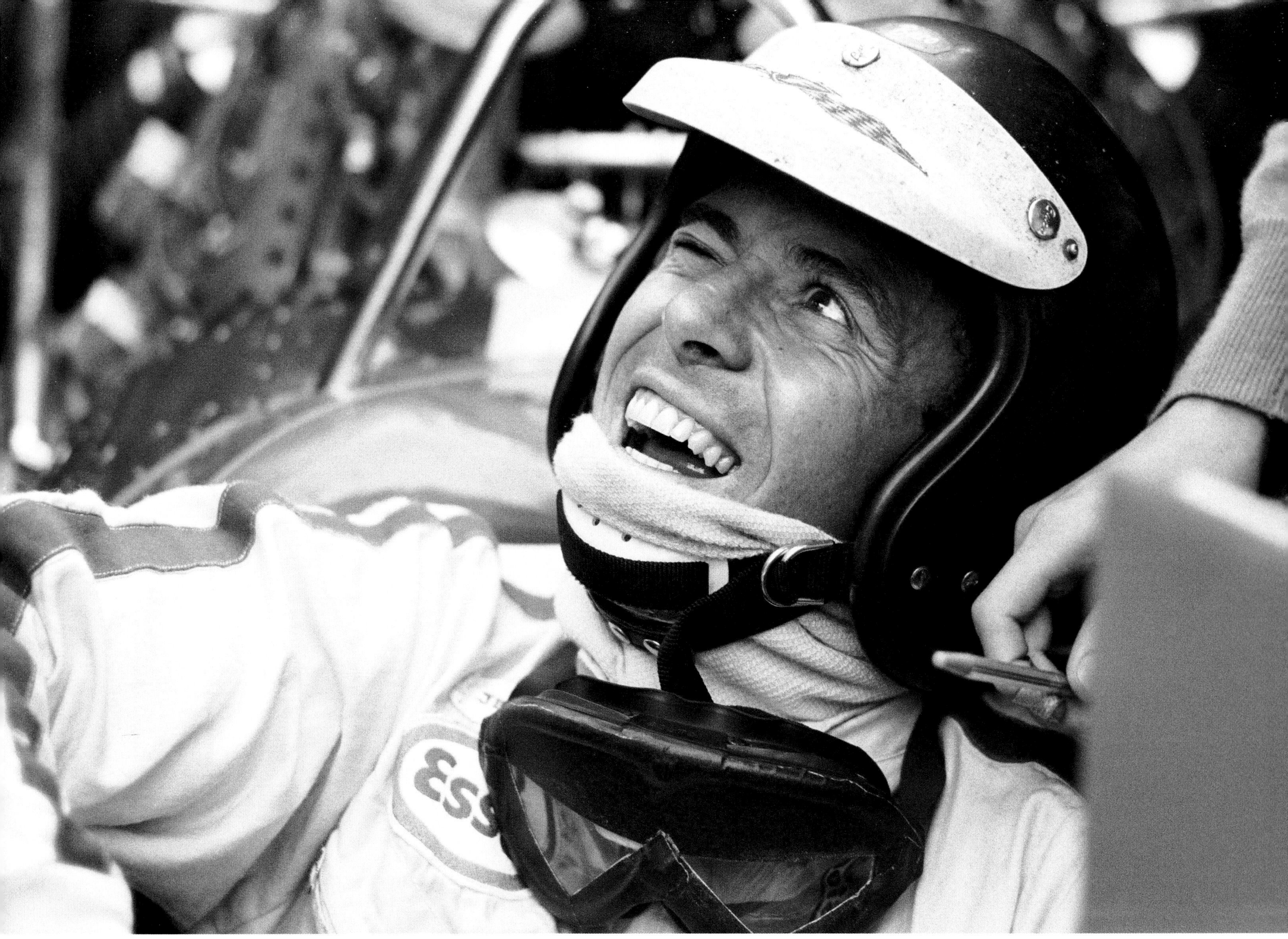

Monza, Italian GP, 1967. Jim Clark shares a joke while sat in his Lotus 49 Ford. Photo: Rainer Schlegelmilch

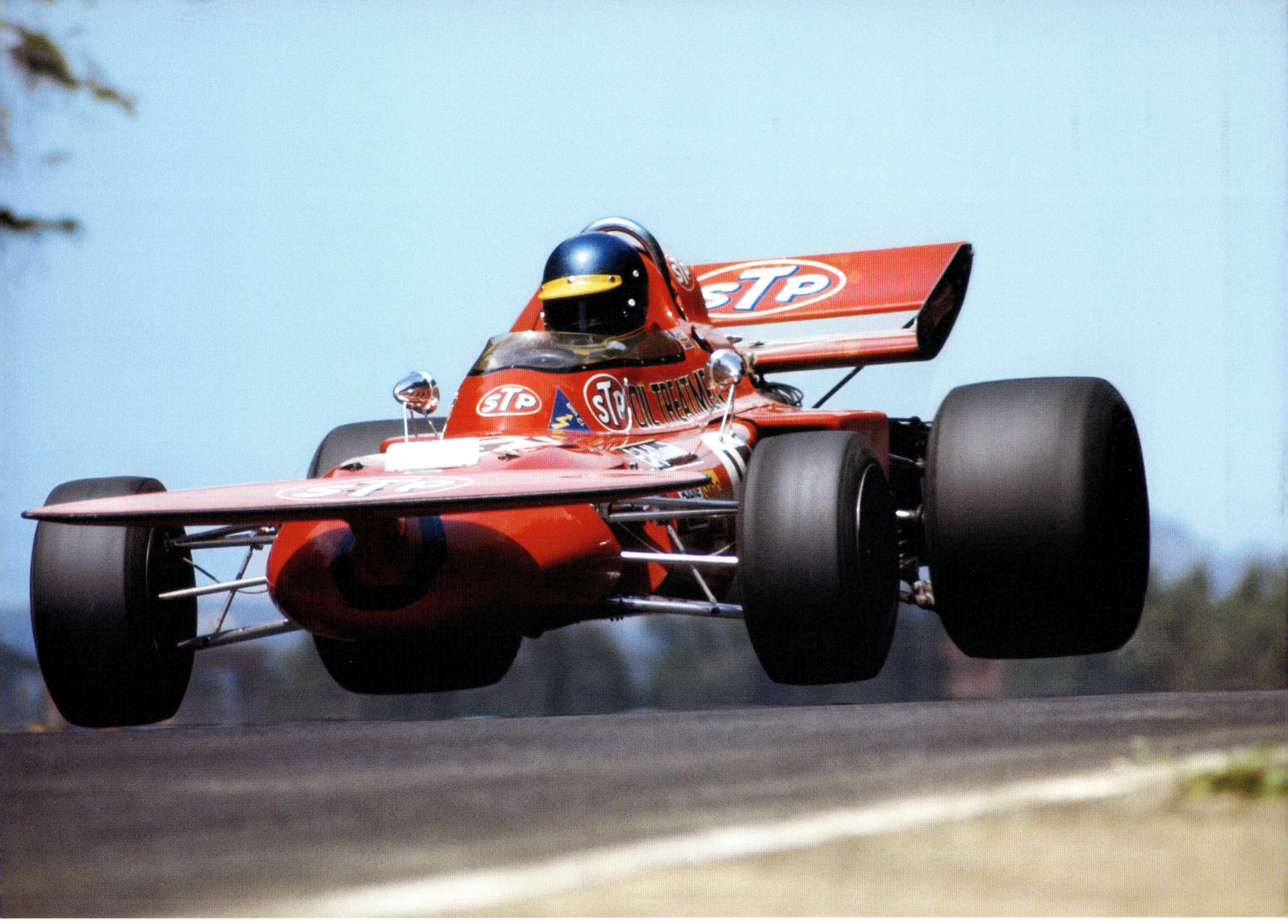

Nürburgring, German GP, 1971. Ronnie Peterson (March 711 Ford) gets airborne over a crest. Photo: Rainer Schlegelmilch

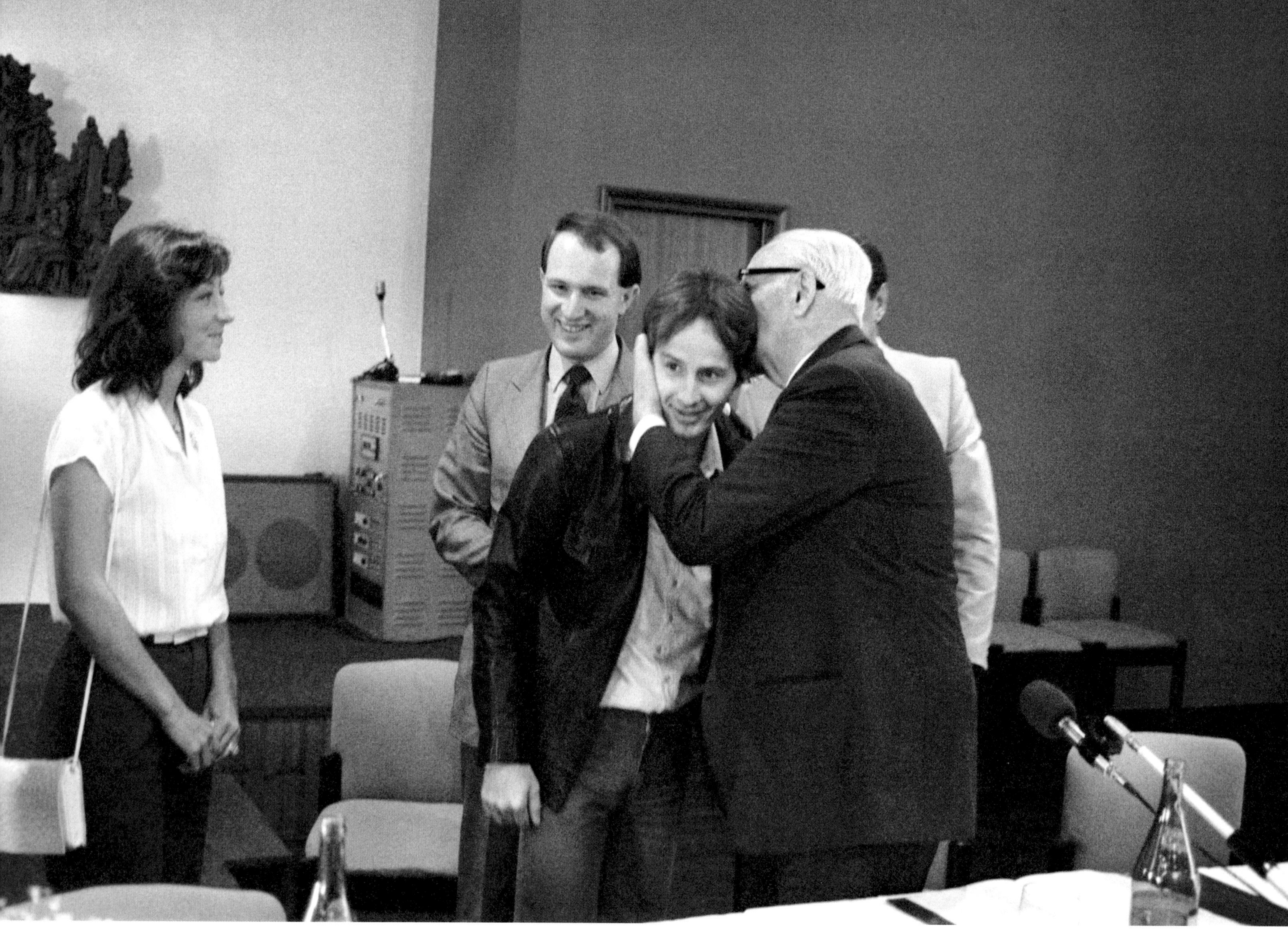

Maranello, 1980. Joann Villeneuve smiles as Enzo Ferrari kisses her husband Gilles, the day after Villeneuve's crash in the Italian GP at Imola. Photo: Ercole Colombo

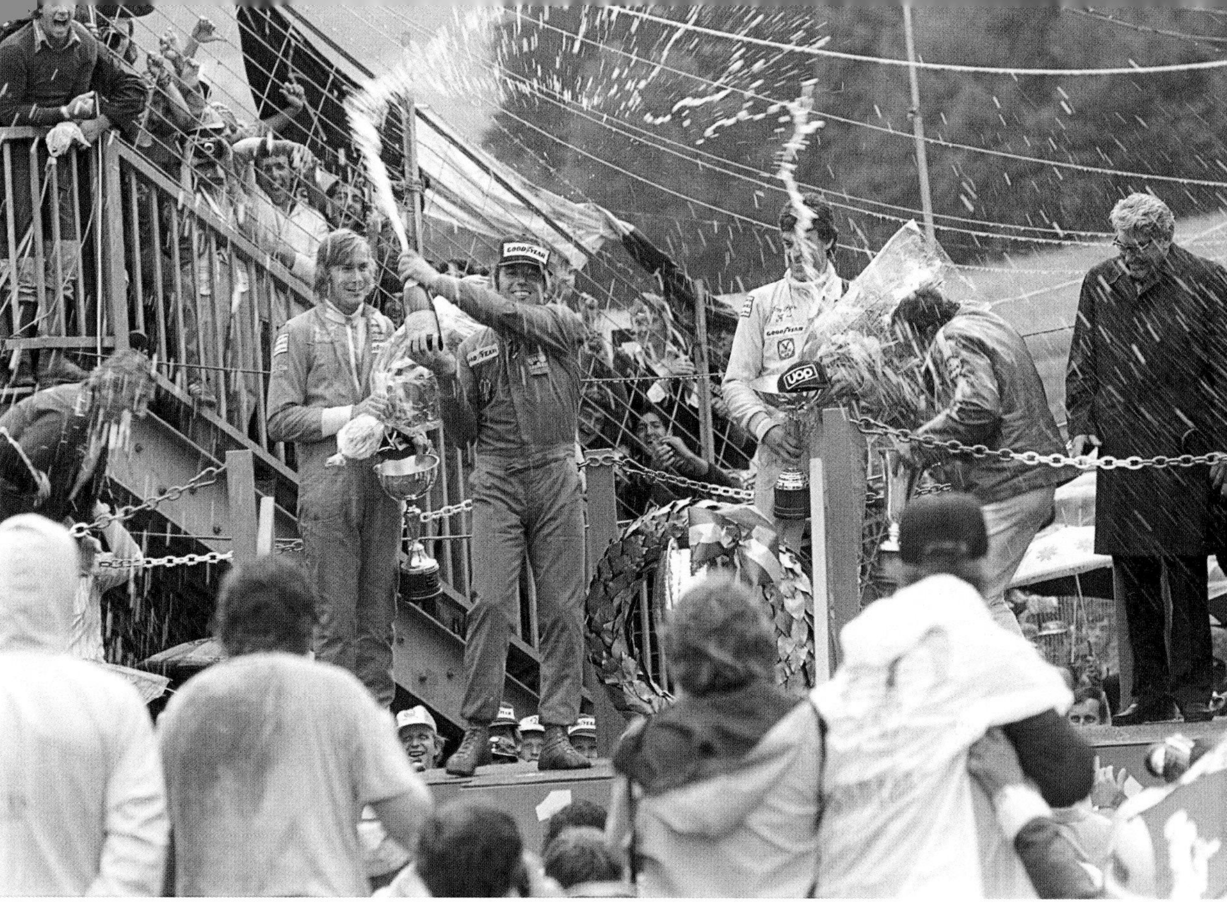

Zeltweg, Austrian GP, 1975. Vittorio Brambilla, happy on the podium after his first victory, with James Hunt and Tom Pryce. Photo: David Phipps

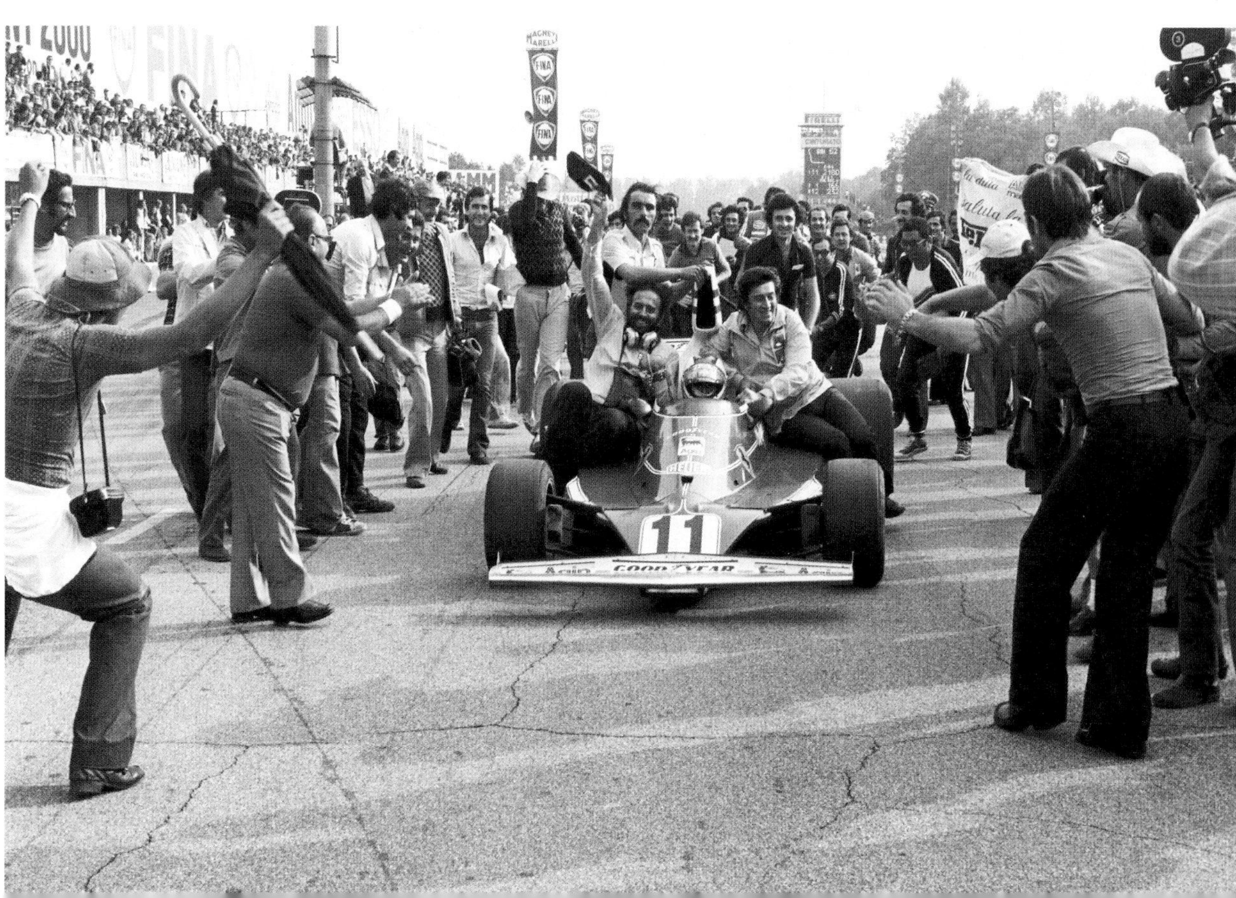

Monza, Italian GP, 1975. Clay Regazzoni (Ferrari 312T) drives down the pit lane with team members riding on his car after his victory, as spectators cheer him on. Photo: Ercole Colombo

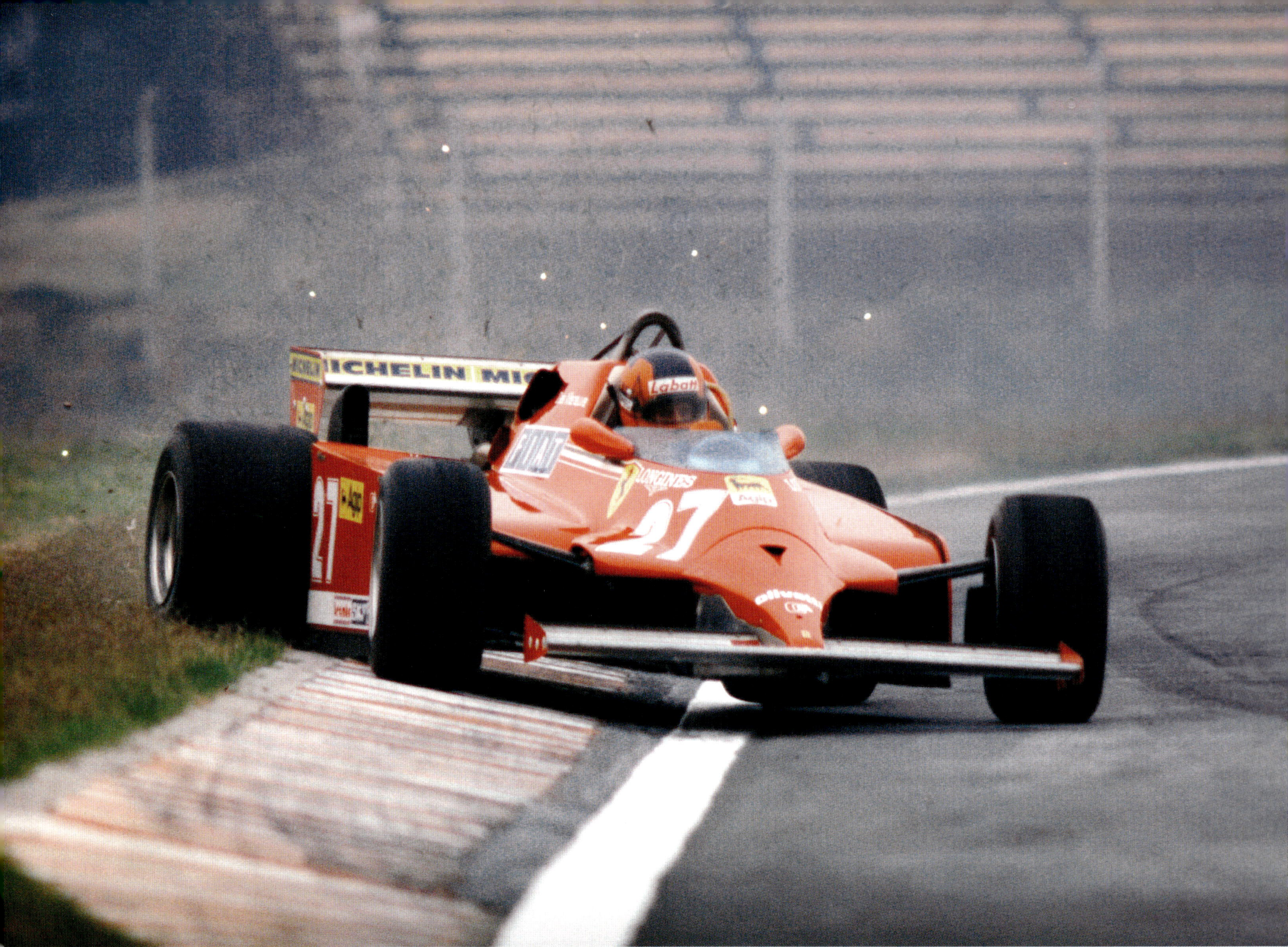

Buenos Aires, Argentinian GP, 1981. Gilles Villeneuve (Ferrari 126CK) corrects a slide as he runs wide onto the grass. Photo: Ercole Colombo

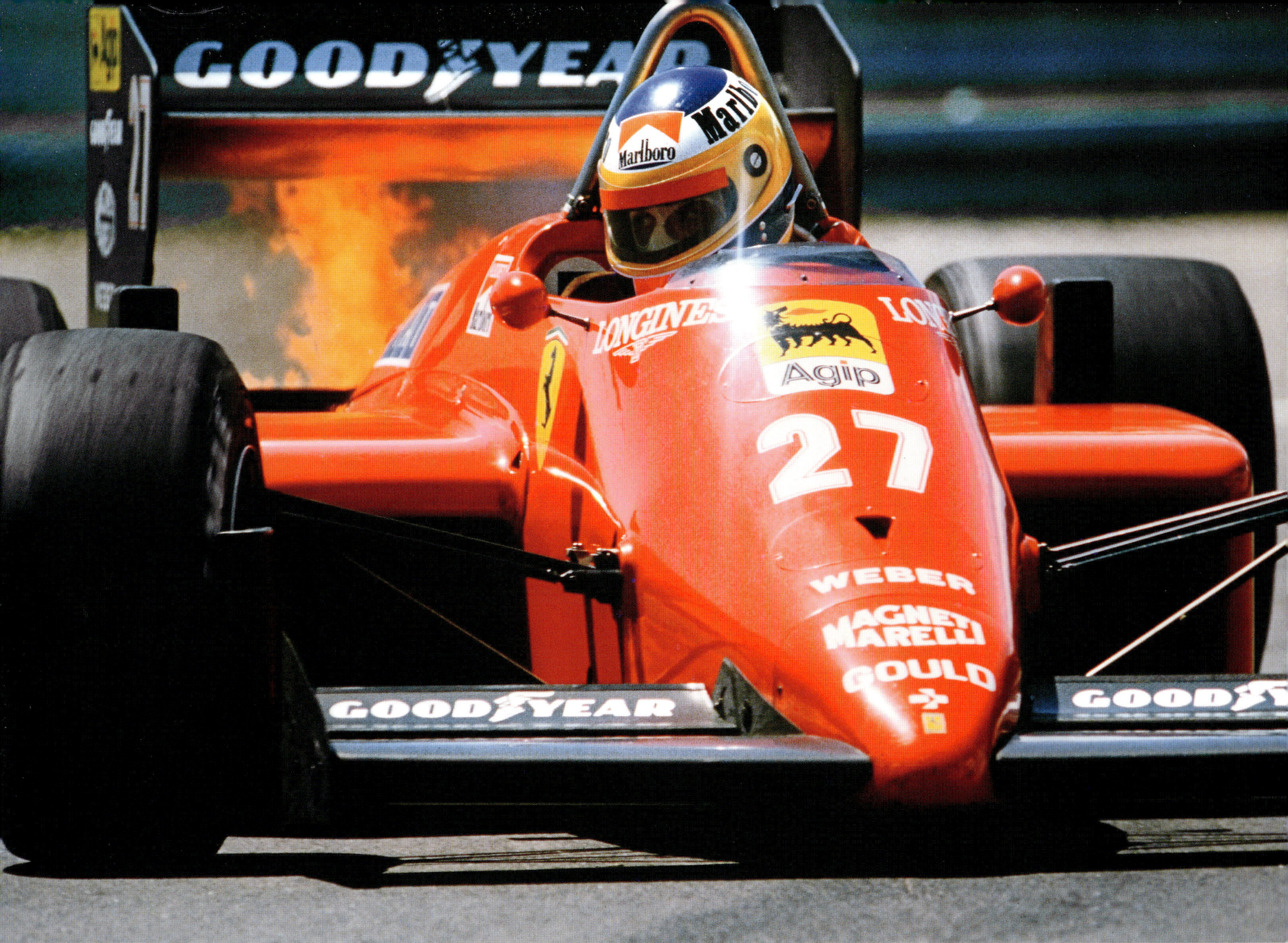

Montreal, Canadian GP, 1985. Michele Alboreto (Ferrari 156/85) with flames rising from his engine as he eyes up the next corner. Photo: Ercole Colombo

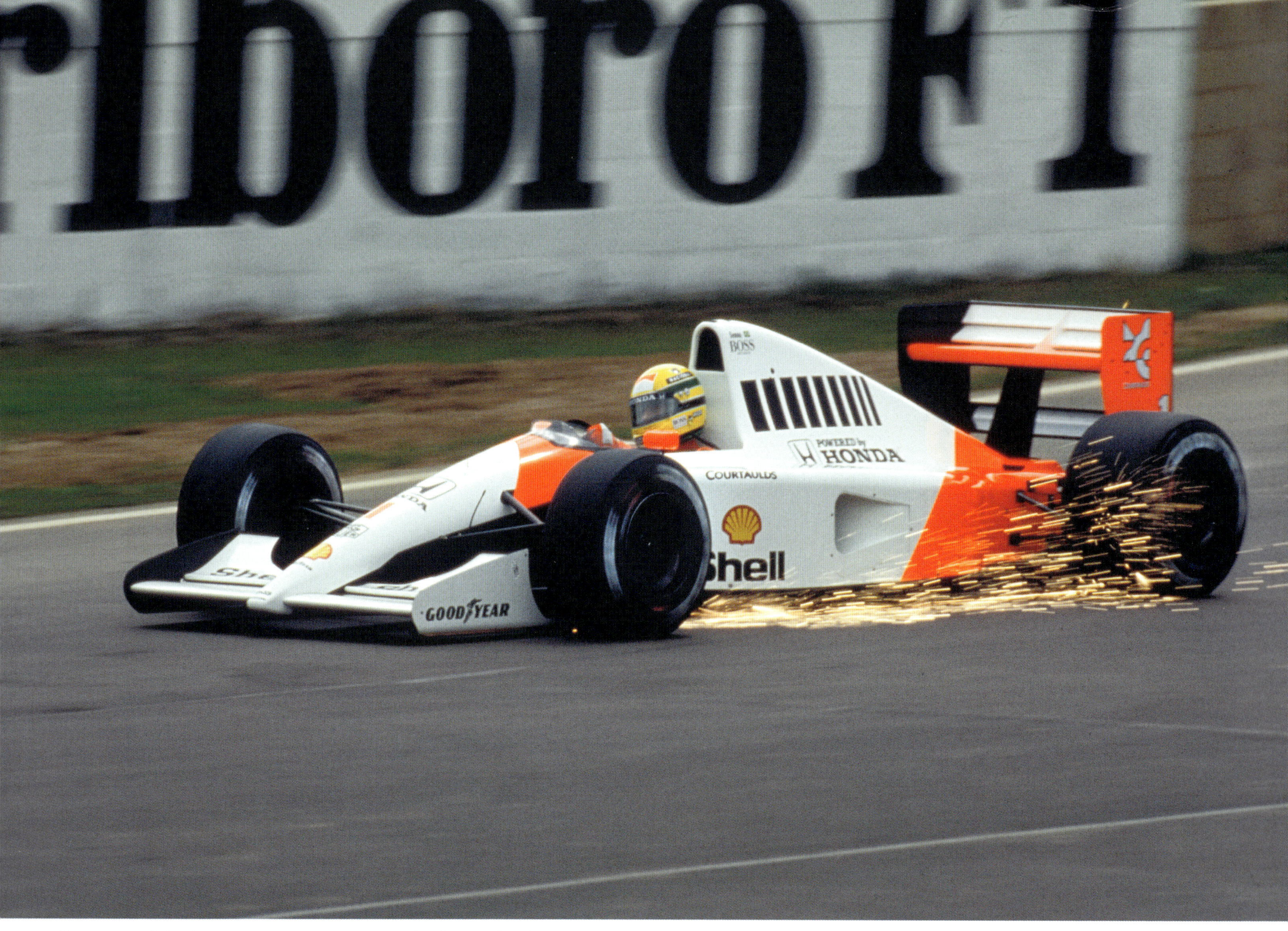

Silverstone, British GP, 1991. Ayrton Senna (McLaren MP4/6 Honda). Photo: Ercole Colombo

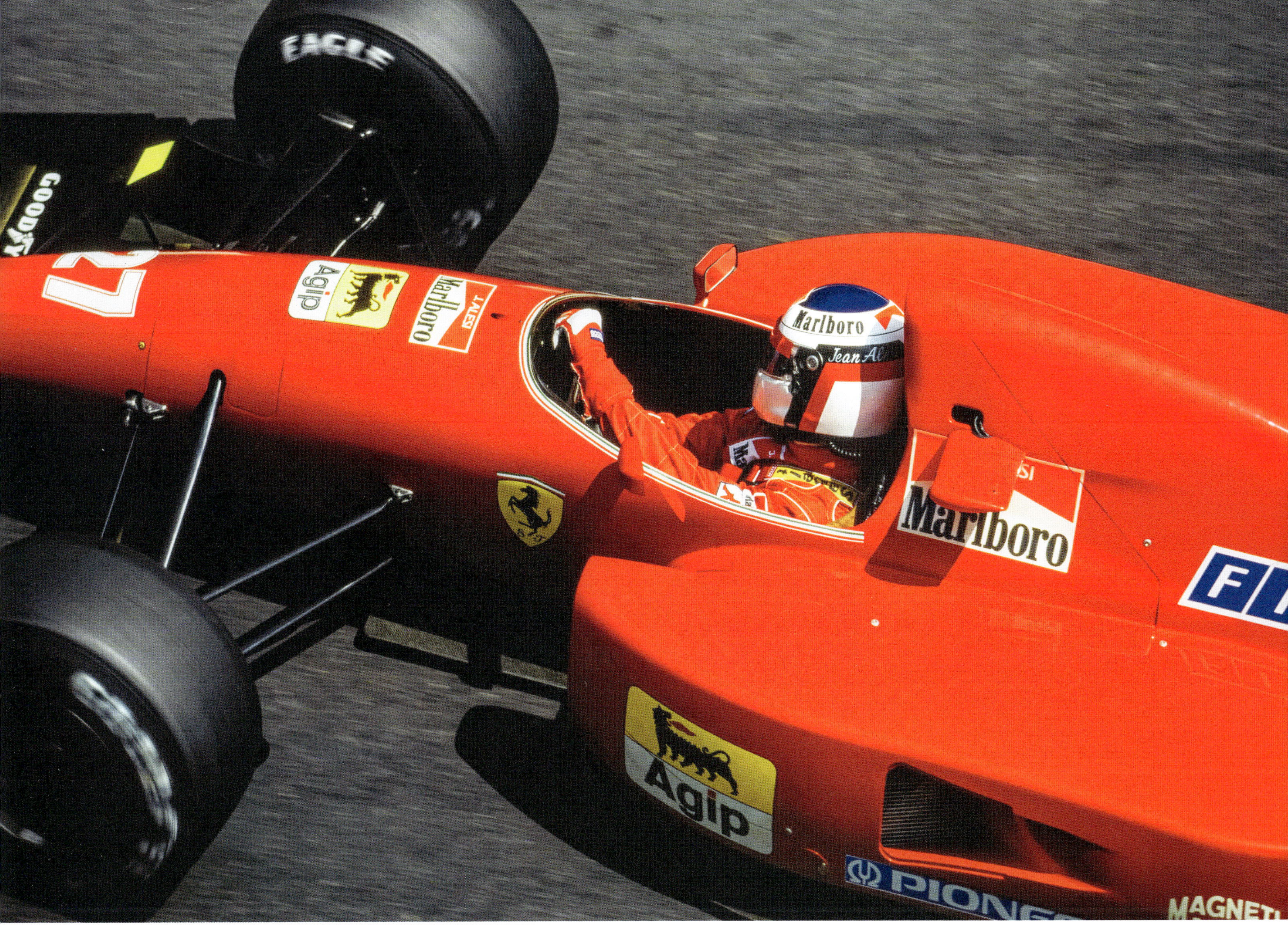

Monaco GP, 1992. Overhead view of Jean Alesi (Ferrari F92A) with his trademark head and steering wheel movements. Photo: Steven Tee

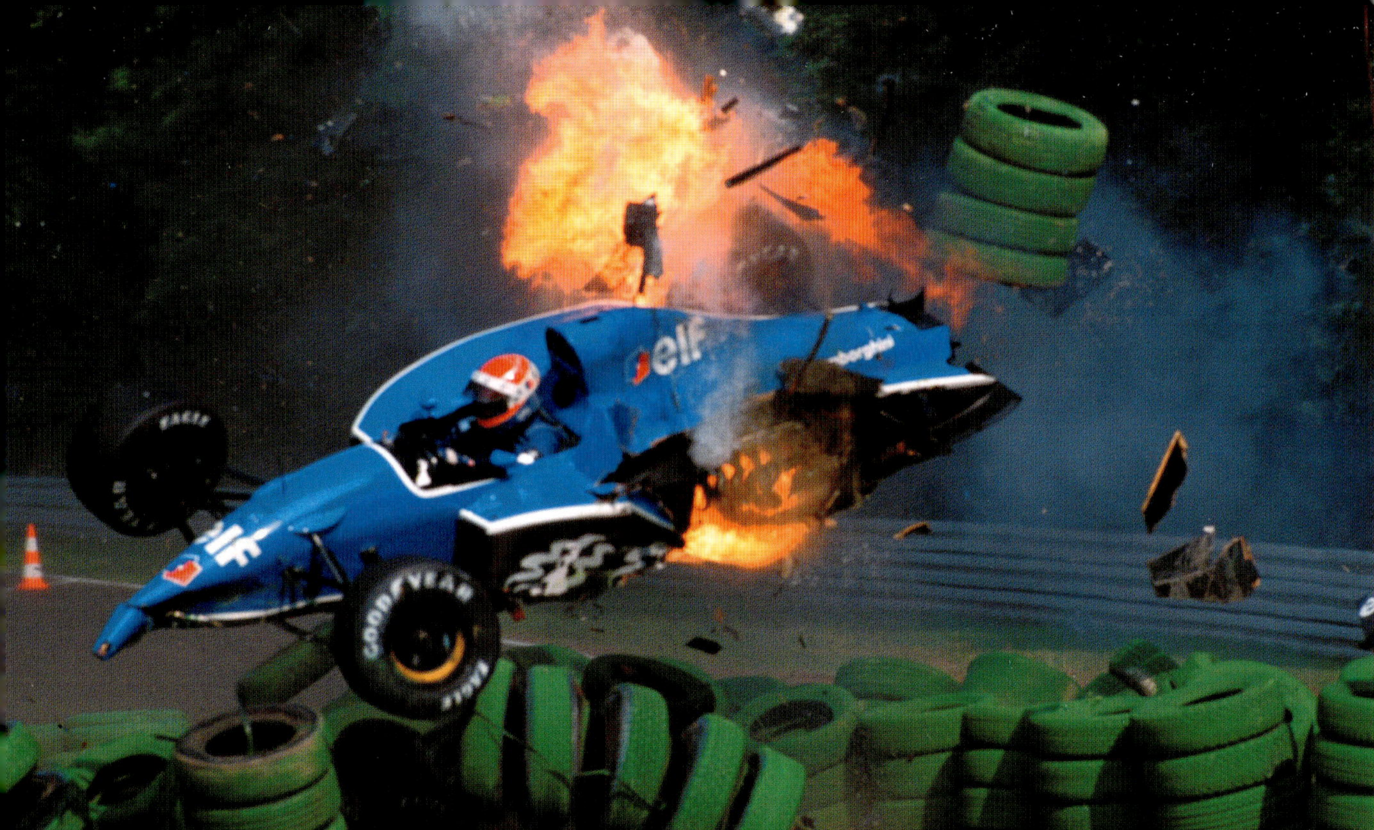

Hockenheim, German GP, 1991. Érik Comas (Ligier JS35B) flying over the Ost corner. Photo: Ercole Colombo

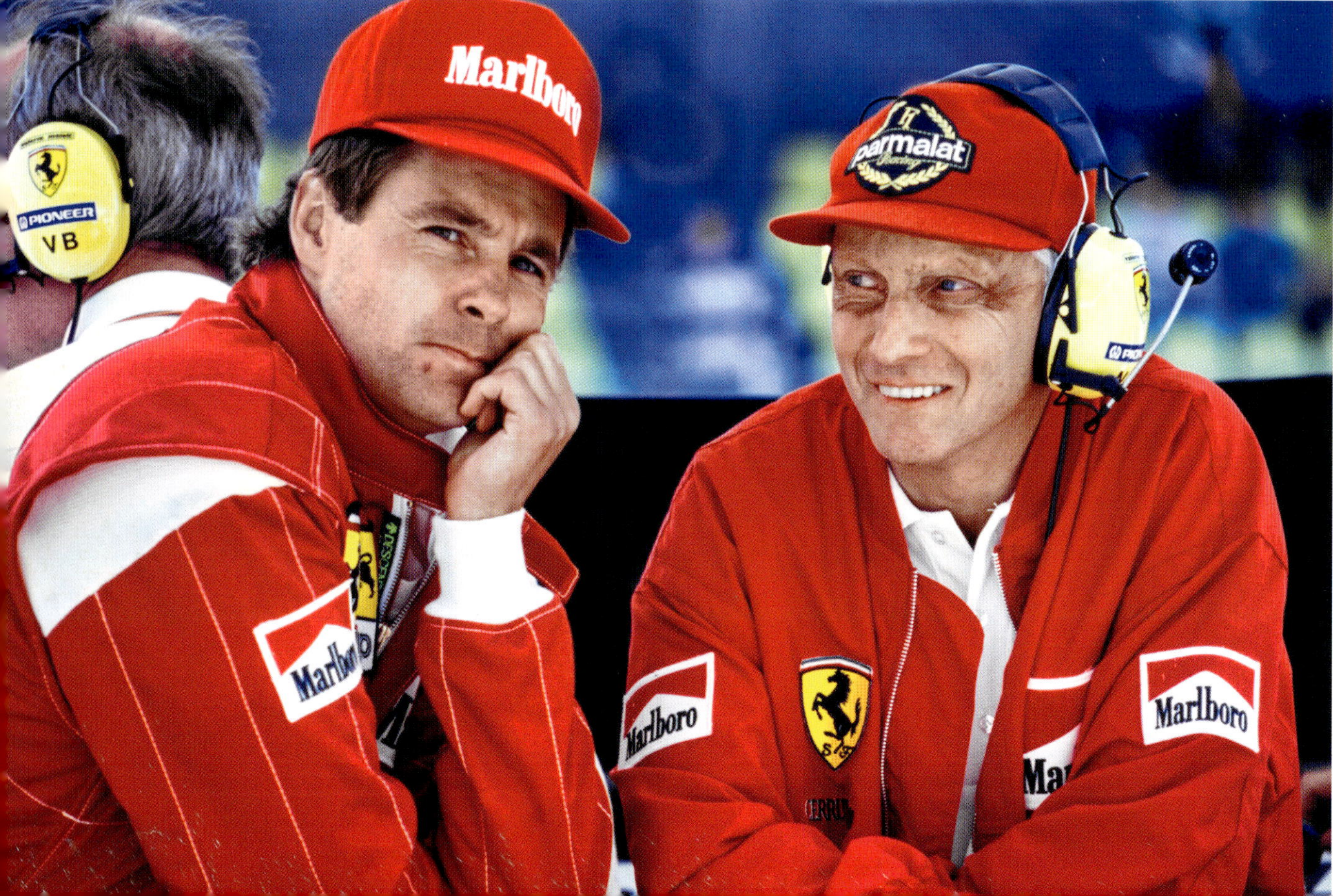

Imola, San Marino GP, 1994. Gerhard Berger and Niki Lauda, Ferrari advisor, in conversation on the pit wall. Photo: Ercole Colombo

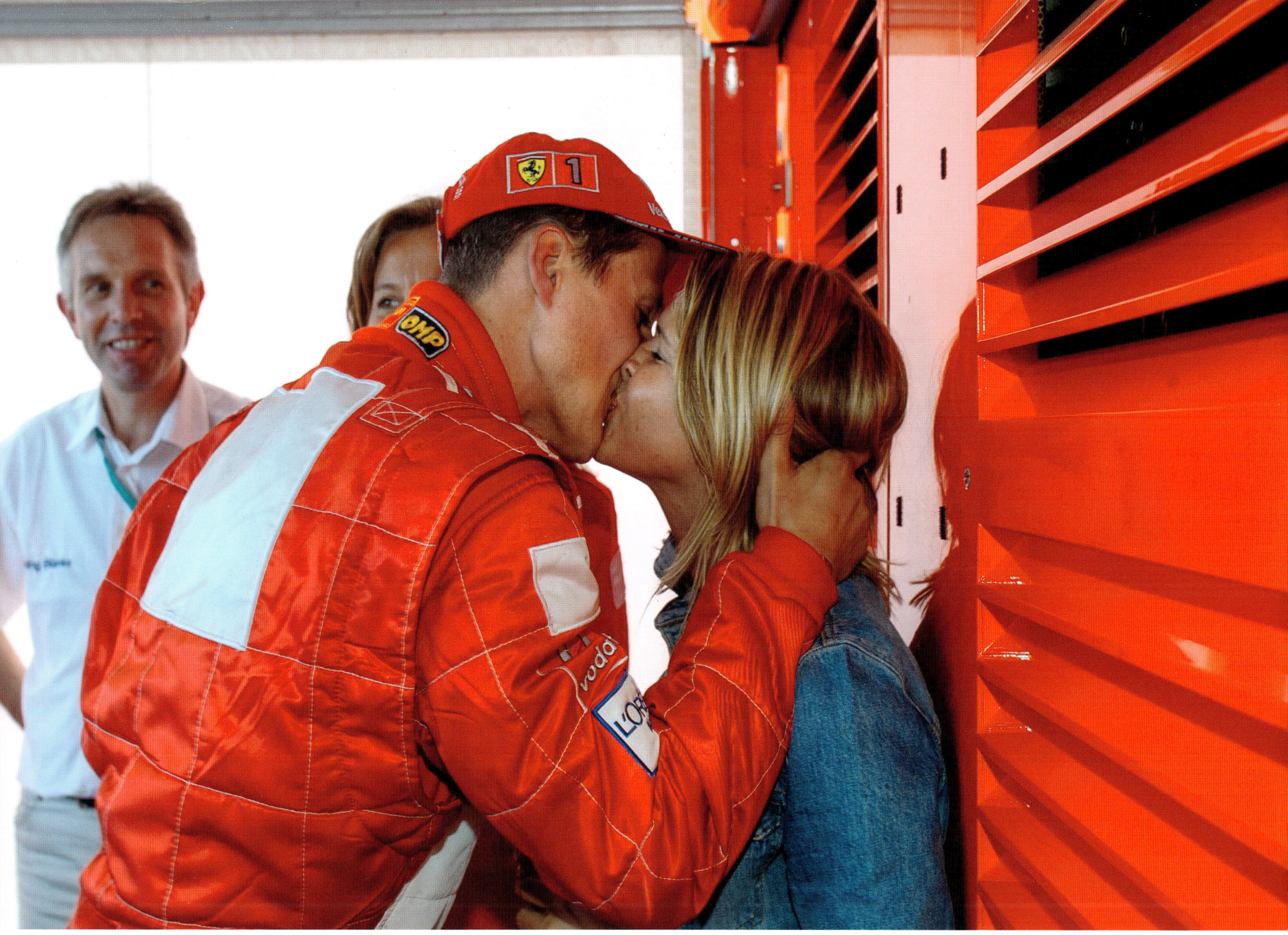

Magny-Cours, French GP, 2002. Michael Schumacher kisses his wife Corinna after winning his fourth title. Photo: Ercole Colombo

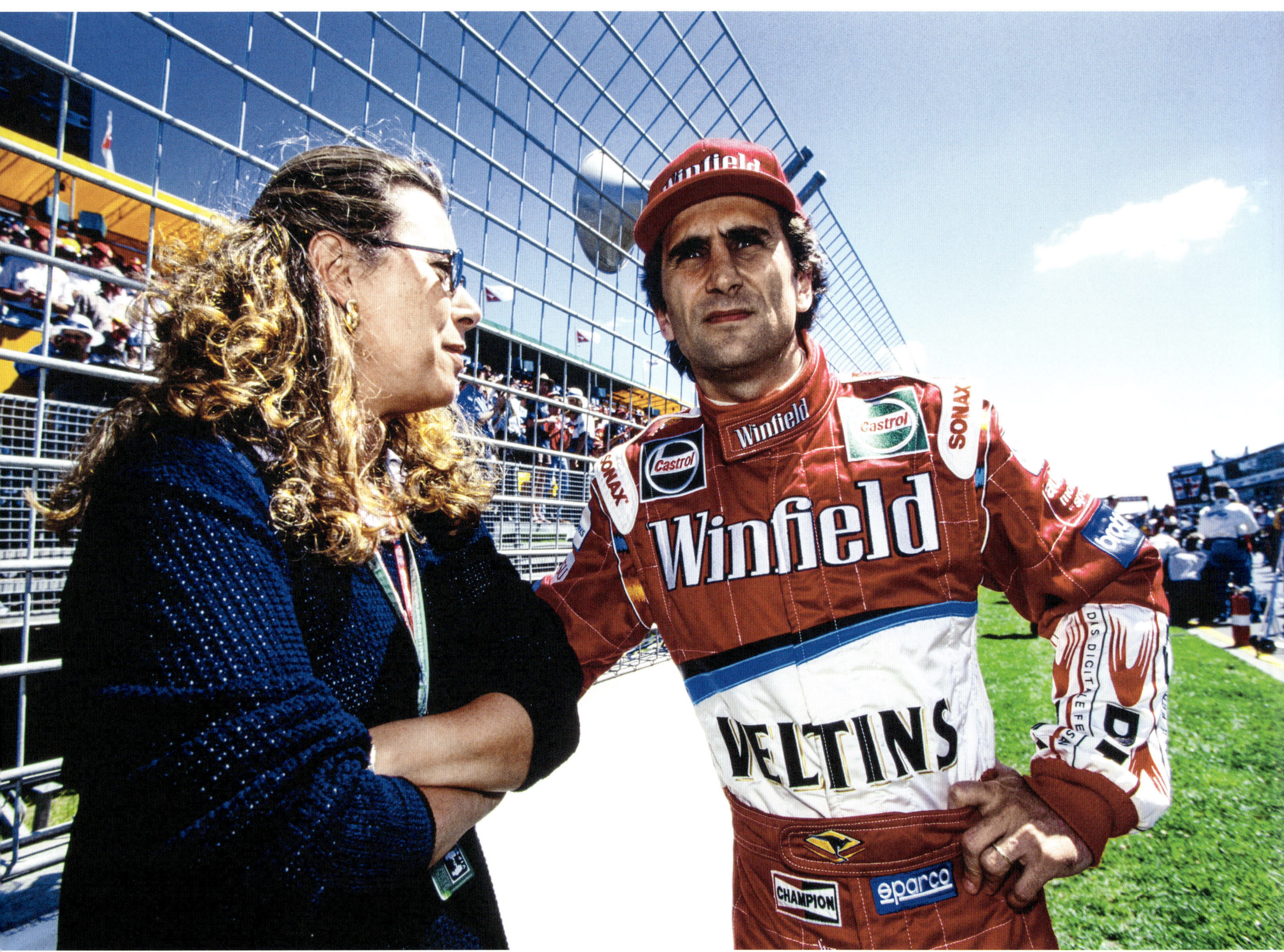

Melbourne, Australian GP, 1999. Alex Zanardi in conversation with his wife Daniela before the first race of his Formula 1 comeback. Photo: Mark Sutton

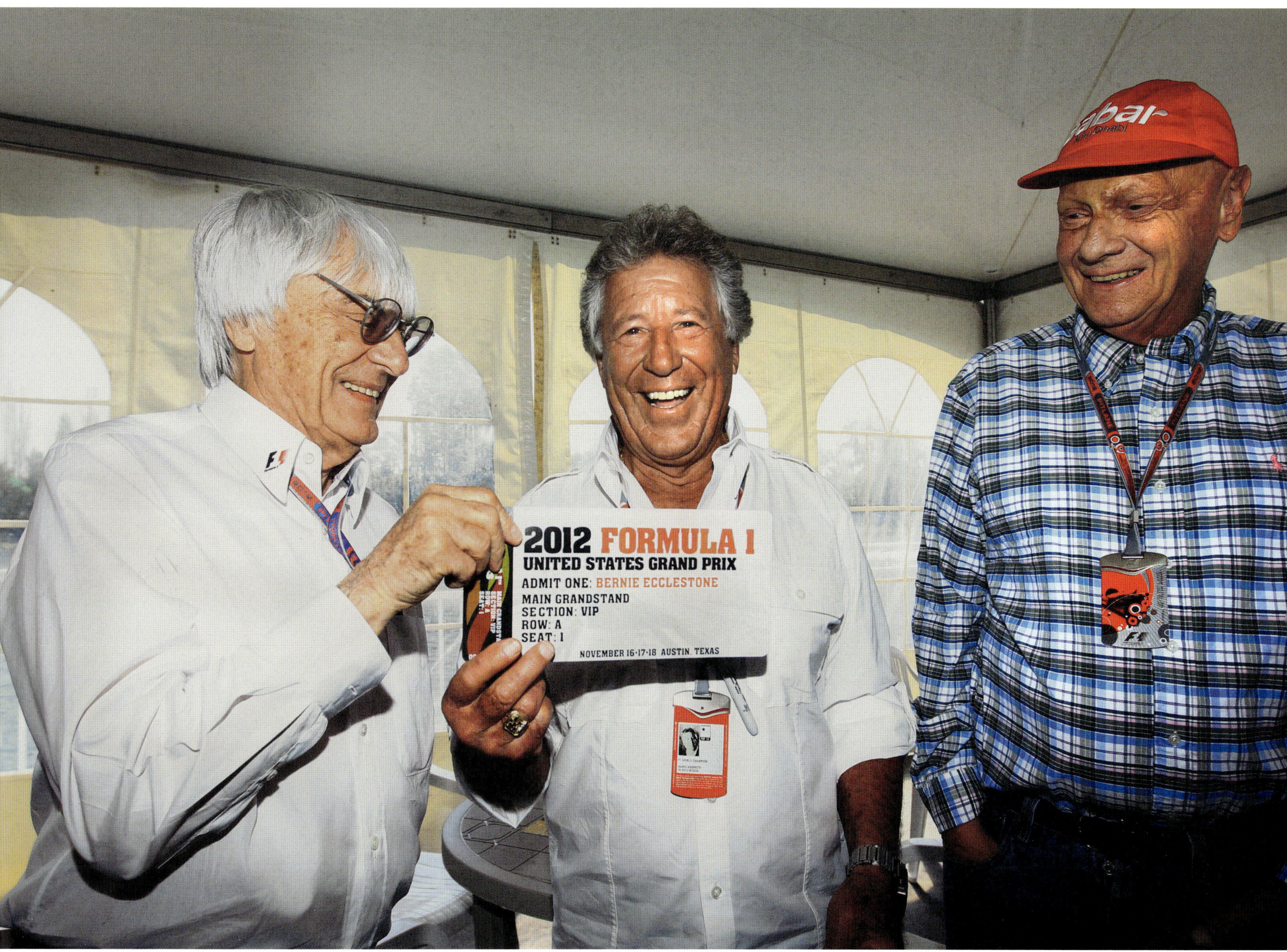

Montreal, Canadian GP, 2012. Bernie Ecclestone, Mario Andretti, and Niki Lauda. Photo: Mark Sutton

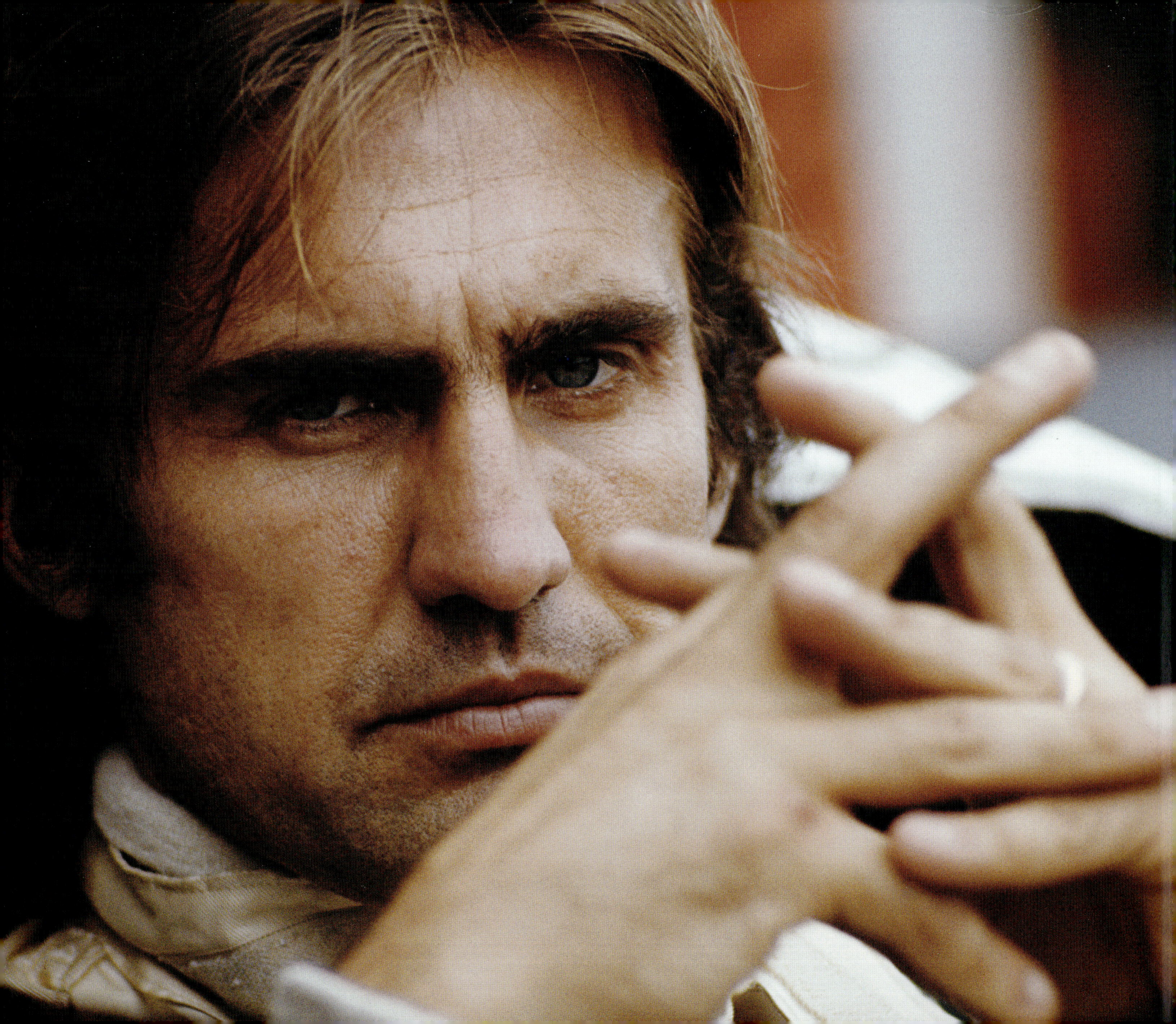

Carlos Reutemann, Argentinian
(Santa Fe, April 12 – July 7,
2021), the winner of twelve
Grand Prix races. A great
champion, a great friend.
Photo: Rainer Schlegelmilch

Motorsport Images

Motorsport Images aims to be the premier specialist supplier of motorsport and automotive photography. With over 28 million images dating from 1895, we have the history of motoring and motor racing covered. And with a team of photographers at every Formula 1 and Formula E race, as well as photographers providing coverage from all the main series around the world, the story is continually being brought up to date.

Using our website, enthusiasts and clients can search through well over 5 million images. Every weekend our team uploads thousands of new photos from the latest events, such as Formula 1, MotoGP, NASCAR, IndyCar, WRC, WEC, and BTCC. And the ongoing digitisation of archive collections means that every day many previously unseen images are being made available for someone to appreciate and perhaps to publish for the first time. The strength of our historical coverage comes not just from the size but also from the variety of our collections.

LAT Images

The LAT Archive is the largest collection within Motorsport Images with over 10 million negatives, transparencies and prints, and millions more digital camera images. The LAT name (standing for London Art Technical) comes from the original photographic arm of Teesdale, set up by Michael Tee, father of current director and chief photographer Steven Tee. This archive was later merged with the photographic archives of *Autosport*, *Autocar* and *The Motor*, adding over 100,000 glass plate negatives which cover events like the 1914 French GP, early racing at Brooklands and Le Mans, hill climbs, rallying, and motor shows.

Sutton Images

Founded by Keith Sutton in 1980 and including images taken by brothers Keith and Mark Sutton as well as many other photographers, Sutton Images was the largest independent motorsport photographic agency in the UK when it was acquired by Motorsport Network in 2017. It had grown to provide contract photographic services in Formula 1, and by the acquisition of the David Phipps archive had extended its coverage back to the early 1960s.

Rainer Schlegelmilch

Rainer Schlegelmilch is one of Formula 1's most famous photographers. He became known for his artistic style, using slow shutter speeds to creative effect. His archive features over half a million images, mostly taken at over 600 Grands Prix from 1962 to 2017, but also covering the 24 Hours of Le Mans and many of the great road cars.

Ercole Colombo

Ercole Colombo grew up within a few hundred metres of the Monza circuit and as a young boy saw legendary drivers such as Fangio, Ascari, and Farina race there. As a photographer he developed a close relationship with the Ferrari team, their drivers, and even with Enzo Ferrari himself. The 2018 Italian GP at Monza marked his 700th GP and his archive contains around 5 million images.

Giorgio Piola

Starting at Monaco in 1969, and with a career spanning into its seventh decade, Giorgio Piola remains one of the foremost technical journalists in Formula 1. His drawings document the sport's technical advances in fine detail, with some of his full car drawings taking up to 45 days to produce.

Maggi & Maggi

Founded in 1984 by Silvano Maggi, and continued by his son Paolo, this is one of the most comprehensive image libraries of Ferrari production cars anywhere in the world. Many hundreds of models are covered, with around 100,000 images in total. Maggi & Maggi is the most recent addition to the Motorsport Images collections.

Martin Lee
Head of Business Development – Images
Motorsport Images
www.motorsportimages.com